THE LOS ANGELES RIVER

CREATING THE
NORTH AMERICAN
LANDSCAPE

Gregory Conniff
Bonnie Loyd
Edward K. Muller
David Schuyler
Consulting Editors

George F. Thompson
Series Founder and Director

Published in
cooperation
with the Center
for American Places,
Santa Fe,
New Mexico, and
Harrisonburg,
Virginia

The
LOS ANGELES RIVER

ITS LIFE,

DEATH,

AND

POSSIBLE

REBIRTH

Blake Gumprecht

The
Johns
Hopkins
University
Press
Baltimore
& London

To Ezekiel

Johns Hopkins Paperbacks edition, 2001
9 8 7 6 5 4 3 2 1

The Johns Hopkins University Press
2715 North Charles Street
Baltimore, Maryland 21218-4363
www.press.jhu.edu

Library of Congress Cataloging-in-Publication Data
will be found at the end of this book.
A catalog record for this book is available from the
British Library.

ISBN 0-8018-6642-1 (pbk.)

Title page photograph by Stephen Callis.
Used with permission.

Contents

Acknowledgments

No author works alone. Many individuals contributed to the making of the book you now hold in your hands. To a few who were especially important, I would like to express my gratitude.

This study, in much abbreviated form, was first produced as a master's thesis at California State University, Los Angeles. Like many graduate students, I was fed up with the members of my thesis committee by the time I was finished; I was so frustrated, in fact, that I didn't even thank them in the thesis. Anger fades more quickly than influence, however, and in the years since I have realized that, while their expectations may have occasionally seemed unreasonable and our disagreements were many, they taught me much and helped me make my study better. Thanks especially to Vincent Mazzucchelli, my committee chair, cartographic mentor, and a taskmaster nonpareil, but also to committee members John Rees and Larry McGlinn and to the rest of the faculty and staff in the Department of Geography and Urban Analysis at CSULA, who helped me recognize almost immediately after I began taking classes there on a part-time basis that geography was that thing for which I had long been searching.

Numerous friends, colleagues, and instructors reviewed the manuscript at various stages in its development and provided invaluable criticism and advice. Karen Oye, a friend and confidante whom I hope one day actually to meet, read every word of numerous drafts and spent countless hours providing comments, suggestions, and encouragement. Dick Nostrand, a historical geographer at the University of Oklahoma and the nicest man on earth, also read the thesis and, more than anyone else, urged me to submit it to publishers. Bill Deverell, a historian at Cal Tech, shared with me his own work about the river, helped me better find my way through several local archives, and patiently answered my endless questions. Dave Snow read the nearly finished manuscript, caught many errors, and helped me to smooth over several rough spots. Others who read parts of the study and provided suggestions include Bret Wallach of the University of Oklahoma and Norris Hundley of UCLA. Special thanks to George F. Thompson, president of the Center for American Places, who saw the potential in the original manuscript, helped me understand its shortcomings, and provided the guidance that enabled me to improve it. Thanks also to Cathryn Harding and Randall Jones at the Center, along with Linda Tripp and Linda Forlifer at the Johns Hopkins University Press.

Like anyone doing historical research, I owe an inestimable debt to the many people who helped me at various libraries, archives, and government agencies. A few went beyond what I had any right to expect. They included Anthony Turhollow, emeritus professor at Loyola Marymount University and staff historian in the Los Angeles office of the U.S. Army Corps of Engineers; Randal Brandt of the Water Resources Center Archives; Kimball Garrett of the Natural History Museum of Los Angeles County; Helen Haskell, Glen Creason, and Carolyn Cole of the Los Angeles Public Library; Hynda Rudd and Jay Jones of the Los Angeles City Archives; Jennifer Watts of the Huntington Library; Scott Fajack of the Los Angeles Department of Water and Power; and Dace Taube of the Regional History Center at the University of Southern California. Lewis MacAdams from Friends of the Los Angeles River provided his time and knowledge whenever asked. Stephen Callis allowed me to use several of his excellent photographs. Elizabeth Van Itallie helped me produce the illustrations in the original manuscript.

I would be remiss if I did not thank a few others who had no direct involvement with this book but whose influence on me personally has been great. My father raised me never to accept anything as "good enough," which made me at least a little crazy but also helped instill in me the high standards I hope are apparent in this book. Rick Musser, a professor of journalism at the University of Kansas and the best teacher I have ever had, taught me never to stop asking questions. Bob Howard, a former editor, and Donald J. Pisani, a professor of history at the University of Oklahoma, made me think about every word and sentence. Miriam Yedvab provided physical and spiritual nourishment when I needed it most. Ed, Trixie, Thistlethwaite, Kurt, and Pablo (may she find an eternally full bowl of milk in the sky) made the long hours sitting in front of the computer a good deal less lonely.

Above all, thanks to my wife, Josephine Lenardi, for her faith and patience. She learned to accept my all-too-common absences (physical and otherwise), tolerated my mood swings, and believed in me when I did not. She also shared my curiosity about the river, accompanied me on walks along its banks, read numerous drafts of the manuscript, made dinner more often than she should have, and paid for most everything. Without her, this book would not exist.

Preface to the Paperback Edition

MUCH HAS HAPPENED SINCE *THE LOS ANGELES RIVER* WAS PUB-
lished in 1999. In fact, the momentum of efforts to make the river more
than just a flood control channel has reached such an intensity that,
to echo the language used in the last sentences of this book, I would
no longer bet against this river, or against people like Lewis
MacAdams, Scott Wilson, Joe Linton, and Dorothy Green, and organizations such as Friends of the Los Angeles River, NorthEast Trees,
and the Mountains Recreation and Conservation Authority. Among
those who care about the river, I have been more cynical than most.
But that cynicism is, like the sandy banks of the old Rio de Porciúncula, rapidly eroding.

The biggest development came in June 2000, when California Governor Gray Davis signed a state budget that provides $83 million for
projects along the river. Reading the news from 1,400 miles away, I
was stunned and humbled. "This feels like we've won the lottery," said
FoLAR board president Melanie Winter. Such a windfall was made
possible the previous March when voters approved a $2.1 billion state
parks referendum, Proposition 12, sponsored by Los Angeles Assemblyman Antonio Villaraigosa. The biggest chunk of the budget allocations, $45 million, will pay for initial work in developing a sixty-
acre state park along the river on the site of the Union Pacific
Railroad's Taylor Yard, long a dream of those seeking to green the
river. What makes this project especially compelling is that it could
result in the first removal of concrete from the river channel, a goal
that so far has eluded river activists.

The most comprehensive vision for such a project had been put
forth in 1998 at the FoLAR-organized "River through Downtown" conference, an event that at the time seemed full of pie-in-the-sky ideas,
but is proving remarkably prescient in its vision. Designs developed
for the conference called for turning the railroad yard, which is gradually being phased out of operation, into a multipurpose flood control, habitat restoration, and recreation site. Crucial to that plan was
the removal of a section of the paved east bank of the river to allow

water to flow into restored wetlands (fig. 6.21). It remains to be seen whether the creation of the park will result in any concrete removal, but flood control officials seem increasingly willing to consider such notions. As FoLAR founder MacAdams says, "You just don't feel that they're quite the enemies they once were."

Money provided in the 2000 state budget will also pay for two other major parks nearby, in the area north of downtown Los Angeles known as the Glendale Narrows, one of only three sections of the river where its channel is partially unpaved and the area that has been the focus of revitalization efforts. The MRCA, a state agency, will develop a five-acre park on the west side of the river just upstream from Taylor Yard and another at the confluence of the river and the Arroyo Seco, one of its major tributaries. The confluence park was one of three other major ideas launched at the "River through Downtown" conference. Together the two projects will cost $10 million.

Two earlier bond issues enabled the MRCA to develop the Los Angeles River Center and Gardens on 6.75 acres of the former Lawry's California Center, a local landmark known for its Mission-style buildings and extensively landscaped grounds. The MRCA spent $8 million to purchase the site and renovate the facilities, and since its formal opening in March 2000, the River Center has become a hub for river activities. Located near the river's meeting with the Arroyo Seco, the River Center features exhibits about the river, a park designed to show what an enhanced river might look like, and is home to offices for the MRCA, FoLAR, NorthEast Trees, and other nonprofit groups.

Numerous additional projects have also been completed in the Glendale Narrows. Although other groups have been more vocal in the debate over the river, no entity has done more to beautify its course than the organization NorthEast Trees, which has quietly created nine small parks, developed 1.3 miles of trails and greenway, and planted five thousand native trees. All of the parks are smaller than an acre, but they are admired locally for their native plantings, sculpted gates, artistic benches, and other innovative features. NorthEast Trees has begun work on a project that will extend the greenway four-and-a-half miles south. Meanwhile, on the opposite side of the river, the city of Los Angeles in August 2000 opened the second segment of a planned seven-mile-long riverside bikeway between Griffith Park and Elysian Park. When all these projects are completed, bikeways and trails will line both sides of the river through the Glendale Narrows and sixteen parks will have been created along its banks since 1995.

Significant work is also under way along the more blighted sections of the river. The city of Los Angeles has created a master plan for beautifying seven miles of the riverside in the San Fernando Valley. A half-mile-long demonstration project will landscape both sides of the river in Studio City and provide trails on its south bank near Ventura Boulevard. Glendale is creating a similar half-mile-long greenway where the river turns sharply south at Griffith Park. South of downtown Los Angeles, Maywood should finally be able to complete its long-planned five-acre Riverfront Park, thanks to $2.4 million in Proposition 12 funds. Farther downstream, South Gate is planning a second confluence park at the meeting of the river and the Rio Hondo, while in north Long Beach two wetlands restoration projects are being considered along the east side of the river. Creation by the state legislature in 1999 of the San Gabriel and Lower Los Angeles Rivers and Mountains Conservancy will likely boost efforts to revitalize the river in the downstream cities, which have been slow to support the greening of its course because of flood control concerns.

Not all has gone the way of the river and its boosters, however. The conservancy formed to oversee planning for the lower part of the river covers only its last nineteen miles and was developed in opposition to a proposal to create a more powerful agency to coordinate all aspects of the river's care for its entire fifty-one-mile course. The proposal, sponsored by state Senator Tom Hayden, won approval from the state legislature but was vetoed by the governor amid opposition from downstream cities that feared such an agency would undermine local authority. In another setback, the MRCA has failed in its bid to implement a project to test alternative flood control methods on one of the river's tributaries, Tujunga Wash. Such a project would have enabled some of the stream's concrete channel to be removed and was designed to show that similar strategies could work on the Los Angeles River. Hydrologists determined, however, that insufficient land was available in the project area to try such methods. River activists are now studying the feasibility of a similar project on the Arroyo Seco.

More contentious has been the battle over a vacant forty-seven-acre parcel near the river in Chinatown known as the Cornfield. The city of Los Angeles in June 2000 approved construction of an industrial park on the site that its developers, Majestic Realty Corporation, claimed would bring a thousand jobs to the area. With the help of Mayor Richard Riordan, Majestic arranged $12 million in federal grants and loans to help pay for the $80 million development. A coalition of community and environmental groups sued the city to stop the project, claiming that its failure to require an environmental impact report violated state law. Drawing on yet another idea first proposed at the "River through Downtown" conference, opponents have called instead for the development on the site of parks, housing, a school, and perhaps even a river walk developed along the historic route of the Zanja Madre, the irrigation ditch that carried water from the river to a young Los Angeles. The federal Department of Housing and Urban Development got wind of the controversy and ruled that it would withhold the loans and grants until an environment impact report was produced. Still, community and environmental groups, lacking the money to fund many of their ideas and without the powerful friends of Majestic (whose president built the Staples Center sports arena), may face an uphill climb to stop the project altogether and implement their more creative vision for the site.

Such developments make clear that the story of the Los Angeles River is still evolving. Significant progress on revitalizing the river has been made, but I am still stuck on one fact that hasn't changed since I finished the original manuscript for this book: All the work so far completed, under construction, or approved is located outside the river's channel. Efforts to remake the river face a seemingly insurmountable barrier at the top of its banks, one that is imposed by the need for flood protection. Perhaps the park that is to be developed at Taylor Yard will change that. Perhaps work done on the Arroyo Seco will make it clear that a re-engineered Los Angeles River is possible. In the meantime, appreciating the river still requires a squint of the eye and a good deal of imagination. It is still too early to say whether it will ever be possible to appreciate the Los Angeles River in anything but relative terms.

Blake Gumprecht
October 2000

Introduction

YEARS AGO, A LOS ANGELES POLITICIAN CAMPAIGNED THAT, if elected, he would paint the bed of the Los Angeles River blue to make it look more like a river.[1] This incident, though politically and historically insignificant, symbolizes just how different the Los Angeles River is from other rivers. From its beginning in the suburbs of the San Fernando Valley to its mouth at the Pacific Ocean, the river's bed and banks are almost entirely concrete. Little water flows in its wide channel most of the year, and nearly all that does is treated sewage and oily street runoff. Chain link fence and barbed wire line the river's fifty-one-mile course. Graffiti mark its concrete banks. Discarded sofas, shopping carts, and trash litter its channel. Weeds that poke through cracks in the pavement are the only plants visible along most of its course. Fish larger than minnows are rare even where the river does contain water. Feral cats, rats, and human transients are the dominant animal life on its shores.

For much of its history, the Los Angeles River has been little more than a local joke. Though millions of people cross it every day on more than a hundred bridges, many do not even realize that the concrete conduit that passes under or alongside some of the nation's busiest highways is, in fact, the bed of a river. A senior government official in a city along its banks was not aware, until asked about it, that a river ran through his town.[2] Some maps of the region do not even show its course. Homes and businesses hide it from view with cinder block walls and tall shrubs. Even parks along the river conceal its presence behind ivy-covered fences. Until recently, if anything at all was said about the river, it was said in ridicule. Even venerable Los Angeles newspaper columnist Jack Smith, a tireless defender of Southern California, once remarked: "When you have grown up beside the Los Angeles River, you don't expect too much of rivers." A radio commentator called it "the Rodney Dangerfield of waterways."[3]

Emblematic of its reputation, the Los Angeles River is probably best known these days as a place where Hollywood movie studios film high-speed car chases. The river's smooth, paved bed looks so much like a roadway, in fact, that every few years some politician or planner actually suggests that it be turned into one as a way of relieving some of Southern California's legendary traffic congestion. Indeed, while urban rivers everywhere have been dirtied and defiled by the cities that grew up along their banks, the case of the Los Angeles River is in many ways unusual. The Cuyahoga River in Cleveland may have once been so polluted that it caught fire, and the Chicago River was so filthy that long ago its flow was reversed to keep it from contaminating Lake Michigan, but at least those rivers, even at their worst, looked like rivers. What other major river besides the Los Angeles River, after all, could you even propose to paint?

The river's image, however, belies its history and importance to the development of Southern California. Three centuries ago, the river meandered this way and that through a dense forest of willow and sycamore, elderberry and wild grape. Its overflow filled vast marshlands that were home to myriad waterfowl and small animals. Steelhead trout spawned in the river, and grizzly bear roamed its shores in search of food. So lush was this landscape and so unusual was it in the dry country that the river was a focus of settlement long before the first white man set foot in the area. Indians relied on the river and the adjacent woodlands for food and the raw materials from which they made almost everything else. They built their villages near the river and bathed each morning in its waters. When the first European visitors passed through the area in the eighteenth century, more than two dozen Indian villages lined the river's course to the sea. The first white visitors, Spanish explorers in search of possible sites where they could establish missions, were also drawn to the river. They marveled at its beauty, named it after a cherished religious site near their homeland, and noted the potential of the gardenlike setting for settlement. Later, when they were looking for places to establish agricultural operations to supply food to their poorly nourished missions and military forts, they founded one of only three such settlements established in California in the eighteenth century on a terrace overlooking the river.

That agricultural village became the city of Los Angeles, which would not exist had it not been for the river. A reliable source of water was the first prerequisite for settlement in the semiarid region and, as one of the few streams in the area that flowed year-round, the river largely determined the location of Los Angeles. The river was the city's nearly sole source of water for more than a century, providing drinking water for a growing population and irrigating the vineyards and orange groves that not only helped to make Southern California the most important agricultural region in the West but also contributed to the development of its reputation as a garden paradise. The exclusive legal right of the city of Los Angeles to the river's waters, furthermore, virtually guaranteed its emergence as the dominant city in the region. As Los Angeles grew, though, demand for water became so great that the river's entire surface flow had to be diverted for domestic use. The floodplain forest that had spread along its banks was cleared for cultivation, its trees cut for fuel and fences, its marshy undergrowth gradually replaced by roads, subdivisions, and industry. Eventually, much of the river's underground flow was also pumped to the surface to meet the rapidly expanding water needs of the growing city, and soon the river was dry most of the year where its flow had once been ample.

Flood control projects made the Los Angeles River what it is today. Despite its usually meager flow—and, in part, because of it—the river was unpredictable and prone to flooding, often shifting its course with each new storm and altering its outlet to the sea by as much as ninety degrees. Two of the factors that made Los Angeles so attractive for settlement, its climate and the tall mountains that surround it, made the river a menace as development spread. The lack of rainfall most of the year limited the dry season flow of the river, which prevented it from establishing a well-defined channel. The mountains, meanwhile, blocked winter storms and squeezed the moisture from them, their precipitous slopes sending torrents of water, mud, and rocks down steep canyons toward the river. Catastrophic floods in 1914, 1934, and 1938 led to the creation of a comprehensive regional flood control program. Devices were built in the foothills to catch rocks, trees, and other debris that would pour from the mountains during storms. Massive flood control reservoirs were constructed on the lowlands to regulate peak stream flows. The river itself was straightened, deepened, and widened and its new channel was lined with concrete to provide floodwaters the quickest route to the sea. Although the facilities that were built to keep the river in place and prevent it from flooding made it the eyesore it is now, large parts of present-day Los Angeles could not have been developed if the vagrant nature of the river had not been controlled.

In the artificial landscape that is contemporary Los Angeles, where even the palm trees were imported, perhaps nothing symbolizes the role of human beings in changing the face of the earth more than the exploitation and transformation of the Los Angeles River. Modified beyond recognition, its flow tapped before it even reached the surface, the river was used, abused, and forgotten. In recent years, however, there has been a growing interest in revitalizing the river—part of an expanding worldwide movement to revive urban rivers. Environmentalists and others are now calling for the removal of the river's concrete channel in some places, the construction of riverside parks and trails, and the establishment of a greenway along its banks. They are advocating that more ecologically sensitive approaches to flood control be implemented and have vigorously opposed new flood control construction along the river. Though progress on efforts to revitalize the river has thus far been limited and the river itself looks much as it has for forty years, its image is changing. A new stage in the life of the Los Angeles River may be just beginning.

I first saw the Los Angeles River on 2 January 1978. It was not a momentous occasion. Like so many other Southern Californians, I encountered the river for the first time while crossing it on a freeway. I was a precocious eighteen-year-old sportswriter on my way from my mother's condo in Marina del Rey to Pasadena to cover the Rose Bowl for a small newspaper in central Kansas. If I noticed the river or even realized what it was, I don't recall. I have lived in the Los Angeles area off and on since then. I worked less than a mile from the river's mouth in Long Beach, but the river made no impression on me. Later, I lived in Hollywood while working as a reporter for the *Los Angeles Times* and certainly must have passed over the river again and again while traveling to assignments, but then, too, it might as well have been invisible. In many ways, my initial response (or lack of one) to the river was typical. I grew up in Delaware, not far from the ample, if hardly scenic, Delaware River. My father was raised along the Mississippi River in Quincy, Illinois, and catfish dinners in a riverside cafe were among the defining events of family trips to Illinois. I have lived in river towns in Kansas, Tennessee, and Louisiana. Like most anyone who has read *Tom Sawyer* or has seen a peeling old boat sitting silently on the Ohio, I've daydreamed of floating down a river on a raft made of driftwood. Consequently, the Los Angeles River was easy to overlook.

My own curiosity about the river was not aroused until many years after I had first seen it. As a beginning graduate student in geography, living just west of the river and going to school five miles east of its course, I realized that the concrete culvert I so often traveled over (and rarely noticed) was the answer to my own question about why Los Angeles—at least its historic center—is located where it is. Why, I had wondered, wasn't it on the ocean? Or at the base of some impressive mountain? Why was it there on the edge of a plain, fifteen miles from the Pacific Ocean, ten miles from the San Gabriel Mountains, with no immediately apparent advantages of location? It was only after I discovered that the river was the reason that its story began to unfold before me. Soon, it seemed as if everywhere I turned I read or heard something new about the river that increased my curiosity about it.

I was amazed to learn, for instance, that, before the river was paved, its course had once been so variable that it had flowed west rather than south from Los Angeles, emptying into the ocean at Santa Monica Bay, and that marshland formed in part by the river's overflow had covered large parts of present-day Hollywood and Beverly Hills. I was astonished to discover that, thanks to the water provided by the river, Los Angeles had been the first important wine-producing center in California and that the earliest oranges shipped east from the state had also been irrigated with river water. I was stunned to find that, during a major flood in the 1930s, the usually tiny river had a discharge at Long Beach equal to the normal flow of the Mississippi River near St. Louis and that, as recently as 1940, two-foot-long trout had been caught in the river. In short, I was surprised to learn that the Los Angeles River had a palpable history, that the ugly, concrete gutter had once been so much more.

In a city that is too often considered not to have a history, my realization that the river had a meaningful past was somehow reassuring. In this light, however, the details of the river's undoing were even more shocking. Flood control officials in general and the U.S. Army Corps of Engineers in particular are blamed for turning the Los Angeles River into an eyesore, when in truth they were little more than undertakers, closing the coffin on a river that was by and large already dead. The destruction of the river had begun half a century before the first concrete was poured, when the river, so unlike the waterways back home remembered by residents in this city of perpetual newcomers, began to be viewed not as a giver of life or a thing of beauty, but as a dumping ground—for horse carcasses, petroleum waste, and the city's garbage. As the river was sucked dry by water developments, many saw its channel as the only logical destination for the city's sewage, and its chief function in the expanding metropolis came to be as a sand and gravel quarry. Despite its preeminent role in the early development of Los Angeles, the Los Angeles River was seldom revered and, even before industrial development transformed the land along its banks, was rarely written about in anything but mocking tones.

My discovery of the river coincided with the blossoming of the movement to revitalize its course, although I do not consider myself part of that movement and my interest in the river has always been more in its past than in its future. Knowing what I know about the river's transformation, I am also somewhat skeptical about the possibilities for its renewal (although less so today than when I first began studying the river). Nevertheless, the new attention being paid to the river does highlight the need for a more complete telling of its history.

Despite all the talk, the multitude of studies and proposals, and the ever-increasing media attention the river has received in recent years, there remains a remarkable ignorance about its past. Most attempts to portray its history have been one-sided and incomplete, seeking chiefly to evoke an image of a "once-enchanted" river and to condemn the engineers who supposedly turned it into something else. The real story of the Los Angeles River is much more complex. Although most of this book is historical, it would be short-sighted to attempt to produce what is, in essence, a biography of the river without also examining current efforts to revive it. This book, then, seeks to tell the story of the Los Angeles River from before the time of European settlement until the present day. Three themes are emphasized—how the river has changed through history, how it has been changed by humans, and how its role in the region has changed over time.

Chapter 1 describes the former character of the river, outlines its importance to the Indians who lived nearby, and tells how the river was perceived by the first Europeans who saw it. Chapter 2 analyzes the river's significance to the selection of a site for the pueblo that became Los Angeles and highlights its development as a water source. Chapter 3 shows that, while the river helped Los Angeles become the largest and most important city in Southern California, the city's increasing reliance on the water it provided doomed the river as the region grew, so changing its appearance that few cared about its ultimate destruction. The focus shifts in chapter 4, which examines the flood risk presented by the river, traces its changing courses over time, and demonstrates how an organized program for flood control became a necessity as the population spread. Chapter 5 tracks the development of a comprehensive flood control program and describes the transformation of the river from a tiny stream with willows on its banks to a huge, concrete channel whose primary purpose is the rapid delivery of floodwaters. Chapter 6 concludes the book by looking at the river today, reconsidering earlier efforts to beautify its course, and contemplating its future.

We can learn much about urban rivers everywhere from the story of the Los Angeles River. From its role in the settlement of a city and its importance as a water source to its ultimate transformation and potential renewal, its larger history mirrors the story of urban rivers the world over. Zoom in closer, however, and the case of the Los Angeles River begins to look unique; and much of that distinctiveness has to do with its setting in a metropolitan area that is unusual in North America—in its climate, in its topography, and in its development. The evolution of the river can also tell us much about greater Los Angeles, not only because the town from which it grew could not have existed without the river, but also because the river's evolution paralleled the growth of Los Angeles from village to city to metropolis. The story of the Los Angeles River is a frequently remarkable, sometimes bizarre, and ultimately tragic tale of how an often overlooked element of the geography of one of the world's great cities shaped its development and was, in turn, remade in its image.

1　The River as It Once Was

WALKING ALONG THE CONCRETE BANKS OF THE LOS AN-
geles River, straight and smooth and wide, it is hard to imagine what
the river might once have been. History creates a vision of a very different waterway, one that has been a magnet for settlement for thousands of years. Long before the river was confined in concrete by flood
control projects, before settlement by the Spanish and the increasing
diversion of its water for irrigation and domestic use, the river flowed
when and where it wanted, often raging out of control during the
winter rains. It did not always empty into San Pedro Bay at Long
Beach, as it does today. Sometimes it meandered west across the
coastal plain, flowing into Santa Monica Bay along the present course
of Ballona Creek.[1]

Much of the river's waters never reached the sea, instead spreading
over the countryside and joining with springs flowing from surrounding hills to form vast marshes, shallow lakes, and small ponds (fig.
1.1). In other places, the river sank into the ground, its bed dry most of
the year. Willow and cottonwood trees covered the overflow lands (fig.
1.2), and a dense undergrowth of shrubs made much of the coastal
plain impassable.[2] Great oak trees lined the stream course in the San
Fernando Valley. This diverse environment provided a rich habitat for
wildlife and helped support one of the largest concentrations of Indians in North America. The first European visitors to Southern California also immediately recognized the potential provided by the
river, noting the rich soil that spread away from its banks and admir-
ing the wild grapes and native California roses that grew nearby. The
plain along the river, one of them wrote, was "so green and lush it
seems as though it has been planted."[3]

Such a landscape was simply the latest stage in the natural history
of a region that had been built in large part by its rivers and shaped by
the water they carried. Much of the Los Angeles Basin is in reality a
broad alluvial plain that stretches from Santa Monica to Newport
Beach in Orange County. The waters of the Los Angeles, San Gabriel,
and Santa Ana Rivers often mingled on the coastal plain in times of

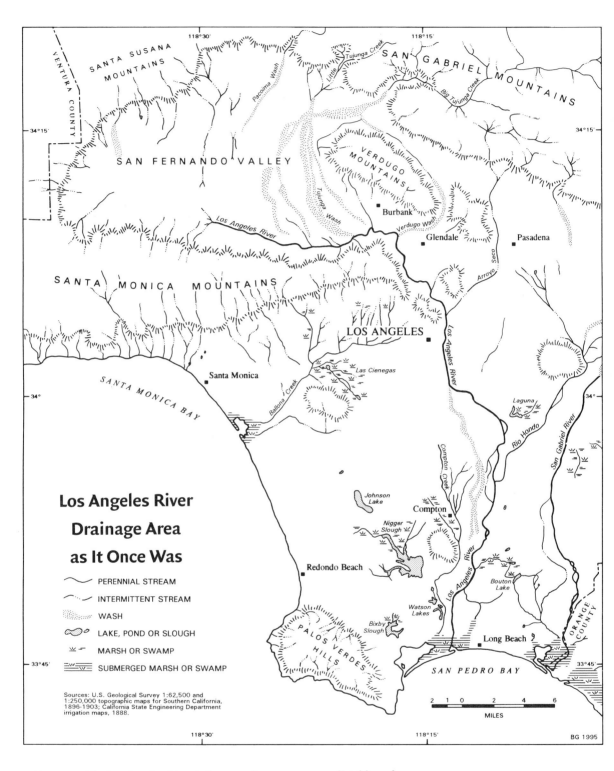

Los Angeles River
Drainage Area
as It Once Was

	PERENNIAL STREAM
	INTERMITTENT STREAM
	WASH
	LAKE, POND OR SLOUGH
	MARSH OR SWAMP
	SUBMERGED MARSH OR SWAMP

Sources: U.S. Geological Survey 1:62,500 and
1:250,000 topographic maps for Southern California,
1896–1903; California State Engineering Department
irrigation maps, 1888.

FIG. 1.1. The Los Angeles River in its natural state was unpredictable and prone to flooding, with its overflow filling vast marshes, sloughs, and shallow lakes. Map by the author.

FIG. 1.2. The river landscape as it probably appeared along much of its course before it was extensively transformed by human settlement and flood control projects. This photograph was taken near present-day Griffith Park, probably in the late 1800s. Used with permission, Seaver Center for Western History Research, Natural History Museum of Los Angeles County.

flood. Floodwaters from these rivers deposited the rich soil that helped make Los Angeles County the most productive agricultural county in the United States until the 1950s. Their braided channels once spread over wide areas, and their courses shifted dramatically over time. The Los Angeles River sometimes flowed south, sometimes west. The San Gabriel River once emptied into the ocean at San Pedro Bay, along a course later occupied by the Los Angeles River. The Santa Ana River also repeatedly changed its path to the ocean.[4]

Twenty million years ago, most of the southern half of present-day Los Angeles County was covered by seawater, and the Palos Verdes peninsula was a distant island off the shore. Seas extended as far inland as Pasadena and Pomona and west to Ventura. The tall mountains that separate the coastal plain from the San Fernando Valley and the inland valleys from the Mojave Desert did not yet exist. As the waters slowly receded, these mountains were gradually uplifted. The granitic slopes of the San Gabriel Mountains, for example, have been continually uplifted since the early Tertiary period, twenty-five to sixty-five million years ago. The greatest period of mountain building, however, did not occur until the mid-Pleistocene, about one million years ago. Most of the mountains that ring the valleys and coastal plain are deeply fractured by faults and, as they grew taller, their brittle slopes were continually eroded. Rivers and streams carried boulders, rocks, gravel, sand, and silt down these slopes to the valleys and coastal plain. As the streams left the mountains, they created broad alluvial fans, their courses swinging back and forth and depositing sediments all the while. It was in this manner that the present ground surface of metropolitan Los Angeles was created. More than half of the soils on the coastal plain, in fact, were deposited in relatively recent time by the region's waterways. In places, these sediments are as much as twenty thousand feet thick.[5]

This pattern of deposition also established the character of Southern California's rivers and streams. As the coastal plain and inland valleys became covered with a thick layer of alluvial deposits, much of the runoff during the rainy season sank into the ground, collecting in underground basins. Only during major storms did stream channels have a significant surface flow. Most of the year, streams flowed both above and below ground, disappearing and reappearing several times between the mountains and the sea. Water rose to the surface when it encountered an underground rock obstruction or when a high water table prevented it from percolating into the sands. So great was the underground flow from the region's three major rivers that it created artesian basins beneath nearly three hundred square miles of the coastal plain.[6]

Because the rivers and streams seldom flowed above ground, their channels were shallow and poorly defined. They were incapable of containing the great quantities of water that would rush from the mountains during winter rains. Sudden storms transformed normally dry streams into raging torrents, often in a matter of hours and sometimes with the sun still shining. Usually placid rivers overflowed their banks, inundating large areas and occasionally turning portions of the coastal plain into a huge lake. Swirling floodwaters, carrying great loads of rock, sediment, and trees, cut new channels through the countryside and dug depressions in the soil, leaving sloughs, marshes, and ponds in their wake.[7] The Los Angeles River was typical in this regard. Before its character was significantly altered by human activity, it was really two different waterways—a small, gentle stream flowing through a broad, sandy bed most of the year and a large, turbulent, unpredictable river for a few days every winter.

The description of a traveler who witnessed the catastrophic floods in Los Angeles in 1884 perhaps best conveys the erratic nature of the river before it was controlled. "The Los Angeles is one of those streams whose bed, at some points, is above the water. In other words, it flows underground, or is lost in the sand," wrote Emma H. Adams in one of a series of letters to an Ohio newspaper. "During the rainy season it enlarges to a broad river, with a powerful current and a dangerous shifting bottom. Widely overflowing its banks, it sweeps away real estate and personal property in a most merciless fashion. Scarcely a season passes in which adventurous men do not lose their lives in attempting to cross it with teams when at its flood. Both driver and horses soon disappear beneath its restless quicksands. But let the early Autumn come! Then the once raging torrent purls along, a narrow, shallow, garrulous brook, which bare-footed children may easily ford."[8]

An Upside-down River

Before it was confined in concrete and its present channel was excavated through wandering sands, the Los Angeles River began much farther east than it does today, its waters first rising to the surface somewhere near the twentieth-century San Fernando Valley suburb of Encino. Water that collects in a huge underground reservoir beneath the valley was here first pushed to the surface by the submerged base of the Santa Monica Mountains, which rise more than a thousand feet above the south side of the valley and project in front of this reservoir like a giant wing dam. The overflow from this natural reservoir supplied most of the dry season flow of the river before flood control. Because the bulk of its flow came not directly from mountain or surface runoff but from this subterranean source, the Los Angeles River has sometimes been called an upside-down river.

This natural reservoir was created by rocks and gravel washed from mountain slopes by seasonal runoff. The San Fernando Valley is a mountain-enclosed basin, twenty-four miles long and twelve miles wide, the sides and floor of which have been covered with thousands of feet of mountain sediment carried by dozens of intermittent streams. The character of deposition determined the location and capacity of the underground storage basin and ultimately influenced the nature of the river the basin supplies. The slopes that rim most of the valley are composed primarily of soft, sedimentary rocks—shales, sandstones, and clays—that produce fine, relatively impervious soils when eroded. These soils cover the central and western part of the valley. Before flood control, seasonal runoff in this area tended to flow above ground because of the compact nature of the fine sediments. Subsurface flow was minimal.

The San Gabriel Mountains, which tower above the northeastern corner of the valley, are much different. Rising to twice the height of the other mountains surrounding the valley, they are composed primarily of granite. Their long, steep slopes, deeply cut by faults, encourage erosion, which leaves mountain soils shallow and rocky surfaces exposed. Debris washed from these mountains is larger and more irregularly shaped, reflecting the nature of the source materials. The soils created from these sediments on the valley floor, as a result, are less compact, more porous, and, thus, more permeable than the soils of the central and western San Fernando Valley. Winter after winter for thousands of years, heavy precipitation washed boulders, gravel, and other debris down the steep mountain canyons to the valley floor. The size of the debris determined how far it was transported because mountain streams gradually lose their carrying power after they emerge from the hills and their gradients decrease. Boulders and other large stones were typically deposited at the foot of mountain slopes. Smaller particles, such as clays, silts, and sands, were carried the farthest. Coarse gravels, too heavy to be carried great distances, spread across the valley floor. The eastern half of the San Fernando Valley, consequently, is composed primarily of porous sediments, which were capable of absorbing most of the mountain runoff before the region was heavily developed.[9]

These pervious materials created the subterranean reservoir that underlies 175 square miles of the San Fernando Valley. Studies have shown that this underground storage basin can hold 3.2 million acre feet of water, roughly one trillion gallons.[10] Only two human-constructed reservoirs in California, Lake Shasta and Lake Oroville, are larger.[11] Water that collects beneath the valley flows southeast with the gentle slope of the underlying topography, rising to the surface when it encounters the impenetrable rock mass that also forms the Santa Monica Mountains. One can visualize the San Fernando Valley as a huge bowl filled with water that has been tipped slightly, causing its contents to overflow. That overflow created the Los Angeles River.[12]

Most of the water that percolates into the aquifers beneath the San Fernando Valley originates in the San Gabriel Mountains. Because these mountains rise much higher than nearby ranges, they receive significantly more precipitation. The Santa Monica, Santa Susana, and Verdugo Mountains, which surround three sides of the valley, seldom reach heights above three thousand feet. The western San Gabriel Mountains, in contrast, have elevations of more than seven thousand feet. These higher ridges often trap eastern-moving winter storms. Although downtown Los Angeles averages just fifteen inches of rain a year, some mountain peaks in the San Gabriels receive more than forty inches of precipitation annually. Nearly all of that falls as rain, and 80 percent occurs during four winter months. Archaeological evidence suggests that the microclimates of Southern California have been relatively stable for the past ten thousand years.[13]

Seasonal rains quickly saturate the shallow mountain soil, and water runs off rapidly, draining into hundreds of mountain canyons that feed three principal streams—Big Tujunga, Little Tujunga, and Pacoima Creeks. Big Tujunga Creek is the largest of the three. It emerges from a canyon north of Sunland and, before its character was significantly altered by human activity, joined with Little Tujunga Creek a few miles west to form Tujunga Wash. Pacoima Creek leaves the hills just east of the city of San Fernando. Until hundreds of small dams and debris basins were built in the mountains to prevent floods, dozens of smaller mountain streams, nearly one per mile, also discharged onto the valley floor. None of these streams reached the Los Angeles River except during extreme floods. Most of the water they carried sank immediately into the porous valley surface, contributing to the vast underground supply that fed the river.[14]

The Native Landscape

The Los Angeles River at its beginning in Encino was but a few feet wide before flood control projects enlarged its channel. It was narrow enough to walk over, really more of a spring than a river or even a creek. Early Spanish explorers noted the presence of marshes and tule patches nearby, no doubt formed from the same underground flow that created the river. The river gradually widened, flowing east for twenty miles, above and below ground, along the base of the north slopes of the Santa Monica Mountains. Much of its flow was subsurface. Its course through most of the San Fernando Valley was ill-defined. On an 1890 map of Southern California, in fact, the river is shown as an extension of Big Tujunga Creek and Tujunga Wash, flowing west after leaving the San Gabriel Mountains before turning south along the west side of the Verdugo Mountains. The river is not shown at all in the western three-quarters of the valley.[15]

The river as it is now recognized meandered east along the base of the Santa Monica Mountains through present-day Universal City and Burbank before turning southeast near Griffith Park, where it followed the eastern terminus of the mountains. Verdugo Wash and the Arroyo Seco, dry most of the year, added to its flow during winter months. The river reached the coastal plain via a gap between two hills known as the Glendale Narrows, the San Fernando Valley's only outlet to the sea, so named because the hills on both sides of the river come progressively closer together farther south until they are but a few hundred yards apart near Elysian Park. The river had its greatest natural surface flow in this area because the ridge that forms the eastern extension of the Santa Monica Mountains dips below ground here but is barely covered with alluvium. Bedrock, sometimes only forty feet deep, is much closer to the surface here than anywhere else along the river's course. As a result, much of the water that flowed underground in the San Fernando Valley was pushed to the surface, a condition that assured an abundant and surprisingly consistent year-round flow in the river between Burbank and downtown Los Angeles. This is the only section of the river that was not dry at least part of the year before diversions from its channel became significant. The subterranean reservoir that supplies the river is so large, in fact, that even during extended droughts the flow of the river through the Narrows rarely fell below 20 percent of its average discharge.[16] The river through this section provided all the water needed by the city of Los Angeles for more than a century.

The river turned more directly south after exiting the Glendale Narrows, sometimes flowing along the terraces that rise gently west of the river, where the pueblo that became Los Angeles was founded in 1781. At other times, it hugged the base of the bluffs (now known as Boyle Heights) on the east side of its valley. South of the original pueblo site, now downtown Los Angeles, the river's course became even more indefinite, shifting back and forth over an area two miles wide, with most of its flow again sinking into the absorbent sands and gravels brought down from the mountains. On a map drawn in the 1830s of a large land grant directly south of the pueblo lands, the river course is labeled as the "Arroyo del Pueblo."[17] *Arroyo* is the Spanish word for a dry wash. The bulk of the water that had been pushed to the surface in the Glendale Narrows disappeared underground beneath the coastal plain, except during winter storms. This underground flow contributed to the vast subterranean supply that for years was the chief source of water for most of the coastal portion of Los Angeles County. The first shallow wells were drilled near the river in the 1860s, and by 1904 there were more than eight thousand wells on the coastal plain.[18] Some of the underground supply returned to the surface in especially low-lying areas or when it encountered a line of hills or a subsurface obstruction. Where this happened, marshes, lakes, and shallow ponds dotted the landscape.

Wetlands created by the river's overflow once covered large areas of the countryside from Los Angeles to the sea. A tule patch once sat in a shallow depression near the present location of Fifth Street in downtown Los Angeles. Early residents said that there were two ponds on the east side of the river near Boyle Heights.[19] An area north of the confluence of the Los Angeles River and the Rio Hondo (see fig. 1.1), now occupied by the city of Commerce, was once known as Laguna for a twisting slough formed by the subsurface flow of the two streams. Old maps also show marshes near Lynwood and in a line west of Compton, where pockets of shallow water and a dense growth of willows and cottonwoods made the area "almost impassable," in the words of a nineteenth-century resident.[20] There was a peat bed in Watts. The city of Paramount, north of Long Beach, used to be called Clearwater because of a lake nearby.[21]

The Los Angeles River is in many ways like a desert watercourse. The Mediterranean-type climate of Southern California produces extremes of surface flow typical of more arid environments, with floodwaters periodically carving new stream channels across the landscape. The Los Angeles River has shifted its path to the sea by as much as ninety degrees. Sometimes, the river turned sharply west near downtown Los Angeles, following a route today approximated by Washington Boulevard, and eventually emptying into the sea at Playa del Rey. This course is now occupied by Ballona Creek. At other times, the river flowed directly south to San Pedro Bay, joining the San Gabriel River seven miles north of its mouth; the combined flow of the two streams reached the ocean through Wilmington Lagoon.[22] This is roughly the river's current course, although its exact route has been significantly altered by port development and flood control projects.

A ridge of hills that stretches forty miles northwest from Newport Beach nearly to Beverly Hills strongly influenced the river's natural route to the sea. This ridge was created by the Newport-Inglewood fault zone and is represented on the surface by a series of intermittent low hills. The tallest of these are the Baldwin Hills, north of Inglewood, which rise four hundred feet above the surrounding countryside (see fig. 3.11). Cheviot Hills, north of Culver City, Dominguez Hills in Carson, and Signal Hill near Long Beach are also formed by this ridge. On its western course, the river inundated a large area when its underground flow encountered the base of the Baldwin Hills and was pushed to the surface. Joined by streams and springs flowing from the south side of the Santa Monica Mountains and swelled by seasonal floodwaters, this overflow helped create a vast marshland labeled on maps even in this century as Las Cienegas, Spanish for "swamps." The name of one of Los Angeles's major streets, La Cienega Boulevard, reflects this legacy. Beverly Hills occupies an area once known as Rancho Rodeo de las Aguas, or "ranch of the meeting of waters." Thick groves of sycamores and other water-loving vegetation were so common in the area that the first Spanish explorers to Southern California named a small stream near the present intersection of

Highland Avenue and Venice Boulevard the Spring of the Sycamores of St. Esteban. Marshes and small ponds extended on both sides of the river for three miles, from near Beverly Hills southeast to roughly the present site of Crenshaw High School, directly east of the Baldwin Hills. These wetlands were popular duck and geese hunting grounds in the nineteenth and early twentieth centuries.[23]

The river was forced into a more narrow course farther west as it passed between the Baldwin Hills and the Cheviot Hills to the north, before again spreading over a wide area at its mouth to Santa Monica Bay. Mud flats and lagoons created by the river's overflow once covered more than twenty-one hundred acres from Santa Monica to the north-facing bluffs at Westchester, forming what eventually became known as the Ballona Wetlands. Most of the year, this was brackish or freshwater marsh, teeming with wildlife. Sea otters may have occasionally moved about on the edges of the marsh. One early naturalist visitor described the tidelands as "unsurpassed by any other on the Pacific Coast."[24] In winter, flood-swollen streams turned the lowlands from Culver City to the ocean into a large lake. Indians called this area *pwinukipar*, meaning "it is full of water."[25]

The ridge created by the Newport-Inglewood fault zone also influenced the river's southerly course. South of Los Angeles, the river swung back and forth across the coastal plain. Most of the year, its bed was dry. Near Compton, however, two sets of hills formed by this ridge confined the river to a more narrow course. The Dominguez Hills prevented the river from wandering farther west. A long line of rolling hills, best known for the abruptly rising Signal Hill, north of downtown Long Beach, kept the river in place on the east. The ridge continues underground between these sets of hills, which forced much of the river's subterranean flow to the surface. Marshes created by this overflow lined the north side of Dominguez Hills. Sloughs and a half-dozen small lakes curved around the base of the hills east of the river. Waterfowl were so abundant in the wetlands that a Pasadena duck hunting club purchased land in the area for the use of its members. Another gun club operated along the base of Signal Hill.[26]

South of the gap between these hills, the course of the river was even more indistinct and impermanent than it had been farther upstream. Sometimes the river meandered east toward Long Beach. More often, it flowed in a fairly direct line south, emptying into the ocean—at least when it carried enough water to reach that far—two miles west of downtown Long Beach. At other times, it occupied the course of Dominguez Creek still farther west and spilled its winter overflow into a line of three lakes northeast of Wilmington, known as the Watson Lakes (see fig. 1.1).[27] As on the river's western route, its seasonal overflow helped create extensive marshes and tidal lagoons near its mouth. Saltwater marsh once stretched from the Palos Verdes hills to Long Beach, a distance of five miles. In such an environment, the location of the river's mouth was in a nearly constant state of flux, shifting this way and that as normal deposits of silt blocked one channel and forced floodwaters to create another.

Eighteenth-century surveys of the coastline, imprecise though such early surveys may have been, nevertheless give some suggestion of the variability and indistinguishability of the river's outlet to the Pacific. A survey of the Rancho San Pedro conducted in 1857 located the eastern shore of the river's mouth 289 feet farther west than had a similar survey conducted twenty-two years before. A subsequent survey, completed in 1866, placed the eastern end of the river's mouth 379 feet farther *east* than had the survey conducted nine years previously. A U.S. Coast Survey map published in 1872, meanwhile, placed the eastern shore of the river's mouth fully 1,275 feet farther *west* than where it had been located in 1866. If that map is to be believed, the location of the west end of a railroad trestle built over the river in 1892 suggests that the mouth of the river had shifted *east* more than fourteen hundred feet during the intervening twenty years.[28]

Such attempts to locate the mouth of the river precisely are exercises in foolishness, however, because it is unlikely that the river carried enough water to reach the sea most of the year. Its sundry channels were probably as insignificant as the summertime flow. Thus, it was only natural that with each new storm floodwaters would seek a new outlet. "The water courses which appear so clearly depicted on the map are in reality shallow beds in readily erodible soil," a U.S. Army engineer wrote in 1915. "Their banks are low and not always well defined, and a single freshet is sometimes able to obliterate the channel at one place and establish a new channel elsewhere."[29] Floodwaters brought down by the river, consequently, often fanned out between San Pedro and Long Beach. Sometimes they backed up along the south and west sides of Dominguez Hills, where they created a stagnant backwater known as Nigger Slough (later renamed Dominguez Slough). The intertwining channels of Nigger Slough once covered some seven thousand acres, stretching all the way to Gardena. Occasionally, floodwaters formed a shallow pond even farther north, known locally as Johnson Lake. Soil believed to have been laid down by the river has been found as far away as Inglewood.[30]

Most of the ponds and marshes that were once such a common element on the Southern California landscape gradually diminished in size or dried up altogether as diversions of water from the region's rivers increased and pumping for underground water intensified across the lowlands.[31] Development also hastened the demise of the wetlands, as marshes and ponds were drained using artificial means. Still, even as late as 1888, according to a report of the state engineer, nearly a third of the coastal plain was covered with soils that were regularly inundated or had been permanently "damaged" by floodwaters. Lands classified as "moist or semi-moist" covered 68,000 acres, almost 15 percent of the surveyed area. Freshwater marshes occupied 5,750 acres. Wetlands bordering the rivers and marshes covered 2,850 acres. Salt marshes and estuaries at the mouths of the rivers occupied 15,200 acres.[32]

Plant and Animal Life

The accounts of early travelers and residents suggest that large parts of Southern California were once covered by a sometimes impenetrable jungle of marshes, thickets, and dense woods. Many modern-day observers often incorrectly assume that the Los Angeles Basin was a nearly treeless plain in its natural state; in fact, large areas of the lowlands seem to have been covered by a floodplain forest before the streams were channelized and the wetlands disappeared. Cottonwoods and several species of willows were thick along the stream courses and amid the marshes, growing to heights of forty to fifty feet (fig. 1.3). Sycamores were also present, though less abundant.[33] One giant sycamore, rising sixty feet above the river near downtown Los Angeles and measuring twenty feet around the trunk, was a landmark for generations and was said to have been a council tree for local Indians.[34] Even as late as 1854, after much of the landscape had been altered by human activity, a U.S. government botanist noted that "nature has peculiarly favored this region. It is well wooded and watered."[35]

Clumps of alder, hackberry, and shrubs formed a dense undergrowth beneath the trees of the willow-cottonwood forest. Masses of thorny California rose grew wild. Native grapes and other vines wound around tree branches and through the shrubs. Briars, brambles, and California blackberries were common. Few trails penetrated the woods. Bears and other wild animals roamed the countryside, making travel dangerous. Horse teams and wagons frequently became bogged down in the mud near the marshes.[36] Felipe de Neve, California's first governor and the founder of Los Angeles, complained in 1777 that, after the first rains in November, it was impossible to move mule trains across the coastal plain and that, "even counting on the rains stopping in February, the roads are impassable for more than a month at a time."[37] At other times of the year, seemingly dry river courses often disguised pockets of quicksand.

This muddy landscape seems improbable when you look at the

FIG. 1.3. Willows shade the river near downtown Los Angeles, probably about 1900. Used with permission, Seaver Center for Western History Research, Natural History Museum of Los Angeles County.

present condition of the coastal plain, which would be predominantly brown most of the year if it were not watered artificially. The geographer Homer Aschmann once wrote that "areas regularly flooded by fresh water never were large in this dry land," but such an observation would seem to be based solely on the climate of the lowlands and fails to take into account the much greater precipitation that falls in nearby mountains and the tremendous changes in the hydrology of Southern California brought about by human beings.[38] Although most of lowland Los Angeles County is indeed semiarid and receives fewer than fifteen inches of rain a year, some areas in the mountains that drain onto those lowlands receive more than forty inches of precipitation annually, as much as many locations in the humid eastern United States.[39] Until the rivers were controlled, excessive pumping lowered water tables, and wetlands were drained, seasonal runoff poured down mountain canyons, spread across the lowlands, and filled underground basins until they were overflowing. Consequently, the true vegetation of large parts of the coastal plain, where subsurface ridges kept much of this water from draining to the sea, was probably not chaparral or other dryland vegetation, but water-loving grasses, shrubs, and trees.

When a catastrophic flood in 1914 prompted the first large-scale flood control investigations in Los Angeles County, the lack of detailed written information about the natural environment prompted engineers to venture out into the field to interview hundreds of old-timers who had lived through earlier floods and had witnessed the gradual transformation of the landscape. One of the most compelling aspects of those interviews is the depiction of an environment that, even by 1900, had largely disappeared. Typical were the comments of George H. Bixby of Long Beach, whose family once owned the Rancho Los Cerritos, which occupied twenty-seven thousand acres east of the river and, together with the Rancho San Pedro farther west, covered half of the coastal plain between Los Angeles and San Pedro Bay. "I once had a Mexican *vaquero* whose father had lived here all his life who said that all of the valley . . . was one tangle of marsh willows, larch, blackberry vines and other tangled undergrowth that was impenetrable," Bixby said. "There were only one or two trails across the valley, and they were not safe for two reasons: on account of the undergrowth and bogs, and there were bears in the tangled jungle. On both sides of Los Cerritos and further up the valley there were a great many springs in the side hills and peat bogs. They were surrounded by tules, willows and other brambles. As the country became more settled and wells were sunk in the upper land, there was less water and the springs flowed less and less until in the final attempt to drain the land, they used tile drains and the springs disappeared."[40] Numerous other accounts in those interviews painted a similar picture.

This floodplain forest formed one of the most biologically rich habitats in Southern California, but it was only one of several that existed along the river. Biologists from the Natural History Museum of Los Angeles County have identified twenty different plant and animal habitats that existed in the Los Angeles River watershed before settlement, including several adjacent to the river's channel.[41] The varied nature of the river greatly influenced the creation of this diverse environment. Where its course was relatively consistent, oaks and walnuts rose above the river. Dense shrubs and water-loving trees such as willows and cottonwoods, which are characteristic of a riparian ecosystem, were more common where floodwaters regularly spread over the landscape. Cattails, bulrushes, and other marsh vegetation thrived where the stream's course was even more indefinite and the river overflow joined with subsurface seeps to leave the soil soggy year-round.

Pickleweed, cord grass, leadwort, and other reedy plants waved in the sea breeze of the open lagoons, salt marsh, and mud flats that spread across large areas near the river's various outlets to the sea. Farther upstream, where sloughs and wetlands wound around the base of the hills that rise along the Newport-Inglewood fault zone, bulrushes and cattails probably grew thick. Edible watercress, water fern, and duckweed could be expected in open water. Patches of marsh vegetation in smaller concentrations were also found all across the coastal plain—bordering intermittent streams, on seasonally flooded lands, and in shallow depressions where floodwaters collected. Cattails and tules sprout not long after an area becomes flooded. On higher ground beside the marshes, several types of willows and other trees grew. One early resident said that trees were still plentiful enough in the late 1880s that he was able to cut four cords of wood a day in the area between the Los Angeles and San Gabriel Rivers, where Bellflower now stands.[42]

Wild grasses, some native but others introduced by humans, often unintentionally, carpeted the terrace lands and spread to the lowlands as the marshes dried up. The native grasses included sage, clover, and pepper grass. Weedy grasses and herbs—wild oats, foxtail barley, and several species of mustard—became dominant as settlement and ranching expanded. Fields of yellow mustard often spread to the horizon after the winter rains, growing so tall that many early visitors marveled at the heights to which the plant grew.[43] "We encountered more than one forest of mustard, whose tall stalks were above the riders' heads, and made, as it were, two thick walls on the two sides of the way," wrote a French traveler, Auguste Bernard Duhaut-Cilly, who visited California in 1827–28.[44]

The landscape was very different north of Los Angeles. An open woodland dominated by oak and California walnut grew on slopes flanking the Los Angeles River in the Glendale Narrows. Though willows, tules, and giant reeds still dominated the riverbanks, yuccas and cacti were likely to grow in areas less prone to flooding, marking the transition to the hotter and drier climate of the San Fernando Valley. One historian described the Glendale Narrows as a "veritable jungle of cactus, tullies and other growth that early pioneers had never dared to travel through, even on horseback."[45] The dry washes that spread north from the river in the San Fernando Valley were home to scattered juniper, prickly pear, and a distinctive leaf succulent known as Our Lord's candle, a yucca whose long, flower-tipped stalk rises up to ten feet above the rocky soil. Early residents of the area reported that clumps of junipers sometimes grew forty feet tall in Tujunga Wash. Junipers are characteristic of alluvial scrub (fig. 1.4), a distinct vegetation type that contains elements of several plant communities, including coastal sage scrub and chaparral. Other plants typically found on the frequently disturbed alluvial fans included greasewood, California holly, and laurel sumac.[46]

The Los Angeles River was less prone to flooding in the San Fernando Valley, where it was held in place by the southerly slope of the valley and the north-facing hills of the Santa Monica Mountains. Although there were several small sloughs between North Hollywood and Burbank, the valley oaks and walnut trees that grew in the rich bottomlands near the upper reaches of the river provide evidence that this area was seldom inundated. Oak trees were so abundant in the San Fernando Valley before European settlement, in fact, that the first Spanish visitors to the area named the valley Santa Catalina de Bononia de los Encinos (*encino* is Spanish for "live oak"). The residential

FIG. 1.4. A distinctive succulent known as Our Lord's candle and other plants characteristic of a vegetation type known as alluvial scrub grew along the dry washes that spread north from the river in the San Fernando Valley. Used with permission, Seaver Center for Western History Research, Natural History Museum of Los Angeles County.

community that later grew up around the site where the Spaniards camped is still known as Encino. Oak woodland occupied the drier sites, interspersed with native prairie, squaw bush, and poison oak. Grasses and wildflowers carpeted the valley floor. Cactus, sage, other small shrubs, and the occasional willow tree interrupted the extensive grasslands. Great valley oaks were scattered throughout the lowlands.[47]

Wildlife was abundant all along the river's course. Deer drank from its waters. Antelope lived near the river in what is today Griffith Park. Representatives of the first Spanish land expedition to Southern California reported that they saw "a great many antelope bands of five, eight or ten apiece" in the lowlands along the Los Angeles and San Gabriel Rivers.[48] Coyotes, gray fox, and mountain lions also roamed widely. Grizzly bears came down from the mountains in search of food, drawn by the steelhead and other fish that spawned in the streams. Hawks and condors hunted all along the river, while myriad other bird species including cuckoos, owls, vireos, and woodpeckers inhabited the willow groves that flourished along its course. Muskrats, prized for their fur, fed on the tules and cattails that grew in the marshes and sloughs. Swans, ducks, and geese swam nearby. Turtles inhabited the small ponds near the river's beginning in Encino, and the native grasses were home to gophers, badgers, shrews, and moles. Sea gulls flew inland in search of food, mingling with doves, pigeons, and quail on the floor of the San Fernando Valley. Later, as dryland farms replaced the grasslands, jack rabbits became so abundant that farmers held periodic drives in what were probably futile attempts to rid their lands of the ravenous hares.[49]

Birds, which remain surprisingly abundant in places along the river today, were no doubt even more numerous in historic times. Records for egg sets and nests in the collection of the Western Foundation of Vertebrate Zoology were analyzed in 1993 by Kimball Garrett, an ornithologist for the Natural History Museum of Los Angeles County. They indicate that the river and its overflow lands were home to numerous species that are no longer present or are now rare. Nighthawks, cactus wren, and roadrunners inhabited the San Fernando Valley. Golden eagles lived in hills overlooking the river across from Burbank. Yellow-billed cuckoos, Bell's vireo, long-eared owls, and California quail nested in the floodplain forest that spread away from the river on the coastal plain, while burrowing owls, green-backed herons, and Savannah sparrows lived in Nigger Slough and other marshes. Clapper rails were once moderately abundant in the lagoons near the river's mouth. Nests for the willow flycatcher were found in Long Beach as recently as the 1920s. In all, more than one hundred species are represented by egg sets collected along the Los Angeles River and its tributaries, primarily between 1890 and 1920. No doubt many more species once existed, since widespread collection of eggs did not commence until more than a century after settlement of the area by Euro-Americans.[50]

At least seven species of fish once lived in the river and its tributary streams, not including the many salt-tolerant species found where fresh and salt water mixed near the river's mouth. Two marine fish, the southern steelhead and the eel-like Pacific lamprey, spawned in the river, and their young spent one or two years in the stream before returning to the sea. They were probably the largest fish to live in the river, both reaching two feet in length. Three smaller freshwater species—Pacific brook lamprey, arroyo chub, and unarmored three-spine stickleback—were widely distributed in the river and in the marshes formed by its overflow. The Pacific brook lamprey grew to about eight inches in length. The arroyo chub, a member of the minnow family, and the threespine stickleback rarely grow longer than three inches. Two other species, the Santa Ana sucker and the Santa Ana speckled dace, occurred primarily in the river's mountain tributaries but were also found in the main river channel.[51]

The Importance of the River to the Indians

The river and the rich diversity of plant and animal life that flourished beside its banks helped support one of the largest concentrations of Indians in North America. The Gabrielino who inhabited the valleys and coastal plain were hunters and gatherers, and the river's waters were crucial to their way of life. The oak trees that covered the river bottomlands in the San Fernando Valley provided the acorns that were a Gabrielino staple. The floodplain forest of the lowlands supported the large animal population they hunted. The sloughs and marshes supplied the raw materials for their huts, clothing, and tools. The Gabrielino relied on the river for drinking water and bathed each day before dawn in the pools beside its banks (fig. 1.5).[52]

At the time of European contact, there are believed to have been more than five thousand Gabrielino in Southern California, spread among perhaps fifty to one hundred small villages, or *rancherias*. They were not the first inhabitants of the region, however. Archaeological evidence suggests that there were humans living in Southern California at least ten thousand years ago. Traveling from inland areas, possibly to escape drought or food shortages, the ancestors of the Gabrielino began to displace or absorb the earlier Hokan speakers between thirteen hundred and four thousand years ago. They spoke a language that anthropologists place in the Uto-Aztecan family, which extended

FIG. 1.5. The Gabrielino often built their villages in close proximity to the region's rivers and streams, reliant as they were on the riparian environment for food and the raw materials from which they made their dwellings, clothing, and tools. Reprinted from Donna Preble, *Yamino-Kwiti: Boy Runner of Siba* (Caldwell, Idaho: Caxton Printers, 1948), between pages 114 and 115.

across the Great Basin region of present-day California, Nevada, and Utah. The transition from the Hokan speakers to the cultural pattern now known as Gabrielino was gradual. The characteristics first described by the Spanish in 1542 are not believed to have crystallized until 350 years before.[53]

The Gabrielino are named for Mission San Gabriel, one of two Spanish missions established much later in what is now Los Angeles County. They include a smaller group, the Fernandeño, differentiated only because they lived closer to the area's other mission, Mission San Fernando, which had its base in the northeastern San Fernando Valley.

The Gabrielino name is not believed to have been applied until 1876, long after most of the Indian population had been extinguished or absorbed into the dominant Euro-American society.[54] It is not clear whether the Gabrielino had a name for themselves. Hugo Reid, a Scottish trader who settled in Los Angeles in 1832, later married a Gabrielino, and wrote the first and still one of the most revealing accounts of local Indian life, said they did not.[55] Later researchers, however, have claimed that the Gabrielino called themselves a variety of names, including Tong-va and Tobikhar, the latter of which means "settlers" and may derive from the Gabrielino name for the earth. Indians living near the original site of Los Angeles reportedly called themselves Kommivet (from *kommi*, meaning "east"), perhaps to differentiate themselves from Indians living in the San Fernando Valley and near present-day Santa Monica. They are believed to have called the Fernandeño Pasheekwarom, a variation on the name of an Indian settlement near the Mission San Fernando.[56]

Gabrielino territory encompassed much of present-day Los Angeles and Orange Counties, as well as parts of San Bernardino and Riverside Counties, stretching from the southern flanks of the San Gabriel and Santa Susana Mountains south to Aliso Creek, near Laguna Beach in Orange County, and from near Malibu on the Pacific Coast as far inland as San Bernardino. They also inhabited the islands of Santa Catalina, San Clemente, and San Nicolas. The lands of the Gabrielino were bordered by the territories of five other groups of Indians. Their neighbors to the northwest along the coast were the Chumash. The Tataviam occupied a relatively small area north of the San Fernando Valley. The Serrano lived in the Mojave Desert to the northeast of the Gabrielino country, while the Cahuilla inhabited the mountains south of San Bernardino. The Luiseño occupied the coast and nearby mountains from southern Orange County south to San Diego. The Gabrielino traded extensively with all of these groups, as well as other Indians still farther afield.

The Gabrielino are considered to have been one of the most culturally advanced and prosperous Indian groups in the Southwest. Their influence reached north to the San Joaquin Valley, east to the Colorado River, and south into Baja California.[57] The anthropologist Alfred L. Kroeber, in fact, called them "the wealthiest and most thoughtful of all the Shoshoneans of the State."[58] The Gabrielino developed an extensive trade network, and many of their technological innovations and societal customs were adopted by other Indian tribes. They are believed, for example, to have been the first Indian group in California to use movable stone mortars extensively for the grinding of acorns and other plants. They are also credited with developing a ritual using the intoxicant Jimson weed practiced throughout the Southwest and with creating a system of beliefs associated with the creator-god Chengiichngech that remained prominent long after the introduction of Christianity.[59] The geographer Homer Aschmann commented that "the clear evidence of borrowing by the Diegueño of Gabrielino songs, stories, and religious ceremonies marks the Gabrielino land as a center of invention and diffusion."[60]

Although the Gabrielino roamed widely according to the season in search of food, they seem to have selected the sites for their villages based largely on the location of water sources (just as did the Spanish, who would eventually displace them), no doubt because of the scarcity of water in the region and the greater food supplies that would have been available near streams and standing bodies of water. Many settlements in Southern California were at the foot of mountain canyons, near year-round springs. Others were located along the region's rivers and streams, though usually at a sufficient distance or on ground high enough to assure their safety in time of flood. The Gabrielino understood the importance of the region's waterways but also knew their dangers. This Indian preference for settlement sites on high ground at a distance from the rivers at first puzzled early Anglo settlers, who had to learn firsthand the nefarious nature of streams in the arid West.[61]

Maps of Indian settlement in Southern California at the time of the first Spanish land expedition show twenty-six Gabrielino villages within a mile of known courses of the Los Angeles River (fig. 1.6). Another nineteen villages were located at a slightly greater distance from the river, though still nearby. One of the largest and certainly the most famous of the Gabrielino villages, because of its location on the future site of Los Angeles, was Yangna, situated in a "delightful place among the trees on the river," according to one Spanish account.[62] Although the exact location of the village has never been determined and has long been debated, it probably occupied a large area west of the river near the present location of Union Station in downtown Los Angeles.[63] Spanish explorers found more than two hundred Indians at the site in 1769. Hugo Reid later wrote that Gabrielino villages usually contained five hundred to fifteen hundred huts, which would suggest that Yangna was home to many more Indians than were seen by the Spanish. The name of this largest Gabrielino village has also been the subject of dispute. Some of the other names applied suggest the importance of the river. John R. Swanton called the settlement at Los Angeles Wenot, apparently the Gabrielino word for "river." J. P. Harrington called it Jangna, the root of which he claimed was *jana*, meaning "the place of salty earth." This could have been a description of the alkaline soil that was sometimes deposited near the river channel.[64]

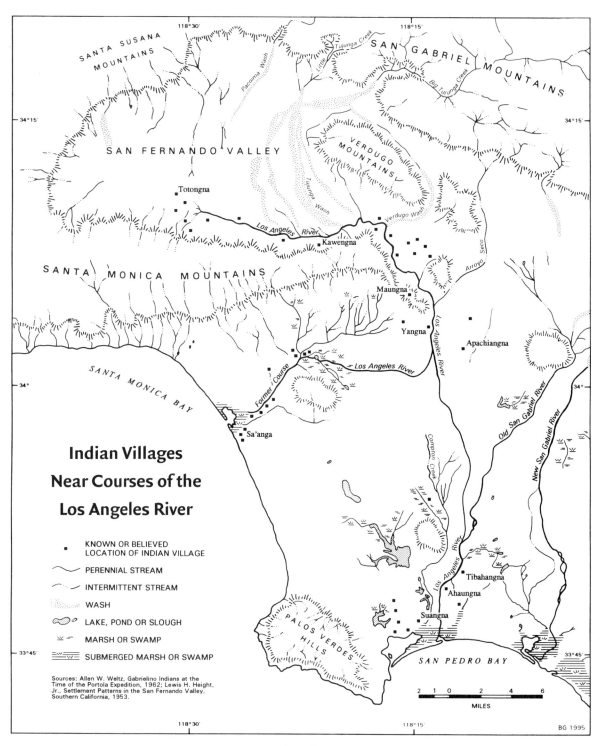

FIG. 1.6. Historical evidence suggests that at least forty-five Gabrielino Indian villages were located near courses of the Los Angeles River. Map by the author.

Gabrielino villages seem to have been most abundant in the San Fernando Valley, in the area north of downtown Los Angeles known as the Glendale Narrows, and around the river's various outlets to the sea. Totongna was a Fernandeño village near the upper reaches of the river in the western San Fernando Valley. Spanish explorers in 1769 found two large Indian villages among the oaks near the present site of Encino, near a spring-fed pool that would have emptied into the Los Angeles River. They set up camp beneath a large white oak tree and spent nearly two days at the site while scouts looked for the best route north. The Spaniards counted more than 215 Indians in the vicinity and described them as "very friendly" and "tractable." The Indians offered the Spaniards beads made from shells, as well as seeds and sage, which grew in abundance along the river. Numerous Indians visited their camp, and some "spent the entire day with us," one of the diarists for the expedition noted, "entirely without weapons or fear, as though they had been dealing with us forever."[65] One of the Indian villages at Encino was known as Siutcanga. Archaeological excavations conducted near the intersection of Ventura and Balboa Boulevards in 1984 and 1985 found the remains of what may have been Siutcanga on the bank of an ancient stream bed. Radiocarbon dating determined that the site had been occupied by a succession of Indian groups beginning at least seven thousand years ago.[66]

The Fernandeño village of Kawengna was located downstream from the settlements at Encino, on the south side of the river at the northern end of Cahuenga Pass. Another Gabrielino settlement, Maungna, is believed to have been located high on a bluff overlooking the Glendale Narrows in the hills now occupied by Elysian Park. The village of Hahamogna may have been located nearby, north of the river's meeting with the Arroyo Seco. Evidence of other Indian villages has been found in several locations beside the marshes that once bordered the river along what is now Ballona Creek and amid the overflow lands between Compton and the sea. The present location of the city of South Gate is believed to have been the site of two Gabrielino villages, both about a mile east of one of the former courses of the river, although neither is shown on available maps. According to Hugo Reid, the largest Gabrielino village, in both population and extent, was Suangna, located near the river's outlet at San Pedro Bay. Suangna was the political center for a cluster of villages in the area, and its name may have reflected the marshy environment of it surroundings. According to one account, Suangna is the Gabrielino word for "rush."[67]

The lands and waters of Southern California provided all that the Gabrielino needed to survive, while the mild climate assured a suffi-

cient supply of food year-round. The Gabrielino did not practice agriculture, but this may have been because the natural harvest of the
country made it unnecessary. The forests, marshes, and grasslands
provided an abundant variety of edible plants and animals. The observations of the first Spanish visitors to the San Fernando Valley suggest
that the Indians did, however, occasionally set fires to encourage the
growth of particular plant species. The Gabrielino diet is believed to
have included some sixty wild plants and more than one hundred
types of seeds. Female tribe members roamed from place to place after the winter rains, gathering seeds, nuts, and fruits and digging wild
roots and bulbs with sticks. Several types of edible berries, including
gooseberries, elderberries, blackberries, and currants, grew near the
river and in the marshes. Watercress, sage, wild celery, and clover
were also eaten. Yucca and prickly pear, found near the river in the San
Fernando Valley, provided sustenance during the dry summer
months.[68] The Gabrielino were remarkably resourceful in their use of
the natural environment, a fact that was probably lost on most Euro-
American settlers, though not all of them. Lt. Edward Ord, who drew
the first map of the city of Los Angeles, wrote of the Gabrielino in
1856: "No wonder they hate us, for you see the generations of them
have only learned to take from the soil and the animals enough to satisfy their few natural wants, but the generations of Americans have
learned to want all the soil (and) animals they can take, and take all
they want, too."[69]

Acorns were the foundation of the Gabrielino diet, and their abundance in Southern California may help explain the relatively advanced
state of Gabrielino society. The importance of acorns derives from
their high nutritional value. Acorns have a fat and fiber content superior to that of corn or wheat and a carbohydrate content equal to that
of those grains. It has been suggested that the relatively nutritious diet
consumed by acorn-harvesting cultures enabled them to reach a com-
plexity equal or superior to that of some aboriginal agricultural societies. Six varieties of acorns were found in Southern California, and
they provided perhaps half the Gabrielino's food. Acorns harvested
from the coast live oak were considered the most desirable, but even
the smaller nuts of the scrub oak were eaten. Acorn mush was the favorite preparation of the nuts. Because acorns contain a bitter, astrin-
gent substance called tannin, this material had to be removed before
the flour created from grinding the acorns could be used as food. The
Indians discovered that boiling water—poured through the flour repeatedly, eight or nine times—leached out the tannin. This was
usually done in a hollow beside a flowing stream using a filter made of
willow twigs and sand. Acorn mush was then created by boiling the

flour in river water. As it boiled, the flour thickened like oatmeal; it was sliced and eaten after it cooled. Other plants that were a significant part of the Gabrielino diet included pepper grass, wild sage, and chia seeds. Chia seeds, which were roasted, ground into meal, and eaten with cold water, were sold in Los Angeles stores as late as 1894.[70]

The Gabrielino also ate nearly everything that moved. They relied heavily for meat on the wide variety of rodents and other small creatures that lived in the wetlands and among the thickets. Rabbits and hares were the most commonly eaten animals, but the natives also ate deer, antelope, squirrel, rat, skunk, gopher, lizard, frog, and some species of snake. Caterpillar and yellowjacket larvae were considered delicacies. Grasshoppers were roasted on a stick in a fire. Only bears and rattlesnakes were safe from most Gabrielino hunters, taboo because of tribal belief. Waterfowl were trapped in the rivers and marshes with nets made from the tule that grew nearby. The natives cut channels through the marshland and stretched nets above the water, allowing enough room for the birds to swim beneath them. The ducks and geese were then gently driven under the nets. When enough had gathered, the Indians on a signal made a great noise, sending the frightened birds skyward and causing them to become trapped in the nets. Sometimes the natives stretched tule nets beneath the surface of the water in shallow, slow-moving sections of the river and spread berries across the channel bottom as bait. Ducks and geese would dive for the berries and become hopelessly entangled in the nets. Fish were also abundant in the rivers and the ponds. The Indians used hooks, nets, baskets, bows, arrows, and even vegetable poisons to catch them. Near the coast and on the islands, marine fishes, shellfish, and sharks were the primary means of subsistence.[71]

The rivers and marshes also provided the raw materials that supported nearly every facet of the Gabrielino existence. Their thatched houses, known as *jacales* or *wickiups* by the Spanish, were made from tule collected from the wetlands, built upon frames of willow or sycamore poles. The ends of these poles were buried in the ground in a circle, and their tops were then bent toward the center and tied together to form a dome-shaped shelter. Tule matting, grass, or brush was then attached to form walls, sometimes a half-foot thick. The doorway and the floor were also typically covered with mats made from tules. The homes of each village were centered around a small, unroofed religious structure known as a *yovaar*, which was also built of willow. Circular and about three feet high, it was made of thin willow branches intertwined like the walls of a basket. Because of the relative scarcity of large timber on the lowlands, tules and rushes were also used to construct rafts and canoes for navigating the region's waterways. Great piles of tules were tied in bundles ten feet in length, thick in the middle and tapered on both ends. These bundles were then lashed together to create a boat that could carry two people. At the time of the arrival of the Spanish, these boats were the natives' sole means of water transport.[72]

The abundant willows, tules, and other plants of the floodplain forest had a wide variety of additional uses, from utilitarian to recreational to ceremonial. Though Gabrielino men and children usually went naked, the women wore skirts woven of tule or grasses. They made aprons from the flexible inner bark of willow, sycamore, and cottonwood trees, cut into strips and worked until it was soft. Gabrielino baskets, renowned for their utility and beauty, were woven from bulrushes, squawbush, and other plants found in the marshes. They were used for food preparation, for storage, or, when coated with asphaltum, to haul and store water. The natural color variations in the plants enabled the basket makers to decorate them with intricate geometric designs. String and cord were wound from the fiber of milkweed and nettle. Bows for hunting were manufactured from the limbs of willow trees. Tules were also used to make a hoop for a popular Gabrielino game.[73] Marsh nettle plants, known for their stinging leaves, were utilized for both medical and ritualistic purposes. Dried nettle stalks were applied to the skin and set afire as part of a cure for rheumatism. Gabrielino men stung themselves all over with nettles before leaving on hunting trips. According to Reid, "This was done to make them watchful, vigilant and clear sighted."[74]

The lives of the Gabrielino were inextricably linked to the wild landscape that thrived in part because of the river and other Southern California streams, but the waterways also may have exerted a symbolic significance. The Gabrielino custom of bathing each day before dawn, for example, was apparently dictated by Chengiichngech, their creator-god.[75] There is also at least one parable in the Gabrielino tradition in which a river plays a central role. In this story a lone coyote, cunning and a little arrogant, approaches the bank of a small river. Seeing its water running slow, he challenges it to a race. "Giving the river one scornful glance, Itaru began to run," goes a modern retelling of the story. "He ran so fast that the other animals gave up trying to keep pace with him. Itaru ran until he was tired, and then looking over the riverbank, he saw the river running along beside him. He could see it stretching way out before him, running and laughing all the way to the sea. So Itaru ran again. He ran until he was so tired he had to stop and lie down. But the river ran on past him. Then Itaru knew that Wenot, the river, had won the race. He had run as fast as he could, and still the river ran ahead of him, untired, quiet, and strong. Itaru walked off with his tail between his legs. How the other animals laughed at him! Every time he saw the river it gurgled and laughed at him, too, and so Itaru did not like the river any more, nor did he feel so proud."[76]

The Arrival of the Spanish in Southern California

As important as the river was to the Gabrielino, it was even more significant to the Europeans and Euro-Americans who would eventually displace the Indians nearly totally from Southern California, dependent as the nonnatives were on cattle and cultivated crops that required a reliable source of water. Spain was the first country to claim California as its own, when an ocean expedition led by Juan Rodríguez Cabrillo, seeking the mythical Northwest Passage to the Atlantic Ocean, landed at San Diego Bay on 28 September 1542. Traveling up the coast, Cabrillo and his crew also visited Catalina Island, San Pedro (which they named the "Bay of the Smokes" for either the fog or the smoke produced by Indian fires), Santa Monica, and Point Magu before continuing north. Cabrillo and his men never ventured far inland, however, and, if they saw the stream we now call the Los Angeles River, they did not mention it. So near its mouth, of course, the river probably did not look much like a river, its scant late-September flow likely spilling over a wide area. Although occasional ships probably anchored along the Pacific Coast, the next thorough exploration of California did not occur until 1602, when an expedition led by Sebastian Vizcaíno surveyed the shore from Acapulco to Oregon, stopping along the way at San Diego Bay (which the party gave its present name), Catalina Island, and San Pedro Bay (which they also named). Written accounts of their travels, like those made on the Cabrillo expedition, did not mention the river.

Spain paid little attention to its newly claimed territory during the first two hundred years after Cabrillo had landed on its shores. Despite favorable reports of the new country from the initial explorers, it wasn't until the mid–eighteenth century that the Spanish made their first overland expedition into what we now know as California. Spurred by exaggerated reports of Russian activity in the north Pacific, the Spanish government in 1768 ordered an expedition to occupy the port at Monterey, whose potential as a harbor had been noted by Vizcaíno more than a century before. The expedition was to secure the port for the crown through the founding of a presidio (military fort) and a mission. Subsequently, it was decided that a colony should also be established at San Diego. The following year, four parties—two by land and two by sea—set out from Baja California for San Diego. From there they were to proceed north to Monterey, looking for other possible sites for missions and presidios en route. Only one of the four parties made it beyond San Diego, however. Both ships sailed too far north in search of San Diego Bay and, by the time they finally arrived, several crew members and passengers had died from scurvy. Many more were sick or disabled. Captain Gaspar de Portolá, governor of Baja California, decided as a result that only a single land party would continue to Monterey.[77]

Portolá led the expedition from San Diego to Monterey and on to San Francisco. His crew consisted of three other military officers, an engineer, two priests, thirty-one soldiers, seven "muleteers," two servants, and fifteen Christianized Indians. Perhaps the two participants in the expedition most important to the future of Los Angeles and the river, other than Portolá, were the two members who kept diaries, engineer Michael Costansó and Father Juan Crespí. Their daily accounts were the first detailed written descriptions of California, and their comments about the river and the wooded lands that spread away from its banks likely influenced the decision to found a pueblo along the river a dozen years later. Costansó's descriptions, terse and largely unemotional, perhaps reflect the more mathematical eye of the engineer, although the relatively large number of existing manuscript copies of his journals suggest that they may have been more widely read in official circles than were the diaries of Crespí. The published narratives of Crespí, however, are the more famous today. They are longer, provide greater detail of the daily activities of the explorers, and are more evocative in their descriptions of the land and its inhabitants. Crespí's diaries have been exhaustively quoted by historians, anthropologists, geographers, and others because they provide the most extensive portrait of the country before it was transformed by European settlement. Ever ebullient in his praise of what he saw, Crespí has, in fact, been called "California's first booster."[78] His journals are even more compelling in their unedited form, which are two-thirds longer than the published versions and considerably less polished. His descriptions of the river and its vicinity are especially rich.[79]

The Portolá expedition left San Diego on the afternoon of 14 July 1769, following the coast before turning inland near present-day San Juan Capistrano on a route today approximated by Interstate 5. They turned more directly north after fording the Santa Ana River and, traveling six to ten miles a day, passed into modern Los Angeles County via the Puente Hills on 30 July, camping that night along San Jose Creek, probably near the current location of La Puente. The next day they proceeded in a west-northwesterly direction through the San Gabriel Valley along the general line of Valley Boulevard, but their progress was slowed considerably by the dense, low woods that, like those that grew along the Los Angeles River, spread on both sides of the San Gabriel River. After traveling about five miles that day, they camped for the night somewhere in the vicinity of the present community of South San Gabriel.

The first day of August was a day of rest for the expedition in honor of the jubilee of Nuestra Señora de los Angeles de la Porciúncula (Our Lady of the Angels of Porciúncula), a plenary indulgence of the Roman Catholic church named for the tiny chapel in Italy where St. Francis of Assisi had received a divine revelation. Crespí and Father Francisco Gómez, the other priest on the expedition, said mass for the men, who also received communion. Several soldiers went hunting for antelope during the afternoon and, upon their return, told the rest of the traveling party of a "very full flowing, wide river," Crespí related, that ran south through a gap in the mountains, perhaps two miles west of their camp. This is the first known written description of the Los Angeles River. Despite the relative closeness of the camp to the river, members of the party were not able to see it from the camp, perhaps because, as Crespí noted, "far across this level there is a great amount of flat land in sight with a great deal of trees running along."[80]

The party resumed their journey the next morning, continuing along the route taken by Valley Boulevard, and, after traveling through a pass between low hills (probably just north of the location of the campus of California State University, Los Angeles), entered "a very green lush valley," Crespí wrote, where they found the river the soldiers had told them about.[81] It was a "good sized, full flowing river," about seven yards wide, he estimated, "with very good water, pure and fresh."[82] It was "a bit smaller," Crespí noted, than the two previous streams they had crossed, the Santa Ana and San Gabriel, but "in no wise inferior." Just upstream from the point where they first saw the river, the explorers noticed another stream that emptied into its channel, but its large bed was dry on the late summer day. This stream we now know as the Arroyo Seco. "The beds of both are very well lined with large trees, sycamores, willows, cottonwoods, and very large live oaks," Crespí wrote. "We found pine-nut cones and a great amount of nut shells."[83] The party stopped for the night on the east bank of the river, probably near the present location of the North Broadway bridge, across from the high hill that forms the eastern edge of Elysian Park. The annual feast of Our Lady of the Angels of Porciúncula, begun the previous day at noon, did not end officially until that evening at midnight, so they named the river and the valley through which it passed in honor of the indulgence. In time, the river became known simply as Porciúncula (little portion), the name of the chapel in Italy that is the cradle of the Franciscan order.

Crespí wrote more than a thousand words in his diary that day, most of them describing the river and the broad, level valley that extended beyond it. He marveled at the "great amount of trees" and the "very large, very green bottomlands" that spread out on both sides of its banks as far south as he could see, "looking from afar like nothing so much as large cornfields."[84] He noted the presence beside its channel of great thickets of brambles, abundant native grapevines, and wild roses in full bloom. Sage was plentiful near the river, and the calls of turtle doves, quail, and thrushes filled the air near the camp.[85] It was "a very lush and pleasing spot, in every respect," he wrote. "To (the) southward there is a great extent of soil, all very green, so that really it can be said to be a most beautiful garden." Remembering, too, that one of the purposes of the expedition was to seek out potential sites for colonization, Crespí concluded that "this pleasing spot among the trees on this pleasant river" was the best site they had so far seen for a settlement. "Good, better than good, and grand though previous places have been," he wrote, "to my mind this spot can be given the preference in everything, in soil, water, and trees, for the purpose of becoming in time a very large plenteous mission."[86]

Shortly after dawn the next morning, as the previous day's fog gave way to bright early morning sun, the party continued its travels. Fording the shallow river, they immediately found themselves in another large field of wild grapes, brightened by "countless rose bushes having a great many open blossoms."[87] The soil, Crespí noted, was dark and brittle, and as they traveled west, away from the river, the floodplain forest gradually gave way to a level, grass-covered plain. As they ascended the terraces west of the river, the extensive coastal plain, unobstructed by the haze of the day before, spread out before them. "We had a clear view of the river's course," Crespí wrote, "with the trees and flat drawing off southward."[88] About a mile from the river, the party came upon a large Indian village, the well-known Gabrielino village of Yangna. The expedition also passed through the future site of the Los Angeles Civic Center before traveling west to about the location of MacArthur Park and stopping for the night a few miles farther west at a thick grove of tall sycamores that surrounded "an exceedingly copious spring."[89] Scholars have placed the camp just east of La Brea Boulevard, about midway between Venice and Washington Boulevards, which means that the spring they camped beside fed the stream we now know as Ballona Creek, which in historic times was the occasional course of the Los Angeles River. Before retiring for the night, engineer Costansó noted in his diary that "all the country that we saw on this day's march appeared to us most suitable for the production of all kinds of grain and fruits."[90]

The Portolá expedition then traveled northwest, perhaps skirting the present boundaries of Beverly Hills, to about where the Veterans Administration Center in Sawtelle now stands. They hiked north over the Santa Monica Mountains via Sepulveda Pass, across the San Fernando Valley (where, if they saw the headwaters of the Los Angeles River, they did not recognize them as such), and up the San Gabriel Mountains through San Fernando Pass. But nothing in their travels through Southern California made so lasting an impression as what they saw on those first three days of August 1769. In fact, when Crespí's diaries, much modified and shortened, were officially transmitted as part of Father Francisco Palou's "Noticias de la Nueva California," Crespí's pronouncements about the future of the river and the plain through which it passes were made even more emphatic. "This plain where the river runs is very extensive," reads the much altered entry for 2 August. "It has good land for planting all kinds of grain and seeds, and is the most suitable site of all that we have seen for a mission, for it has all the requisites for a large settlement."[91] Such words would prove prophetic, if not a little ironic. In 1781, drawn by the ample supply of water provided by the river and the fertile soil beside its banks, Spain established El Pueblo de la Reina de Los Angeles on a site not far from where the Portolá expedition had first forded the Río de Porciúncula. The river provided drinking water for the nascent settlement and irrigated the agricultural land that helped the village grow. The river, furthermore, would prove integral to the transformation of that pueblo into the largest and most important city in the American West. But the rise of Los Angeles would also doom the river and the Arcadian landscape that once thrived along its course.

Sustenance for the Young Pueblo

LOS ANGELES WAS ONE OF THREE AGRICULTURAL VILLAGES founded by Spain in California during the late eighteenth century to help provide food to the missions and especially the presidios that had been established to help secure the territory for the Spanish crown. The eight missions and three presidios set up by Spain along the California coast from 1769 to 1777 were unable initially to raise enough food to supply their own needs and soon became a burden to the Spanish government.[1] They were dependent almost entirely on food brought more than a thousand miles from central Mexico by ship. Delays in shipments could be disastrous. In 1772, for instance, several settlements were threatened with starvation when shipments were late and, after reaching San Diego, could not continue to Monterey. Mule trains could seldom travel from the ports during winter months, as soils turned to mud and trails became impassable. Until the establishment of the agricultural settlements, formally known as *pueblos* by the Spanish, the missionaries and soldiers sometimes had to survive on milk, bear meat, and whatever provisions they could obtain from various Indian tribes.[2]

The problem was especially acute at the presidios, built on the ocean and therefore often farther from consistent supplies of the freshwater necessary for the raising of the most basic of crops. The presidios also lacked the ready labor supply that the missions had in the Indians. "I remain frustrated at the presidios, afflicted as they are by the irregularity of rains in this country, the scarcity of arroyos, springs of water, and running streams," wrote Felipe de Neve, first governor of California.[3] But even the missions experienced severe difficulties in supporting themselves the first few years. Spanish authorities soon realized that the abundant rains they witnessed in 1770 and 1771, as the first missions and presidios were being established, were unusual. The following three years were dry up and down the coast, and only one of seven Spanish settlements was able to produce a crop. Mission San Diego and Mission San Antonio de Padua, in fact, were not able to raise any wheat during their first six years of existence.[4]

As a result, de Neve, in the summer of 1776, petitioned the viceroy of New Spain, Antonio Maria Bucareli y Ursúa, for authorization to establish an agricultural operation on Baja California to supply the colony with food. A few years earlier, Father Junípero Serra had suggested to the viceroy that Spain consider establishing civilian settlements in what was then Alta, or Upper, California. The viceroy directed de Neve instead to seek fertile lands farther north in what is today the state of California. The following winter, de Neve rode north from San Diego to look for possible sites, examining valley after valley for a location that had not only abundant arable land but also access to a convenient and, he hoped, year-round supply of water. In a letter written to Bucareli in June 1777, he made favorable comments about the Santa Ana, San Gabriel, and Porciúncula Rivers in the south and the Guadalupe River down the bay from San Francisco, and he asked permission to establish towns at sites on the Porciúncula and Guadalupe Rivers. The first pueblo, San José de Guadalupe (present-day San Jose), was founded even before the viceroy could reply on 29 November 1777.[5]

De Neve's request for colonists to found a pueblo on the Río de Porciúncula was not initially granted, but on 3 September 1778 Spanish authorities approved the establishment of a presidio at Santa Barbara and, to make sure that the presidio would have enough food, a second pueblo.[6] The pueblo that became Los Angeles was founded three years later. No doubt influenced by the earlier descriptions from Father Crespí and engineer Michael Costansó, de Neve selected a site for the southernmost pueblo on a broad terrace one-half mile west of the river. The pueblo was to include all land suitable for irrigation. De Neve further stated that the settlement should be "slightly elevated [and] exposed to the north and south winds. Measures shall be taken to avoid the dangers of floods. The most immediate vicinity to the river or vicinity to the principal zanja (irrigation ditch) shall be preferred."[7] No other site near the river so closely met the requirements. North of the pueblo location, water in the river's subterranean source is pushed to the surface by the same ridge that forms the Santa Monica Mountains, so the stream provided an abundant supply of water even during dry summer months. The lowlands along the river, meanwhile, offered plenty of fertile land for farming, while the terrace upon which the core of the town was to be built seemed to be beyond the reach of floods.

Though it is unknown why de Neve chose to establish a pueblo along the Río de Porciúncula rather than at a site along the Santa Ana or San Gabriel Rivers, it is clear today that the location he selected better fit the needs for settlement than did any other site in Southern California. Both the Santa Ana and the San Gabriel posed greater flood risks in their uncontrolled states than did the Los Angeles River, since they spread over wide areas as soon as they left the mountains. Much of the water they carried, moreover, sank immediately underground and therefore would not have been available for irrigation using the primitive diversion methods relied upon at the time.[8] Other locations along the Los Angeles River were similarly unsatisfactory. The flow of the river in the San Fernando Valley was barely a trickle most of the year. The current location of Glendale provided access to the river's increased flow through the Glendale Narrows, but this area was at a higher elevation than the river, a characteristic that would have prevented the distribution of water by gravity to the pueblo lands. The narrow strip of land that straddles the river between Glendale and Los Angeles—site of the present communities of Atwater and Elysian Valley—also had access to the river's greatest surface flow, but the river's course here was unstable and prone to flooding and the area did not provide much land for growth. South of the pueblo site on the coastal plain, the supply of water was inadequate because most of the river's flow disappeared underground except during winter storms.

Spanish authorities in northern Mexico hoped to recruit twenty-four colonists, plus their families, to settle the pueblo but were able to sign up only fourteen. Just twelve of those actually made the trip north, and one of them ran away before the formal founding of El Pueblo de la Reina de los Angeles on 4 September 1781.[9] The eleven *pobladores* brought thirty-three family members. Within six months, however, three settlers and their families—sixteen people in all—were expelled as "unfit."[10] Each of the remaining families was given a house lot and four fields for planting crops, only two of which were to have access to irrigation water. In addition, they were promised a monthly salary of ten pesos for three years and received, as a loan, thirteen farm animals, a variety of agricultural implements, a musket, a knife, and a leather shield. Settlers were required in return to sell any surplus agricultural products to the presidios at fair prices. They were also responsible for the construction of a dam to divert water from the river and for the digging and maintenance of ditches that would transport that water to the pueblo.[11]

The original pueblo occupied four square leagues, roughly twenty-eight square miles, and utilized a plan adopted by Spain in her colonies throughout North and South America.[12] Twelve house lots, or *solares*, surrounded a common square, or *plaza*, which sat in the geographic center of the pueblo, its corners facing the cardinal points of the compass (fig. 2.1). Thirty-six fields for cultivation, or *suertas*, were laid out between the plaza and the river. The planting fields were square, 200 *varas* (500 feet) on each side, and together occupied about 250 acres. A vacant area was left between the town site and the fields to allow for future growth. Lands east of the river belonged to the Spanish government and were known as the *realengas*, or royal lands.[13]

Upon their arrival, the settlers built primitive dwellings formed by palisades of sticks (probably willow cut from the river bottomlands) and covered the roofs with mud (perhaps also hauled from the river). These were eventually replaced by houses constructed of adobe, much of which was probably also made using river water and mud. The first community task, meanwhile, was the construction of a simple water delivery system. The Spanish were accustomed to the feast-or-famine rainfall cycle characteristic of the region's Mediterranean-type climate and understood well the importance of irrigation. Most of the settlers, furthermore, were from the Sonoran desert region of Mexico, where rainfall is even more sporadic than in Southern California. They erected a dam of sand and willow poles two miles upstream from the pueblo where the river rounds a steep bluff of the Elysian Hills. The intake was just north of the location of the present North Broadway bridge, near where the Portolá expedition had crossed the river a dozen years before. The diversion had to be constructed upstream from the pueblo at a higher elevation than the settlement so water could flow by gravity to the town site and the agricultural lands. The pool that formed behind the dam was a popular swimming hole in Los Angeles for generations.[14]

The main irrigation ditch, or Zanja Madre ("mother ditch" in Spanish), was completed by the end of October 1781 and ran south from the river to a point just north of the plaza, where it split into two ditches. One transported water for irrigation to the fields that had been laid out between the plaza and the river. The other ran just behind the house lots on the southeastern corner of the plaza to provide for the domestic needs of the settlers, although this ditch is not shown on the original plan of the pueblo. Rather than haul it from the ditches themselves, many early residents preferred to buy water from local Indians who peddled it door to door in clay and terra cotta urns. Shouts of "*Agua! Agua! Agua!*" rang through the dusty streets of the infant pueblo (fig. 2.2). Some of the water carriers obtained their water directly from the river, which offered a more pure supply than was available in the often stagnant ditches. Once the irrigation ditches were completed and the settlers had built primitive dwellings, they began planting a few crops—wheat, beans, and maize, most likely.[15]

The Development of Agriculture

The steady supply of water from the river and the fertile soil beside its banks appear to have helped the pueblo attain self sufficiency by 1786, when the Spanish government discontinued financial support. Los

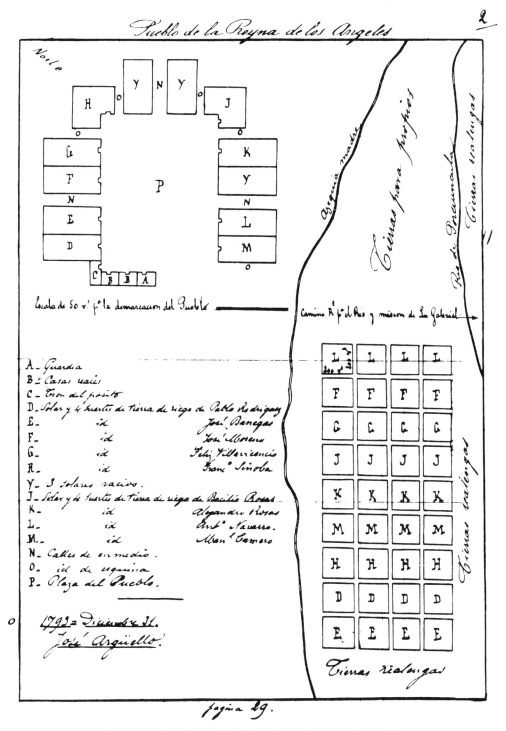

FIG. 2.1. Plan of El Pueblo de la Reina de los Angeles. *Top left,* twelve house lots face the plaza. The *top left* corner of the plaza points north. The Zanja Madre (mother ditch) runs vertically through the *center* of the plan. *Bottom right,* agricultural lands sit between the main ditch and the river. The scale used to map the plaza area is four times larger than that used for the fields. Courtesy, The Bancroft Library, University of California, Berkeley.

FIG. 2.2. Indian water carriers in the days of the pueblo. Drawing by Orpha Klinker Carpenter. Reprinted from Boyle Workman, *The City That Grew* (Los Angeles: Southland Publishing, 1935), 1.

Angeles was soon producing more grain than any California mission except San Gabriel. In 1790, some 4,500 bushels were produced. Six years later, the harvest was 7,800 bushels. Nearly all of that was maize. The early agricultural success of the pueblo has been largely credited to the work of the Indians. The original colonists have been widely characterized as lazy. Two early mission priests commented in 1796, in fact, that "whatever is effected in those pueblos is due more to the gentile Indian of the neighboring rancherias than to the settlers. It is the hired Indian who plows, sows, harvests, in a word does nearly everything. The Indian for his labor is given his meals and a blanket."[16]

Indian labor helped Los Angeles become the most important agricultural settlement on the Pacific Coast by the early 1800s. By then, the pueblo was producing surpluses of wheat, corn, barley, and beans that it exported to the presidio at Santa Barbara. Although production varied significantly from year to year, the harvest reached an early peak of 13,700 bushels in 1811. Of that total, 4,920 bushels were maize, 430 bushels were wheat, and 230 bushels were beans. By 1831, the pueblo was harvesting more corn and beans than any mission or pueblo in California except San Luis Rey. Los Angeles also had ample grazing land and, fifty years after its founding, had greater numbers of cattle, horses, and mules than any Spanish or non-Spanish settlement on the Pacific Coast. Los Angeles residents owned an estimated 80,000 cattle, 25,000 horses, and 10,000 sheep. Indians were used to maintain the water ditches. In 1836, after receiving complaints that the volume of water in the Zanja Madre was no longer sufficient, the town government ordered that all drunken Indians be arrested and required to work on the ditches until the amount of water they carried increased.[17]

Though it is difficult to imagine today, Los Angeles remained an isolated, predominantly agricultural village for much of its first century, and farming was integral to the local economy until well into the 1900s. Growth of the pueblo was steady, but slow. The population remained small. Few travelers stopped at Los Angeles, preferring the more welcoming accommodations provided by the missions. At the end of its first decade, Los Angeles had a Spanish-speaking population of just 139. The pueblo included about thirty adobe houses, twelve of which were clustered around the plaza. Thirty-six years later, it seems likely that there were still not more than a few hundred non-Indian residents, at least judging by a report of the number of dwellings at the settlement. Auguste Bernard Duhaut-Cilly, a Frenchman, counted eighty-two houses on a visit to the pueblo in 1827. He noted an "air of cheerfulness, ease and neatness" about the town.[18] The population of Los Angeles probably did not rise above one thousand until several years after California had become the property of Mexico and the city had been made the territorial capital in 1835. As late as 1844, more than half the workers in the pueblo were still engaged in agricultural pursuits.[19]

By then, many of the settlers grew grapes or made wine, often using Indian labor to both maintain the vines and produce the wine. Few recognize that Los Angeles, not San Francisco or the Napa Valley, was California's first important wine-producing center. The earliest grape crop in Southern California was grown at Mission San Gabriel, but an unidentified man is believed to have planted a large vineyard in Los Angeles about 1803. Before long, vines blanketed the lowlands along the river. By 1817, there were an estimated 53,686 vines under cultivation. Tithes to the church in 1820 suggest that secular production of wine had grown to about 325 gallons a year. Between 1824 and 1826, a United States–born sailor named Joseph Chapman planted 4,000 vines in the pueblo, the largest single vineyard in Los Angeles at the time. Within five years, there were twenty-six vineyards in Los Angeles and 100,000 vines covered an estimated 112 acres.[20]

Most of the vineyards were located between present-day San Pedro Street and the river. As the pueblo grew, farms spread north and south from the original pueblo site, eventually occupying nearly all of the triangular area between the river and the terrace lands upon which the town was built. Vineyards irrigated with river water also lined the stream course south of the pueblo boundary. Another 100,000 vines grew outside Los Angeles, many of them along the west side of the river just beyond the pueblo limits in what is now the city of Vernon.[21] Grapes and maize were the principal crops in Los Angeles when the Frenchman Duhaut-Cilly passed through the pueblo. "The vine succeeds very well," he wrote. He cautioned, however, that the wine and brandy extracted from the grapes was "very inferior to the exquisite taste of the grape used for it," but added, "I think this inferiority is to be attributed to the making rather than the growth."[22]

Another Frenchman, Jean Louis Vignes, helped alter that perspective. A native of the Bordeaux region of France, Vignes left his ancestral home in 1827 after his family had fallen on hard times. He traveled first to Hawaii, where he was employed by a trading firm. When the firm went bankrupt, he apparently migrated to Monterey in California, selling a number of religious statuettes and medals he had been given as final payment by the trading company. Vignes settled in Los Angeles in 1831 and bought a tract of land adjacent to the river two years later. There, on 104 acres of land east of the present location of Alameda Street and south of Aliso Street, he laid out El Aliso Vineyard, named for the same giant sycamore beside the river that had been a council tree for local Indians. It is not known what prompted Vignes to settle in the pueblo, but it seems likely that, by the time he reached Monterey, the early success of Los Angeles in raising grapes had become more widely known.[23] "With my knowledge of vine and orange cultivation and of the soil and climate of California," he told a visitor in 1833, "I foresee that these two are to have a great future; this is just the place to grow them to perfection."[24] Vignes, however, was not satisfied with the quality of the vines already growing in the pueblo, so he imported cuttings from France. Watering his vines from canals dug directly from the river, he reportedly produced his first wine in 1837. Before long, he began chartering steamers at San Pedro and shipping wine and brandy to Santa Barbara, Monterey, and San Francisco. In 1841, he shipped a barrel of wine to the king of France.[25]

By 1847, Vignes had some forty thousand vines and El Aliso Vineyard had emerged as one of the cultural centers of local life. The elite of the town often gathered under a quarter-mile-long grape arbor that stretched from Vignes's adobe home. Edwin Bryant, a Kentucky newspaperman who visited Los Angeles that year on a tour of California, remarked, "Mr. V's vineyard is doubtless a model of its kind. It was a delightful recreation to stroll through it, and among the tropical fruit trees bordering its walks. He set out for our refreshment three or four specimens of wines, some of which would compare favorably with the best French and Medeira [sic] wine." Another visitor who sampled wine produced in the Vignes vineyards that year wrote that "many bottles were drunk, leaving no headache or acidity on the stomach."[26]

Vignes, whose name means "vines" in French, became the most important winemaker in the West, producing as many as forty thousand gallons a year, and is today considered a pioneer of California viticulture. In 1857, he advertised some of his wine as twenty years old. Two of his nephews, Pierre and Jean Louis Sainsevain, came to Los Angeles to help their uncle in 1839 and purchased the vineyard in 1855, carrying on the family tradition. They shipped the first California wine to New York in 1861 and were the first vintners in California to produce a champagne-like sparkling wine.[27]

French immigrants such as Vignes, the Sainsevain brothers, Louis Bouchete, Remi Nadeau, and Louis Lemoreau transformed the lowlands on both sides of the river (fig. 2.3). The area south of present-day Aliso Street, in fact, became known as French Town. Vignes encouraged friends and relatives from France to join him in California and, at the dawn of statehood in 1850, one in five Los Angeles residents reportedly claimed French ancestry. Grapes were the dominant crop. There were more than one hundred vineyards in the city, containing some 400,000 vines. All of these were watered from the river or one of the numerous zanjas that carried its supply to the agricultural lands. Vineyards surrounded the plaza area and occupied most of the preferred acreage along the main irrigation ditches, extending south beyond where Jefferson Street is today (see fig. 2.7). Led by the city of Los Angeles, Los Angeles County was the number one wine-making county in the nation in 1850, producing 57,355 gallons, a third more than its nearest competitor.[28] Vineyards were central to the image of Los Angeles, which became known as the "City of Vines." The road from the city to San Pedro passed through so many vineyards and orchards that it was sometimes called "Vineyard Lane." One of the local newspapers of the day was the *Southern Vineyard*. The first Los Angeles city seal, furthermore, was adorned with a cluster of grapes and, during the harvest, grapes were even occasionally stored in the basement of the original Los Angeles City Hall.[29]

William P. Blake, a U.S. government geologist who visited Los Angeles in November 1853, observed that "the most important production of the soil, at this time, is the grape." Blake arrived during the harvest and, though he stayed only two days, saw enough to predict that California would become as well known for its wine as it was for its gold. During his visit, the vineyards along the river were beehives of activity. The vines, he wrote, grew in rows about five feet apart and, because they had been closely trimmed, were stout and thick and required no support. Bunches of grapes weighing one to three pounds hung from the vines. Workers crossed the vineyards in every direction, carrying baskets of grapes to packing sheds, where the fruits were spread on clean white sheets and laid gently on a bed of sawdust in redwood crates. Many of the grapes, Blake reported, were shipped to San Francisco, where they were sold for eighteen to twenty-five cents a pound, six times what they sold for locally. "The region is very well adapted to the growth of the grape and other fruits," the geologist concluded. "The genial climate and the character of the soil are favorable, and there is nothing to prevent the multiplication of vineyards to an almost unlimited extent. I believe that when the adaptation of that portion of California to the culture of grape and the manufacture of wine becomes known and appreciated, the state will become celebrated not only for its gold and grain, but for its fruits and wines."[30]

True to his forecast, the production of grapes and wine in Los Angeles increased dramatically. In 1854, a San Francisco wine house, Kohler & Frohling, opened a branch winery in Los Angeles. That year, an estimated 100,000 gallons of wine and brandy, worth $200,000, were manufactured in Los Angeles County, nearly twice the volume that had been reported just four years earlier. Another $50,000 in un-

FIG. 2.3. Vineyard and orchard owned by Jean Louis Vignes, the pioneer of California viticulture. Although Vignes's principal vineyard was on the west side of the river, this property seems to have been located east of the river in what is now Lincoln Heights. Used with permission, Los Angeles Public Library/ Security Pacific Collection.

processed grapes were shipped to San Francisco and the mining towns near Sacramento. In 1857, 250,000 gallons of wine and 945,000 pounds of grapes were shipped to northern markets. As the city grew under U.S. rule, the zanja system was expanded and more and more of the pueblo lands were cultivated for the production of grapes. By 1861, wine was also being shipped to New York and Boston.[31] A catalog of California wines published in 1863 listed sixty-five vineyards each containing 1,000 or more vines in the "town of Los Angeles." Together these vineyards contained more than one million vines. Twenty different vineyards each contained more than 20,000 vines; five had more than 45,000 vines each. William Wolfskill, a Kentucky-born trapper and carpenter who had planted his first vines south of El Aliso Vineyard in 1838, was the largest grower, with 85,000 vines.[32] Matthew Keller, an Irish merchant who had established a winery in Los Angeles about 1852 (fig. 2.4) and who later opened a sales office for his wines and brandies in Philadelphia, had 61,600 vines on Aliso Street.[33] Dr. H. R. Myles and J. R. Scott had 50,000 vines each. The Sainsevain brothers, who had taken over El Aliso Vineyard from their uncle a few years earlier, had 45,000 vines.[34]

The city's blossoming as a wine center was integral to helping Los Angeles avoid economic disaster after the collapse of the cattle industry, which was precipitated by drought in the early 1860s. Perhaps more important in historic terms, the export of Los Angeles wine to the eastern United States no doubt helped foster the city's image as a semitropical paradise. A Boston newspaper remarked in 1862 that "no one acquainted with the soil and climate of California can doubt that it is to that state we are to look for the wines that are to make us forget Bordeaux, Rheims, Epernay, Tokay, and Oparto." U.S. Secretary of State William H. Seward, speaking in the city in 1869, proclaimed to thunderous applause that the vineyards of Los Angeles were the best in the world. By 1870, there were six million grapevines growing in and around Los Angeles. Forty-three local wineries produced four million gallons of wine that year and accounted for three-quarters of all manufacturing employment.[35]

The ample supply of water provided by the river enabled farmers to diversify and experiment with a variety of crops. Blake, the government geologist, wrote that "it is almost impossible . . . even to enumerate the variety of fruits and vegetables that can be abundantly produced here with great ease."[36] Oranges, introduced in 1815, were among the most notable. The first orange grove in Los Angeles was laid out in 1834, when Jean Louis Vignes planted near the river a small plot of seedling trees from the Mission San Gabriel. A few years later, William Wolfskill planted sixty orange trees on two acres where

FIG. 2.4. Winery established about 1852 by Matthew Keller, who owned one of the largest vineyards in Los Angeles, as it appeared in the 1880s after it had been taken over by the Los Angeles Vintage Company. Used with permission, The Huntington Library, San Marino, California/Matthew Keller Collection.

Fourth Street now crosses Alameda. Wolfskill steadily expanded the size of his orchards, and by the 1850s they occupied seventy acres (fig. 2.5).[37] "This grove was one of the showplaces of Los Angeles," recalled early historian J. M. Guinn. "It had been for years an unfailing source of revenue for its owner. It was the pride of the native, the lure of the tourist, and an incentive for the prospective orange grower."[38] Encouraged by Wolfskill's success, others also began planting oranges. Andrew Briswalter, for example, planted twenty-five hundred trees. Matthew Keller imported orange seeds from Central America and Hawaii. Soon, most of the city south of Third Street was a succession of orange groves. Wolfskill alone had more than fifteen hundred bearing trees (fig. 2.6), some of which were as high as forty feet tall. At one time, he was reported to have owned more than two-thirds of the orange trees in California. Wolfskill's son Joseph, who took over the family operation after his father's death in 1866, was responsible for introducing California oranges to the eastern United States when he shipped a boxcar of oranges from his Alameda Street groves to St. Louis in 1877.[39]

Grapes and oranges were the most valuable agricultural products produced in Los Angeles before the arrival of the railroad in 1876, but at least forty-four other crops were also cultivated. Hemp, used to make rope, canvas, and paper, was introduced in 1805 after insects had reduced the corn and bean crops; within five years, 173,200 pounds of hemp were produced in Los Angeles. Corn flourished in the bottomlands that were too wet for any other crop. Growers began to cultivate walnuts in 1847. William Wolfskill was the first person to plant almonds, laying out a small orchard in 1855. He also introduced persimmons to Southern California and had small stands of several other exotic fruits and nuts—bananas, figs, Italian chestnuts, and quince. Tobacco, peanuts, peaches, pears, asparagus, and an assortment of peppers were also raised. One farmer even tried to grow cotton, planting eighty acres and building a cotton gin north of Jefferson Street. A nursery near the southern border of the city was reportedly home to seventy-five thousand young fruit trees.[40] "Nearly every householder had a garden," recalled H. D. Barrows in 1911, "and eventually, a small vineyard and orchard, adjoining his home." None of this would have been possible without the river, which, as historian J. Gregg Layne observed, was "the blood of life" to Los Angeles in those early days.[41]

A Garden Paradise

The river not only helped to make Los Angeles one of the richest agricultural regions in the nation, but its water enabled the physical environment of the town to be transformed to such a degree that it left a deep impression on travelers and settlers. What those visitors and residents wrote about the city contributed greatly to the development of its reputation as a garden paradise. The landscape of Southern California by 1850 was very different from that first encountered by the Spanish. The once tree-covered plain was now barren and desolate. The willows and cottonwoods that had lined the river courses and marshes had been cut for lumber and firewood or cleared to make room for farms and ranches. Cattle had sheared the countryside of its luxuriant growth of native grasses. Much of the wetlands had dried up because of increasing use of surface water. Verdant and inviting, Los Angeles was visible from a great distance, a fertile oasis amid a sea of dust. The geologist Blake, arriving in Los Angeles in 1853 as part of an expedition to determine the best route for a railroad from the Mississippi River to the Pacific Ocean, remarked, "It was very delightful, after having been so long in the mountains, far from civilization, and for a part of the time traveling over the arid wastes of the Great Basin, to arrive in this vine-clad valley, and to walk through gardens and

FIG. 2.5. Fruit orchards of William Wolfskill, located a mile west of the river, as they appeared about 1880. Reprinted from J. Albert Wilson, *History of Los Angeles County, California* (Oakland: Thompson & West, 1880), between pages 16 and 17.

FIG. 2.6. Orange trees irrigated with river water in the groves of William Wolfskill, who once owned two-thirds of the orange trees in the state and whose family shipped the first oranges from California to the eastern United States. Used with permission, Department of Special Collections, University Research Library, University of California, Los Angeles.

vineyards where the purple fruit hung in luxuriant and tempting clusters."[42]

An ever-increasing number of Americans visited and settled in Los Angeles after California was acquired by the United States in 1848. Nearly all who recorded their impressions commented on the delightful setting. Vineyards and orchards adorned the pueblo with a necklace of green. Flowers bloomed in gardens, and celery grew wild along the irrigation ditches. Fences formed by live willow trees, planted inches apart in a row, shaded the roadsides. Groves of oranges, lemons, and olives were interspersed with feathery palms. Acres of apples, peaches, walnuts, pears, and pomegranates brightened the horizon. Fences made from transplanted cactus surrounded fields of wheat, beans, and barley. Travelers and residents alike marveled at the varieties of produce cultivated and the sizes to which the fruits and vegetables grew. One young New Englander wrote relatives back home that he had seen cabbages that weighed fifty pounds, beets ten inches round, and corn growing eighteen feet tall along the river. Another early resident claimed that he had seen pumpkins that weighed 214 pounds and that he raised one himself that weighed 206 pounds. Squash, onions, beans, peas, cauliflower, carrots, and turnips also flourished. To newcomers, the zanjas that wound through the agricultural lands, so unlike anything back home, also sometimes became part of the romantic appeal of Los Angeles.[43]

When U.S. Army Lt. Edward Ord arrived in Los Angeles in 1849 to survey the city under contract to the new town government, he observed that the bottomlands along the river were blanketed with vineyards, orchards, and gardens for four miles up and down its banks. He estimated that there were sixty to one hundred cornfields and at least as many vineyards along the river.[44] Seven years later, he described the approach to Los Angeles as seen on a stage trip from San Pedro:

> Rising the slope . . . we see the city of Los Angeles. Someone points across the plain to a thin line of green some 15 miles off. Where are the houses? Oh, they are surrounded by trees and vineyards. The little white spot you see above the green is the cupola of the church. By and by we rode between willow hedges, and zanjas . . . of flowing water went perling along the roads and thro the fields of corn and the long rows of vines, the almond and orange groves. All around us was a refreshing green, so grateful to the eyes and nose after the arid brown and yellow of the hot plains.[45]

The accounts of visits to Los Angeles before the arrival of the transcontinental railroad in 1876 resound with such descriptions. Many were more effervescent in their praise, more extravagant in their use of adjectives, setting the tone for the promotional literature that soon became commonplace and would help draw millions to Southern California. Ironically, it was these same romantic portrayals that helped assure the ultimate demise of the once-tiny pueblo as a semitropical paradise and the destruction of the river that watered the vineyards, orange groves, palm trees, and flowers. "The song of Mignon came vividly to me as I walked through the gardens of the city of Los Angeles," wrote John S. Hittel, in one of the more poetic examples, published in 1863. "Luscious fruits, of many species and unnumbered varieties, loaded the trees. Gentle breezes came through the bowers. The water rippled musically through the zanjas. Delicious odors came from all the most fragrant flowers of the temperate zone. The general impression upon my mind, after spending the last week in September in the place, is that it is one of the most pleasant places in the world."[46]

After the Gold Rush

The discovery of gold near Sacramento in 1848 was the first step in the transformation of Los Angeles from a sleepy agricultural village into a regional trading center and eventually a city of much greater importance. The demand for food and equipment from the hordes of fortune seekers who flooded the gold fields spurred the city's development as a supply center and shipping point for cattle. After California became a state in 1850, more and more people migrated to the city from points east. The newcomers would not tolerate the primitive conditions that had characterized Los Angeles from its first days as a pueblo. They demanded better streets, improved sanitation, police and fire protection, schools, and water piped directly to their homes.[47] Water, in fact, would become the most crucial factor in the city's initial expansion under U.S. rule. As Los Angeles grew, demand for water increased and, for the first time, there was competition for the river's supply, stirring division and provoking crime, even murder. The network of irrigation ditches was gradually expanded, and a domestic distribution system was created. Increasingly, access to water determined the value of real estate and shaped the direction of development.

To better understand the metamorphosis of Los Angeles during the last half of the nineteenth century and the changing role in local life played by the river and its water supply, it is helpful to first glimpse what the city was like at the time of statehood. Los Angeles in 1850 was still very much a small town, although its sudden gold- and cattle-inspired wealth had given it a decided Wild West spirit. The first census of the city conducted that year by the U.S. government counted 1,694 people living within its limits—1,610 whites, 70 Indians, 12 blacks, and 2 Chinese. The population was concentrated around the plaza, the business and social center of the town, and extended north two blocks in the vicinity of Main Street and south slightly farther along Main and Los Angeles Streets. Most of the houses were small, one-story adobe structures with flat, asphalt-covered roofs, although the added income derived from the booming market for cattle had prompted a few residents to add second stories to their homes. The new money had also given rise to many saloons and gambling halls, the most notorious of which sprouted along a narrow, block-long street southeast of the plaza. During the Mexican period this street had been called Calle de los Negros, but as English speakers began to predominate it became known as Nigger Alley. Most of the more traditional businesses were located on Main Street, south of the plaza and north of First Street.[48]

Outside the plaza area, agricultural uses prevailed. Lt. Edward Ord's 1849 map of Los Angeles provides the best depiction of the character and geographic dimensions of agricultural development in the city at the time of statehood.[49] It has been redrawn in figure 2.7 to clarify the symbolization, so that the use of each field can be more easily understood. On Ord's map, the cultivated lands stretched north along the main irrigation ditch and south almost to the pueblo limits, encompassing nearly all the land between the present route of Main Street and the river. The agricultural lands ended abruptly west of a line extending from Main Street because these lands were at a higher elevation than the main dam on the river and, therefore, could not be irrigated from the city's zanjas. Calculations made from Ord's map indicate that between 1,500 and 1,600 acres were under cultivation in Los Angeles at the time, roughly one-tenth of the original pueblo lands. Vineyards covered much of the northern two-thirds of the cultivated area. Corn and pasture occupied larger plots farther south. Vegetable gardens and a few small orchards were sprinkled throughout. Most of the cattle shipped from Los Angeles were raised outside the city limits on the numerous large *ranchos* that extended in every direction from its borders.[50]

The river, which by this time had assumed the name of the town through which it passed, formed the eastern limit of the settled area.[51] Aliso Street ended abruptly at El Aliso Vineyard, where it narrowed to a willow-lined lane extending as far as the river's edge.[52] No bridges had yet been built across its channel, and cultivation had not yet spread east of its course. The flow of the river, furthermore, was still ample. There seems to have been little concern at the time about whether it carried enough water to satisfy the future needs of Los Angeles. The Zanja Madre and three smaller irrigation ditches were the principal method of distributing water from the river. Farmers whose land did not border one of the zanjas dug their own ditches to the public canals, while property owners whose farms sat next to the river often cut channels directly from its banks. There had been few regulations governing use of the water supply through the Spanish and Mexican periods. Private water carriers remained the exclusive means of obtaining water for domestic use for those who did not want to haul water from the river or one of the ditches themselves. Water carriers, many of them women, were the principal source of domestic water for many residents of the city for more than seventy-five years.

Ord's map of 1849 also provides the earliest known view of the irrigation system of Los Angeles. It shows the Zanja Madre following the base of the bench along which Main Street runs, terminating near the plaza. En route the Zanja Madre powered the first flour mill in Los Angeles, built in 1831 and still standing on North Spring Street in Chinatown.[53] Water wheels in the zanjas also reportedly provided power for the printing press of one of the town's first newspapers. On Ord's map, another ditch begins south of the Zanja Madre and follows the same southwesterly course as the main zanja, splitting in two about Ninth Street. Its two branches continue south to about where the Santa Monica Freeway now runs. Ord's contract with the city, however, reveals that he was required to map the zanjas only where they crossed unfenced land. Knowing this, it seems likely that these two ditches were actually the same ditch and that the south zanja was merely a continuation of the Zanja Madre.[54]

An offshoot of the Zanja Madre begins north of the present location of Chinatown and briefly splits in two before disappearing on the map east of the town site. Assuming that this ditch also extended across fenced farmland, it seems probable that it connected with another ditch shown farther south on the map. This ditch begins about where Fifth Street runs today and approximates the route of San Pedro Street. It extends south on the map to about Ninth Street, where it splits in two before disappearing at a hedge fence. Two smaller ditches are also visible on Ord's map. One runs midway between the Zanja Madre and the river, terminating north of the present location of the Los Angeles County Jail. Another begins near the river and extends across pasture to a vineyard and other scattered farms in the southeast corner of the mapped area, east of the present location of Alameda Street.

In the city's first decade under U.S. control, the population of Los Angeles nearly tripled and the zanja system assumed increasing importance. City officials began to impose fees for water use and to establish rules governing the zanjas. They also created a full-time posi-

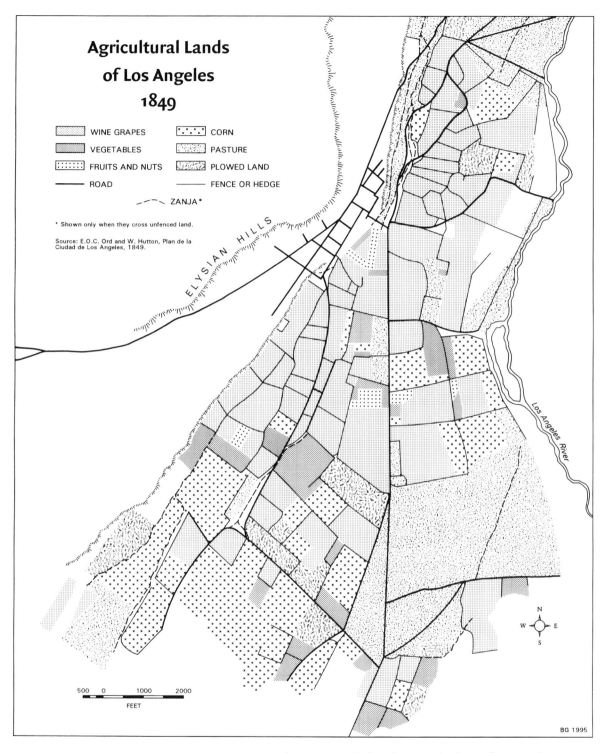

**Agricultural Lands
of Los Angeles
1849**

WINE GRAPES   CORN

VEGETABLES   PASTURE

FRUITS AND NUTS   PLOWED LAND

——— ROAD   ——— FENCE OR HEDGE

– – – ⌐ ZANJA*

* Shown only when they cross unfenced land.

Source: E.O.C. Ord and W. Hutton, Plan de la
Ciudad de Los Angeles, 1849.

ELYSIAN HILLS

Los Angeles River

N
W   E
S

500   0   1000   2000
FEET

BG 1995

FIG. 2.7. Los Angeles was an agricultural town at the dawn of statehood,
with farms occupying at least fifteen hundred acres in the city. Vineyards occupied most of the prime irrigable land north and south of the town center.
Corn fields, vegetable gardens, fruit orchards, and pasture were more common further south. Map by the author.

tion to oversee the network of ditches. On the recommendation of Mayor Stephen C. Foster, the Los Angeles Common Council in 1854 established the position of *zanjero*. During the Spanish and Mexican periods, administration of the city's water supply had been lax, supervised only by a standing committee of the pueblo government. Each week a different city official had been placed in charge of the zanjas. Landowners who drew water from the ditches seem to have been required in return only to supply Indian laborers for occasional maintenance of the zanjas or repair of the city dam.[55]

Water was so important in the arid country that the zanjero soon became the most powerful public official in Los Angeles. His salary in 1860 was $1,200 a year, more than that of any other city employee. The mayor received just $800, and three mayors went on to became zanjero. The authority of the zanjero was so great that eventually the city council gave him permission to purchase goods using city funds without having to obtain approval from the council, a right held by no one else. The duties of the position, moreover, were broad. The zanjero issued permits for the use of irrigation water, scheduled water deliveries, collected fees, and enforced all ordinances pertaining to the zanjas. He coordinated maintenance of the ditches and arranged for any necessary repairs to the city dam. He had policing powers and could arrest individuals who illegally diverted water, damaged the zanjas, or dumped garbage into the ditches. He even issued permits for fishing in the zanjas. The zanjero also coordinated some of the earliest publicly funded flood control work on the Los Angeles River.[56]

As cultivation spread, new zanjas were built. In 1855, the Common Council approved a request for the construction of a private ditch on the east side of the river. It carried water to the Rancho San Antonio, just south of the city limits; when demand for water later became more intense, however, the city halted diversions into the ditch. In 1857, Zanja No. 1, an offshoot of the Zanja Madre that wound between Alameda Street and the river, was completed (see fig. 2.11). It supplied the first public bath in Los Angeles and powered Aliso Mill, located on a site now occupied by Union Station. Still another zanja, crossing Spring Street near Fourth Street, was built about 1860, although this one does not appear on later maps and may have ultimately been relocated. The following year, the Common Council approved the creation of a ditch (probably Zanja No. 2) branching from Zanja No. 1. Irrigation was extended to the southwestern part of the city in 1864 when a ditch twenty-four hundred feet long and three feet wide was dug from the Zanja Madre southwest to Ninth Street by a hardware merchant and nurseryman named O. W. Childs. Later known as Zanja No. 8, this ditch ran between Main and Los Angeles Streets before zigzagging across Spring and Hill Streets to Central Park, now Pershing Square. From there, it turned southwest and meandered to the then-rural district around Figueroa Street. Childs was given a two-hundred-acre parcel of land between Main and Figueroa Streets as payment for his work. There he planted fifty acres of orange trees.[57] "That irrigating canal, figuring the land at its present value," historian J. M. Guinn later wrote, "cost the city almost as much as the Panama Canal cost the nation."[58]

By 1870, there were eight zanjas in Los Angeles, with a total length of about fifty miles. Zanja No. 2 was the longest, running at least six miles south of First Street along Alameda Street. Zanja No. 1, which ran between Zanja No. 2 and the river, was about three miles in length. The individual ditches varied in width and capacity. They were typically about three feet wide and a foot deep, with water flowing through them continuously at a speed of about five miles an hour. The Zanja Madre was larger; it was maintained to a width of ten feet along its entire length. All were open earthen ditches dug through porous, sandy ground. As a result, much of the water they carried was lost. As the amount of water diverted from the river increased and the network of zanjas grew, theft of water also became a problem. Diversions were not monitored. Irrigators simply paid the zanjero for the right to divert water for a twelve-hour period. In 1870, for instance, the fee was $1.50 a day for daytime service, $1.00 at night.[59]

The ditches were neither covered nor lined, and residents whose properties bordered the zanjas could easily cut an opening in the side and divert water to their land when the zanjero was out of sight. Since a single zanjero was responsible for the entire system until 1873, there was little risk of getting caught. Others might pay for daytime service, cut the zanja to divert water to their property, and then, at night, while the zanjero slept, take additional water, closing the opening before the arrival of the zanjero at daybreak. Competition for water also led to more serious crimes. A man who owned a small farm south of the city was shot to death after a disagreement over use of water in a nearby zanja. The suspected murderer was later hanged by an angry mob. Some irrigators, meanwhile, hired armed guards to watch over their ditches.[60]

The zanjas were also unsanitary and posed a health hazard. There were no bridges over the ditches, so livestock, wagons, and pedestrians regularly splashed through the public water supply. Dead animals were frequently removed from the ditches. Human bodies were also occasionally found. In 1851, the body of an Indian was found in a zanja in the northern part of the city. Several years later, a twenty-three-month-old child was found drowned in the Zanja Madre. Local vigilantes sometimes used the zanjas as a means of punishment, dragging their victims "up and down the water ditch" until they were "more dead than alive."[61] Not surprisingly, dysentery was common. Residents bathed, washed clothes, and disposed of garbage in the same zanjas from which the community drew its drinking water. This continued even during an outbreak of smallpox. Nevertheless, some local residents used the ditches to perform an old Hispano-California custom intended to guarantee health for the coming year. They celebrated El Bano de las Virgenes (the Bath of the Virgins) by bathing in the running water of the zanjas at dawn.[62]

As early as 1836, the pueblo government, after having received repeated complaints of Indians bathing and washing clothes in the Zanja Madre, prohibited such activities. The Committee on Zanjas required the Indians instead to dig a pool beside the ditch and divert a small amount of water into the pool, so that the public supply would not be contaminated. Two weeks later, however, a member of the committee reported that it was nearly impossible to prevent women from doing their laundry in the main zanja. That didn't keep city leaders from trying, though. In 1841, the city government instituted a fine of one dollar for anyone caught washing clothes or otherwise polluting the main irrigation ditch. In 1852, soon after the city came under U.S. rule, the first Los Angeles Common Council enacted ordinances that prohibited bathing, washing clothes, dumping refuse, and the slaughter of cattle in the zanjas. The fine for washing clothes in the zanjas was three dollars.[63]

The laws seemed to be of little consequence, however. "Day after day, from sunrise till evening, groups of females, from 'snowy white to sooty,' can be seen at the daily avocations of washing clothes through nearly the entire length of our water canals," the *Los Angeles Star* observed on 10 June 1855. "A stranger would be very apt to suppose that our water canals were built for the purpose of carrying off the garbage and foul matter that is continually accumulating within the precincts of a city, instead of being the source from which a large portion of the inhabitants are supplied with water for domestic purposes." In the 1860s, the situation became still more serious when it was discovered that the sewer from a local hotel was emptying into one of the zanjas. Similar complaints were made about Zanja No. 8 in the 1870s. The city health officer, in fact, called it a "foul nuisance" and recommended that efforts be "made to cut off the many foul drains that now do and have for years connected with the various zanjas." Disposal of the city's liquid wastes continued to confound city officials until 1892, when voters approved a bond issue to pay for the construction of a sewer system, storm drains, and an outfall sewer that emptied into the ocean at Playa del Rey.[64]

Before the development of a domestic water system, more affluent residents often refused to obtain their water supply from the increasingly filthy zanjas. As Los Angeles grew, water carriers sold, by subscription, water drawn directly from the river. In the early 1850s, water carriers charged fifty cents a week, due each Saturday night, for one bucket a day. No deliveries were made on Sunday. They increased the amount of water they could deliver by using barrels pulled through the streets by horses or swung between the handles of a wheelbarrow. Later, ox-drawn carts were also used. One water carrier, advertising his services in the *Los Angeles Star* of 25 June 1853, said that he was "ready and willing to supply the citizens of Los Angeles with this very necessary element on very reasonable terms. Having a good horse and cart, he will be punctual in all arrangements." Legend tells the tale of Bill the Waterman, a tall American, thirty to thirty-five years old, who wore a walrus mustache and rubber boots that came almost to his waist. From house to house, he led two worn-out horses pulling a rickety wagon that carried a sixty-gallon barrel full of river water.[65]

The Development of a Domestic Water System

The first proposal to distribute water directly to the homes of Los Angeles in pipes was made in 1853 by the clerk of the Common Council, William G. Dryden, a former county judge. In return, he requested a twenty-one-year franchise for the water system and two square leagues of land—nearly nine thousand acres—an area equal to half the size of the original pueblo. The offer was rejected.[66] "We want water, to be sure," the *Star* remarked in opposing the proposal, "but we cannot afford to give ourselves away for it." Four years later, however, the council granted Dryden a franchise to distribute water in pipes to the northwestern part of the city from a series of springs known as the Abila Springs. Located on low ground near the current intersection of College and Alameda Streets in present-day Chinatown, these springs were formed by the underground flow of the Los Angeles River.[67]

Dryden formed the Los Angeles Water Works Company in 1858, erected a forty-foot water wheel in the Zanja Madre (fig. 2.8), and built a fifteen- by thirty-foot brick reservoir in the plaza (fig. 2.9). The water wheel provided the power necessary to lift water from the springs into an elevated flume that carried it to the reservoir, which was located at a higher elevation than the springs. Water was supplied to homes of the city's elite near the plaza through underground pipes made of pine logs brought down from the San Bernardino Mountains. Three-inch holes were bored through the center of the logs. Storms in December 1861, however, destroyed the water wheel and the dam that diverted

water from the river into the Zanja Madre, crippling the city's first domestic distribution system. Residents had to rely again on water
hauled in carts from the river. Dryden eventually installed a new water
wheel, but by that time the city had decided to develop its own domestic water system.[68]

Three years earlier, the Common Council had hired two engineers
to devise a plan for diverting water directly from the river and distributing it to homes in the city through iron pipes, but the council was
unable to come up with the $45,775 required to implement the plan.
After the failure of the Dryden system, city officials in August 1862
contracted with Jean Louis Sainsevain, nephew of pioneering vintner
Jean Louis Vignes, to construct an improved system, though one less
elaborate than that which had originally been recommended. Sainsevain built a more substantial dam on the river and a line of flumes to
transport water to a small reservoir. Two rows of piles, fifteen to eighteen feet long, were driven six feet apart into the river bed so that the
top of the piles protruded above the river bottom. Two-inch planks
were then nailed to the piles to form parallel bulkheads seven feet

FIG. 2.8. This water wheel, built about 1858, lifted water from the Abila
Springs, located where Chinatown is today, to an elevated flume, which
transported the water to a brick reservoir in the plaza. The system provided
the first water distributed in pipes to the homes of Los Angeles. Used with permission, Los Angeles Public Library/Security Pacific Collection.

FIG. 2.9. The plaza area, about 1869. The brick building in the center of the plaza is the reservoir of the city's first domestic water system. The cupola of the pueblo Catholic church is in the foreground, just to the left of the reservoir. Note the lush agricultural lands that spread east from the plaza area toward the river. Used with permission, Department of Special Collections, University of Southern California Library/Title Insurance & Trust Co. Collection (USC 1-1-1-3827).

high designed to block the river's flow and form a reservoir behind the dam. The area between the bulkheads was filled with rock. At the same time that the dam was being built, some fifteen thousand feet of wooden pipe was being laid beneath the city streets and, by 5 November 1864, the new system was delivering water directly to homes in the city. The following February, the city leased the domestic supply system for four years to David W. Alexander, a longtime Los Angeles merchant and former president of the Common Council, at an annual rental rate of $1,000.[69]

Alexander transferred his lease to Sainsevain six months later. With the assistance of former mayor Damien Marchessault, Sainsevain erected a water wheel at the dam and built a small reservoir, with a capacity of about 700,000 gallons, near a Catholic cemetery that stood at the intersection of North Broadway Street and Bishops Road. The water wheel raised water thirty-six feet so it could be transported by flume to the reservoir. Distribution pipes were extended along Macy Street and as far south as First Street, encompassing most of the business district (then still concentrated along Main and Los Angeles Streets) from the plaza south for four blocks. The residential district had by this time begun to expand. Residential areas were developing between First and Fourth Streets, west of Main Street—beyond the reach of the new water system—and along Aliso Street, where Matthew Keller had subdivided the front of his vineyard into twenty- by one-hundred-foot lots in 1861. The majority of the Hispanic population in Los Angeles, meanwhile, lived north of the plaza church, along Main and Eternity (now Broadway) Streets in an area known as Sonoratown, so named because many of its earliest residents had migrated from the Mexican province of Sonora during the Gold Rush. The population of Los Angeles had grown to about five thousand in the previous fifteen years, but the new water system was inadequate even for a town of that size. The wooden pipes, connected only by wires, leaked continually and frequently burst from pressure. As a result, streets were often flooded and were filled with mud even during dry summer months. Many residents in the newly settled areas, moreover, still had to obtain their domestic water from water carriers or the irrigation canals.[70]

In November 1867, Sainsevain signed a contract with the city to replace the wooden pipes with iron conduits and to extend the distribution system by five thousand feet. But severe floods that began the following month again washed away the dam and destroyed the water wheel. There was no water in the pipes for four months. The zanjas dried up. Discouraged and embarrassed by the continued problems with the water system, former mayor Marchessault committed suicide in the chambers of the Common Council on 20 January 1868. The next month, Sainsevain, in despair, sold his lease to a triumvirate composed of Dr. John S. Griffin, a surgeon and the city's first superintendent of schools; Prudent Beaudry, a French Canadian who was the first true real estate promoter in Los Angeles; and Solomon Lazard, a prosperous local dry goods merchant. About the same time, William G. Dryden relinquished his franchise for the separate Los Angeles Water Works Company.[71]

Griffin, Beaudry, and Lazard immediately sought to renegotiate their contract with the city. They proposed to lease the domestic water works for fifty years. In return, they would lay twelve miles of iron pipe, build a reservoir capable of holding a twenty-day supply of water, install fire hydrants at every intersection, and pay the city

$50,000 in gold coin. They also offered to erect an ornamental fountain in the plaza, build new ditches from the river to the two reservoirs, and supply all city buildings with water for free. The proposal was referred to a council committee, which recommended acceptance. The ordinance submitted to the full council by the majority of the committee, however, went one step further than the original proposal. The water works, it advised, should be granted to the group in perpetuity; in other words, they should be sold outright. "We do not believe it advisable or prudent for the city to own property of this nature," the majority report said. "It is well known by past experience that cities and towns can never manage enterprises of that nature as economically as individuals can; and besides it is a continual source of annoyance and is made a political hobby."[72]

On 1 June 1868, the council voted 3 to 2 in favor of the proposal. The ordinance, however, was vetoed a week later by Mayor Cristóbal Aguilar, a former zanjero, who claimed that the sale of the water works was tantamount to selling the city's rights to the water in the river and that such an action would threaten the future needs of irrigators in the city. He also thought the price offered was too low. Disagreeing with the water works committee, moreover, he said that the city would be better off leasing or managing the system itself. "It has always been considered by my predecessor, as well as myself . . . that the prosperity of the city of Los Angeles depends entirely upon the proper management and distribution of the waters of the Los Angeles River," he said in a message accompanying his veto. "First in magnitude will be the supply of water for domestic use, properly managed to avoid waste. But I cannot conceive the necessity of a sale of this water franchise in order to secure a supply for domestic use. I find the latter term so indefinite as to [the] extent that in the course of time great questions may arise with other vested rights, [such as the] cultivators of the soil, all of which we should endeavor to avoid."[73]

Griffin and his associates then proposed to lease the domestic water works for thirty years for an annual payment of $1,500, offering essentially the same improvements included in the first proposal. This time, the city received offers from several other parties as well. Some contained significantly better terms than the Griffin proposal. Juan Bernard and P. McFadden, who had taken over Dryden's Los Angeles Water Works Company, for example, offered $2,000 a year for a twenty-year lease. Council President John King, however, denied all requests from citizens to speak before the council about the issue and forced a quick vote. On 20 July 1868, the council approved by a 4-2 vote the thirty-year lease of the city water system to Griffin, Beaudry, and Lazard. This time Mayor Aguilar gave his support. Historian J. M.

Guinn later suggested that council members may have accepted the Griffin offer, despite its less lucrative terms, because they had become so rankled by the water question that they were anxious to dispose of the water system to the party that would take it off their hands for the longest period.[74] After obtaining the lease, Griffin, Beaudry, and Lazard immediately transferred control of the water system to a new corporation called the Los Angeles City Water Company.

Over the next thirty years, the Los Angeles City Water Company made many improvements and built the framework for a more modern water distribution system. The company's most important initial decision was to build its diversion on the river farther upstream from previous dams, at a higher elevation than the town site, thus eliminating the need for the fragile water wheels and flumes that had proven so susceptible to damage from floods. The company purchased land near the southeastern corner of what is now Griffith Park and dug a canal from the river through the Crystal Springs, a marshy area formed by the subsurface flow of the river.[75] The canal then wound along the hills on the west side of the river for six miles before emptying into three small reservoirs on Eternity Street (Broadway) in the northern part of the city. From there, water was transported south in an eight-inch cast iron main as far as First Street, while individual homes were supplied through galvanized 1-1/2-inch iron pipe connected to the main. By November 1869, seven miles of water pipe had been laid beneath city streets. The following year, the three small reservoirs on Eternity Street were replaced by a larger storage facility formed by the construction of a small earthen dam across a ravine in the Elysian Hills. The reservoir, which was located near the southeasternmost tip of present-day Elysian Park, eventually became known as Buena Vista Reservoir (fig. 2.10).[76]

Diversions from the river for domestic use increased in 1868 when the Los Angeles Canal and Reservoir Company was formed to supply water to an undeveloped area on the west side of the city. The company paid the city for the right to build a twenty-foot dam across a ravine at the present location of Echo Park. A ditch was excavated through a winding pass in the hills west of the river to transport water to a reservoir created by the dam. Water was diverted into the ditch from the river where it rounds the bend of Griffith Park, five miles north of what were then the city limits. Another ditch was built to transport water from the reservoir south to Figueroa Street, providing water for the fledgling suburbs atop Bunker Hill and powering the first woolen mill in Los Angeles. In 1872, a third water company was created to supply water to the hilly areas northwest of the business district. Prudent Beaudry, who had been one of the founders of the Los Angeles

FIG. 2.10. Buena Vista Reservoir, built in the Elysian Hills just west of the river in 1870. The river would have been just below the dam and, in this photograph taken in 1876, is blocked from view by the dam. What was probably streamside vegetation can be seen just above the dam on both sides of the photo. Used with permission, Los Angeles Public Library/Security Pacific Collection.

City Water Company, excavated a large basin at the corner of College and Alameda Streets to collect the underground flow of the river that rose to the surface at the Abila Springs, by this time also known as the Dryden Springs. A sixty-horsepower engine pumped the water uphill to two reservoirs built at an elevation of 240 feet in the Elysian Hills. Water was supplied to homes via iron pipes. The Beaudry franchise was purchased by the Citizens Water Company in 1886 and was acquired by the Los Angeles City Water Company in 1892.[77]

The Expansion of the Irrigated District

The zanjas remained under the control of the city government and were still the sole source of water for irrigation. They also supplied water to homes and businesses beyond the reach of the three domestic service systems. As demand for irrigation increased and the service area expanded, the zanjero was authorized to hire several deputies and, in 1870, the cultivated area was divided into irrigation districts and the deputies were each put in charge of a district. Construction of Zanja No. 7 about this time enabled cultivation to spread east of the river. Water was diverted into the ditch from the river using a sand-and-brush dam built just north of the Macy Street bridge. From there, water ran south three miles along the base of the bluff upon which Boyle Heights was built. Before long, vineyards and fruit trees covered much of the area between the river and the bluff. Although construction of the Aliso Street Railway across the river in the 1880s helped Boyle Heights become a streetcar suburb of Los Angeles, Zanja No. 7 was still in use as late as 1903. Only one other irrigation ditch remained in use longer.[78]

Improvements to the zanjas until this time had been haphazard and disorganized, but in 1877 the city for the first time created a comprehensive plan for development of the river's resources, issuing $75,000 in bonds to improve and expand the zanjas. Overly optimistic promoters of the proposals claimed that the improvements would enable 100,000 acres outside the city limits to be irrigated with river water. A local newspaper, on the eve of an election for the bond issue, predicted that "the plains below the city would be turned into orange orchards and vineyards, and from here to the sea would be a stretch of country as beautiful as the Vale of Cashmere seems from Moore's description." A board of engineers was created to coordinate the improvements. The city bought and enlarged the Canal and Reservoir Company ditch to supply irrigation water to two areas that had been beyond the reach of the zanjas—the uplands west of Figueroa Street and the plains on the east side of the river in what was then the northeastern part of the city (present-day Cypress Park and Lincoln Heights). Ditches were also extended beyond the city limits. An additional $40,000 in bonds were issued in 1878 to help pay for the improvements.[79]

Prior to these developments, irrigation from the river had largely been confined to the bottomlands along its banks and to the first bench above the bottoms, areas that could be reached by inexpensive ditches that required no engineering knowledge to construct. The vast majority of the irrigated land was within the corporate limits of Los Angeles. The most heavily watered district extended in a fan shape four miles south from the beginning of the Zanja Madre and stretched three and one-half miles wide at its southern end. It included an area of about 4,500 acres. The new work expanded the area within the city that had access to water from the zanjas to about 10,000 acres. It also extended irrigation well beyond the city's southern and western boundaries. By 1880, an estimated 4,922 acres in the city were irrigated with river water. Another 3,456 acres outside Los Angeles were watered from the city's zanjas. Ditches fanned in every direction from the river (fig. 2.11), at least nine of them extending beyond the city limits. Within Los Angeles, nearly half the irrigated acreage was devoted to the raising of fruits. Vineyards covered about a third of irrigated land. Vegetable gardens occupied slightly less than a quarter. Outside the city limits, fruits and vegetables each occupied about 40 percent of the irrigated acreage, with vines covering 12 percent and alfalfa 8 percent.[80]

In 1885 and 1886, the city provided another $187,000 from the sale of real estate, the issuance of bonds, and general taxation to continue the improvements to the zanja system. As urban development intensified, many of the open ditches were replaced in the most congested areas by closed cement conduits and iron pipes. Iron pipes were also extended across the river to improve service in East Los Angeles. The new work helped boost the total amount of land irrigated from city zanjas to 11,136 acres in 1886, more than in any other year for which data are available. By 1888, fifteen city-maintained zanjas and nine branches meandered more than fifty-two miles within the corporate boundaries of Los Angeles. City-owned ditches also extended more than four miles south of the city limits. Another forty miles of privately owned conduits connected to the city system to distribute surplus water from the zanjas to the fruit and vegetable farms in the outlying districts. In all, about ninety-three miles of open ditches, cement conduits, and iron pipes transported irrigation water from the river.

Even after the arrival of the railroad, the zanjas remained one of the most romantic and frequently written-about images in Los Angeles, despite their once-squalid reputation and occasional association with disease. Harry Carr, a Los Angeles newspaper columnist, fondly remembered playing as a child in the zanjas that ran along Figueroa and Adams Streets. A visitor from Ohio wrote in 1884 that "the soft murmuring of water as it glides through the zangas [sic] in some of the beautiful suburbs of the city is sweet music to the ear, a happy voice sending out joy and gladness." An 1893 travel guide written by Karl Baedeker, the influential German guidebook author, even recommended that tourists visit "one of the open Zanjas, or irrigating canals, in the suburbs."[81] At least two postcards produced around the turn of the century prominently featured an ornamental zanja on Figueroa Street. Well into the twentieth century, furthermore, a painting of a zanjero digging an irrigation ditch hung on a wall in the headquarters of the Los Angeles Department of Water and Power (fig. 2.12).

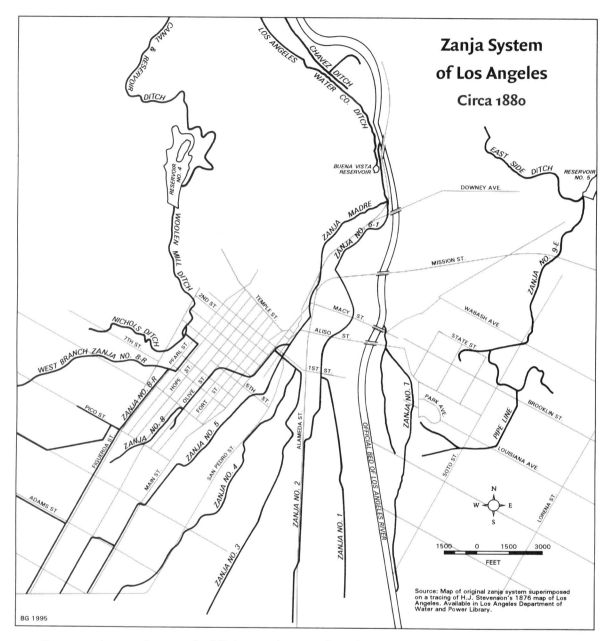

FIG. 2.11. An extensive network of ditches carrying water from the Los Angeles River irrigated 8,378 acres in and around Los Angeles in 1880. Map by the author.

A thorough investigation of irrigation works in Southern California by state engineer William Hamilton Hall in 1888 provides the most complete view of the zanja system of Los Angeles, although it is important to remember that, by the time Hall made his study, development had already forced significant changes to the zanjas.[82] Nearly half of the total length of conduits in the system, for instance, was by then made up of what were called "tight" conduits—cement or iron pipe or wooden flume—rather than open ditches. In describing the system, Hall divided the city irrigation works into upper and lower service areas, according to the point on the river at which water was diverted. The upper and lower works could then each be subdivided into an eastern and western system, based on the side of the river to which they supplied water.

The upper, or high-service, works took water from behind a sand-and-brush dam located five miles north of what were then the city limits, at a point on the south side of the river just before it turns sharply southeast at today's Griffith Park (fig. 2.13). Water was distributed to both the east and west sides of the river from the same diversion. An open canal twelve feet wide and three feet deep carried water south on a route today approximated by Crystal Springs Drive. Known as the Main Supply Ditch, this ditch turned away from the river at a pass through the hills near the present intersection of Riverside Drive and Glendale Boulevard. From this division point, the east-side waters were piped across the river, while the west-side supply continued south in the old Canal and Reservoir Ditch to Reservoir No. 4 (see fig. 2.11), a remnant of which today forms the lake in Echo Park. The Canal and Reservoir Ditch was about eight feet wide. From the division point it followed a course that approximated the present routes of Glendale and Silver Lake Boulevards, before turning east and following a winding route to the reservoir. Reservoir No. 4 was built to provide storage for 150 million gallons of water, but by this time never held more than a third of that amount because the dam was considered unsafe.

From the reservoir, water was transported for most of the rest of its route within the city limits in iron or cement pipes or in open concrete conduits. It was carried south 1.75 miles in an iron pipe known as the Woolen Mill Ditch, so named because it supplied a mill near Figueroa Street. At the mill, a shaft gave the water a drop of seventy-eight feet, producing the energy that ran the mill. Cement pipe and open concrete conduit, which had replaced the earthen ditch of Zanja No. 8-R, carried water south along Pearl and Figueroa Streets. The concrete ditches were two feet wide and eighteen inches deep and were enclosed by ornamental walls where they passed through residential ar-

FIG. 2.12. The symbolic importance of the zanjas to the early development of Los Angeles is represented in this painting of a zanjero at work by Hernando Villa. It hung for years in the headquarters of the Los Angeles Department of Water and Power. Used with permission, Department of Special Collections, University Research Library, University of California, Los Angeles.

eas (fig. 2.14). Concrete bridges were built over the ditches at carriage entrances. Zanja No. 8-R had five branches, all veering west from the main conduit, one extending all the way to Vermont Avenue and another stretching beyond Western Avenue, more than fourteen miles from the original diversion point. Water in the branches was transported in cement pipe as far as the city limits. Outside the city, water was again carried in earthen canals.

A wrought iron pipe, 7,836 feet long and built atop a pile trestle, carried the high-service supply across the river from the division point in a southeasterly direction to the base of a steep hill, now known as

Mount Washington. From there, a cement pipe wound around the hill and across the Arroyo Seco to Zanja No. 9-E, a pipe that followed the route of the old East Side Ditch, which, according to Hall, had been "of low grade, insufficient capacity, constantly choking up with weeds, and very wasteful of water."[83] Zanja No. 9-E emptied its supply into Reservoir No. 5, which was located near the present intersections of Mission and Soto Roads and had a capacity of 120 million gallons. Zanja No. 9-R (Zanja No. 9-E in fig. 2.11) transported water south from the reservoir, following the base of the hills on the east side of Boyle Heights. It was still an earthen ditch in 1888, although a pipeline built that year extended its length eight hundred feet.

Water for the west-side, low-service irrigation system was diverted from the river by a brush-and-wing dam built across from where the

FIG. 2.13. An 1895 photograph shows an irrigation ditch that takes water from the river on the north side of what is now Griffith Park. This is probably the beginning of what was known as the upper, or high-service, works, which distributed water to the more elevated areas on both sides of the river. Used with permission, Los Angeles Public Library/Security Pacific Collection.

FIG. 2.14. Zanja No. 8-R, which carried water south along Pearl and Figueroa Streets (1890). This ornamental concrete conduit replaced an earthen ditch in the 1880s. Used with permission, The Huntington Library, San Marino, California.

Arroyo Seco empties into the Los Angeles River. The dam diverted the river's water into the Zanja Madre, which then carried it south, parallel to the river, for a short distance. The Zanja Madre turned southwest where the Elysian Park hills back away from the river. At this point, Zanja No. 6-1 split off from the main ditch, continuing south between Alameda Street and the river for about 1.5 miles, where it split in two near First Street (see fig. 2.11). Before the land in this area was subdivided for residential and industrial development, the course of Zanja No. 6-1 was lined with pear trees. The Zanja Madre, meanwhile, followed the bluff of the Elysian hills for about a mile through present-day Chinatown before turning south. Water was carried for thirty-three hundred feet in a masonry-lined canal and then for another mile in a brick conduit. Along the way, an eighteen-foot drop provided power for the Capitol Milling Company on Spring Street. The main irrigation ditch also powered the first ice plant in Los Angeles.[84]

At First Street, the Zanja Madre divided into four conduits—Zanja No. 3, Zanja No. 4, Zanja No. 5, and Zanja No. 8. Although Zanja No. 8 originally terminated just east of Zanja No. 8-R (as shown in fig. 2.11), by the time Hall conducted his study it had apparently been extended to meet the main conduit of the upper-service system. The other three zanjas ran southwest, each of them extending two to three miles beyond the city limits. By 1888, among the four conduits formed near First Street from the Zanja Madre, only Zanja No. 3 still carried water in an open, earthen channel from its head. The others, all passing through the center of the business district, had been converted to cement pipe for much of their lengths.

The east-side, low-service system, the least extensive of the four systems identified by Hall, diverted water with a dam built from the east bank of the river about 1.75 miles downstream from the beginning of the Zanja Madre. Zanja No. 7, an open ditch for most of its length, was the only low-service canal still in use on the east side of the river in 1888. Following the base of the Boyle Heights bluff, it extended about two miles south of the city limits.[85]

The zanja system in 1888 was administered by a chief zanjero, who was assisted by a secretary and three deputy zanjeros. The chief zanjero was paid $1,800 a year, while each of his assistants were paid a salary of $900. The chief zanjero was responsible for overseeing all diversions from the system, as well as coordinating maintenance and improvements. Water was sold by an imprecise unit called an *irrigating head* ("as indeterminate a volume to-day as it was twenty years ago," according to Hall), for a designated period of service. Rates in 1888 were three dollars for a day (sunrise to sunset), two dollars for a half-day (sunrise to noon, or noon to sunset), and fifty cents for an hour. Irrigators were required to apply in writing to the zanjero by the twenty-fifth of each month, stating the number of acres they owned, the zanja from which they sought water, and the dates and hours they wanted service the following month. The zanjero then scheduled the diversions. After all diversions for city irrigators had been scheduled, surplus water was sold to irrigators outside the city limits at rates roughly double those for city residents. The zanjero and his deputies were also responsible for enforcing a "quite voluminous" set of regulations governing the zanjas, and even in 1888 were still sworn policemen with arresting powers.[86]

Though considerable improvements had been made to the zanja system during the twelve years before Hall conducted his study, he nevertheless found a system impaired by the same administrative inefficiency and engineering ignorance that had plagued the zanjas for decades. "The Los Angeles city irrigation works," he wrote, "are a gradual development of the crudest possible system of irrigation ditches—the old Mexican low-land zanjas—and much of the general character of the primitive works themselves, as well as the generic name they bore, adheres to the work of the present day." There was still no accurate method for measuring water use. Despite planning by successive teams of engineers, no definite program for improvements had been followed. A submerged dam that was to be built in the river, for example, was never finished. A tunnel intended to replace part of the Zanja Madre collapsed and was abandoned. Other work was completed, only to be replaced almost immediately. "Much has been done only to be abandoned, commenced only to be stopped, or planned only to be upset," Hall wrote.[87]

The Influence of the River on Development

As the city and region grew, access to water often shaped the direction of development. Land that did not border a river or a zanja was often considered worthless. Andrew Boyle, for instance, paid three thousand dollars an acre in 1851 for a plot of riverfront land east of the river. He paid just twenty-five cents an acre for unirrigated hill land nearby, which would become Boyle Heights. A decade later, the city sold two thousand acres in what is today Lincoln Heights for fifty cents an acre, "and it was not considered a bargain at that," according to early historian J. M. Guinn. City officials in 1883, moreover, decided to create Elysian Park on 746 acres of hill land west of the river because the property, beyond the reach of the zanjas and the city's domestic supply system, could not be given away. "It is the water, and not the land, comparatively speaking, that is the source of so much wealth in Los Angeles County," Ben C. Truman, editor of the *Los Angeles Star*, remarked in 1874. "The question is not 'how much land have you got?' but 'how much water?' An acre of land, bounded by rich, swelling irrigation ditches, is worth from $30 to $1,000 unimproved; lands which cannot be irrigated may be purchased for the same number of half-dimes."[88]

The situation was similar elsewhere in Southern California. Many of the earliest towns in Los Angeles County—Downey, Compton, El Monte, and others—were founded in the rich bottomlands along the county's three principal waterways. The Santa Ana River provided water for the communal vineyards of the Anaheim colony in present-day Orange County. Settlers at Riverside used canals built from the same stream to water their apple orchards and orange groves. Meanwhile, the absence of water inhibited the growth of agriculture elsewhere. At the time of the first federal census of California in 1850, just 2,648 acres were under cultivation in all of Los Angeles County—barely one one-hundredth of 1 percent of the total land area of the county, which then encompassed eight times as much area as it does today.[89] Huge cattle ranches covered nearly a million acres; more than 100,000 cattle roamed the landscape. Overgrazing and drought led to the decline of ranching and the subdivision of many of the ranches in the 1860s. Still, as late as 1871, only 18,000 acres were being irrigated in the county, less than 1 percent of the total land area.[90]

Perhaps half of this irrigated land received its water from the Los Angeles River, but even it proved an unreliable source of water south of the city. The river, furthermore, would become legally off limits to farmers in the San Fernando Valley, north of Los Angeles, because of court rulings that gave the city exclusive right to tap its flow. Near Compton and Dominguez, the braided channels of the river were dry most of the year. Farmers who wanted to grow anything other than wheat had to rely on water drawn from wells, the first of which was drilled near Downey in the 1860s. Some tapped water at depths of up to 250 feet. In other places, the water came to the surface naturally from artesian basins. Soon, windmills, steam pumps, and flowing wells became defining characteristics of parts of the Southern California landscape. Most of the rest of the irrigated farmland in Los Angeles County was located along the San Gabriel and Santa Ana Rivers.[91]

Until water was imported from the eastern slopes of the Sierra Nevada in the early twentieth century, the San Fernando Valley looked a little like Kansas, with dryland farms stretching from the north side of the Santa Monica Mountains to the foothills of the San Gabriels (fig. 2.15). Wheat, which required no irrigation, once covered thirty-one thousand acres (fig. 2.16). Although grapes, figs, olives, and a variety of garden crops were planted at the Mission San Fernando after its founding in 1798, irrigation was not widely developed in the valley until after the opening of the Los Angeles–Owens River Aqueduct in 1913. The Los Angeles River could have provided sufficient water for irrigation in the southeast San Fernando Valley, but the city's exclusive right to its flow, repeatedly confirmed in court, effectively prohibited diversions north of Los Angeles. As late as 1888, fewer than six thousand acres in the San Fernando Valley were artificially irrigated— less than a tenth of the total land area. Nearly all of that water was from mountain springs and underground sources. The Lankershim Ranch, for example, raised peaches and other non-dryland crops on six thousand acres located along the river around present-day North Hollywood, but these were watered not from the river's channel but from natural subirrigation. Vineyards, melons, fruits, and vegetables grown in present-day Burbank were dependent on water drawn from wells.[92]

The Los Angeles River would prove to be an inadequate source of water as Southern California grew. Residential and industrial development would displace farmland and, in the mad rush to Southern

California that followed the arrival of the transcontinental railroads, the landscape would be forever changed. Demand for water increased so much that the Los Angeles City Water Company and later the city of Los Angeles were forced to tap the river supply even before it reached the surface. The once-beautiful stream, its flow plentiful near downtown Los Angeles even in summer, would soon become a dry wash for most of the year there as well. In 1876, the year that the Southern Pacific Railroad completed its line to Los Angeles, an Austrian visitor observed on a drive along its course, probably in the Glendale Narrows, that the river, "on whose banks many graceful willows attain an extraordinary height," passed through "country that is still virgin, uninhabited, and where the silence of Nature is unbroken," but that, too, would soon change.[93]

FIG. 2.15. Cattle graze on a sand bar (*center*) in the Los Angeles River in the San Fernando Valley, probably about 1900. The exclusive right of the city of Los Angeles to the water of the river slowed the development of irrigation in the valley. As a result, dryland farming and ranching were the predominant forms of agriculture practiced there until after the opening of the Los Angeles–Owens River Aqueduct in 1913. Used with permission, The Huntington Library, San Marino, California.

FIG. 2.16. Harvesting wheat in the San Fernando Valley before the completion of the Los Angeles–Owens River Aqueduct, which opened up much of the area to irrigated agriculture and urban development. Used with permission, Los Angeles Public Library/Security Pacific Collection.

The importance of the river to the development of Los Angeles cannot be overestimated, however. The river made settlement possible in the semiarid country. The unique physical characteristics that created it assured an abundant and consistent supply of water year-round. The river was the sole source of drinking water for a young Los Angeles and irrigated the grapevines and fruit trees that first made Los Angeles County one of the most productive agricultural areas in North America. But the significance of the river surpassed even its usefulness as a water source. Twentieth-century Los Angeles also owes much to the river because it was the gardens and vineyards watered from its channel that helped create the reputation of Southern California as Eden, and this image would draw hundreds of thousands of people west. It may have been a tiny stream, unpredictable and unimpressive compared to the mighty rivers of Europe and the eastern United States, but, as one nineteenth-century writer noted, without the Los Angeles River, "we could bid farewell to this beauteous home of the Angels, and fold our tents and follow the lead of the absquatulating Arab in his silent march away."[94]

Draining the River Dry

THE COMPLETION OF A TRANSCONTINENTAL RAILROAD link to Los Angeles in 1876 changed Southern California forever, and the increased development that resulted eventually forced the city to search elsewhere to meet its water needs. Newcomers poured into Los Angeles, and demand for water increased exponentially. Farmland was replaced by residential and commercial development. New water supply reservoirs had to be built, and the subsurface flow of the river was tapped. The zanja system was dismantled ditch by ditch. Water became a controlling factor in development, and the exclusive right of the city of Los Angeles to the flow of the Los Angeles River helped it to become the dominant city in the southern half of the state. The river had long been thought capable of supplying all the water the city would ever need. But, as development spread, the river's reserve dwindled and, little by little, its surface flow disappeared.

The population of Los Angeles nearly doubled between 1870 and 1880, the decade when the Southern Pacific Railroad came to town. The completion in 1886 of a second cross-country line, the Atchison, Topeka, & Santa Fe, spurred a fare war that inspired an even greater boom, driving demand for real estate to unprecedented heights. For a single day, it was possible to travel from Kansas City to Los Angeles, a trip that normally cost $125, for a single dollar. The one-way fare between St. Louis and Los Angeles was just $25 for an entire year. Towns sprang up overnight to meet the demand for new homes. In 1887 alone, sixty new town sites were platted, many of them along the two railroad lines that ran east from Los Angeles. An estimated $100 million in real estate was sold in the county that year, and the assessed value of property more than doubled.[1] "The whole country went off its head for a season in the rush for sudden wealth," recalled one man who witnessed the frenzy.[2]

Many of the new towns and subdivisions never existed except on paper, and unscrupulous promoters, in an effort to persuade outsiders that Southern California was indeed the promised land, presented images of the region's rivers that were always exaggerated and at times fanciful. A subdivision map circulated in Eastern cities, for instance, offered docking space on the Los Angeles River.[3] Bird's-eye views from the period typically portrayed the river as a deep, wide, full-flowing waterway—and, if the image was printed in color, the river was bright blue—looking more like the Ohio River as it flows through Pittsburgh or the Mississippi as it passes St. Louis than the intermittent stream it was in fact.[4] A brochure advertising home lots in a subdivision south of Monrovia called Chicago Park, meanwhile, depicted ocean-bound steamers on the mostly dry San Gabriel River. Still, much of the new development was real. The population of Los Angeles County grew from 33,881 in 1880 to 101,454 a decade later. Towns like Hollywood, Pasadena, Burbank, Redondo Beach, and Covina had their origins during this time. In the city of Los Angeles, the population grew from 11,183 in 1880 to an estimated 80,000 during the peak of the boom, before settling to 50,395 at the time of the 1890 Census.[5]

Land that had been farmed since settlement of the pueblo suddenly became too valuable for agriculture. City lots that had sold for $500 in 1886 brought ten times that amount a year later. Joseph Wolfskill, whose father had developed the most successful orange-growing operation in the state and who had himself shipped the first boxcar of oranges east a decade before, subdivided his family's 120-acre plot near the river into twenty-five-foot-wide residential lots (fig. 3.1). Many others did the same. A 54-acre tract on Main Street was offered for $100,000. Lots near a planned Santa Fe passenger station brought $200 per frontage foot. Even flood-prone home lots in the river bottom sold for $500. Parcels subdivided from the former lands of Jean Louis Vignes, once home to the most prized vineyard in California, were advertised in the *Los Angeles Tribune* as ideal for "parties desiring a home." As developers bought up productive agricultural lands for residential lots, the number of farmers irrigating crops within the city limits of Los Angeles fell from 337 in 1886 to 125 two years later. Irrigated acreage declined from 6,697 to 2,937 during the same period.[6] "The land was divided into city lots and the trees fell before the woodsman's ax and were cut into cordwood," said early historian J. M. Guinn, who had migrated to Los Angeles seven years before the arrival of the first cross-country railroad line. "All that was left to Los Angeles of its living border of green and gold was the blackened stumps of trees."[7]

The needs of the growing population, however, spurred agricultural development outside the city. Irrigated acreage increased tremendously throughout the coastal basins of Southern California, and demand for irrigable land caused real estate prices to skyrocket far

FIG. 3.1. Sales office for house lots subdivided from the Wolfskill orange groves (1889). The large palm tree is being moved to the site of a new Southern Pacific Railroad depot, built on land donated by the Wolfskill family.
Used with permission, Department of Special Collections, University of Southern California Library/Title Insurance & Trust Company Collection (USC 1-1-1-534).

from the settled areas. Unimproved land adjacent to Los Angeles that had sold for $100 an acre before the arrival of the Santa Fe Railroad changed hands in 1887 for $1,500 an acre. Soon, vegetable gardens, vineyards, orange groves, fruit orchards, and grain fields spread north and south from the city along the river (fig. 3.2). Alfalfa, walnuts, blackberries, and strawberries were grown in the river bottomlands in the Glendale Narrows. The area south of the Los Angeles city limits that is today the industrial city of Vernon was devoted to the raising of fruits—oranges, apples, peaches, and pears. Nine irrigation ditches carried water from the river to farms beyond the city limits. By 1888, more than eight thousand acres outside Los Angeles were being irrigated from city-owned ditches, nearly twice the acreage that had been irrigated two years before. The number of farms outside the city limits that received water from the zanjas more than tripled between 1880

FIG. 3.2. Farms line both sides of the river near Elysian Park about 1900. Alfalfa, vegetables, and a variety of fruits were raised in this area. The San Rafael Hills and the San Gabriel Mountains rise above the river in the background. Used with permission, Department of Special Collections, University of Southern California Library/Title Insurance & Trust Company Collection (2209).

and 1888.[8] As urban development spread, however, this trend too would be reversed.

The Enlargement of the Domestic Water System

The sudden growth of Los Angeles necessitated the rapid expansion of the domestic water system. When the Los Angeles City Water Company first leased the domestic waterworks in 1868, it inherited a broken-down system that consisted of an antiquated water wheel, a deteriorating diversionary dam, a tiny brick reservoir in the plaza, and two miles of wooden pipes. Although the company immediately built a new dam farther upstream and constructed a reservoir in the Elysian Hills, facilities remained insubstantial into the 1880s. As late as 1883, the company's equipment consisted of just two horses, two small wagons, a few hand-operated pumps, and several water buckets. The company had just ten employees and its superintendent, Fred Eaton, was on the payroll only half-time. It served about 1,900 customers. Over the next two decades, however, the number of homes and businesses supplied by the company increased tenfold, and its facilities were expanded accordingly. After the arrival of a second cross-country railroad line, orders for new connections rose rapidly and, by 1892, the company had 9,000 customers. That number continued to rise and, in 1902, when the water company relinquished control of its facilities to the city of Los Angeles after a lengthy battle, the domestic water system provided service to 23,180 customers. Facilities had grown to include six reservoirs, 325 miles of iron pipe, and 676 fire hydrants.

As demand for water increased, the Los Angeles City Water Company first sought to enlarge its storage capacity to allow more of the river's rainy season flow to be stored. Buena Vista Reservoir, built in 1870, was enlarged in 1884, its capacity expanded from about one million gallons to thirteen million gallons. Between 1889 and 1891, the company acquired three more reservoirs and an additional fourteen million gallons of storage when it purchased three small water companies that had supplied water to Highland Park, Boyle Heights, and the hills north of downtown. Growth around Westlake Park, now MacArthur Park, became so swift that in 1894 the company began building another reservoir in a ravine on what was then the western edge of the city. Bellevue Reservoir, with a capacity of thirty-nine million gallons, was completed in 1895 one-half mile east of the present site of Los Angeles City College. Water was transported to the reservoir from the river through a 5,700-foot tunnel that began near the southeastern tip of Griffith Park and ran southwest, roughly paralleling Hyperion Avenue.[9]

Despite the added reservoir capacity, the surface flow of the river alone gradually became insufficient to supply the needs of the growing city. East of downtown, diversions left the river so dry most of the year that its bed became the source of much of the sand and gravel used by local construction crews. To increase the amount of water available, the water company in 1886 installed a double line of perforated pipes ten to fourteen feet below the river bottom in the Glendale Narrows to capture the river's subsurface flow—a development known as an infiltration gallery. The pipes were 3,656 feet long and extended well beyond the river channel on both sides of its banks near the southeast corner of what is now Griffith Park. The Crystal Springs Galleries, as the facility became known, provided an additional five million gallons of water a day at first; by 1892 it provided up to ten million gallons daily.

Conservation also become more important. The city's first water meter was installed in 1889 at a winery on Macy Street, west of Mission Road. To diminish loss of water through evaporation and percolation, reservoirs were lined with concrete and one was covered with a wooden roof. To reduce such losses further, the company also replaced the so-called Power Ditch that carried water from Crystal Springs to the Buena Vista Reservoir. Originally an open earth canal, it was replaced first with a closed redwood conduit and, in 1897, by a forty-four-inch sheet iron pipe. The city, meanwhile, lined the Zanja Madre with concrete for eight thousand feet and replaced its open channel through the business district with underground pipe.[10] Efforts also intensified to enclose the other zanjas through the most heavily developed parts of the city. The chief water overseer, as the position of zanjero had become known, recommended in the early 1890s, for example, that an open ditch that ran through the former Wolfskill orchard west of Alameda Street, subdivided and built with homes a decade before, be replaced by pipes because it "endangers the lives of children who gather about the zanja to play in the water." Maintenance of the ditch through the "thickly populated" district, meanwhile, had become increasingly difficult, the water overseer complained, because it had become a dumping ground for "tin cans, boards and other debris."[11]

Greater diversions from the river for domestic use began to tax the ability of the city to supply irrigation water to farmers. In 1894, the water overseer had noted that "there is plenty of water in the river," but three years later, after three winters of subnormal rainfall, his successor reported to the city council: "I wish to call your attention to the fact there is an apparent shortage of water in the river. Irrigators are clamoring for water and it seems impossible for me to furnish the same to them." Overseer E. H. Dalton complained in 1899 that the Los Angeles City Water Company was using more than its share, "at times taking almost all of the water in the river." As the drought worsened, the city was sometimes unable to supply water it had contracted to deliver and for which it had already been paid. In 1900, Mayor Fred Eaton, former head of the water company, said in his annual report that the supply of water flowing in the zanjas had been reduced so greatly that "the past two years have taxed [the] department [of the water overseer] to keep on speaking terms with the irrigator." That spring, the shortage became so serious that city officials were forced to spend $1,700 to hurriedly install three pumping plants in the river bed to augment the city's irrigation supply.[12]

The zanjas, however, were gradually filled in and built over. The need for irrigation diminished as farmland was swallowed up by residential and commercial development. Zanja No. 5, which had wound through the center of town, was the first to disappear when it was abandoned in 1888. Zanja No. 4 was abandoned south of First Street in 1897. A branch of Zanja No. 8-R that ran along the south side of Adams Street was abandoned in 1901. City council minutes throughout the late 1890s and early 1900s, furthermore, are filled with requests from property owners seeking the official abandonment of rights of way for zanjas that had long before ceased to be used.[13]

The inefficiency of the zanjas and the imprecise way in which water use was regulated also came under increasing criticism. An engineer for the state of California in 1901 recommended that a state officer be placed in charge of the irrigation system. "The methods of distributing irrigation water practiced by the city of Los Angeles," he said, "are astonishingly crude and unsatisfactory. It would be impossible to find another system in California—in the southern portion at least, and probably not elsewhere in the state—where such unscientific methods are still employed." His suggestion was ignored, however, as demand for domestic water caused the entire zanja system, in the words of one early resident, "to disappear almost as completely as if it never existed."[14]

A few years after the last of the zanjas had been abandoned, H. D. Barrows, who had come to Los Angeles in 1854 as a schoolteacher and later cultivated an extensive vineyard east of the river, lamented the changes that transformed Los Angeles from the "City of Vines" into a burgeoning metropolis. "The rapid increase of population required all the water from the river, especially in dry years, for domestic purposes; and the issue was squarely brought home to the people of the city: Shall we suffer in our homes for want of water . . . or shall we cut off its somewhat wasteful use in irrigation by open ditches," he wrote in 1911. "The alternative was a severe one, and our orchardists met it at first with some flinching; but they quickly saw that not only was the absolute necessity of water for domestic use overwhelming . . . but that their land was worth more vastly for *homes* than it was for raising vegetables or even orange trees. They realized that, financially at least, they were fully compensated for what seemed a cruel thing to do, to cut down bearing orange orchards and dig up by the roots bearing vineyards."[15]

The Pueblo Water Right

As demand for water escalated, the city of Los Angeles also sought to strengthen its legal right to the water in the Los Angeles River. Los Angeles had claimed, as early as 1810, when the pueblo was still under the control of Spain and had a non-Indian population of just 415, that it had a superior right to the water of the river. It first asserted this claim in an attempt to halt diversions from the river by the Mission San Fernando, founded in the northern San Fernando Valley sixteen years after the pueblo's founding. The mission had initially obtained most of its water from nearby artesian springs. As its agricultural needs had increased, these sources had proven insufficient and the mission had begun to divert water from the river at a dam built near the present location of North Hollywood. Pueblo officials protested to the Spanish government, complaining that the diversion threatened the livelihood of the town. Mission fathers denied the allegation, maintaining that the dam had been used for fourteen years by a former occupant of the land and insisting that the mission had equal right to water in the river. Spanish authorities, however, upheld the superior right of the pueblo. In 1817, they granted the mission permission to use enough water to irrigate a small field of corn on condition that the mission agree to discontinue use if the pueblo found its supply of water lacking.[16]

California came under the control of Mexico in 1822, and the missions were secularized. In 1836, Los Angeles city officials again sought to halt diversions from the same dam, by this time being used by the Rancho Ex-Mission San Fernando, a cattle ranch that eventually occupied more than 117,000 acres in the San Fernando Valley. The city attorney of Los Angeles investigated complaints that the diversion was reducing the amount of water available to the city but found that, despite the dam, the river still supplied plenty of water to city zanjas. He obtained a promise from the dam's owner, however, that the dam would be removed if the town ran short of water. In 1848, California was acquired by the United States after the Mexican War, and the terms of the treaty that concluded the war called for the recognition of all property rights that had been established when the territory was under Spanish and Mexican law. This provision helped to assure continued recognition of the city's preeminent right to the water of the river, a right that would become known, however erroneously, as the "pueblo right."[17] The California Assembly in 1874 sought to strengthen this principle when it approved an amendment to the Los Angeles City Charter granting the city "absolute ownership" and "the full, free, and exclusive right to all of the water flowing in the river," from its source to the city's southern boundary.[18]

After two early setbacks, the city's supreme right to the water in the river was repeatedly validated in court. The interpretation of that right, moreover, has continually been expanded. The city's preeminent right to the river's waters was first confirmed by the California Supreme Court in April 1881 in *Feliz v. Los Angeles.* Two years earlier, after a drop in the river's flow, the city had cut off the supply of water flowing from the river into a ditch that transported water to the former lands of the Rancho Los Feliz, located on the west side of the river just upstream from Los Angeles. The city claimed that the flow of the river had been so diminished by upstream diversions that it no longer supplied enough water for the needs of the town. Diversions from the river in this area had frustrated city officials for years and, beginning in the 1860s, Los Angeles newspapers had suggested that the city buy the land to prevent future conflicts.[19]

When Los Angeles, fed up by the continued use of what the city claimed was its water, finally cut off the supply flowing into a ditch owned by Anastacio Feliz in 1879, Feliz filed suit against the city, arguing that, as the owner of property adjacent to the river, he had the right to use a reasonable amount of its flow, a concept known in water law as the *riparian right*. Feliz testified, moreover, that previous owners of the land had diverted water from the river for irrigation and domestic purposes for thirty-five years. The Los Angeles County Superior Court upheld the right of Feliz to divert water from the river, but that decision was overturned by the state Supreme Court, which stated that, since the founding of the pueblo, the city had claimed the exclusive right to use all of the water in the river and that owners of land along the river since that time had recognized this right. The original owners of the Rancho Los Feliz, the court said, had first obtained permission from the pueblo to divert the river's flow. The court concluded that the city held "the paramount right to the use of the waters of the river." Three other state Supreme Court decisions issued before 1900 further confirmed this right.[20]

Feliz v. Los Angeles did not, however, as has sometimes been asserted, establish the city's "pueblo right," which is based on the belief that Spanish authorities, when they founded Los Angeles in 1781, had granted the pueblo exclusive ownership to the water in the Río de Porciúncula. The city claimed such a right in its defense, but the court skirted the issue, saying only that upstream irrigators had long "recognized" the city's premier right. The court did not issue an opinion explicitly supporting the existence of a pueblo right until 1895, in *Vernon Irrigation Co. v. Los Angeles*. In that case, the court ruled that the pueblo right did, in fact, exist and said that it guaranteed Los Angeles "all the waters of the river." As Los Angeles sought in subsequent legal actions to expand its right to the underground basins that supplied the river, that decision became, in the words of the historian Norris Hundley Jr., "the bedrock for Los Angeles's claim to all the water of a five-hundred-square-mile area."[21]

But the court's ruling in *Vernon Irrigation Co. v. Los Angeles* now seems to have been based on insufficient evidence and a questionable interpretation of that evidence. Hundley, for example, wrote that the decision "transformed the Hispanic preference for community rights into a rigid formula favoring a specific community." In fact, the document that formed the basis for governing Alta California throughout the Spanish period, Gov. Felipe de Neve's *Reglamento*, issued in 1779, seems directly to contradict the idea of the pueblo right. Outlining the privileges of the pueblos, de Neve stated that the natural resources of a region, including the water flowing in its streams, were to be shared by all residents, not just inhabitants of the original pueblo. "The residents and natives shall enjoy equally the woods, pastures, water privileges, and other advantages of the royal and vacant lands that may be outside of the land assigned to the new settlement, in common with the residents and natives of the adjoining and neighboring pueblos."[22]

The lack of firm evidence to substantiate the city's claim of exclusive right to the flow of the river has continually confounded the courts. A Los Angeles County Superior Court judge in 1968 went so far as to declare that the pueblo right had no support in Spanish or Mexican law. The state Supreme Court agreed in part, noting in 1975 that "data on Spanish-Mexican law and history" did not demonstrate conclusively "the existence of the pueblo right." Nevertheless, justices refused to reverse a century's worth of decisions predicated upon it, fearing that such a decision would "unjustly impair legitimate interests built up over the years in reliance of our former decisions."[23] In California water law, the pueblo right is still considered superior to all other water rights, including riparian rights and appropriative rights. Appropriative rights award the right to water to the first person who uses it, so long as that person continues to use it.

The Return of the Water System to City Control

The Los Angeles City Water Company's thirty-year lease of the domestic waterworks expired on 22 July 1898. Private control of the water system, by this time, had become increasingly unpopular, and the growing belief that the waterworks should be returned to public control reflected a nationwide trend.[24] As early as 1890, city officials had begun to investigate the possibility of the city building its own water system, claiming that the company had failed to fulfill the terms of its lease. The system was woefully inadequate for a city the size of Los Angeles. Seventy percent of the distribution system was made up of two-inch pipe, far too small for a system of its extent. As a result, water trickled from faucets and water pressure was often insufficient for fighting fires. The company did not even have a map of its distribution system. Rates for water service were considered high by local residents, and the company's profits were seen by some as exorbitant.[25] Two years into the lease period, the city had agreed to reduce the company's annual lease payment from $1,500 to $400. Its earnings, meanwhile, had risen from about $20,000 in 1868 to roughly $425,000 in 1898. As the lease neared expiration, a local engineer, Joseph B. Lippincott, calculated that sixty cents out of every dollar paid for water service in Los Angeles went to the company's profit.[26]

Under the terms of the lease, the city of Los Angeles was required upon expiration of the contract to pay for any improvements that had been made to the water system. When negotiations for the return of the waterworks to city control began in 1893, however, the city and company disagreed about the value of improvements and even what was covered by the lease. The company claimed, for instance, that its developments at Crystal Springs and the water they supplied were not part of the original agreement because they were built on private land and did not tap the river's surface flow. Shortly after leasing the domestic waterworks in 1868, in fact, the water company had transferred ownership of the Crystal Springs site to a holding company, the Crystal Springs Land and Water Company. City officials, nevertheless, contended that, because the infiltration galleries collected the underground flow of the river, the water they provided legally belonged to the city.

When negotiations began in 1893, the water company offered to sell the entire water system, including the Crystal Springs developments, for $3.3 million. A special committee of the city council, however, said that the facilities that could reasonably be claimed by the water company were worth only $1.49 million.[27] Persistent efforts to reach a compromise not only failed to bring the two sides together, but also drove a wedge between them. In an attempt to assess the worth of the existing system more accurately, for example, the Los Angeles City Council in 1897 ordered City Engineer Henry Dockweiler to investigate the works and then appraise their value. After conducting a detailed examination of the system, with full cooperation of the water company, Dockweiler estimated that it was worth only $1.19 million, $300,000 less than the earlier council estimate. He was also strongly critical of the distribution system, which he said "seems to be designed irrespective of engineering rules." He added that it contained "a great number of pipes . . . deteriorated by age or the action of the soil." The engineer's findings did little to dissuade the water company of the value of its holdings, however. Within days of the release of the report, company officials lowered the asking price for the waterworks, but only slightly, offering the system for $3 million, $1 million of which was for the Crystal Springs facilities. With the two sides so far apart, a Pasadena newspaper remarked that "the water works war can be said to be fairly launched in Los Angeles."[28]

The report of City Engineer Dockweiler further undermined negotiations by insisting that the city could build an entirely new system that duplicated the extent of the water company works for $1.43 million, not much more than he claimed the antiquated and worn-out equipment of the existing system was worth. He recommended that a much improved system, more in line with what the city actually needed, could be built for $3 million. Almost immediately, petitions began to be circulated calling for the council to call an election for the issuance of bonds for building an entirely new system. The following January, Los Angeles Mayor Meredith P. Snyder threatened that the city would seize possession of the waterworks if no agreement was reached. The dispute even became a statewide issue. The *San Francisco Call*, in a story headlined "The Plant Is of No Value to Anybody," charged that the water company works were "made up of the most complete mass of worn out, rusty pipe, rotten timbered conduits and old broken-down buildings . . . that can be conceived."[29]

The lease expired without agreement, but the water company refused to relinquish the waterworks. The stalemate continued until October 1898, when the two parties, as stipulated in the lease, selected a three-person board of arbitration to settle their differences. Both the water company and the city supplied one member of the board, and the first two arbitrators then selected a third, impartial member. The board spent seven months investigating the waterworks to determine their value. In May 1899, the arbitrators recommended a settlement price of $1.18 million—even less than the city's estimate of the water system's value. The board's decision, however, was not unanimous. The company's representative thought the price too low, and the company, as a consequence, refused to abide by the decision of the board, announcing that it would honor only a unanimous decision.[30]

A ruling by the California Supreme Court in June 1899, however, significantly reduced the water company's bargaining power. From the outset, the major stumbling block in negotiations had been the company's claim to ownership of the water supplied by its developments at Crystal Springs. In 1893, in fact, the city had filed suit against the water company and its subsidiary, the Crystal Springs Land and Water Company, seeking to halt their diversions of the river's subsurface flow. Arguments in that case were postponed, pending the outcome of a related suit. In anticipation of regaining control of the water system, the city had also filed suit against several property owners on the north side of Griffith Park, seeking to condemn a two-mile strip of land along the river for the purpose of building a new headworks for the water system. The defendants in the case, *Los Angeles v. Pomeroy*, claimed that, because of abundant ground water resources in the area, they should be suitably compensated by the city for their land. The Supreme Court, however, ruled in favor of Los Angeles, judging that the rights of the city to the river's waters also extended to its underground flow.[31]

Soon after that decision, the city council passed an ordinance approving the construction of an entirely new water system, while simultaneously addressing a conciliatory appeal to the water company. Realizing its claim to the water at Crystal Springs had been significantly undermined by the court's decision in *Los Angeles v. Pomeroy*, the water company reduced its demands. In July 1901 the two parties reached a compromise, with the city agreeing to pay $2 million for the complete system, including the Crystal Springs Galleries. The following month, voters approved a bond issue to pay for the purchase, along with other improvements, and the city formally assumed control of the domestic water system on 13 February 1902. To gain the confidence of water users, the new city water department immediately reduced water rates by as much as 50 percent. Hoping to prevent a recurrence of the lease fiasco, the Los Angeles City Council approved an amendment to the city charter that prohibited any future lease or sale of the waters of the Los Angeles River.[32]

The river held a special place in the heart of the man who was appointed superintendent of the new city water department, a self-taught, Irish-born, forty-seven-year-old engineer named William Mulholland (fig. 3.3). Mulholland had come to Los Angeles in 1877 and a year later had secured a job with the water company as a ditch tender, living in a cabin beside one of its supply ditches, just west of the river.[33] He had spent many evenings and weekends strolling along the river's banks, observing its characteristics. Years later, he wrote that, when he first had seen the river, "it at once became something about which my whole scheme of life was woven, I loved it so much." Mulholland described the river, as it looked to him in 1877, as a "beautiful, limpid little stream with willows on its banks" and called it the city's "greatest attraction."[34] A merchant seaman by trade, Mulholland had pored over engineering texts at night in his cabin, slowly climbing through the ranks at the water company, and was its superintendent when the city regained control of the waterworks. In the twenty-five years after he had arrived in Los Angeles on horseback, Mulholland watched as the river that had so drawn him to the city was sapped of its life and verdure. "Our population climbed to the top," he said later, "and the bottom appeared to drop out of the river."[35]

FIG. 3.3. William Mulholland, Los Angeles's most famous engineer, who once described the river as "a beautiful limpid, little stream with willows on its banks" and called it the city's "greatest attraction." Used with permission, Los Angeles Department of Water and Power.

The Los Angeles City Water Company had made few improvements
and performed only essential maintenance during the three years between expiration of the lease and settlement of the contract dispute.
Water resources development during that time had failed to keep pace
with the growth of the population, and the domestic waterworks had
fallen into even greater disrepair. It has been suggested, in fact, that
the system was in such disarray that the primary reason Mulholland
was hired to lead the new city water department—he had, after all,
been the water company's chief executive during the years of acrimonious negotiations—was that he was the only person who knew
enough about the system to oversee its operation.[36] The population of
Los Angeles, meanwhile, had risen to about 128,000 in 1902 and
would grow to more than 300,000 by the end of the decade.[37] Increased demand had reduced the flow of the river near downtown to
a trickle, and a water shortage seemed inevitable. The once-ample
stream had become a local joke. A newspaper columnist later remarked that its channel was "so dry eight months out of the year that
a pollywog would have to stand on his head to get enough moisture to
soothe a headache." Even booster publications began to find humor at
its expense. One such publication referred to the river in quotes: "This
'river'—as the tourist scoffingly emphasizes it—generally only flows
underground."[38]

In a region such as Southern California, where stream flow varies
significantly from season to season and year to year, the potential of a
river as a water source is largely dictated by its average dry season flow.
Using this as a guide, water department officials estimated in the early
twentieth century that the Los Angeles River could be counted on to
provide forty-five to fifty million gallons of water a day.[39] In other cities, a source of this volume might have been expected to supply a residential population of perhaps 400,000 people. But Los Angeles,
when it was served by the Los Angeles City Water Company, was believed to have the highest per capita rate of water consumption of any
major city in the nation. In 1901, city residents consumed 306 gallons
of water per person each day, three times the rate of consumption of
many eastern cities.[40] Angelenos consumed so much water that, unless consumption was slowed, domestic demand alone would have
exceeded the expected supply when the population of Los Angeles
reached 150,000, which it did in 1904. There was little incentive for
consumers to limit consumption because just 319 homes and businesses had water meters when the city regained control of the waterworks. Most customers had been charged a fixed rate for water service
regardless of the amount of water they used.[41] An engineer hired by
the city as a consultant wrote that "there are few, if any, cities in the

United States, consuming and wasting as much water per capita as the city of Los Angeles."[42]

Compounding the situation at the turn of the century was a prolonged drought that had begun in the winter of 1893-94. Downtown Los Angeles receives an average of 15 inches of rain a year, but during the worst of the drought, from 1897 to 1900, seasonal rainfall averaged 6.9 inches. Between 1893 and 1904, precipitation was 28.5 percent below normal. Desperate farmers in the vicinity even hired rainmakers in an attempt to squeeze moisture from the reluctant clouds. The volume of water supplied by the river, which usually remained relatively consistent even during periods of below-normal rainfall because of the tremendous size of the natural reservoir beneath the San Fernando Valley, fell 20 percent below normal. The crisis reached its peak in the summer of 1904, when the entire surface and subsurface flow of the Los Angeles River had to be tapped to meet the rapidly expanding needs of the city. During one ten-day period that July, consumption of water in Los Angeles exceeded inflow into the city's reservoirs by 3.5 million gallons a day. Water use averaged 39.3 million gallons a day. The combined capacity of the city's reservoirs at the time was about 72 million gallons, less than a two-day supply.[43]

Conservation and New Development

With dwindling resources and ever-increasing demand, the new city water department immediately sought to curb consumption and develop new ways to augment the river's surface flow. Between 1902 and 1905, it installed more than eight thousand water meters, and by 1908 nearly half of the water services in the city were metered. The meters helped lower per capita water use to 136 gallons a day, a 56 percent reduction from usage in 1901. City officials also discontinued the relatively inefficient use of water for irrigation even in those parts of Los Angeles where urban development had not completely displaced agriculture. Zanja No. 7, built east of the river in the 1870s, was abandoned about 1903, and the last two zanjas, the Woolen Mill Ditch and Zanja No. 8-R, were eliminated in the spring of 1904.[44] The head of the city's irrigation system, whose position had once been the most powerful in the city, was given an office job in the water department. That same year, Los Angeles initiated legal action to stop two hundred farmers in the San Fernando Valley, still largely agricultural, from pumping water out of the river's underground source. City officials claimed that pumping by upstream irrigators had reduced the flow in the river by 6.4 million gallons a day.[45]

The city worked feverishly to increase the amount of water available to it. It built a new diversion dam and main supply conduit on the northwestern side of Griffith Park, across from Burbank. Constructed on lands acquired after the resolution of *Los Angeles v. Pomeroy*, this development became known as the Headworks site. The water department also sought to increase its use of the river's underground flow. As early as 1896, the city had drilled test wells into the riverbed to obtain information on the depth of saturated materials. After the city regained control of the water system, wells were driven into the river at three different points in the Glendale Narrows, increasing the city's water supply by 14.8 million gallons a day. The water department also began to tap ground water reserves away from the river. In 1903, the city bought the West Los Angeles Water Company, which had serviced an area west of the city limits at Hoover Street, obtaining a set of wells south of Jefferson Street as part of the deal. This marked the first time in Los Angeles history that the city obtained water from a source other than the Los Angeles River, although the river no doubt contributed to the aquifers that supplied the wells. Two years later, the city drilled several new wells and installed pumps near the intersection of Slauson and Compton Avenues, south of downtown Los Angeles, boosting its supply by another four million gallons a day.[46]

To assure that every last drop of the river's subsurface flow could be captured, the city installed new infiltration galleries beneath the river near the outlet of the Arroyo Seco in 1904. A 1,178-foot tunnel was driven into bedrock 115 feet beneath the riverbed. Nine wells were then drilled in the river gravel to allow water to percolate into the tunnel (fig. 3.4). From the tunnel, water was pumped to a reservoir in Elysian Park. Infiltration galleries were installed in 1905 at the Headworks dam, across from Burbank, and in 1906 the Crystal Springs Galleries were extended 2,000 feet. By removing the subsurface flow of the river, the infiltration galleries sucked the river dry. A series of photos taken a few years later by Los Angeles County flood control officials dramatically illustrate the influence such developments had on the character of the river (fig. 3.5). One shows the river near Griffith Park, its flow ample, its banks lined with brush and willows. In another, taken "200 feet below [the] filtration galleries," the river is a dry wash, with a small puddle in midstream the only reminder of its former state.

The additional water supplied by the new developments required the city to expand its reservoir capacity. Four new reservoirs were built in five years, increasing the system's total storage capacity by more than 838 million gallons. Solano Reservoir, with a capacity of 10 million gallons, and Elysian Reservoir, which could hold 5.8 million gallons, were built in Elysian Park in 1903. Two much larger reservoirs were built west of the river, midway between Griffith Park and Elysian Park. The first of the two, Ivanhoe Reservoir, was completed in 1906 and had a capacity of 50 million gallons. The much larger Silver Lake Reservoir (fig. 3.6), for which the residential area that now surrounds it is named, was built next to Ivanhoe Reservoir in 1907 to allow greater retention of peak winter flows. It was built to hold 773 million gallons of water.[47]

But nothing the water department did could overcome the fact that local water resources were simply insufficient to meet the needs of an ever-increasing population. In the first four years after the city took control of the water system, the population of Los Angeles nearly doubled, from 128,000 in 1902 to 240,000 in 1906. The number of homes and businesses seeking water service increased at an even faster rate. Although the installation of meters helped reduce per capita water use significantly, total consumption nevertheless inched upward because of the rapid growth of the population, climbing from 31 million gallons in 1902 to 34.9 million gallons a day four years later. The heightened demand reduced water pressure so much that water service to the hilly sections of the city sometimes had to be interrupted during periods of peak consumption. To compensate for reduced surface water supplies all over Southern California, pumping for water increased throughout the coastal plain and inland valleys, so much so that the level of the water table at the city's pumping plant south of downtown dropped nine feet in four years. At a private well nearby, the water level dropped twenty-nine feet in twelve years. Between 1898 and 1904, in fact, the area from which artesian water could be obtained on the coastal plain shrunk by 33 percent.[48]

As drought sapped the river supply and each week brought requests for water service from areas that had never before been served, the tone of Superintendent Mulholland's comments in the Board of Water Commissioners' annual reports became increasingly frantic. The physical expansion of the distribution system simply could not keep pace with the building of new homes and commercial development. Despite the drought, the city expanded its corporate territory by nearly 50 percent between 1895 and 1899. All these areas required service from the city water department. Mulholland, in response, urged the city council in 1903 to limit the future growth of Los Angeles. "It is respectfully suggested that great care should be exercised in making any further additions to the corporate limits of the city," he said. "Such added area should be capable of being supplied from the works of the city as at present designed." He also requested that new reservoir construction be accelerated to provide greater safety during drought years. That year, one new reservoir was completed and a second was roofed to slow evaporation. Still, he remarked, "there is a narrow margin . . . between us and a water famine."[49]

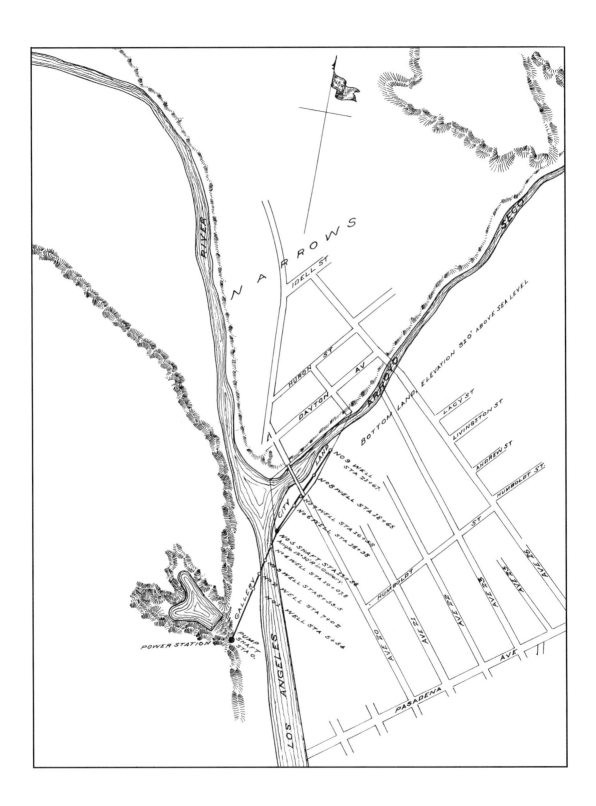

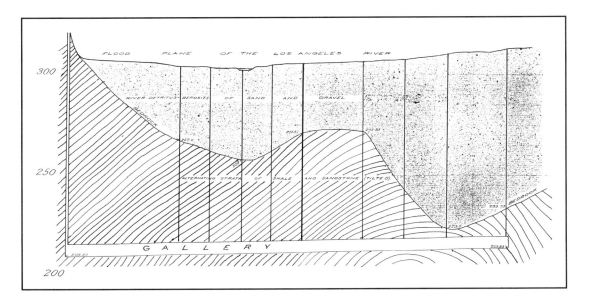

FIG. 3.4. Map and cross-section showing the location and design of what was known as the Narrows Gallery, which enabled the subsurface flow of the river near the outlet of the Arroyo Seco to be captured. A 1,178-foot tunnel was excavated in the bedrock beneath the river, and nine wells were drilled into the riverbed. *Left:* Map detail shows the location of the power station at Buena Vista Reservoir in the *lower left;* the gallery is indicated by the *diagonal line* running under the river toward the Arroyo Seco. *Above:* The *vertical lines* on the gallery cross-section are the wells that allowed water in the saturated deposits beneath the riverbed to percolate into the gallery, from which it was pumped to the reservoir. The bed of the Los Angeles River is indicated by the *horizontal line* at the top; the *shaded and hatched areas* are river detritus and bedrock. Courtesy, Los Angeles Department of Water and Power.

The following year, Mulholland reported that the water supply had become so strained that it would no longer be possible to fill the lakes in city parks. Wells that the city had drilled in the San Fernando Valley to augment the river's surface supply proved to be no help because they only tapped the river's underground source and ultimately reduced its flow. It had become evident that no number of new reservoirs or wells would enable the river to furnish enough water for a city that was growing so fast. "This is certainly a noble stream to be found running in the semi-arid country after a long succession of dry years, and speaks volumes for its constancy and reliability as a source of municipal supply," Mulholland wrote in 1904. "The time has come, however, when we shall have to supplement its flow from some other source. Earnest and immediate steps are necessary to produce additional water."[50]

FIG. 3.5. Two photographs taken by Los Angeles County flood control officials in 1914 show the effect of water developments on the flow of the river. *Top:* The river at Griffith Park, upstream from the Crystal Springs and Narrows Galleries. *Bottom:* The river further downstream, just below the infiltration galleries near Elysian Park, the final diversion point on the river.
Reprinted from Los Angeles County Board of Engineers, Flood Control, *Report of the Board of Engineers, Flood Control, to the Board of Supervisors, Los Angeles County, California* (Los Angeles, 1915), 127-28.

FIG. 3.6. Silver Lake Reservoir, under construction in 1907 adjacent to Ivanhoe Reservoir, was built to provide storage for 773 million gallons of river water. Used with permission, Water Resources Center Archives, University of California, Berkeley/Joseph Barlow Lippincott Collection.

Even in the midst of the drought, Mulholland displayed an attitude that helps explain why Los Angeles became and remains the enemy of all other water users in the West. Even as thousands of new water meters were being installed and progress on conservation was improving dramatically, Mulholland defended the city's extravagant use of water. Per capita water consumption in Los Angeles, he cautioned, could never be expected to fall to eastern levels. "It is not desirable that [it] should," he said, "a bountiful supply of water being necessary to the maintenance of the beauty for which [the city] is famous."[51] Conserve they might, but then, as now, Angelenos insisted on watering their lawns and continued to plant flowers, shrubs, and trees ill-suited to the semiarid environment. Los Angeles might still have been Eden in the eyes of some, but long after the draining of the marshes and the diversion of most of the surface streams for human use, it took the artificial application of water to make it so. And if the lawns and gardens of Los Angeles were to stay green, the city needed much more water.

As early as 1898, Los Angeles officials had begun to investigate the possibility of importing water from outside the city as a means to supplement the river supply. They first considered Big Tujunga Creek in the San Gabriel Mountains, Piru and Alamos Creeks in Ventura County, and Lake Hemet in the San Jacinto Mountains southwest of Palm Springs. Big Tujunga Creek, they soon realized, helped replenish the subterranean reservoir beneath the San Fernando Valley, which was the natural source of the Los Angeles River, so any attempt to capture its flow before it left the mountains would ultimately reduce the volume of water carried by the river. The other sources were judged too small to help satisfy the city's future water needs. As the threat of a shortage grew greater, the city renewed its efforts to find new sources of water, both in Los Angeles County and elsewhere. City officials looked to the San Gabriel River but found that most of its supply was already being used by local irrigators and decided that the cost of obtaining water rights in the area and transporting that water to Los Angeles would be too expensive. Ground water basins on the coastal plain that might have once provided the city with abundant additional water were by this time being tapped by more than eight thousand wells, and the shrinking of aquifers during the drought raised questions about the adequacy of the future underground supply. Studies were also undertaken to determine the feasibility of transporting water to Los Angeles from the Mojave River, north of San Bernardino, the Kern River near Bakersfield, and the San Luis Rey River in San Diego County, but all were eliminated from consideration because of concerns about existing water rights or the uncertain nature of available supplies.[52]

For years, former Los Angeles Mayor Fred Eaton had been trying to convince anyone who would listen that the solution to the city's water problems lay still farther away—in the Owens Valley, on the eastern side of the Sierra Nevada range, more than two hundred miles from Los Angeles. Eaton, a longtime Los Angeles city engineer and Mulholland's former superior at the Los Angeles City Water Company, first began promoting a plan to build a canal from the Owens Valley to Los Angeles in 1892, after reading two private surveys showing that the building of such a canal was technically possible. Most (including, it would seem, Mulholland) thought the idea foolish. A U.S. Bureau of Reclamation official, in fact, wrote that "such a project is as likely as the City of Washington tapping the Ohio River." But, when all the other sources he investigated proved unsatisfactory and the city appeared on the verge of disaster, Mulholland in 1904 agreed to make a trip to the area with his old boss. Once there, Eaton was able to convince Mulholland that the Owens Valley could provide enough water to support Los Angeles even if its population grew to two million.[53]

The Owens River collected the flow of some forty mountain streams draining the eastern slopes of the Sierras, fed by the melting snows from nearby peaks, including 14,495-foot-high Mount Whitney, the tallest mountain in the continental United States. From its source near Mono Lake, the Owens River flowed south for about 120 miles before emptying into Owens Lake, south of Lone Pine. Because it had no outlet, the lake was heavily laden with salt. Suitably impressed with what he saw on his trip to the area with Eaton, Mulholland in September 1904 obtained approval from the Los Angeles Board of Water Commissioners to conduct a detailed investigation of Eaton's plan. After three months of work, he reported that it would cost $23 million in construction costs alone to build an aqueduct to carry water across the Mojave Desert, through the San Gabriel Mountains, and into the San Fernando Valley. The project was nevertheless thought to be worthwhile because studies determined that it could supply Los Angeles 325 million gallons of water a day, seven times the normal flow of the Los Angeles River.[54]

Water commissioners in May 1905 endorsed the plan to build a 233-mile aqueduct from the Owens Valley to Los Angeles. On 29 July the *Los Angeles Times* publicly announced the proposal under the headline, "Titanic Project to Give City a River." In September, voters approved by a 14-1 margin a $1.5 million bond issue to pay for the purchase of land and water rights along the proposed aqueduct route (fig. 3.7). In June 1907, they approved a second bond issue, this one worth $23 million, to fund the building of the project. Construction began the next year and, on 5 November 1913, as thousands of spectators watched, the first water carried by the Los Angeles–Owens River Aqueduct poured out of a tunnel cut through the mountains and splashed into an open ditch that emptied into a reservoir built on the north side of the San Fernando Valley (fig. 3.8). In effect, the Los Angeles–Owens River Aqueduct *did* become the new Los Angeles River, as the earlier headline had suggested, making it easy for residents to forget about the stream that had supplied the city for more than a century. The aqueduct was extended 105 miles to near Mono Lake in 1940, and a second aqueduct, built parallel to the first, was completed in 1970. Today, runoff from the eastern Sierras that is carried to Los Angeles through the various aqueducts supplies about 40 percent of the city's water.[55]

Much has been said and written and still more has been speculated about the clearly underhanded methods used by the city of Los An-

One can be seen with the naked eye; the other hard to find with a spyglass.

FIG. 3.7. The *Los Angeles Times* ran this cartoon on the eve of an election in which the city sought approval to sell $1.5 million in bonds to pay for the purchase of land and water rights along the proposed route of the Los Angeles–Owens River Aqueduct. The bonds were approved by a 14-1 margin. Reprinted from the *Los Angeles Times*, 18 August 1905.

FIG. 3.8. Thousands of spectators watch water pour out of a tunnel and into an open ditch in the San Fernando Valley as the Los Angeles–Owens River Aqueduct delivers its first water to Los Angeles on 5 November 1913. Used with permission, The Huntington Library, San Marino, California.

geles to secure the Owens Valley water supply and transport it south. Critics of the city have questioned the accuracy of streamflow data supplied by the water department during the drought of 1893-1904, with some charging that officials manufactured a crisis to build support for the aqueduct proposal (although some of these claims have themselves been built on a faulty interpretation of the evidence).[56] A few have even suggested that department officials drained water from reservoirs to heighten fears—a scenario depicted in the movie *Chinatown*. But there is little doubt that the city would soon have required more water than the Los Angeles River and local ground water resources could supply. The population of Los Angeles more than tripled during the first decade of the twentieth century. By the summer of 1913, with the opening of the aqueduct imminent, nearly a half-million people lived in the city. Consumption during a ten-day period that June averaged 61.3 million gallons a day, 20 percent more than the normal flow of the river and 50 percent more than the river, diminished by two years of below-normal rainfall, had supplied during the those same ten days. Without the reserves provided by city reservoirs and the additional supplies obtained from underground sources, the city would have certainly run out of water. Completion of the Los Angeles–Owens River Aqueduct, in the words of William Mulholland, came just "in the nick of time."[57]

The Territorial Growth of Los Angeles

Water from the Los Angeles River not only was crucial to the development of Los Angeles, but also helped assure the city's emergence as the dominant city in Southern California. Although Los Angeles was the first and always the largest city south of the Tehachapi Mountains, its evolution into the metropolis of the southern part of the state did not always seem certain. Its growth was remarkably slow at first. Whereas San Francisco became an urban center almost in an instant, Los Angeles remained a small town for most of its first one hundred years. San Diego, in fact, grew faster in the initial years following statehood and was more important as a trading center than its northern rival until Los Angeles officials convinced the Southern Pacific Railroad to build a line to the city. Located fifteen miles from the ocean on a stream that didn't carry enough water to allow boat travel, Los Angeles had few natural advantages other than its water supply. It had no port. It had no coal, iron, or timber.[58]

Other towns could have given Los Angeles serious competition. Anaheim, founded as a German agricultural colony in 1855, once rivaled Los Angeles as a wine center. In 1860, both the Santa Ana and El Monte districts had populations larger than that of San Diego. Although no natural harbor existed on the coastal plain, the town of Wilmington was founded on San Pedro Bay in 1858, and if it and the neighboring city of San Pedro had been able to retain their independence from Los Angeles, they would now be home to the most active port on the Pacific Coast. At the same time that major port improvements were being proposed for San Pedro, the Southern Pacific Railroad was fighting to develop a harbor site on Santa Monica Bay. Had the railroad been successful, Santa Monica would no doubt be a much different city than it is today. Long Beach might have become more than the county's second largest municipality if initial efforts to develop a town on the site had not gone broke and if the city had developed its port and naval base sooner. Most of the early-twentieth-century oil discoveries in Los Angeles County, furthermore, were made outside the city of Los Angeles, and the movie industry developed initially in Hollywood, once an independent city.[59]

Los Angeles became the most important city in Southern California in large part because of its water supply. Its access to the most reliable source of fresh water in the region—first from the river and later via the aqueduct—enabled it to grow progressively larger through accession. This helped the city grow in population to a size comparable to more densely populated cities while still retaining its largely residential character. The added population boosted the city's tax base, which allowed it to consider expensive public works projects, such as the building of a port at San Pedro or an aqueduct from the Owens Valley. And though manufacturing development in the city lagged behind that of other urban centers and even smaller towns in Los Angeles County such as Vernon, Torrance, and Burbank, Los Angeles continued to grow because it had what most other cities in the region lacked—a plentiful supply of water.

In the years after the arrival of the railroads, many of the communities that had been developed near Los Angeles during the boom discovered that they lacked adequate water resources. Most obtained water from wells, but underground reserves shrank each year and were insufficient to meet the needs of the burgeoning population. Towns located near the river were no better off because they were prohibited from tapping its flow by court decisions that had given Los Angeles exclusive right to the river. Many farmers in areas adjacent to Los Angeles relied for years on irrigation water supplied by the city's zanjas, but this also was ultimately outlawed by the courts. The paramount right of Los Angeles to the waters of the river, consequently, limited growth elsewhere, and existing small cities and unincorporated areas often had no choice but to become part of the city if they wanted to survive.

Three court decisions that helped define the city's rights to the water of the Los Angeles River were key to the areal expansion of Los Angeles. In 1895, the California Supreme Court, in a suit brought by a downstream property owner who claimed riparian and appropriative rights to water in the river, ruled that the city was entitled to as much water from the river as it needed for its own supply but forbade it from selling surplus water outside the city. The plaintiff in *Vernon Irrigation Co. v. Los Angeles* had challenged the city's right to provide river water through its irrigation ditches to farmers outside the city limits.[60] A few months after the decision, residents in a large agricultural area south of Los Angeles who had received water from the zanjas voted to become part of the city. Annexation was also approved by residents of Highland Park, a small community northeast of Los Angeles that since 1889 had received its domestic water from the Los Angeles City Water Company. Several years later, two more communities that had relied on the city's water supply in their initial development elected to become part of Los Angeles. In 1899, as the city fought to regain control of its water system, Garvanza, a community near Highland Park, and the University district, southwest of the original pueblo limits, approved annexation. These four actions increased the total area of Los Angeles by more than fourteen square miles but also heightened demand for water in the midst of a severe drought and, thus, helped to assure that the city would have to search elsewhere to meet its future water needs.[61]

In 1899, the California Supreme Court ruled that the city's rights to the water in the river were not limited to the amount of water required to supply the original boundaries of the pueblo. The city, in *Los Angeles v. Pomeroy*, had sought to condemn a two-mile strip of land along the river, outside the city limits, for the purpose of extending its waterworks. The court ruled in the city's favor, saying that Los Angeles was entitled to any water it needed from the river as it grew in area. The state Supreme Court issued its most far-reaching interpretation of the city's rights to the waters of the river in 1909 when it halted pumping for water by two hundred farmers in the San Fernando Valley. Settling a suit filed five years before, the court ruled that the city's rights also extended to the underground basin that supplies the river. "The San Fernando Valley is the great natural reservoir and supply of the Los Angeles River," Justice Frederick H. Henshaw wrote in *Los Angeles v. Hunter*. "Unquestionably the cutting off of this supply would as completely destroy the Los Angeles River as would the cutting off of the Great Lakes destroy the St. Lawrence."[62] These decisions triggered a new wave of annexations. Between 1899 and 1910, the communities of Colegrove, Hollywood, East Hollywood, and Arroyo Seco voted to become part of Los Angeles, largely to satisfy their water needs. By 1912, the city, which originally had covered twenty-eight square miles, encompassed more than one hundred square miles.[63] The city's access to water would prove crucial to its continued expansion long after the river ceased to be its primary water source. The added supply provided by the Los Angeles–Owens River Aqueduct prompted the city in 1915 to annex 170 square miles in the San Fernando Valley. Piecemeal land additions, many of them water inspired, eventually gave Los Angeles the largest area of any city in the United States.[64]

Legal battles over rights to the water in the river, however, did not end there. It was not until 1979 that continued challenges to the city's so-called pueblo right were finally resolved. The end came twenty-three years, three months, and twenty-seven days after the city of Los Angeles, in the midst of a severe drought, had filed suit against the cities of San Fernando, Glendale, and Burbank, plus more than two hundred other parties, seeking once more to halt pumping for water from the river's underground source in the San Fernando Valley. The case, *Los Angeles v. San Fernando et al.*, had the most voluminous record in the history of Los Angeles County Superior Court at the time. Transcripts required nearly fifty thousand pages—more than the transcripts for the O. J. Simpson murder trial of 1996. The appeal brief alone consisted of eleven printed volumes with a combined thickness of ten inches.[65]

The case was actually decided in 1975. A lower court had once again rejected the concept of the pueblo right. The state Supreme Court then overturned that decision and awarded most of the water beneath the San Fernando Valley to the city of Los Angeles. It was not until 1979, however, that a Los Angeles County Superior Court judge delineated the exact amount of water to which each party in the suit was entitled. The city of Los Angeles was given the exclusive right to all native water in the San Fernando Basin and is also allowed to extract an additional amount believed equal to the quantity of water it imports into the area that percolates into the ground water. The cities of Glendale and Burbank are also permitted to withdraw water derived from supplies each imports into the area. In addition, the cities of Glendale and San Fernando are allowed to continue pumping from two underground basins in the San Fernando Valley that are physically separated from the San Fernando Basin by underground obstructions.[66]

The Changing Perceptions of the River

Vital though the Los Angeles River was to the growth of the city and region, its significance was always more economic than aesthetic. The often-quoted comments of William Mulholland about the river were atypical. Although the utility of the river was certainly appreciated, its appearance rarely seems to have been. For the most part, in fact, the river was ignored. It was never the center of local life, as some modern-day environmentalists have supposed. The earliest commentators about Los Angeles rarely mentioned the river, except when it turned vicious and overflowed its banks. Booster publications marveled at the bountiful harvests its water produced but said little about the river itself, except in brief historical passages. Guidebooks may have sent tourists this way and that across its channel, to visit picturesque vineyards or steep mountain slopes, but the river seldom received even passing notice. Despite its utilitarian importance, the river also seems to have been one of the least-photographed sites in early Los Angeles. Among the hundreds of images that chart the development of the city in the late nineteenth century, the river is almost never seen, except far in the background.

As the Southern California landscape was transformed after the arrival of the railroads, the character of the river was also significantly altered, and soon it was as much deplored as it was ignored. It carried no water in its wide bed near downtown Los Angeles because of diversions of its surface and subsurface flow farther upstream. Railroad tracks and freight yards lined both banks. Warehouses and manufacturing plants were built nearby. The river landscape, in fact, became the antithesis of the Arcadian ideal so central to the promotion of the region. Elsewhere, palm trees were planted in great numbers to confirm the country's reputation as a Mediterranean paradise, or "our Italy," in the words of one prominent promoter. Homes and gardens became inseparable. People could sleep outside year-round, or so one popular song said.[67] But even in the enlightened metropolis, an industrial base had to be developed and the refuse of city life had to go somewhere. Like so many urban waterways, the river became a dumping ground. In other ways, however, the plight of the Los Angeles River was unique. Because it carried no water for much of its course, its use as a dump was more conspicuous, and the other uses of its channel were unusual. People actually lived in its bed. Not only was the river lined with industry, it became an industrial site itself, a use that remains prevalent today.

In Los Angeles, as in other cities, industrial development naturally followed stream courses, though in Southern California this did not occur for all of the usual reasons. Elsewhere, rivers provided a means to transport industrial products. They supplied the water that powered turbines and provided a convenient way to dispose of liquid industrial wastes. The flow of the Los Angeles River, however, was too insignificant and irregular to enable water-borne commerce. By the time industry became widespread in Los Angeles, moreover, the river had been so deprived of its surface flow that power generation was no longer a possibility. The river also had limited potential as an outlet for industrial sewage because there was too little water in its channel to dilute effluents or wash them downstream. Consequently, water pollution was not a problem initially. In Los Angeles, industry developed first along the river because it was there that the earliest railroads were built, probably because the riverfront lands were prone to flooding and, therefore, were less desirable for other uses. Southern California's first railroad, the Los Angeles and San Pedro, was built in 1869 to link Los Angeles and the future port. Its tracks were laid along Alameda Street, about a mile west of the river, and its depot was constructed at the southwestern corner of Alameda and Commercial Streets. Although the effect on development of the Los Angeles and San Pedro was far less dramatic than that of the national lines that came to Los Angeles a few years later, the railroad did inspire the first significant subdivision of agricultural lands in the city. Warehouses, lumber yards, blacksmiths, foundries, and wagon manufacturers began to displace the vineyards and orchards near the railroad's depot.[68]

When the Southern Pacific came to Los Angeles in 1876, it took over the Los Angeles and San Pedro Railroad. The Southern Pacific built its line south from San Francisco along the eastern side of the San Fernando Valley and parallel to the east bank of the river through the Glendale Narrows (where it built the huge Taylor Yard facility beside the river in the 1920s). The Southern Pacific crossed the river just upstream from its confluence with the Arroyo Seco and ran south through present-day Chinatown to its meeting with the old Los Angeles and San Pedro tracks, constructing its first station on land donated by the Wolfskill family at the southwestern corner of Alameda and Fifth Streets. Within a few years, a small manufacturing complex made up of a gas plant, flour mills, slaughterhouses, and freight yards developed in the vicinity. Railroad development along the river intensified in 1886, when the Los Angeles City Council gave the Atchison, Topeka, & Santa Fe a fifty-foot right of way on the west side of the river for its tracks. The Santa Fe completed its line to Los Angeles the following year and built its depot and freight yards on the south side of First Street. Before long, spur lines crisscrossed the former agricultural lands immediately adjacent to the river. Industry was most heavily concentrated in the area between Macy and Seventh Streets from Alameda Street to the river. This area was home to planing mills, foundries, lumber yards, fuel plants, food and beverage manufacturers, warehouses, and the like. Development of the downtown riverfront was completed in 1891 when the Los Angeles Terminal Railroad built a line to San Pedro on the east bank of the river. That line was taken over by the Union Pacific in 1905.[69]

Railroad and industrial development so changed the landscape beside the river near downtown that, as the stream channel was gradually robbed of most of its surface flow, there was little demand for its care or improvement. Perception of the river had been so altered that in 1887, when eighty horses were killed in a stable fire, their carcasses were unceremoniously dumped in the riverbed south of Seventh Street.[70] Thus, as Los Angeles city officials wrestled with the problem of what to do about the growing volume of sewage produced in the city, many thought it only logical that the city's liquid wastes be discharged into the river. Perhaps realizing that the river would do little to carry the sewage away from Los Angeles, city engineers proposed instead that a comprehensive sewer system be built at a cost of $1 million. The proposal called for the construction of an outfall sewer that would transport the city's sewage fifteen miles across the coastal plain, where it was to be discharged into the Pacific Ocean. Some saw this as an unnecessary expenditure with the river so close. One local resident wrote that "the course of the Los Angeles River is the . . . proper outlet for the sewage of Los Angeles. To such disposition of the sewer water, no one would have a right to complain, for it would be precisely the drainage provided by Nature." The *Los Angeles Times*, in an editorial, agreed: "A fair investigation will make it apparent to all reasonable persons that the building of the outfall sewer would involve a needless expense. The river route . . . is the natural route and is inexpensive."[71]

The comprehensive sewer system was eventually approved by voters in 1892, but that did little to prevent the future degradation of the river. In August 1896, for example, the city council received complaints that rubbish was being dumped in the riverbed. A few years later, the Board of Health reported that the river channel was becoming a health hazard because of "pollution by pigeons and other species of fowls," likely a reference to a large pigeon farm that existed beside the river across from Elysian Park. (Though it may seem strange by today's standards, the pigeon farm was a far more popular attraction than the river.)[72] In 1904, five local residents complained to the council that large amounts of tar and oil dumped in the riverbed by the Los Angeles Gas Company posed a threat to humans and livestock. So much tar and oil had been dumped in the river, one man said, that a pool two to ten feet deep and thirty by eighty feet in area had formed. Because it was covered by a thin layer of dust, he added, it was largely invisible and, as a result, human beings and livestock had repeatedly become mired in the muck. Four cows, in fact, were trapped in the sludge when they sunk up to their necks and had to be rescued by men working on the nearby Aliso Street bridge. "Only about four to six inches of the cows were visible above the tar," the man said. "In order to save them from perishing it was necessary to fasten ropes to their heads and with the aid of about forty men, and a team of horses, the animals were dragged from the deposit."[73]

With so little water in its bed near downtown, the river also became home to an increasing number of transients. The *Los Angeles Times* on 6 January 1901 featured a long article on the "ever shifting class that inhabits the river bed." They included thieves, "men of morose disposition with ambition dead," a drug "fiend," and even an ex-millionaire. Three photos published with the article show that some of the dwellings were remarkably substantial. One looks two stories tall, perhaps to enable its owner to survive high water. Two years later, the city health officer complained that "manure, garbage, etc." left by "squatters" living in the river threatened the health of local residents and recommended that the city council pass an ordinance prohibiting people from living in the river channel. Just such an ordinance was passed in 1911, but people continued to live in the riverbed, particularly during hard times. A newspaper reporter during the depression years of the 1930s found migrant laborers, the unemployed, and even an ex-major in the British army living among the willows in the riverbed near Compton. Folk singer Woody Guthrie, commenting on a song he wrote about the 1934 New Year's Day flood in Los Angeles, claimed that many more people were killed than were counted in official death tolls—dirt poor "Okies" living in the riverbed.[74]

As industrial development spread along its banks, the most common use of the river was as a sand-and-gravel quarry (fig. 3.9). City council records from the late nineteenth and early twentieth centuries are filled with requests from local contractors seeking permission to remove sand and gravel from "the pits" in the riverbed. In 1901, the council even approved the construction of a bridge into the bed of the river at Aliso Street to make it easier for teams to haul gravel from its channel. So much sand was hauled from the river that a few years later the city street superintendent warned that the stability of bridge supports and levees along the river was being threatened. In 1907, Los Angeles Mayor Arthur C. Harper, seeing a potential new source of revenue for the city, reported that 1,000 to 1,200 truck loads of sand and gravel were being taken from the riverbed every day by contractors. "If the gravel pit was owned by some individual or company it would pay enormous dividends," he said. "I see no reason why the city should not operate such a gravel pit."[75]

FIG. 3.9. Mule-drawn teams haul sand and gravel from the riverbed near the Olympic Boulevard bridge in the 1920s. A sand- and gravel-processing plant is located on the opposite side of the river and is visible along the right edge of the photograph, beneath one of the arches of the bridge. Photograph by Dick Whittington. Used with permission, Los Angeles Public Library/ Security Pacific Collection.

The Los Angeles City Council in August 1910 sought to gain some control over activity in the river when it approved an ordinance prohibiting the dumping of "market refuse and rubbish" in the riverbed. The law, however, was clearly a failure. Two years after passage of the ordinance, a Los Angeles parks commissioner remarked that the river was "unsightly to the extreme." He reported that, not only were huge volumes of sand and gravel being hauled from the river, but "teams engaged in removing gravel frequently haul back trash and dump it into the river bed." The parks department conducted a study of such activity and reported that an average of 670 truckloads of gravel were being removed from the river each day, while an average of 27 loads of rubbish were being dumped back into it.[76] Even city officials ignored the law prohibiting the dumping of trash in the river. An official of the Los Angeles County Flood Control District complained in 1920 that a city-operated dump near the Macy Street bridge projected into the river channel (fig. 3.10), thus reducing the flood-carrying capacity of the river. City officials responded that it would be too expensive to relocate the dump. City council records indicate that the Board of Public Works continued dumping refuse into the riverside dump until at least 1925.[77]

There were occasional proposals not only to clean up the river but to beautify its channel, but these seem to have been isolated suggestions, the most sweeping of which, perhaps not coincidentally, were made by nonresidents and newcomers, whose ideas about the river may not have been so shaped by local attitudes. The earliest proposal to improve the river was made by Dana Bartlett, a New England min-

FIG. 3.10. The smoldering Los Angeles city dump protrudes into the river channel near downtown Los Angeles (1923). Tin cans, wood boxes, barrels, and other refuse from the dump are mired in the river's muddy bed. For scale, note the men at *center left*. Used with permission, Water Resources Center Archives, University of California, Berkeley/Joseph Barlow Lippincott Collection.

ister and settlement house worker who moved to Los Angeles in 1896. He suggested ten years later that, "despite the fact that its banks are lined with factories and the river bed itself is sought by utilitarian corporations," the river could be "made into a line of beauty." In 1910, another easterner, Rochester, New York–based planner Charles Mulford Robinson, a leader in the City Beautiful movement that was then sweeping urban planning, recommended as part of a broad plan of improvements for Los Angeles that the river be cleared of trash and that trees be planted on its banks. The most ambitious program for beautifying the river was suggested in 1930 by two eastern landscape architects, Massachusetts-based Frederick Law Olmsted Jr. and Harland Bartholomew, whose main office was in St. Louis but who also maintained an office in Los Angeles. In a $230.1 million parks plan for Los Angeles County, Olmsted and Bartholomew recommended that the river—at this late date already confined along part of its length by flood control revetments—be made into a series of parkways. None of these proposals ever gained significant support, however.[78]

The nature of still other proposals, moreover, suggests much about local perceptions of the river. Joseph Mesmer was an Ohioan who had moved to Los Angeles as an infant in 1859 and who had later become an influential local merchant. About 1910 he recommended that the river, the "most unsightly sight in the city" in the words of an article describing his plan, be transformed into a series of parks, lakes, and esplanades. To men like Mesmer, the improvement of the river was an economic necessity because the river was the first thing many visitors saw when they arrived in Los Angeles by train. This same line of thinking would also inspire proposals for the enhancement of the river channel made in the 1930s as the Los Angeles Union Passenger Terminal was being built.[79] More interesting, though, was what Mesmer proposed to do to the river. To create a park six miles long, he recommended that the riverbed and sides be "lined solidly with concrete."[80] About the same time, a member of the Los Angeles Board of Park Commissioners made a more modest proposal, recommending only that quarrying activities in the river be regulated and that steps be taken to prevent further dumping in the riverbed. His comments are even more telling. "It would be expensive and difficult, if not impossible, ever to make the river bed a thing of beauty," he said, "but it is not necessary to have it so ugly and unsanitary."[81]

The Continued Reliance on the River

Despite its blighted state near downtown, the Los Angeles River farther upstream remained an important source of water for the city of Los Angeles even after the opening of the Los Angeles–Owens River

Aqueduct in 1913, although its role has been largely overlooked. The river and its subsurface supply provided nearly one-fifth of the city's water until the 1940s, when a second major aqueduct, from the Colorado River, began delivering water to Southern California. The percolation of imported water used to irrigate agricultural lands in the San Fernando Valley, meanwhile, actually increased the amount of water destined for the river. In fact, by 1960, according to water department annual reports, the river provided more than twice the volume of water it had in 1902.[82] These statistics give a somewhat misleading impression of the river, however, because by 1930 most of its underground supply was tapped by wells and other devices before the water even reached the river.

The city of Los Angeles steadily expanded its use of wells and infiltration galleries because of increasing concerns about the quality of the river's surface water. Such concerns were first expressed in water department annual reports in 1911; in 1914, a year after the opening of the Los Angeles–Owens River Aqueduct, the city hired a biologist to monitor water quality.[83] Owens Valley water enabled the rapid subdivision of the San Fernando Valley and, as intensive agriculture and urban development gradually replaced the dryland farms and ranches that had bordered the river, the quality of the water flowing in its channel began to be threatened by agricultural pollution, industrial discharges, and street runoff. Irrigated acreage in the San Fernando Valley grew from about 3,000 acres in 1915 to more than 70,000 acres ten years later. Residential development also increased significantly, particularly in the southern part of the valley near the river. The Los Angeles Suburban Homes Company, a syndicate headed by *Los Angeles Times* owner Harrison Gray Otis and his son-in-law Harry Chandler, bought 47,500 acres south of present-day Roscoe Boulevard in 1909, in anticipation of the opening of the aqueduct, and subdivided much of this land for homes. It paid the Pacific Electric Railway $150,000 to extend its commuter rail line across the valley and founded the towns of Lankershim (now North Hollywood), Van Nuys, and Owensmouth (now Canoga Park) along its tracks (fig. 3.11). The Pacific Electric also provided a boost to the cities of Burbank and Glendale, both products of the Boom of the Eighties, and, by 1930, more than 100,000 people lived in communities along the river in the San Fernando Valley. The population was most heavily concentrated in the southeastern corner of the valley, the same area from which the city of Los Angeles, since 1904, had diverted the flow of the river for its water supply.[84]

As development spread in the land areas tributary to the Los Angeles River, surface water supplies required increasing treatment to be made drinkable, so city officials did all they could to prevent water in

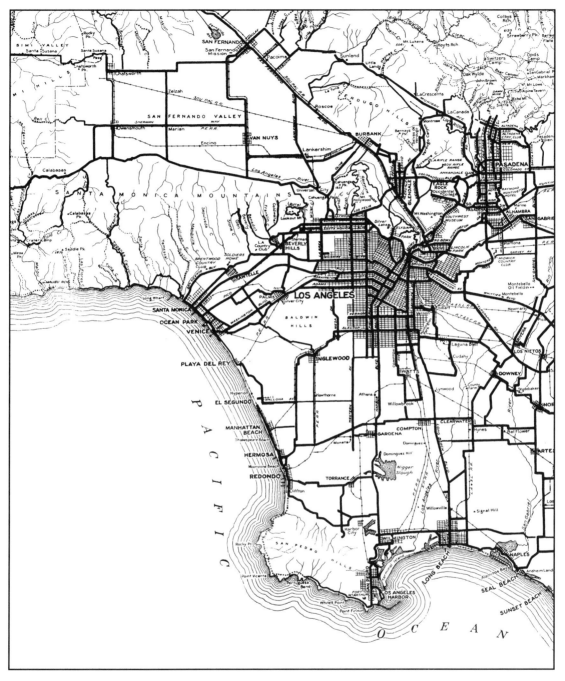

FIG. 3.11. Map of the Los Angeles area in 1919 shows the new suburbs developed in the San Fernando Valley after the opening of the Los Angeles–Owens River Aqueduct: from the left, Chatsworth, Owensmouth, Van Nuys, and Lankershim. The growth of these and other communities north of Los Angeles undermined water quality in the Los Angeles River and also heightened the flood risk. Excerpted from Security Trust and Savings Bank, *Automobile Road Map of the Los Angeles Region* (Los Angeles, 1919).

the underground reservoir that supplied the river from ever reaching the surface. Water obtained from underground sources required no treatment because it was naturally clean, and supplies drawn down from the river into infiltration galleries were purified by the sands and gravels that underlay the valley floor. The Headworks infiltration galleries, first installed opposite Burbank in 1905 to capture the river's subsurface flow on the north side of Griffith Park, were expanded in 1916. Soon after, the capacity of the Crystal Springs Galleries, originally developed in 1886 near the southeastern corner of the park, was also increased. These developments enabled the city in 1917 to halt all surface diversions from the river in the Glendale Narrows and to discontinue the use of two chlorination plants that had been built to disinfect the river supply.[85]

The volume of water supplied by the Los Angeles–Owens River Aqueduct was gradually increased, however, and soon existing facilities were not enough to capture the river's entire flow. Expanded aqueduct deliveries meant that more water was available for irrigation; after irrigation water percolated into aquifers, it eventually found its way to the river. As a result, the surface flow of the river increased so considerably that, by 1918, as much as five million gallons of water a day were flowing in the river channel beneath the Macy Street bridge, east of downtown. To water department officials, any water that flowed downstream from its final diversion point on the river was water that was wasted. To prevent water from traveling that far, infiltration galleries were installed in the riverbed near Macy Street and, in 1920, a third Headworks gallery was built. Well development along the river also intensified. By 1925, there were eighteen wells at Crystal Springs and fourteen at the Headworks plant. That year, fourteen more wells were drilled three miles north of the river in North Hollywood. In 1930, ten new wells were drilled in the San Fernando Valley and the Glendale Narrows. "The object of these wells," said the Los Angeles Board of Water and Power Commissioners in its annual report, "is to lower the water levels enough to prevent any surface water from flowing under the Dayton Avenue bridge, except during flood periods."[86] The Los Angeles River, such statements made clear, had become a river in name only (fig. 3.12).

By this time, flood control projects had also begun to transform the river and industrial development had increased along its banks. Levees, protected by stone or concrete, had been built along more than a third of its length. Wire fence, a means of temporary flood protection, lined portions of the channel. The river's course had been straightened and its bed excavated in places to provide greater carrying capacity. Trees and brush that might obstruct flood flows had been cleared

FIG. 3.12. The dry, sandy bed of the Los Angeles River near Seventh Street in downtown Los Angeles (about 1930) shows that efforts to prevent any water from flowing on the surface of the river during the dry season were successful. Used with permission, Department of Special Collections, University of Southern California Library/California Historical Society Collection (31076).

from its bed. Movie studios had begun to line both sides of the river from Cahuenga Pass to Griffith Park. Farther downstream, heavy industry became more prevalent. The Southern Pacific Railroad's massive Taylor Yard facility, which eventually employed more than ten thousand people, occupied three miles of riverfront opposite Elysian Park, while the riverside through downtown was clogged with railroad tracks, warehouses, and factories. The city's industrial core had expanded south, with brickyards, glass plants, furniture manufacturers, and oil field suppliers spreading between Alameda Street and the river. Warehouses congregated around the three railroad depots.

Industrial development escalated throughout Southern California after World War I, as growing demand for products caused by the exploding population prompted many eastern manufacturing companies to open branch operations. This was especially true of the auto-

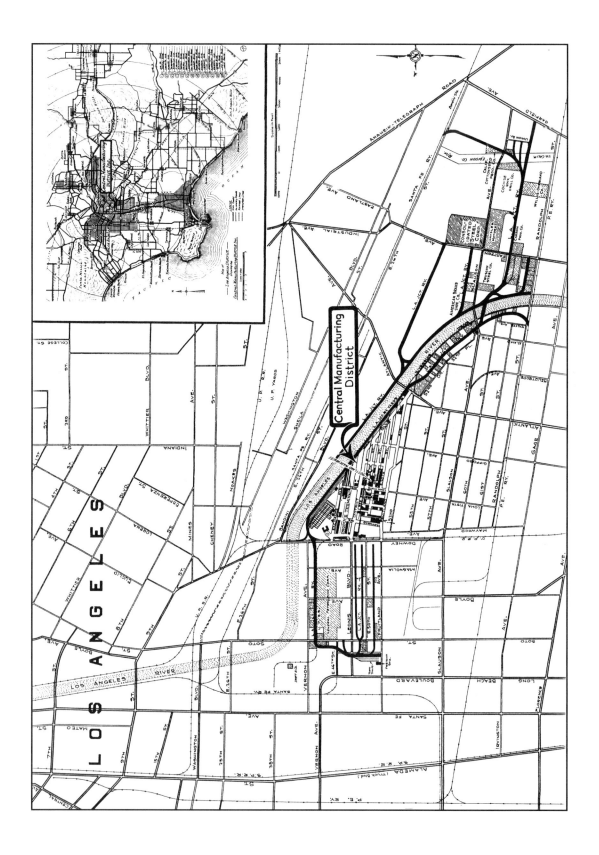

mobile industry, which in the Los Angeles metropolitan area first developed in close proximity to the river. Henry Ford built a plant in Long Beach in 1927. That same year, the Willis-Overland Company, an important early manufacturer, opened a factory one mile east of the river in what is now the city of Commerce. Chrysler Motors opened a plant one block west of the Willis-Overland factory in 1932. Four years later, Studebaker established its first branch plant in the United States across the river from Chrysler in the city of Vernon. Several steel manufacturers, including U.S. Steel, Bethlehem Steel, and Consolidated Steel, built in the vicinity to supply the automobile plants. Vernon became the heart of what was known as the Central Manufacturing District (fig. 3.13). Incorporated in 1905 as an "exclusively industrial" city, after court decisions cut off the flow of water into the zanjas that had watered the vineyards and fruit trees in the area, Vernon had more than three hundred industrial plants employing twenty thousand workers by 1927. In addition to the auto plants and steel manufacturers, it was home to Owens Glass, Alcoa Aluminum, American Can, and General Mills. The Los Angeles Union Stockyards, located on the south bank of the river at Downey Road in Vernon, was the largest such facility in the western United States. In 1937, more than 1.4 million cattle, calves, and hogs were sold from the yard.[87]

The Pollution of the River's Waters

With railroads, factories, and stockyards occupying much of the riverfront from the San Fernando Valley to Long Beach, industrial discharges into the river channel became more prevalent and, by the 1940s, what little water occasionally flowed in its channel was often toxic. Chromium wastes from San Fernando Valley aircraft plants, for example, were discovered in the river in 1941. They had been discharged illegally into storm drains that emptied into the river. The Long Beach Department of Health, meanwhile, was forced to quarantine a section of beach just east of the river's mouth in 1941 and again in 1947 because of contamination from the river. The contaminants were later traced to two paper mills in the city of Vernon; the mills had

Facing page

FIG. 3.13. The Central Manufacturing District, centered upon the city of Vernon south of downtown Los Angeles, was the source of much of the pollution in the Los Angeles River. Excerpted from Central Manufacturing District, *Central Manufacturing District and Los Angeles Junction Railway* (Los Angeles, 1932).

been discharging into the county storm drain system wastes that contained *Escherichia coli*, the same bacteria that in recent years has been linked to deaths of persons who have eaten beef.[88]

Such problems were widespread. Excessive oil and grease were reaching the river from railroad yards in Los Angeles. Urine, manure, and other animal refuse were draining into the river from feedlots, livestock holding pens, and slaughterhouses in Vernon. Compton Creek, which empties into the river in north Long Beach, was so overloaded with wastes that government officials were besieged with complaints about offensive odors coming from its channel. Oil field brines were found in the river near Wardlow Road in Long Beach. As the problems began to be noticed, subsequent testing detected concentrations of iron, boron, chromium, and alkaline substances all along the river's course, indicating that industrial plants were occasionally discharging untreated wastes into storm drains and the river channel. Untreated sewage was also sometimes allowed to flow directly into storm drains during heavy rains. Between 1930 and 1940, in fact, the volume of sewage carried by the river more than doubled. "Many reaches of the river," said a hydraulic engineer for the California Division of Water Resources, "had become foul and septic."[89]

The Los Angeles River was especially prone to potentially harmful levels of pollution because it contained so little water that it was not able to satisfactorily dilute wastes discharged into its channel. The problem reached a crisis level when contaminated water began to turn up in ground water basins on the coastal plain. In 1943, the city of Los Angeles Bureau of Sanitation, in response, began to study the quality of water flowing in the river. Three years later, the U.S. Engineer's Office began to conduct chemical analyses of the liquids carried in sixty-nine storm drains that emptied into its channel. Finally, in the fall of 1947, meetings were held by state, city, and county officials, along with several private parties, to address the situation. The California Department of Public Health agreed to coordinate efforts to clean up the river and, in February 1948, the Los Angeles River Pollution Committee was created. It included representatives from the state Department of Public Health, the Los Angeles County Flood Control District, the Los Angeles Department of Water and Power, the City of Long Beach Engineering Department, and several other governmental agencies. Smaller cities along the river were represented by the Los Angeles County Department of Public Health. The city of Vernon declined initially to participate despite the fact that, according to a committee report, the river received "its greatest volume of industrial wastes" from that city and the city of Los Angeles.[90]

The Los Angeles River Pollution Committee established tentative standards for waste discharges into the river and initiated a program of river sampling and waste discharge surveys. Sampling stations were established at seventeen locations along the river from Van Nuys to Long Beach. Monthly samples were taken. Sources of illegal discharges were located, and responsible parties were ordered to correct the problems. Within twelve months of the committee's formation, it claimed that, as a result of its efforts, toxic wastes from fifteen different industries had been eliminated from the river. The number of incidences of odorous discharges were reduced from seventeen in the final six months of 1948 to one in all of 1949, nine in 1950, and one in 1951. Organic wastes that had caused the odor problems in Compton Creek were eliminated, and the oil field brines that had been discharged into the river in Long Beach were redirected into sewers. Still, new concerns emerged just as other problems were being overcome. The total volume of dissolved solids present in the river water, for example, increased between 1948 and 1952.[91] Swimming and bathing in the river were outlawed. Signs were posted along the river's course warning that its waters were contaminated.

And though the most flagrant water quality concerns were overcome and the threat to ground water resources was reduced, pollution of the Los Angeles River, like that of most urban streams, has remained a persistent problem. A sampling of the reports of the various government agencies that monitor water quality shows that most of the early problems were never truly solved and many new sources of contamination developed. Unsafe levels of arsenic were found in the river in 1958. Oil field brines were again discovered in its channel near Long Beach. Chromium wastes were found in the river's tributaries in the San Fernando Valley in 1961. That same year, water in the river a mile north of its mouth was found to be toxic to fish. In 1965, the California Department of Water Resources remarked that the water in the river at Long Beach "is usually of such poor quality that it is unusable for any recognized beneficial use." In 1968, gasoline believed to have leaked from underground pipelines was discovered in wells along the river across from Burbank.[92]

Pollution eventually forced the Los Angeles Department of Water and Power to eliminate its last remaining surface diversion on the river and to discontinue pumping for water all along its course. The Headworks Deep Gallery, a vertical pipe that captured part of the river's subsurface flow, was shut down in 1971 because of water quality concerns. Diversions from the river into the Headworks Spreading Grounds on the north side of Griffith Park were halted in 1982 because of increased discharges of treated sewage into the river. More serious contamination, this time threatening the river's underground supply, was discovered in 1979. Most of the wells near the river were closed in the 1980s after tests ordered by the California Department of Health Services revealed that large areas of the ground water in the southeastern San Fernando Valley had been contaminated by industrial chemicals. The most common contaminants were the solvents trichloroethylene and perchloroethylene, widely used in a variety of industries, including metal plating, machinery degreasing, and dry cleaning. Subsequent investigations found that more than two thousand small industrial plants had no connections to municipal sewer systems.[93]

The U.S. Environmental Protection Agency (EPA) began its own inquiry in 1984 and, two years later, three groups of wells along the river were included within the boundaries of an area designated for cleanup using federal funds. That area became known as the San Fernando Valley Superfund Site. Superfund is a program, created by Congress in 1980, to coordinate the cleanup of the worst hazardous waste sites in the United States. The extent of contamination was not immediately known, but in May 1987 the last five wells in use at the Headworks plant were shut down. Two months later, the remaining four wells still in use at the Crystal Springs pumping plant were closed. The last active wells along the river—five wells located on the east side of the river north of Fletcher Drive, known as the Pollack wells—were shut down in February 1990. The EPA-coordinated cleanup program is continuing.[94]

Although it is not part of the EPA program, the Los Angeles Department of Water and Power is building a new water treatment plant that will allow it to resume pumping from the Pollack wells. The treatment plant will enable the city to draw three thousand gallons of water per minute from wells along the river. Chemical contaminants will be removed from the water using liquid-phase, granular-activated carbon filters. The plant was expected to be in operation by late 1998. The treatment plant was developed for the same reason that so many wells were drilled near the river after the opening of the Los Angeles–Owens River Aqueduct—to prevent any water from spilling out of aquifers into the river. In other words, the goal of local water agencies is still to make sure that no water flows in the river from its natural source, the huge subterranean reservoir beneath the San Fernando Valley. The shutting down of wells because of contamination had allowed some water from the San Fernando Basin again to reach the river. The Upper Los Angeles River Area Watermaster, a court-appointed official who oversees court-adjudicated ground water allocations in the area, told the city of Los Angeles that, unless it did something to prevent water from upwelling into the river from the aquifer, it might lose its rights to that water.[95]

Although 10 to 15 percent of the Los Angeles city water supply is still pumped from beneath the San Fernando Valley, nearly all of the water that now flows in the river is treated sewage, authorized industrial discharges, and street runoff. Very little water from the source that originally formed the river ever reaches its channel, except during the rainy season. Sewage treatment plants alone provide nearly half of the dry season flow. The greatest single supplier is the Donald C. Tillman Water Reclamation Plant in Van Nuys, which began operating in 1984 and now provides about a third of the river's flow (fig. 3.14). Consequently, the true "source" of the transformed Los Angeles River is not some mountain stream in the Santa Susana or San Gabriel Mountains. Rather, it is the huge concrete treatment tanks that clean the city's wastewater and discharge it into an outflow channel that empties into the river just upstream from Sepulveda Dam. Smaller amounts of treated wastewater are discharged from a city of Burbank reclamation plant and a combined Los Angeles–Glendale treatment facility located near the outlet of Verdugo Wash. Another 30 percent of the river's flow, even in summer, comes from the hundreds of storm drains that empty along its banks. Ironically, less than 5 percent of the dry season flow of the river comes from the ground water basin that was its historic source.[96] Though efforts to revitalize the river are increasing, the primary purpose of the river today is as a conduit for urban waste and a means to deliver seasonal floodwaters safely to the sea.

Even so, the Los Angeles River is now a very different river than it was two decades ago because of the large volumes of treated wastewater discharged into its concrete channel. This reclaimed water has greatly increased the amount of water flowing in the river and, in fact, the volume of water carried may now be greater than ever before. The average annual surface flow in the river between 1988 and 1993 was more than twice the average during the previous twenty years. In July 1993, the average flow in the river near the Arroyo Seco was 109.5 million gallons a day, more than double its flow upstream from all diversions in 1902. The river now also flows year-round—though meagerly—in places where in a relatively undisturbed state it was probably a dry wash except after winter storms. The added water has boosted the growth of vegetation in three soft-bottom sections of the river and, though the product of urban sewage, it has actually improved water quality by diluting the street runoff and contaminated ground water. This has led to other unexpected changes. The cleaner, faster-moving stream has attracted increasing numbers of gnats in the Glendale Nar-

FIG. 3.14. Concrete sewage treatment tanks at the Donald C. Tillman Water Reclamation Plant in Van Nuys, source of much of the dry season flow of the Los Angeles River today. Photograph by Stephen Callis. Used with permission.

rows, aggravating golfers in Griffith Park and even baseball players at Dodger Stadium. The growing insect populations have also led to a rise in the number of birds living near the river, since they feed off such insects. It has even been suggested that the cleaner, faster-moving water has reduced frog populations across from Elysian Park—an area long known as "Frogtown"—because the frogs prefer dirtier, more stagnant water.[97]

The treated wastewater has improved the quality of water flowing in the river so much that in 1993 the Los Angeles Department of Water and Power conducted an $800,000 study to determine whether water diverted from the river to the Headworks Spreading Grounds and later pumped to the surface by wells would be clean enough to drink. An inflated black rubber dam was placed across the bottom of the river's concrete channel, near the intersection of the Ventura Freeway and Forest Lawn Drive, to block part of the river's flow. Water that accumulated behind the dam was then diverted into the Headworks Spreading Grounds, a series of dry, shallow basins beside the river on the north side of Griffith Park, where it was allowed to percolate underground. Once underground, the water seeped slowly downward and back toward the river channel. It was pumped out from test wells six months to a year after it had first been diverted. The natural filtering action of the soil was all that was used to clean the water. The study found that the extracted water, which contained 45 percent reclaimed water, complied with all drinking water standards. The reclaimed water has the potential to provide up to 10 percent of the city's water supply. It is ironic that the treated wastewater has improved water quality so much that, for the first time in years, the surface flow of the Los Angeles River, however unnatural, may again contribute to the city's domestic water supply. The project has been put on hold, awaiting the construction of new treatment plants and resolution of the EPA-sponsored cleanup program of ground water in the area.[98]

Recent developments have, in effect, created an artificial waterway that has little in common with the intermittent stream that wandered back and forth across the landscape for thousands of years. Although the degradation of urban rivers is an old and familiar story, the destruction of the Los Angeles River is in many ways unique in North America because of the very different native character of the stream and the ways in which Euro-American settlers, their ideas about rivers shaped by waterways that had deep channels and carried abundant water year-round, reacted to it. Early residents viewed the river as a resource and little else. They took from it all they needed to survive until its channel was drained dry. And then they took some more. Flood control projects are generally blamed for turning the river into an eyesore, but in truth it was the city's increasing reliance on the river for its water supply that first transformed it from a thing of beauty into an object of ridicule. Water projects so changed the river that, by the time flood control became a necessity, few cared whether it was covered with cement. Concrete channels merely became the coffin for a river that had already been sapped of nearly all its life.

DESPITE ITS REPUTATION AS A LAND OF PERPETUAL SUN-shine and little rain, Southern California probably faces a greater natural hazard from catastrophic floods than any other metropolitan area in the nation.¹ More than half of the nonmountainous portion of Los Angeles County was once threatened by floods. Before the region's waterways were confined and controlled, rivers and streams overflowed often, carving ravines through fertile farmland, destroying homes and businesses, crippling transportation and communication lines, and occasionally washing away entire towns. Rivers became torrents, sometimes breaking through their banks and cutting completely new courses to the ocean. Periodically, the floodwaters from dozens of streams would join on the coastal plain and spread across the landscape to form huge lakes. Such floods were also deadly; in fact, more people have been killed in Los Angeles County in floods than by earthquakes. Flooding became an increasing hazard as the population grew and development expanded. Human beings made matters worse by building on the floodplain, removing trees and vegetation that had kept soils in place, cutting openings in stream banks to divert water for irrigation, erecting levees that constricted flood flows, and constructing railroads that interrupted natural drainage patterns.²

Southern California has experienced more than sixty significant floods since settlement by the Spanish. Many of those occurred on the Los Angeles River. The earliest written report of a flood in California, in fact, concerned the Río de Porciúncula. Representatives of the first Spanish land expedition to California in 1769 found trunks of numerous trees on the banks of the river near its confluence with the Arroyo Seco, "giving clear indication of great floods in the rainy season." When the Portolá expedition returned to the area on 17 January 1770, representatives noted that the river's banks were littered with uprooted trees and debris, evidence that "a few days previous there had been a great flood, which had caused it to leave its bed." Historical climate studies have since estimated that the Los Angeles area received more rain that winter than at any time in the next forty years.[3] Though details about many early floods are unknown, the Los Angeles River has overflowed its banks at least two dozen times since then. Floods, moreover, have altered the course of the river again and again.

Los Angeles is naturally flood prone because of the region's topography and climate. Mountains ring the valleys and coastal plain, trapping storms and speeding runoff (fig. 4.1). Elevations rise to more than 7,000 feet in the area drained by the Los Angeles River. Though some portions of the coastal plain receive as few as ten inches of rain a year, a few mountain peaks receive more than forty inches of precipitation annually. It has been estimated that nearly 75 percent of the runoff in the county originates in the mountains. Nearly all of the precipitation occurs during four winter months, and most falls as rain, concentrated in brief but often violent storms. Drainage lines are short, and their fall to the ocean relatively rapid. The watershed of the Los Angeles River drops more than 7,000 feet in a little over forty miles, from its highest point at 7,124-foot Mount Pacifico to the river's mouth at Long Beach. The river itself falls 795 feet on its fifty-one-mile course, a seemingly insignificant slope but comparatively abrupt for a major lowland waterway passing through a heavily urbanized area. The Mississippi River, in contrast, falls just 605 feet in more than two thousand miles.[4]

The San Gabriel Mountains, which contribute the greatest runoff to the Los Angeles River system, are composed primarily of igneous rock that is cut by numerous faults and is heavily fractured. The mountains are relatively young in geologic terms, so their slopes are extremely steep and rugged, rising 1,000 to 3,000 feet per mile. They are taller from base to summit than the Rocky Mountains by three thousand feet. Because they are in a nearly constant state of disintegration, moreover, craggy ridges and narrow V-shaped canyons are common.[5] In places, the inclines are nearly vertical. As a result, soils are thin and rocky, and the lack of rain most of the year inhibits vegetation growth. Few trees can survive in such conditions. Scattered chaparral and coastal sagebrush cover most of the mountains, with small pockets of conifers in the higher elevations. A state government engineer in 1888 wrote that "bare granite slopes, great crumbling masses of rock, and glistening ridges innocent of a tree, are the ruling features of the landscape."[6] Before flood control work began in the mountains, there was little to absorb or slow runoff. Fire only made matters worse, frequently burning the brushy slopes bare. The mountain soils were subject to intense erosion.

The winter storm systems that stall over these mountains often produce torrential rain, with precipitation rates of two inches per

FIG. 4.1. The San Gabriel Mountains, rising to more than seven thousand feet in the watershed of the Los Angeles River, dwarf the giant Rose Bowl in Pasadena, which seats 104,000 people. The lined channel of the Arroyo Seco, a major tributary of the Los Angeles River, is visible in the foreground. Photograph by the author, 1997.

hour not uncommon.[7] Some of the most concentrated rainfall ever recorded in the United States has occurred in the San Gabriel Mountains. During such storms, the mountain soils quickly become saturated. Rainfall runs off rapidly, carrying mud, rocks, and trees down the precipitous slopes and narrow canyons, many of which are often blocked by boulders that had been transported during earlier storms. Even today, massive, catastrophic debris flows—moving mixtures of boulders, mud, sand, and water that can wipe out entire residential subdivisions in minutes—are a fact of life in foothill communities.[8] Until dams and other flood control works were built in the mountains and foothills, this debris was often carried to the valleys and coastal plain below, clogging stream channels. The rivers and streams of the lowlands were ill-equipped in their natural state to carry the great quantities of water and other materials that cascade from the mountains during heavy storms. The result was floods of such fierceness that an anonymous U.S. government engineer likened their power to "the discharge of a bursting dam."[9]

Precipitation is rare in lowland Southern California except during winter, so until stream channels were lined with concrete by flood control projects, most were dry except during the rainy season. Lacking a continuous flow, they were unable to dig deep channels or establish well-defined courses. Their banks were low and their beds wide. Even in moderate storms, floodwaters quickly spread over the landscape. Before a comprehensive program of flood control was developed, at least 215,300 acres in Los Angeles County, more than 336 square miles, were subject to inundation (fig. 4.2). Floods threatened most of the eastern half of the San Fernando Valley, vast areas of the San Gabriel Valley, and much of the coastal plain from Los Angeles to San Pedro Bay and along Ballona Creek.[10] Silt, sand, and gravel carried from the mountains during the rainy season gradually filled stream channels to capacity, eventually raising channel bottoms above the level of the surrounding countryside. When this happened, swollen streams would cut new channels across lower ground. Even as late as the 1890s, the braided channels of Tujunga Wash, for example, wandered over an area seven miles wide in the eastern San Fernando Valley.[11] As development spread, the area subject to flooding actually increased because buildings and pavement prevented natural runoff from sinking into the ground. The porous ground surface of the San Fernando Valley had served as a natural regulator of flood flows, but as it was covered by homes, businesses, and streets, its absorptive ability was seriously reduced. By 1940, in fact, with the county's population approaching three million and despite the millions of dollars that had already been spent on flood control work, the area subject to inundation had increased by 50 percent. Some 325,000 acres in Los Angeles County, 59 percent of the nonmountainous area, were subject to overflow. In the Los Angeles River Basin alone, 160,000 acres were threatened, 44 percent of the lowlands.[12]

Before flood control projects dramatically altered natural drainage patterns, the Los Angeles River and its eighteen principal tributaries drained roughly 890 square miles. The bulk of storm runoff destined for the river was carried by just five streams, all but one draining the west end of the San Gabriel Mountains. The floodwaters from three of these streams—Pacoima Creek, Little Tujunga Creek, and Big Tujunga Creek—often mingled on the floor of the San Fernando Valley, inundating a vast area north of the river. During one major flood in 1914, the discharge from these three streams alone was equal to three-quarters of the flow in the Los Angeles River near downtown Los Angeles. Big Tujunga Creek, all by itself, carried half as much water as the river. Farther downstream, Verdugo Creek, emptying into the river opposite Griffith Park, had a flow equal to one-quarter of the river's

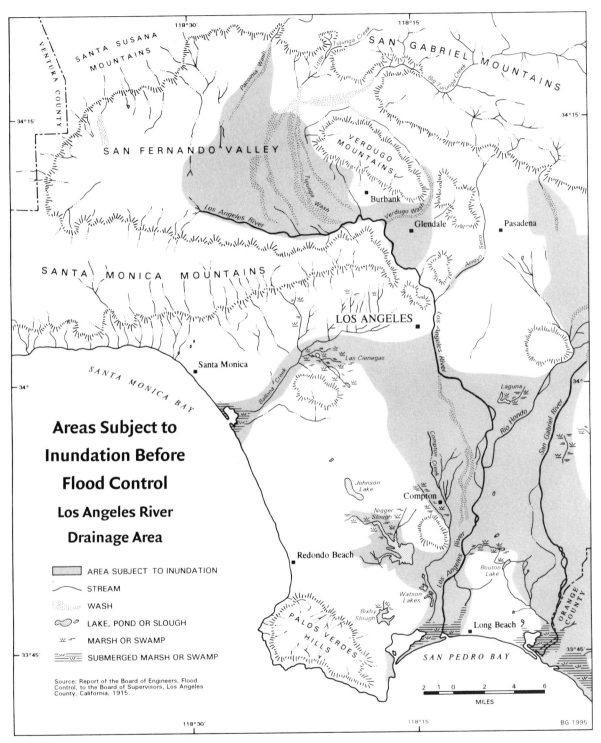

**Areas Subject to
Inundation Before
Flood Control**

**Los Angeles River
Drainage Area**

▨	AREA SUBJECT TO INUNDATION
⌇	STREAM
⠿	WASH
⬡⬦	LAKE, POND OR SLOUGH
⩜	MARSH OR SWAMP
≋	SUBMERGED MARSH OR SWAMP

Source: Report of the Board of Engineers, Flood
Control, to the Board of Supervisors, Los Angeles
County, California, 1915.

FIG. 4.2. More than 336 square miles of Los Angeles County were threatened by floods before a comprehensive flood control program was developed. Map by the author.

flood volume. The peak discharge of the Arroyo Seco, draining the south side of the San Gabriels above Pasadena, was 36 percent of the river's maximum flow. The combined flow of these five streams was greater than the peak discharge of the Los Angeles River because some of the water they carried spread across the landscape, never reaching the coastal plain.[13]

The Los Angeles River had seldom been visible west of Encino before flood control, even during heavy runoff. It was here that water in the subterranean reservoir beneath the San Fernando Valley, forced above ground by the submerged base of the Santa Monica Mountains, first spilled to the surface to form the river. The river slowly widened as it flowed southeast and met the divided channels of Tujunga Wash. Held in place by the gentle slope of the valley and the mountains that prevented it from drifting farther south, the river remained relatively narrow and its course comparatively consistent through the San Fernando Valley. Once the river rounded the bend of the Santa Monica Mountains at Griffith Park, however, its path became much more circuitous. Between the mouth of Verdugo Wash and the Arroyo Seco, the river spread over a broad depression two thousand feet wide, its course meandering considerably from year to year. One early resident reported that the river had no defined bed in the Glendale Narrows until 1825, when the region was hit by a major flood that changed drainage patterns throughout Southern California. Floods were so common in the Narrows that once-fertile bottomlands along the river were eventually abandoned as unsuitable for cultivation because they were so regularly covered with sand. The river also had its greatest dry season flow through this section because the bedrock that forces its underground flow to the surface—the same rock that forms the Santa Monica Mountains—is sometimes only forty feet deep.[14]

The flood risk from the Los Angeles River was greatest on the coastal plain, where the river's meager year-round flow prevented it from establishing a well-defined course and few obstructions hindered the movement of floodwaters. Once the river emerged from a narrow gap between the Elysian and San Rafael hills, just north of downtown Los Angeles, its channel widened considerably and its banks diminished in size. S. B. Reeve, a nineteenth-century Los Angeles city surveyor, once said that, until the first primitive levees were built near downtown, the river had "practically no banks" south of Seventh Street.[15] As a result, floodwaters sometimes stretched more than a mile wide, from the terrace upon which the pueblo was built to the bluffs of Boyle Heights. Even after settlement of the pueblo, the river sometimes flowed along what is now Alameda Street (fig. 4.3). At other times, it hugged the base of the Boyle Heights bluffs (fig.

4.4). A decade after the founding of Los Angeles, in fact, floods forced pueblo officials to move the town to higher ground.[16]

The Changing Courses of the River

Before its channel was deepened, widened, and confined between walls of concrete, the Los Angeles River changed its course between the city and the sea again and again. Many of these changes were minor, but others altered the entire drainage of the coastal plain and helped transform the character of vegetation that grew on the lowlands. It is generally acknowledged that the river once flowed west after leaving Los Angeles, emptying into the ocean at Santa Monica Bay, before shifting its mouth twenty miles down the coast to San Pedro Bay. Reports of early settlers suggest that, at an earlier time, the river may have emptied into the sea at Alamitos Bay, another six miles down the coast. Throughout the first half of the nineteenth century, the main channel of the lower Los Angeles River shifted at least nine times. The most significant known changes in the course of the river occurred in 1815, 1825, 1889, and 1914 (fig. 4.5).[17]

Until 1825, the river is believed to have flowed west from the pueblo along the present course of Ballona Creek. There is much evidence to support this view. A member of the prominent Sepúlveda family, whose ancestors had first arrived in Los Angeles shortly after the pueblo was founded in 1781, told an interviewer in 1914 that the river once flowed southwest through the pueblo along what is now Los Angeles Street (which could help explain the general southwesterly orientation of many of the streets in downtown Los Angeles) before turning more sharply west and following the route of Ballona Creek to Santa Monica Bay. Several witnesses in an 1897 hearing in Los Angeles County Superior Court also said that the river once took this route. When a historic palm tree was transplanted in 1914 from downtown Los Angeles to Exposition Park, more than three miles west of the river's present course, gardeners at its new home found river sand and gravel just a foot below the ground surface.[18]

River sand has also been found stretching westward from the intersection of Twenty-fourth Street and Maple Avenue, south of downtown Los Angeles, more than two miles west of the river's current channel. Construction of Hamburger's department store at the corner of Eighth Street and Broadway in 1906 also unearthed significant quantities of river sand and gravel. Dozens of interviews conducted by Los Angeles County flood control officials in the early part of the twentieth century provide further anecdotal evidence of the river's former courses. "There is no doubt that the Los Angeles River once flowed out through Ballona Creek," said one man, who had arrived in

FIG. 4.3. Even after levees were built in downtown Los Angeles, floodwaters often turned Alameda Street into a river. In this photograph, taken during a storm in December 1897, water flows in a wide channel near the Southern Pacific Railroad's Arcade Depot at Fifth and Alameda Streets. Used with permission, Los Angeles Public Library/Security Pacific Collection.

Los Angeles in 1886. "An old stage driver by the name of Gorton who was here in the very early years, and who carried mail from here to Santa Barbara, has told me many things of the early days and that the Los Angeles River flowed out through the southwest into the Cienega and on into Ballona [Santa Monica] Bay."[19]

It is uncertain whether the Los Angeles River always flowed into Santa Monica Bay before it shifted south, though this seems doubtful. Juan Crespí was diarist for the first Spanish land expedition to California in 1769. After crossing the river near the present location of downtown Los Angeles, he wrote in his journal that "from what we could see of how [the] trees wound along, we guessed" that the river emptied into "the Bight of San Pedro." A subsequent visitor to Southern California in 1776 wrote that the river, "running toward the Bay of San

Pedro, spreads out and is lost in the plains a little before reaching the sea."[20] Maps depicting the underground flow of water beneath the coastal plain suggest that the river probably alternated between its route via Ballona Creek and its southerly course to San Pedro Bay.[21] Artesian basins fed by the Los Angeles, San Gabriel, and Santa Ana Rivers once underlay nearly three hundred square miles of Los Angeles and Orange Counties, from Beverly Hills south nearly to Long Beach, east to Whittier, and southeast as far as Mission Viejo.

The first recorded shift in the course of the Los Angeles River occurred in 1815. In the midst of ten days of nearly continuous rain, the river overflowed its banks and abandoned its former channel, then located east of the agricultural lands of the pueblo. It veered southwest through the vineyards and cornfields, along the present route of North Spring Street. The plaza was flooded and several adobe houses were destroyed. An Indian village beside the river was washed away. The pueblo church, its walls weakened by floodwaters, had to be rebuilt on higher ground three years later. Since the pueblo church was

FIG. 4.4. The prominent meander scar visible in the foreground of this photograph, taken about 1880, shows that the river in relatively recent times had run near the base of the bluff that forms Boyle Heights, east of its present channel. The river runs horizontally from the *center* to the *left*, defined by a line of dark vegetation, in this view. Used with permission, Department of Special Collections, University of Southern California Library/Title Insurance & Trust Company Collection (USC 1-1-1-2255).

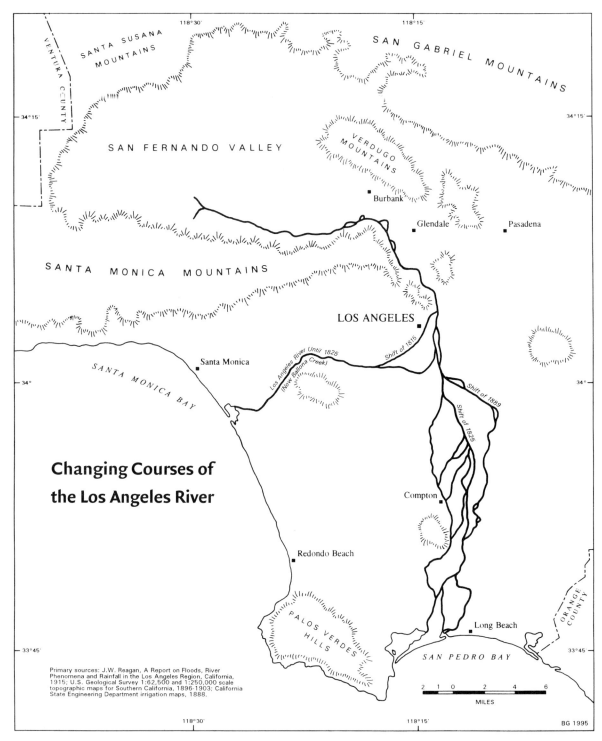

FIG. 4.5. The Los Angeles River shifted back and forth across the coastal plain before it was controlled. This map shows a few of the river's channels and courses during the last two hundred years, as disclosed on historic maps and suggested by anecdotal evidence. Map by the author.

supposed to front on the plaza, the plaza was also moved. Early residents said the river flowed for a decade along an embankment sixteen to eighteen feet high between the present routes of Main and Los Angeles Streets, curving slowly southwest to about where Seventh Street is today. A well-defined channel six to eight feet deep and fifteen to twenty feet wide was once visible near the current intersection of Ninth and Hope Streets in downtown Los Angeles. The river then flowed toward Exposition Park before turning west and rejoining its normal course through the sloughs and marshlands known as Las Cienegas. From there, it followed the route of Ballona Creek to the sea.[22]

The most dramatic change in the course of the river occurred in 1825, when the flood-swollen waterway broke through its banks near the pueblo and cut a new channel directly south. At least some of the river's water has emptied into San Pedro Bay ever since. The flood began on a clear spring night. Torrential rain had fallen in Los Angeles and the surrounding mountains two days earlier, but lingering showers had stopped that morning. The heavy mountain runoff, however, was delayed in reaching the town. Suddenly, about midnight, a torrent of water surged through the sleeping pueblo. Don Jose del Carmen Lugo, a member of one of Southern California's most prominent ranching families and then a twelve-year-old boy, had been sleeping under the stars in the pueblo:

> My father heard a great noise. The river ran about 100 *varas* [275 feet] from our house. I went to the bank, and discovered that it was a sea of water which was overflowing vegetable gardens, fences, trees and whatever was before it. The water was running with great violence, making enormous waves. I warned my father immediately of the terrible danger. He . . . sent me without a moment's delay to inform the commissioner of the pueblo.
>
> My brothers and some of my father's servants were already running through the town warning the people. Orders were given speedily for all the inhabitants of the town to move to a place of safety. They did so, everyone loading family and belongings into *carretas* drawn by oxen, along with their cows and other animals. At daybreak I saw that the water in the old channel of the river was subsiding, and was running toward the other side of the narrow valley—which is where the river has its bed today. The channel changed.[23]

The force of the water carried by the river in the 1825 flood was reportedly so powerful that it cut a new channel directly south to San Pedro Bay. Old timers said the shift changed the drainage of much of the lowlands and helped to alter the landscape of the coastal plain. Until that time, large parts of the countryside between the city and the ocean had been covered by a willow and cottonwood forest, interspersed with marshes, sloughs, and small ponds, with the river's floodwaters often spreading over the lowlands. Now, with most of the river's waters traveling in a more direct line south, many of the marshes and ponds began to dry up. The floodplain forest gradually disappeared and was replaced by wild mustard and native grasses. Floods in 1832 deepened the newly cut stream channel just enough to hasten the demise of the wetlands still further.[24] The grazing of cattle and the removal of trees by settlers intensified the transformation of the coastal plain, so much so that a traveler from San Pedro to Los Angeles in 1843 wrote that there was not "a single tree or shrub of any kind to be seen on this extensive tableland."[25]

Many of the factors that made the river so prone to shifting its course were exacerbated as diversions from the river for irrigation and domestic use increased and the use of wells became more prevalent on the coastal plain. Diversions near Los Angeles reduced the dry season flow of the river, which further limited its ability to dig a definite channel for itself and build banks of sufficient height to contain heavy winter runoff. Ground water use lowered the water table, reducing the subsurface flow of the river that had helped it maintain a more consistent course. Previously, even where the river channel had been dry in summer, water often continued to flow just below the surface, but as water use escalated the wetlands formed by its underground supply disappeared altogether and the river bed looked like a beach. A U.S. government surveying team that visited the city in 1854 reported that "a few hundred yards below the town of Los Angeles, the river, in summer time, ceases to flow."[26] The draining of the river intensified after the arrival of the railroads. Detailed irrigation maps published in 1888 show the river as a dry wash for most of ten miles from the city limits to its meeting with the old San Gabriel River, southeast of Compton.[27]

The flow of the river south of Los Angeles became so meager during most of the year that it was unrecognizable as a river. "Many times I was up to Los Angeles, and on crossing the valley just below town, I would ask where the Los Angeles River was," recalled an early Long Beach resident, who had settled in Southern California in the 1880s. "They would tell me I was in it and that it never flowed except in extreme high water."[28] As a result, the river could not contain even moderate increases in runoff, and its course therefore became more unpredictable. Floodwaters quickly spread over the countryside, cutting new channels with each storm. Before the river was confined in a narrow path by flood control projects, its overflow "spread out annually" between Downey and Compton. Sometimes the river broke southeast toward the San Gabriel River. At other times, it followed the routes of

Cerritos and Dominguez Creeks to the sea. Old maps show a dozen dry stream courses between Los Angeles and Compton.[29]

The vagrant nature of the river led to many boundary disputes during the early 1800s between two of the largest ranches in Southern California, the Rancho San Pedro and the Ranchos Los Nietos, which became the Rancho Los Cerritos. The Rancho San Pedro once occupied 75,000 acres on the west side of the river, from Wilmington halfway to Los Angeles. Rancho Los Nietos spread across 167,000 acres on the east side of the river. The river served as the boundary between the two ranches, but that boundary was altered almost every year as the braided channels of the river shifted and subdivided during winter runoffs. After one flood had moved the main channel of the river east, draining marshy land and creating rich grazing land on the new west bank, heirs to the Nieto property began grazing their cattle on the San Pedro side of the river channel, insisting that the land still belonged to them.[30] Elsewhere, changes in the river's course spurred similar disputes, which sometimes ended up in court. Legal remedies proved short-lived, however, because, as one U.S. government engineer noted, "the river can change faster than our courts could follow."[31]

The course of the Los Angeles River was most ambiguous just above its mouth. South of Compton, the bed of the river was coincident with the level of the water table, so even though its flow here was enlarged by the outflow of the Rio Hondo, it was unable to dig a distinct channel. As a result, floodwaters carried by the river often spread fan-shaped over the flatlands between San Pedro and Long Beach. Lagoons and marshes swelled by the river's overflow once extended from the Palos Verdes Hills all the way to the high lands near Long Beach before they were reduced in size by deposits of silt carried by the river during floods. Detailed maps drawn as late as 1919 show that the Los Angeles River had no definite course south of the present route of the San Diego Freeway, four miles north of its mouth. Floods were so common in this area that even residents who lived far inland and away from any permanent lake or stream kept boats at their homes so they could get around during high water.[32]

A Litany of Floods

Much more is known about flooding in Los Angeles after California became a state in 1850 and migration to the region increased. The city had no newspapers during the Spanish and Mexican periods, and many official records from those years have been lost. Those that remain are brief and short on nonadministrative details. Firsthand accounts of any type about Los Angeles before 1850, in fact, are scarce. Most of the descriptions of floods that occurred before that time were

simply part of the local lore, vague on specifics and a little more dubi-
ous with each telling. But Los Angeles got its first newspaper, the Star,
in 1851, and the city has had newspapers continuously since then. The
first precise measurements of rainfall were made in 1857, and regular
records began to be kept soon after that. Before long, the new class of
settlers who came to Los Angeles after the Gold Rush, weary of continually being stranded during the rainy season, demanded that bridges
be erected over stream courses. As they built homes and businesses
and planted vineyards and orchards in close proximity to the river, they
also began to petition city officials for the construction of the first rudimentary flood protections. Information about floods and the public
reaction to them, consequently, became much more plentiful.

Available records indicate that Los Angeles County experienced
significant floods—the sort that would overflow rivers and streams—
about once every four and a half years during the last half of the nineteenth century. The Los Angeles River flooded eleven times. The first
flood on the river during the American period occurred in the winter
of 1851–52. That January, rain fell for twelve straight days. The city
dam that diverted water into the Zanja Madre was washed away. The
flood inspired Abel Stearns, a leading local landowner and the richest
man in early Los Angeles, to build a block of buildings in the business
district on stilts, five feet above the level of Los Angeles Street. With its
storefronts higher than the usual level of floodwaters, Arcadia Block,
as the development was named, became the most exclusive block in
the city. Natural forces of a different sort caused the river to flood in
January 1857, when the Fort Tejon earthquake on the San Andreas
Fault, believed to have been more severe than even the catastrophic
1906 San Francisco quake, created fissures in the river's bed and
caused the river to spill over its banks.[33]

In December 1859, rain was again the culprit. During one storm
that winter, a foot of rain fell in Los Angeles in twenty-four hours,
nearly a year's supply, "the most disastrous rain known in the history
of the Southland," according to one witness. Vineyards and orange
groves beside the river washed away. Numerous houses in town were
damaged, and a few collapsed. The destruction of the original pueblo
church, begun with the flood of 1815, was completed. "The front
of the old Church, attacked through a leaking roof, disintegrated,
swayed and finally gave way," recalled a city resident, "filling the
neighboring street with impassable heaps."[34] The deluge came after
four winters of subnormal rainfall had left pastureland surrounding
Los Angeles parched. Cattle and sheep, starving after the prolonged
drought and unsheltered from the cold rain and accompanying wind,
died by the thousands. The river was impassable for months, and the

Los Angeles Common Council, in response, agreed to build the first footbridge over the river thirteen months later.[35]

Flooding in January 1862, called "the Noachian deluge of California floods," may have been the most extensive in the history of the state.[36] Rain had begun to fall in Los Angeles on the previous Christmas Eve and continued almost without interruption for thirty days. The weekly Star remarked on 4 January that "there has been one shower since our last publication, but it lasted all the time. Morning, noon, and night—day in and day out—it has been rain, rain, rain." After one brief break, the paper dead-panned, "On Tuesday last, the sun made its appearance. The phenomenon lasted several minutes and was witnessed by a great number of persons." But the respite was short-lived. The following Saturday, the ground saturated by three weeks of nearly constant rain, another downpour brought the most severe damage yet. "Rivers were formed in every gulch and arroyo," the Star wrote on 25 January. "The Los Angeles River already brimful, overflowed its banks, and became a fierce and destructive force." Elijah Moulton, one of the first persons to settle on the east side of the river when he had bought thirty acres north of the Aliso Street crossing a few years before, lost everything he owned—his house, vineyards, and orange groves. T. J. White watched as five thousand of his vines on the west bank of the river were uprooted and carried downstream. The vineyard of William Wolfskill was also heavily damaged. At least four people drowned.[37]

All told, the city received an estimated fifty inches of rain during the series of storms. The Los Angeles River in flood stretched from Alameda Street to Boyle Heights, splitting in two below present-day Vernon, its overflow again spilling west through Ballona Creek. The coastal plain from the city to the sea was a great lake. Much of Los Angeles was under water. Adobe houses crumbled, and businesses were ruined when their walls caved in. The city dam, rebuilt just months before, was again washed away. There was no mail service for five weeks, prompting a local wag to hang a "To Let" sign on the door of the post office. A U.S. government survey team, camped beside the river before embarking on a trip across the desert to establish the eastern boundary of the new state, was delayed for weeks after floodwaters swept away their tents, saddles, and equipment and killed one of their camels. The normally dry Arroyo Seco, swollen to a raging river, carried great piles of trees from the mountains to the Los Angeles River and then onto the plains. The driftwood that remained when floodwaters subsided supplied firewood to local residents for years.[38]

During the same series of storms, the Santa Ana River broke out of its banks and washed away the town of Agua Mensa, the first nonmission settlement in present-day San Bernardino County. The river, according to a history of the county, "became a raging torrent which, washing, swirling, and seething, swept away everything from its path."[39] Though town residents had received enough warning of the impending flood to evacuate and there were no fatalities, the town was never rebuilt. The devastation could have been a valuable lesson to the inhabitants of Los Angeles. Agua Mensa, too, was an agricultural settlement built beside a river, the bottomlands along its banks covered with productive farms watered from its channel. Los Angeles Judge Benjamin Hayes visited the town site, located about two miles south of the present city of Colton, two weeks after the flood, and his recollections of Agua Mensa before its destruction sound remarkably like many descriptions of early Los Angeles:

> A dreary desolation presented itself to my eye, familiar dwellings overturned, or washed way; here only a chimney, there a mere door-post or a few scattered stakes of a fence, lofty and stout trees torn up, a mass of drifted branches from the mountain cañons, and a universal waste of sand on both banks of the river, where a few months before all was green and beautiful with orchard and vineyard and garden, the live willow fence enclosing every field and giving a grateful shade for the pleasant lanes and roads.[40]

Damage to private property in Los Angeles during the 1862 floods was estimated at $25,000, nearly all of that incurred by five property owners who had built their farms close to the river. But it was the destruction of the city diversion dam that stirred the greatest public outcry and prompted what were probably the first serious calls for the government to protect its citizens from future floods. As had almost become a routine after significant storms, Los Angeles again had to rely on water hauled from the river in jugs and barrels after the dam was destroyed. Irrigation ditches filled with sand during the storms and then promptly dried up, since water was no longer being diverted into the Zanja Madre. Almost as soon as the sun started shining, the *Los Angeles Star* urged the city to build a more substantial dam farther upstream, out of the path of the outflow of the Arroyo Seco. The newspaper also recommended that the channel of the Los Angeles River be straightened and its banks strengthened. "This the property holders interested will surely now do, after the severe lesson taught them," the paper wrote. "Without such permanent improvements . . . no reliance can be placed on a supply of water from the river."[41]

With no experience in such matters and without an engineer in its employ, the city government was slow to react, but in December 1865 the Common Council agreed to pay a local judge, Murray Morrison, himself a former council member, $225 to "erect a sufficient dam to turn the water of the Los Angeles River" at the northern boundary of the White vineyard (about where Mission Street crosses the river today). The ledger book entry for the expenditure says simply, "For expense of altering course of river." Whether this work was done is not clear, but it seems doubtful in light of future developments. A year later, Mayor Cristóbal Aguilar ordered that the city begin "necessary work for the straightening of the Los Angeles River," and in September 1866 the Common Council approved the establishment of a special tax to create a "River Fund" to pay for future flood protection work. It appropriated $500 to pay for initial work, but construction was postponed until the following spring because of concerns that work could not be completed in time for the winter rains.[42]

As it turned out, the work does not appear to have been done for several years, and in January 1868 the Los Angeles River again overflowed its banks. The story was beginning to sound awfully familiar. The city dam, which had been repaired after the flood of 1862 at a cost of $3,000, was the first thing swept away. The debris from the dam then destroyed the footbridge that had been built across the river a few years before. (A more substantial, covered bridge would be built at the foot of Aliso Road two years later.) Floodwaters first broke out where North Broadway now crosses the river, destroying "several acres of choice vines" owned by Louis Willhart. Pouring across the lowlands between Alameda Street and the river, floodwaters then washed over the vineyards of Vincent Hoover and swept away the entire front of the White vineyard, carrying away vines that were as much as twenty years old and coming within a few feet of the family's brick residence. The vineyard, according to the *Los Angeles News*, was "lost forever." Three adobe houses on San Pedro Street were destroyed, and water was a foot deep on Main Street. All roads leading into the city were rendered impassable.[43]

Floods that winter caused the San Gabriel River to cut a new course to the sea. Until that time, the San Gabriel and Los Angeles Rivers had joined north of the present location of Long Beach. From that point south, this waterway was generally known as the San Gabriel River. Surging waters that winter, though, forced the San Gabriel to leave its bed farther upstream, where its channel turned southwest after emerging between two hills south of El Monte, a gap known as the Whittier Narrows. Floodwaters washed away the town of Galatin, settled a few years earlier near the present site of Downey, and dug an entirely new channel south to Alamitos Bay, which straddles the bound-

ary between Los Angeles and Orange Counties. This new channel, initially known as New River, is approximately the course of the San Gabriel River today. Water continued to flow in the river's former channel, which became known as the Rio Hondo. The last seven miles of
the old San Gabriel channel, downstream from its meeting with the
Los Angeles River, meanwhile, gradually assumed the name of that
river.[44]

The inclination for the rivers of Southern California to shift their
courses dramatically in times of flood was, of course, part of an ancient and very natural tradition. The problem was that, as the region
became increasingly populated, such movements became a greater
hazard to humans. The potential danger in Los Angeles was laid out
with remarkable clarity in 1870 by a city surveyor named Frank Lecouvreur in a report that accompanied a detailed topographic survey
of the city. The survey had been ordered to provide data to help in the
grading of the city's streets. Nevertheless, because the topography of
much of the city had been shaped by past floods and the sediments
they carried, Lecouvreur's report also included considerable information about the river. It made quite clear that Los Angeles was in a
most precarious position. Lecouvreur's report, in fact, may have been
what finally provoked the Common Council to build its first flood
control works along the river.

The existing west bank of the river, Lecouvreur said, was a "feeble
barrier" to keeping the river on its present course. It was about thirty
feet high where the river left the Glendale Narrows but quickly diminished in size and, about Ninth Street, "it loses its identity" altogether.
From that point south, the only thing that prevented the river from
wandering still farther west were the tablelands that began just east of
Main Street and turned slowly southwest. All of the wedge-shaped
area between the Elysian Hills, the tablelands, and the river he called
"river bottom." His surveys found, moreover, that Alameda Street was
in places actually lower than the existing riverbed. The ground surface
between Alameda and the river, he added, was "dead level, excepting a
low rise or swelling of the ground, somewhat nearer the river than the
street."[45] This low rise was all that kept the river from returning to the
course it had occupied from 1815 to 1825 and submerging year-round
the agricultural lands east of the plaza. Such a shift would also have
threatened the city's first railroad station, built at the corner of
Alameda and Commercial Streets the year before, and the growing industrial district that was developing around it.

The past behavior of the river certainly suggested that such a shift
was possible. Future floods would, too. Floodwaters so consistently
poured southwest instead of south after leaving the gap that formed

the river's outlet from the Glendale Narrows that, during a flood in the 1880s, a local newspaper remarked that Alameda Street was "as usual" a river.[46] The location of the Zanja Madre, dug from the river along the bluff at the head of the floodplain, only encouraged this. The channel the river occupied until 1825, Lecouvreur said, had gradually filled with sediments until, in the flood of that year, "the river completely damned up its old bed," forcing it to open a new channel farther east. "In this channel now the same process is repeating itself, and a slow but steady filling in of the river wash takes place." This could be witnessed on a smaller scale, even during the dry season, in the river's wide bed near downtown, where the river's waters, laden with sediments, were carried by numerous intertwining, ever-shifting, small channels, meandering back and forth across its sandy bed. "The velocity of the water is more than sufficient to keep the fine and light particles of sand on which it flows in constant motion, lifting them up in one place and depositing them in another," wrote Lecouvreur. "This tendency of the river to fill up old channels and open new ones, being a mere playful and harmless one at the usually low state of the water during the dry season, becomes threatening and dangerous when, swollen by storm waters, the same action takes place on a scale proportionate to the increased volume of water."[47]

Soon after Lecouvreur had issued his report, new appeals were made for the city to do something to keep the river in its existing channel. In September 1870, J. J. Warner, an early Los Angeles newspaper editor and one of the founders of the Canal and Reservoir Company, recommended that a "breakwater, or some effective protection" be built "without delay." Three months later, fifteen property owners along the river petitioned the Common Council to "take immediate steps . . . to avert the threatened danger."[48] Finally, in 1872, the council's Committee on River Improvement reported that the long-contemplated work had been completed. It did not amount to much, however. In all, $386.75 had been spent, $356 for tools and the rest for labor. The exact nature of the work was not specified, but the fact that no money was spent on materials suggests workers simply used shovels to build up the riverbank. Even the members of the committee, in their report to the council, hinted that they were not entirely satisfied with the results, saying that they had made "all the improvements that could be made for the amount of funds that were placed at their disposal." Others were far more critical. The Finance Committee of the Common Council said in 1873 that "the money was spent to no purpose and entirely thrown away."[49] Future floods would prove that the work was grossly inadequate.

The Impact of Development

Until the boom of the 1880s led to rapid subdivision of the agricultural lands and increased urban development throughout Southern California, floods were often seen as beneficial, despite the damage caused by a few major storms. Floodwaters deposited a fresh layer of silt on agricultural lands, enriching the soil. They also restored moisture to parched ground and washed away salts that had accumulated as a result of irrigation. "A flood might be a temporary evil," remarked early historian J. M. Guinn, "but like the overflow of the Nile, a year of plenty always followed." Most of the floods on the coastal plain, moreover, did little damage because rivers and streams, their banks low, usually overflowed before water levels rose significantly or flood flows had the opportunity to intensify. Flood depths outside main stream channels, consequently, were rarely greater than a foot, and the velocity of floodwaters was usually minimal. "In those days, the water would spread all over the country," recalled one early resident in 1914. "It did no damage, and in many ways did good. It was not necessary to fertilize the land, as they are now doing."[50]

There was also less potential for damage from floods before the arrival of the railroads because most of the lands near the river were still devoted to agriculture and few structures had been built on the most flood-prone lands. Maps show that, as late as 1876, nearly all of the land between Main Street and the river and from the river to the Boyle Heights bluffs, was still devoted to farming. Homeowners, for the most part, knew enough not to build in the areas that were regularly inundated. The earliest residential subdivisions in Los Angeles were laid out on the benchlands that stretched beyond Main Street and on the terraces east of the river.[51] This helps explain why, after the flood of 1862, which anecdotal evidence suggests may have been the most extensive in the history of Southern California, the *Los Angeles Star* of 25 January commented that "the losses . . . on the whole . . . have been quite insignificant."

Like so much else in Southern California, the risk from floods changed dramatically after the Southern Pacific Railroad extended its line from San Francisco to Los Angeles in 1876 and a second cross-country line was built to the city a decade later. Newcomers descended upon Los Angeles, and the changes they made increased the flood threat. Urban development intensified beside the river, not only in Los Angeles but all along its length. Both Burbank and Glendale were founded near the river in the San Fernando Valley during the boom. Compton was established a mile west of the river as a station stop for the Los Angeles and San Pedro Railroad but grew more rapidly after the Southern Pacific took over the line. Long Beach was founded east of the river's mouth in 1888 and by 1900 was the fourth largest city in the county. Efforts to create a deepwater port at San Pedro Bay grew in response to the greater trade the new population brought. Agricultural development, meanwhile, increased in the open country between the cities and towns.

The newcomers heightened the flood hazard by building homes and businesses not only on the floodplain, but sometimes directly in former channels of the rivers and streams. Willows and cottonwoods that had lined the river and anchored its banks were cut for fuel or to build fences. Scattered trees and shrubs that kept the soil in place and slowed the flow of water across the lowlands in time of flood were cleared to enable cultivation and to improve grazing. Plowing by farmers also removed the soil's natural grass cover, causing runoff to increase and heightening erosion, while irrigation canals dug directly from stream channels weakened riverbanks. Individual property owners built levees in an attempt to keep streams from overflowing, but these were often inadequate and only increased the threat elsewhere.[52] "Each man builds his levees as strong as he can and hopes and prays that his neighbor's levees will break," remarked one engineer at an early meeting about flood control. In downtown Los Angeles, the removal of sand and gravel from the bed of the Los Angeles River by construction crews lowered the riverbed by twenty feet. This forced runoff into a more narrow channel, which increased the velocity of flood flows and, therefore, their destructive power.[53]

But nothing exacerbated the flood danger more than the railroads. The most serious problem caused by the three national rail lines built across Los Angeles County during the last three decades of the nineteenth century was their use of trestle bridges, which often obstructed the free flow of water in the rivers and streams. Such bridges were typically built upon wood piles driven at close intervals into riverbeds (fig. 4.6). The bridge supports were so close together that they frequently acted as dams during heavy storms, when rain-swollen streams carried large quantities of trees, brush, and other debris. If enough material accumulated behind the trestles, water was forced out of stream channels and over nearby lands. Sometimes, when the pressure upon the trestles became great enough, the bridges themselves gave way, unleashing a torrent of water and debris that endangered bridges, buildings, and human lives downstream.

Even railroad bridges that did not rely on trestles for support often impeded the free flow of storm waters. The Los Angeles and San Gabriel Valley Railroad bridge over the Los Angeles River, for example, was built so low to the ground that it would seem to have been designed by someone who had seen the river only in summer. It was clearly destined to fail. Railroads further heightened the flood danger by building their tracks across floodplains, thus confining flood-waters that would have formerly spread unimpeded over a wide area. Such tracks were often built on artificial embankments several feet high (fig. 4.7). Where natural stream banks were low, these embankments, in effect, became set-back levees and, by forcing floodwaters into an area smaller than the river's natural floodplain, increased the depth, speed, and cutting power of flood flows. The purpose of levees built for flood protection is to keep water away from development, but these embankments sometimes enclosed already settled areas.[54]

The changes that occurred after the arrival of the Southern Pacific were greatest in Los Angeles. After 1876, urban development began to seriously encroach upon the floodplain. The first significant subdivision of agricultural lands had begun a few years earlier, when the Los Angeles and San Pedro Railroad had built its depot at the corner of Commercial and Alameda Streets. This had spurred a small property boom in the area. Businesses had begun to spring up along Commercial Street, and the Aliso Homestead Association had started to sell

FIG. 4.6. Trestle railroad bridges, like this Los Angeles and San Gabriel Valley Railroad bridge built over the Arroyo Seco, often acted as dams during heavy storms, when stream-carried debris backed up behind bridge supports. Used with permission, The Huntington Library, San Marino, California.

FIG. 4.7. Railroad embankments, such as this one built across the river floodplain south of Los Angeles, confined floodwaters into a smaller area, which increased the intensity of flood flows and heightened their destructive power. Used with permission, Department of Special Collections, University of Southern California Library/Hearst Newspaper Collection.

home lots in the vicinity. Development intensified in the area when the Southern Pacific took over the Los Angeles and San Pedro and continued to use its depot. Warehouses and factories were constructed near the depot, and the area immediately surrounding the incipient industrial complex was subdivided for residences to provide homes for workers. Within a few years, much of the area between Macy and First Streets, from Alameda Street to the river, was occupied by small homes (fig. 4.8). By 1884, residential development had also begun to spread south of First Street, along Alameda, and between Main and San Pedro Streets sporadically all the way to the city's southern limits. Farther north, homes began to be built on the west side of the river near the Southern Pacific's freight yards, northeast of present-day Chinatown. Urban development also spread east of the river. Boyle Heights was subdivided in 1876 and became a streetcar suburb of Los Angeles after a horsecar line was built across the river at Aliso Street. East Los Angeles (now Lincoln Heights) was developed at the same time.[55]

As Los Angeles filled up with homes, few paid much attention to the river that flowed gingerly through the center of the city. One who did was J. J. Warner, the same man who in 1870 had urged city officials to strengthen the west bank of the river to prevent its overflow. As development moved closer to the river, he warned in a series of letters published in the *Los Angeles Times* in 1882 "of the risk to which many . . . are exposing themselves, their property and their families in the selection of places upon which to build their dwellings." Warner had arrived in Southern California in 1831 at the age of twenty-eight and had heard many firsthand accounts of the floods of 1815 and 1825 that had so altered the course of the river. He had himself witnessed the great floods of 1832, 1859, 1862, and 1868. "There are many now living in Los Angeles," he wrote, "who do not know the magnitude of the volume of water which flows through this city when the river is flooded." He castigated the "reckless and crafty" real estate agents who had sold property in the low-lying areas between Alameda Street and the river and cautioned that "the many obstructions" that had been placed in the river channel (the nature of which he did not specify) increased the likelihood of an overflow. If a flood of the magnitude of previous great floods occurred again, he said, "such a flood would destroy a large part of the property situated in that part of the city."[56]

Such warnings did little to deter newcomers from buying lots in the Aliso, Johnston, Sanchez, and Alanis Vineyard Tracts—all south of Aliso Street and east of Alameda Street—some of whom scoffed at the idea that the harmless-looking river could possibly be a threat. The case of Alfred Moore is especially telling. Moore had arrived in Los Angeles in 1876, the same year as the Southern Pacific, and had bought a large lot on Lazard Street in the Aliso Tract, where he had built a house. An auctioneer by trade, Moore kept a few horses on his land and raised some chickens.[57] As he became more established, he bought several other lots in the neighborhood. Some he sold, but he built small homes on others and began renting them out. After Warner's letters were published, Moore responded with a letter of his own, thumbing his nose at the danger. "We need not, I think, feel at all alarmed about a flood," he said. "I have lived on the Aliso Tract, the most central part, for the past eight years and never saw a flood yet." He boasted that he had recently sold six lots "within a few feet of the river" to a woman who was "plucky enough" to disregard the warnings of her soon-to-be neighbors about the possibility of an overflow. "I am selling bottom land lots, so-called, rapidly ever since," he wrote.[58]

FIG. 4.8. This photograph, taken from a balloon in June 1887 and looking east across the Los Angeles River, shows that urban development had encroached on the west side of the river from Macy Street south to First Street. The plaza is the circular feature in the *left center*. Alameda Street roughly parallels the course of the river a mile west of its banks, running just east of (*above*) the plaza. The northernmost crossing on the river in the photo is Mission Street (*far left*). Moving south, the other crossings are at Macy Street, Aliso Street, and First Street. Used with permission, Seaver Center for Western History Research, Natural History Museum of Los Angeles County.

The arrogance of Alfred Moore is emblematic of the attitudes of many then and many more since, who have ignored dire predictions of floods, fires, landslides, and earthquakes and have built their homes in places that were ill-suited for them, later demanding that the government bail them out and protect them from future disasters. Although the storms Warner said would happen again, of course, did reoccur, floods were still seen as an exception in a place where the sun shone nearly all the time, flowers bloomed year-round, and the worst cold was jacket weather. What people saw when they looked out their windows—mountains, beaches, palm trees—only cemented their resolve to stay where they were. The occasional flood or other disaster might scare off a few. Some in the more flood-prone areas would sell their land, perhaps to the railroads so they could build depots and freight yards or to industrialists for whom a foot of water was less a cause for alarm. Others would move to higher ground and rent their properties to people who could not afford to be so choosy. A few might even move back to Iowa or Indiana, perhaps deciding that paradise had too high a price. But they were clearly in the minority. Most probably laughed at the stream that ran through their city when they thought of the *real* rivers back home. A little stream like that, they assured themselves, could certainly be controlled.

Boom Years Are Flood Years

Contributing to the false sense of security of many of the newcomers was the fact that the late 1870s and early 1880s were relatively dry years in Los Angeles. Rainfall was below normal in five of seven winters, and from July 1879 to June 1883 precipitation averaged 30 percent below the mean. The winter of 1883–84 broke the spell, however, and the next seven winters still constitute one of the wettest stretches on record in Southern California. Abundant rainfall does not necessarily mean floods, if the storms are spread out and lack intensity, but the boom years were also one of the most flood-plagued periods in the region's history. As newcomers poured into Los Angeles, the city experienced six heavy floods, four moderate floods, and one light flood in seven years. The Los Angeles River overflowed five times, altering its course with each new storm and eventually breaking through its banks near Vernon, where it created an entirely new course two miles east of its former route.[59]

The first heavy floods came in 1884, when three major storms in two months led to flooding that destroyed forty-three homes, severed railroad and telegraph lines, and washed away all bridges over the river except one.[60] Floodwaters stretched from downtown to Boyle Heights, with the river overflow again reaching Ballona Creek and its former outlet at Santa Monica Bay. Water was two feet deep on Main Street, and houses on Alameda Street were flooded to a depth of six feet. The cities of Compton, Downey, and Clearwater (now Paramount) and the San Fernando Valley from present-day Chatsworth to Glendale were also under water. Floodwaters mixed with ocean currents near the river's mouth, causing tides more than a mile inland.

Estimates of damages from the floods ranged from about $150,000 to $1 million ($2.4 to $16.3 million in current figures). Rain fell in every month that year, with Los Angeles receiving more than thirty-eight inches in all. Climatologists now blame the above-normal precipitation on a cyclical phenomenon known as El Niño, which is caused by periodic changes in the direction of trade winds that result in the warming of sea temperatures in the Pacific Ocean. El Niño can spur unusual weather patterns worldwide.[61]

The Los Angeles River in flood washed barns, houses, household belongings, railroad cars, livestock, and even caskets downstream. Forty-three homes in Los Angeles were destroyed in 1884. Several people drowned. Forty-one horses were washed into the river when a stable near First Street was inundated. A winery at Ninth and Alameda Streets was also washed away. The power of flood flows was so great that, according to legend, a ten-gallon keg of brandy washed from the winery was found six years later buried in the soil several miles downstream by a farmer plowing his fields. The keg was reportedly still filled with brandy.[62] Years later, Boyle Workman, a prominent Los Angeles banker and one-time city council president, remembered watching the floods as a boy from the back porch of his family's Boyle Heights home. "Day after day it rained in great sheets," he wrote in his memoirs. "The river became a boiling yellow lake. Houses, torn from their foundations, floated downstream with the smoke still escaping from their chimneys. Horses, cows, sheep, and now and then the ghastly form of a human being, were part of the strange driftwood. Sometimes the water came in waves fifteen feet in height."[63]

The first storm began about 1:00 A.M. on 26 January 1884, and on 6 February the Evening Express reported that the city had received ten straight days of rain. Rail connections between Los Angeles and Santa Ana were cut off. The San Gabriel River overflowed its banks and inundated the town of Downey. A second storm began on 13 February. Two days later, the paper said that "Alameda Street is a veritable river."[64] The next morning, the steady showers turned into a downpour. About noon, as debris backed up behind the bridges, the supports to a bridge at Aliso Street gave way and the bridge began to break up. A large section became lodged in the channel of the river, causing water to back up behind it and flow westward into the city. By 4:00 P.M., most of the residential neighborhood south of Macy Street and east of Alameda Street, the same area about which J. J. Warner had issued his warnings, was under water. A laundry on Weill Street was the first building to go, washing out into the center of the river and downstream. Three small homes that had stood nearby went soon after. Eventually, thirty-five houses in the Aliso Tract alone were washed away. "House after house was gradually loosened from its foundation, and in many cases the occupants had barely time to get out before the building was afloat," the *Los Angeles Times* reported in an extra edition published on 18 February 1884. "The river rose all night and created a scene of destruction, at points close to its banks, which can hardly be pictured. Numbers of families lost everything they had. The destruction is immense."

Among the hardest hit was Alfred Moore, who had so cavalierly dismissed Warner's warnings two years before. Moore's home on Lazard Street was washed downstream with all its contents still inside. His son and brother-in-law living next door also lost everything, and a rental property Moore owned on Turner Street was destroyed. Two horses and several chickens he kept on his property were killed. Nearly as ironic was the case of J. P. Widney, a surgeon and local civic leader who had witnessed the flood of 1868 and in 1876 had co-written with Warner the first history of Los Angeles. Widney lost the most expensive house in the area, built fifteen months before at the foot of Sainsevain Street at a cost of $2,000. Moore and Widney were hardly alone in their suffering, however. Joseph Mozet and his wife, for example, lost three houses they owned on Center Street. Another woman lost three new houses built, according to the *Times*, "right in the bed of the river."

Many of the victims were newcomers. Several French families living on Sainsevain Street were left homeless. A German who had recently relocated from New Mexico lost his house and most of his possessions. One of the dead was a twenty-eight-year-old milkman named George Stoltz, who had moved to Los Angeles just three weeks before. He drowned when he tried to cross the river near the Arroyo Seco in a wagon drawn by two horses. "The swift current was too much for the strength of the animals and in a short time the wagon was overturned and Stoltz then began a fierce struggle for his life," the *Times* said. "He was borne for a distance of nearly half a mile, still holding on the bridle reins of the animals, when, to the horror of the excited spectators who had lined the banks, he was seen to throw up his hands and sink beneath the waters. Nothing more was seen of the unfortunate man, and he is doubtless many miles from the spot where he came to his unfortunate end."

The levees built by the city in 1872, if they had been able to withstand the normal rains of the previous dozen years (and even that is not clear), were certainly no match for the floods of 1884. No mention of the work was made in news accounts of the floods and, within days of the first overflows, people began to demand more substantial levees. After the second overflow in mid-February, the Los Angeles City

Council erected a wing dam made of sandbags on the west side of the river, just downstream from the covered bridge at Macy Street, to protect the already devastated area west of the river. New storms a few days later, though, washed away the sandbags. The council then created a committee to study alternatives for preventing future floods and ordered a survey to delineate an "official" three-hundred-foot-wide channel for the river. Many in the hardest hit area seemed certain to abandon their properties until the city agreed to erect a more sizable levee on the west side of the channel. The council allocated $10,000 for the work, and the new levee was completed in the summer of 1885. The Los Angeles and San Gabriel Valley Railroad, which built a line to Pasadena on the west side of the river that year (it was taken over by the Atchison, Topeka, & Santa Fe in 1886), increased the protections by lining the front of the levee in places with rocks, trees, and sand. Convinced that the new work provided adequate safety, many property owners west of the river, including Alfred Moore, decided to rebuild their homes. One-half mile of levees were also constructed on the east side of the river.[65]

But the new levees proved no more capable at protecting the city than had earlier efforts. A storm in January 1886 caused the Los Angeles River to rise two feet higher than it had in 1884, and the new municipal levees were, in the words of the Los Angeles Times of 21 January, "washed away like so many playthings." Although flooding was not as severe or prolonged as it had been two years before, fifty families were nevertheless driven from their homes when the same neighborhoods so heavily damaged in that flood were inundated again. At least four people were killed, including an old Scotsman who had been living for more than a year in a tent in the riverbed and, according to the Times, "died from fright." Los Angeles was completely isolated for seven days, as telegraph, telephone, and railroad lines were washed out. Seven bridges over the river were destroyed. Published estimates of the damages ranged from $58,000 to $250,000 ($988,000 to $4.3 million in current figures).[66]

The sequence of events in the flood demonstrated the effect of railroad development on flood risk. As the waters in the river rose, driftwood and other debris began to back up behind the Southern Pacific Railroad bridge, the northernmost bridge on the river, located just upstream from the Arroyo Seco. Just before dawn on 19 January 1886, the build-up of debris behind the bridge became so substantial that the river began to wash over the top of the tracks, and about 6:00 A.M. the bridge gave way, its wooden supports adding to the great load of material already carried by the river. This started a chain of events that caused the river to overflow. The swirling water and wood rushed toward the new bridge of the Los Angeles and San Gabriel Valley Railroad, built a few months earlier. Both approaches to the bridge were swept into the river, adding still more timbers to its load. The debris-laden river then washed out the approaches to the Downey Avenue (now North Broadway) bridge, causing a horse-drawn streetcar to fall into the river. The driver and a passenger inside had to be rescued by a sheriff's deputy, who rode his horse into the raging waters. Soon after, the depot of the Los Angeles and San Gabriel Valley Railroad, built just north of the Downey Avenue bridge on the west bank, toppled into the river. It floated downstream until it rammed into the Downey Avenue bridge, knocking out one hundred feet of its length (fig. 4.9). With the depot and the horse car lodged in the river channel, the river began to overflow.

FIG. 4.9. Remains of the Downey Avenue bridge, partially destroyed during the flood of 1886. It was in this area that the Los Angeles River first broke out of its channel and inundated the lowlands west of the river. Its normal path was partially blocked by a horse-drawn streetcar and a railroad depot that had toppled into its channel. Used with permission, Department of Special Collections, University of Southern California Library/Title Insurance & Trust Company Collection (USC 1-1-1-31).

Floodwaters poured south and broadened as they spread across the lowlands, stretching two-thirds of a mile wide by the time they reached Seventh Street. Once again, the greatest damage was experienced between Aliso and First Streets adjacent to the river, an area that, according to the *Los Angeles Times* of 20 January, "was occupied mainly by small frame houses which had sprung up since the flood of 1884." Most of the residents were able to evacuate, but at least two people in the area were killed. One was a young child who drowned during a rescue attempt by a sheriff's deputy (the same man who had saved the two passengers stranded in the horse car) after the deputy fell from his horse. The other was a woman who lived at the corner of Center and First Streets in the Aliso Tract, a block from the river. Trying to escape her house, she immediately found herself waist deep in water and had to hang on to a small tree to keep from being pulled under by the current. She was about to be rescued by a mounted police officer, when, the *Times* wrote, "a small house came floating down and struck the unfortunate woman. She was knocked over, and was seen no more."

As before, numerous homes were swept away. Alfred Moore, who had rebuilt after losing three houses in the flood of 1884, lost five houses this time and estimated his losses at $3,000. Two of his houses were washed completely downstream. The other three were knocked from their foundations and seriously damaged. All that was left where his home had once stood was a steam laundry deposited there by floodwaters. The same man who had, four years earlier, dismissed warnings about the river now demanded that the city take immediate action to control it. "He was emphatic in his declaration," the *Times* said, "that the city ought to build a substantial bulkhead along the riverfront, first widening the official channel to 600 feet." The lesson of two disastrous floods in three winters was not lost on others, either. "This last flood is another warning to the people of Los Angeles," the *Times* wrote. "The river, though a small stream ninety-nine hundredths of the time is still capable of foaming freaks when maddened by the Storm God's lashings. It is a treacherous stream and cannot be trusted. It needs to be restrained within its banks. It pays no attention to the 'official' riverbed, but breaks out just where it pleases, each time doing damage which, aggregated, would soon pay the cost of necessary levees to keep it within its bounds."[67]

Unable to protect its citizens from floods, the city responded the same as it had two decades before, when the establishment of a domestic water system had proven so difficult—it sought assistance from private parties. In December 1886, the Los Angeles City Council agreed to give the Atchison, Topeka, & Santa Fe Railroad, through its subsidiary the Southern California Railway, a fifty-foot right of way on the west bank of the river on the condition that it build and maintain a levee from Mission Street south to First Street. The city also agreed to pay the railroad $12,000 for its work. As it turned out, the Santa Fe did even more than was required. It erected a levee from Downey Avenue (now North Broadway) all the way to the city's southern boundary, a distance of 3.7 miles, protecting its front with piling and wood planks. The levee was completed in March 1888. Realizing that a levee on only one side of the river would mean certain flooding on the opposite side of its channel, the city itself built one mile of new levees on the east side of the river at a cost of $31,389.[68]

The new railroad- and city-constructed levees were almost immediately put to a test. Los Angeles was hit by four major storms in 1889, one in the spring and three in the weeks before Christmas. As the rainy season began in December, City Engineer Fred Eaton reported that storms the previous winter had left the Santa Fe levee in "dangerous condition at many points north of First Street."[69] Rainfall was greatest between 21 December and 27 December; on Christmas night the Los Angeles River rose at a rate of eighteen inches an hour. "Eastern thurists [sic]," remarked the *Evening Express* on 26 December, "are complaining." Once again, storm-induced damage to the railroad bridges precipitated destruction and contributed to flooding farther downstream. Half of the Santa Fe bridge was washed out, and the debris from it weakened the piers and badly damaged the Buena Vista (now North Broadway) Street bridge, just downstream. Swelled by ever-increasing debris from the bridges, the river then washed away the approaches to a bridge at Kuhrts Street (now North Main Street). The Southern Pacific bridge at Mission Road was also carried off. By this time, the river was a swirling mess of timbers, rocks, sand, and other debris, and its current cut away at the new levees. The wooden bulkhead built by the Santa Fe to protect its levee was broken in places, and fifteen hundred feet of the city-built levee on the east side of the river was washed away. Where the levees were destroyed, water spread over the low-lying areas, damaging houses and streets. "The scene along the river," commented the *Evening Express*, "was a melancholy one." This latest flood finally persuaded some riverfront residents, including Alfred Moore, to move to higher ground. A few years later, Moore was living on Workman Street in the new suburbs of East Los Angeles (now Lincoln Heights), well above the floodplain on the east side of the river.[70]

Still, news reports suggest that the damage incurred at Los Angeles was not as severe as in the previous two floods. The new levees, although undermined in places, still prevented flooding in large parts of the city. Other areas were not so fortunate; in fact, the city's levees heightened the flooding elsewhere. The floods came as Southern California was experiencing the most intense growth in its history. The population of Los Angeles County tripled between 1880 and 1890, with much of that increase coming in 1887, after completion of the Santa Fe line to Los Angeles instigated a fare war that reduced the cost of a one-way ticket from Chicago to Los Angeles to pocket change. The total assessed value of property in the county rose from $40 million in 1886 to $102 million in 1888.[71] During the two years before the floods, the cities of Burbank, Compton, and Long Beach had been founded. The number of farms in Los Angeles County, meanwhile, more than doubled during the boom decade.

Because so much of the settlement was new, few outside Los Angeles were prepared for the great quantity of water that the river carried during the storms. Only sporadic levees had been constructed south of the city. The Santa Fe levee, meanwhile, ended abruptly at the city limits. The city-constructed levee did not extend even that far. Thus, when the river emerged from the partially confined channel south of Los Angeles, it again widened, which caused its velocity to diminish and its ability to carry debris and sediment to decline. As a result, the river dropped much of the sediment it carried. Sand slowly built up in the riverbed until, during the flood, its channel was blocked entirely, causing the river to break through its banks two miles south of the city. The river swerved sharply southeast, digging a new channel as much as a quarter of a mile wide and twelve feet deep. One man in the Fruitland section south of Los Angeles lost fifty acres of grapevines, walnut trees, and fruit trees when the rampaging river left his farm a wash of sand and debris. The shift dramatically altered the future course of the river. From then on it flowed southeast instead of south after leaving the city of Los Angeles, before turning more directly south near the present city of Maywood, its channel meeting with the Rio Hondo four miles farther upstream.[72]

Near Downey, the river overflow joined with floodwaters from the San Gabriel River and the Rio Hondo to form a waterway five miles wide that swept away everything in its path, emptying into the sea through both Alamitos Bay and San Pedro Bay. "The country between the city and the sea is in places covered with water," the *Evening Express* reported on 26 December 1889. "Many ranchers will lose heavily." Residents around Compton and Downey were forced to use boats to obtain food and supplies.[73] Farther downstream, the infant city of Long Beach was completely surrounded by water. All communication with the outside world was cut off, and many of its new homes were inundated. "A dismal wail comes up from Long Beach," wrote the *Eve-*

ning Express on 27 December. County officials later estimated that the peak flood discharge of the Los Angeles River during the 1889 floods, based on observations of stream velocity, was between 38,000 and 54,000 cubic feet per second—more than five hundred times its normal dry season flow.[74] Damages from the floods were estimated by one newspaper at $398,700 ($6.9 million in current figures).[75]

Soon after the floods, the Los Angeles County Board of Supervisors commissioned a group of engineers to make recommendations for curbing the flood risk throughout the county. The Santa Fe Railroad, meanwhile, spent $15,000 to repair and strengthen the levee on the west bank of the river through the city of Los Angeles. Railroads also improved the levees on the east side of the river. In 1891, the Los Angeles Terminal Railroad, a subsidiary of the Union Pacific, built a line from the city to San Pedro to compete with the Southern Pacific for harbor traffic and built its tracks through Los Angeles on the east side of the river. It spent $93,000 to construct a levee from near the Arroyo Seco to the city's southern boundary. A photograph taken a year after the levee was completed shows that the railroad built a wooden bulwark in front of the levee to increase its strength along at least part of its length (fig. 4.10). In 1903, the successor to the Terminal Railroad, known as the San Pedro, Los Angeles and Salt Lake Railroad, agreed to build a levee protected by rock riprap north of the existing levee on the east side of the river. The city gave the Salt Lake a triangular plot of land beside the river, north of Mission Road, as payment for its work. The railroad built its station and freight yard there. To reduce obstructions to the free flow of the river, meanwhile, the Los Angeles City Council began regularly to use chain gangs from the city jail to remove trees and brush from the bed of the river.[76]

As is so typical of the climate of Southern California, the wet years of the 1880s were followed by an extended dry spell. Seasonal rainfall was below normal eight out of the next ten winters. Although poorly drained streets regularly flooded during cloudbursts and high water on the river occasionally knocked out bridges or overflowed agricultural lands, no major floods were recorded in Los Angeles County for the next twenty-one years.[77] Persuaded that the string of floods during the boom years might have been a fluke, the county put off plans to initiate any large-scale flood control program of its own. The proposals of the engineers it hired after the 1889 flood were set aside. Money was diverted to more pressing needs, like the building of highways to connect the rapidly expanding metropolitan area. While the rains slowed, the migration to Southern California most definitely did not. Few of the new arrivals recognized the flood risk any more than their predecessors had during the Boom of the Eighties. Even if they heard

FIG. 4.10. Wooden bulwark built in 1891 by the Los Angeles Terminal Railroad to protect the levee on the east side of the river. Employees of the Southern California Packing Company, which occupied land to the east of the levee, stand atop the train. The banner on the first boxcar reads: "This entire train loaded with canned fruit." Used with permission, The Huntington Library, San Marino, California.

stories, the appearance of the river—drained by drought and diversions of its flow—made it easy for them to ignore what they heard. As demand for land grew, building intensified beside the river, not only near downtown, where the riverfront lands became the center of the city's first industrial district, but all along its course.

Over the next two decades, the population of Los Angeles County increased fivefold to more than 500,000 and the city of Los Angeles grew from what was still basically a small city into the sixteenth most populous municipality in the United States. Other cities in Southern California grew even faster than Los Angeles. Henry Huntington, nephew of Southern Pacific magnate Colis P. Huntington, built the first line of his Pacific Electric commuter railroad from Los Angeles to Long Beach in 1902. The line became an immediate success and helped Long Beach grow from a small town with about 2,000 residents to the third largest city in the county by the end of the decade, with a population of nearly 18,000. Numerous other towns also developed along the line, including Vernon, which would become the most important industrial city in Southern California, and Huntington Park. Indicative of the amnesia Angelenos had about their river was the fact that parts of both Vernon and Huntington Park were platted directly in the former channel of the river, as it had existed until the flood of 1889 (fig. 4.11). Within a few years, a General Petroleum Corporation plant was built right in the old bed of the river, just south of the point where its channel had shifted sharply east in 1889.[78] Near Elysian Park, meanwhile, some 250 "Mexican" families were by 1913 living in shacks "mostly in the river bottom," according to a prominent local attorney and Progressive politician.[79]

Much of the San Fernando Valley, meanwhile, was cut up into small farms and even smaller residential-sized lots in anticipation of all the

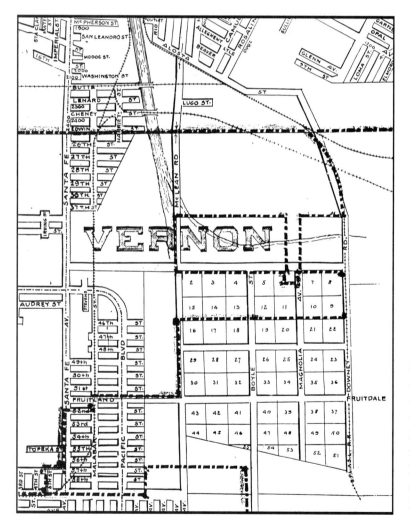

FIG. 4.11. Early twentieth-century map shows industry-sized lots platted in the former channel of the Los Angeles River in Vernon. Note the riverbed running under McLean Road in the center. Excerpted from Félix Violé, "Map of Los Angeles and Surroundings," 1916.

water the Los Angeles–Owens River Aqueduct would bring. The Pacific Electric extended its tracks to Glendale in 1904. A year later the town got its first newspaper, and by 1910 it had a population of 2,742. Perhaps 10,000 people lived in the surrounding area, including the town of Burbank, which had a population of about 500. The Pacific Electric extended its tracks to Burbank in 1911, and that city began to grow steadily as a result. The same year, the railroad built a new line through Cahuenga Pass to the San Fernando Valley to serve the new residential subdivisions that would become North Hollywood, Van Nuys, and Canoga Park.[80] Amid all this new development, however, almost no attention seems to have been paid to the possibility that the river could overflow. That quickly changed, however, in 1914.

The Flood of February 1914

The winter of 1913–14 was an El Niño season, as the flood year of 1884 had been. Had the relationship between the periodic warming of ocean currents and weather patterns been more widely recognized at the time, floods in Texas, which left 177 people dead in December 1913, might have been considered a preview of coming attractions.[81] In Los Angeles, rain fell heavily in November and throughout January. Shortly after midnight on 18 February 1914, the ground already saturated from a month of regular showers, rain again began to fall. This time it did not stop for three days. Even as the rain came down, however, some in Los Angeles remained in denial about the potential for the river to overflow. The first day of the storm, officials of the city water department said that "there is positively no danger of a flood."[82]

By the time the storm ended, however, some locations in the San Gabriel Mountains had received more than nineteen inches of precipitation, and every major river and stream in Los Angeles County had overflowed. The city of Los Angeles got just over seven inches of rain, including an inch and a half in a single hour. Floodwaters from Tujunga Wash, Pacoima Creek, and Verdugo Creek spread over much of the San Fernando Valley. The peak discharge of the Los Angeles River was 31,400 cubic feet per second, equal to the normal flow of the mighty Colorado River and far more than its small channel could contain. Long Beach again became an island. Nearly twelve thousand acres in Los Angeles County were flooded (fig. 4.12). Given all the new development since the great floods of the 1880s, it is hardly surprising that the flood of 1914, while not the most intense in terms of rainfall or the land area inundated, was the most damaging in history. Miraculously, no humans were killed.[83]

Nearly all the flooding occurred outside the city of Los Angeles. Railroad-constructed levees on both sides of the river from the Arroyo

Seco south to the city limits for the most part kept the Los Angeles River in its channel, though the levees themselves were seriously damaged, numerous bridges were washed out, and some property losses occurred near the river. A pigeon farm across from Elysian Park was swept into the raging waters, and many of the estimated 500,000 birds housed there were killed. The river also threatened the Los Angeles city gas supply, and the cutting away of levees near several giant gas tanks that had been built west of its channel gave hint of the potential for even greater disaster. Elsewhere, damages were more severe. An entire street of houses along the Arroyo Seco toppled into that stream when its banks gave way. South of Los Angeles, the Los Angeles River overflowed its banks and inundated large areas between the city and the sea (fig. 4.13). East of Watts, according to news accounts, "the river became a great lake, encompassing in its broad expanse hundreds of ranches."[84]

Shifts in the river's channel again wreaked havoc. Relatively minor changes nevertheless left bridges high and dry near Vernon. East of Compton, a sheet of water a mile across covered the area; when floodwaters finally receded, the main channel of the river had moved a mile west. Long Beach was the hardest hit. Hundreds of houses there were inundated. All railroads, highways, and telephone lines into the city were washed out. Even as the storm toll mounted, however, some remained ignorant that such a flood certainly had historical precedence and continued to judge the river by its dry season appearance. "The flood was wholly unexpected," the Los Angeles Times wrote. "Even those most familiar with the rainfall and topography of the country never had reason to think that so destructive a torrent could come rolling down from the hills and through the gully that has been lightly termed the 'Los Angeles River.'"[85]

The public and private infrastructure of the county suffered the greatest financial losses. Floodwaters from the river dumped four million cubic yards of silt into Los Angeles and Long Beach Harbors, which had been transformed into one of the busiest port complexes on the Pacific Coast after the arrival of the railroads. The silt significantly raised the bottom of channels in the harbor area, stranding ships and rendering some channels unnavigable. Transportation lines throughout Southern California were also damaged. Thirty-five bridges were washed out. More than one hundred roads and highways were destroyed. Railroad service was suspended, and communication with the outside world was cut off for nearly a week. Total damages from the flood were initially estimated at $10.1 million ($162.1 million in current figures). County assessors later calculated that flooding had reduced the aggregate value of property in the county by another $20 million.[86]

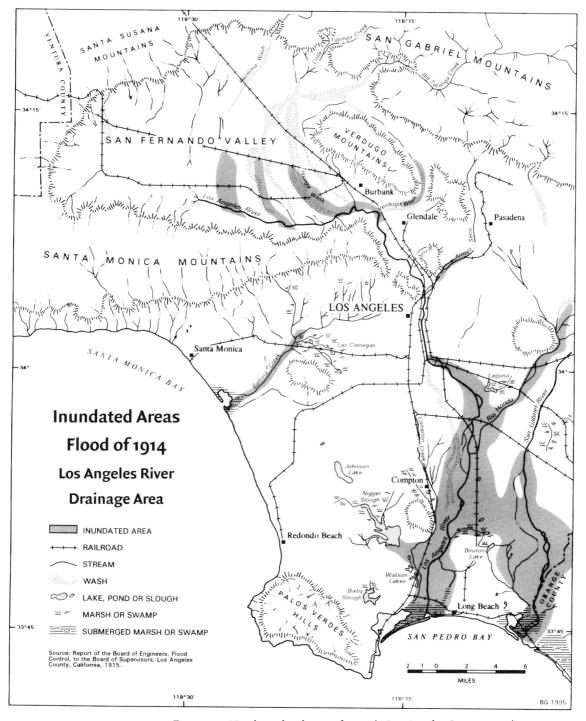

Inundated Areas

Flood of 1914

Los Angeles River

Drainage Area

▓	INUNDATED AREA
+++++	RAILROAD
⌒	STREAM
⋯⋯	WASH
⌒⌒⌒	LAKE, POND OR SLOUGH
↯	MARSH OR SWAMP
≡↯≡	SUBMERGED MARSH OR SWAMP

Source: Report of the Board of Engineers, Flood
Control, to the Board of Supervisors, Los Angeles
County, California, 1915.

MILES

BG 1995

FIG. 4.12. Nearly twelve thousand acres in Los Angeles County were inundated during the flood of 1914. This map is based on a 1915 map, produced by a county flood control board, which was more approximate in its delineation of the flooded area than similar maps produced for later floods. As a result, the flooded area appears larger than statistical estimates issued by the same board would indicate. Still, the map provides a good sense of the geographic dimensions of the flood. Map by the author.

RH 86487

More than ever before, the railroads were a factor in the flooding. By this time, three major railroads and an extensive network of commuter rail lines crisscrossed Los Angeles County. In the years since the last major flood in 1889, the Pacific Electric Railway had built hundreds of miles of commuter tracks that radiated in every direction from Los Angeles. The Los Angeles River was crossed in sixteen places by railroad bridges, many of them trestle bridges, which slowed and sometimes blocked debris-laden flood flows. After the flood, county flood control officials received "a large number" of letters from residents critical of the railroads for their continued use of trestle bridges.[87] Within days of the flood, furthermore, the Los Angeles County Board of Supervisors passed a resolution calling on the railroads to replace their pile bridges with more permanent span structures that would allow stream flows to pass more freely. Railroad representatives expressed a willingness to cooperate. An official of the Santa Fe Railroad said, "The Santa Fe follows the policy of erecting permanent bridges wherever possible. But it is handicapped in this country by the fact that the stream bed of today may be a mile from the stream of tomorrow."[88]

A map of the areas inundated in the 1914 flood, replicated in figure 4.12, gives some suggestion of the impact of the railroads. In seven different places, floods began very near where railroads crossed stream channels. This is especially noticeable in the San Fernando Valley, where three tributary channels of the Los Angeles River flooded. All three breakouts began near Southern Pacific Railroad crossings. The Los Angeles River, meanwhile, overflowed its channel south of downtown Los Angeles in a location where railroad-constructed levees confined floodwaters to a narrow course and two railroad bridges crossed the river within a mile. In addition, three other waterways—the San Gabriel River, Ballona Creek, and the Arroyo Seco—all first flooded near where their channels were crossed by railroads.[89] Although the exact role of the railroads in these outbreaks is not known, the impediments caused by the railroad bridges and embankments were clearly a contributing factor.

Silting of Los Angeles Harbor was also caused in part by the inadequacy of railroad bridges. The east approach to a Southern Pacific bridge between Wilmington and Long Beach, built in the 1880s before human activity forced much of the flow of the upper San Gabriel River into the Rio Hondo and out to sea via the Los Angeles River, was too short to allow debris-filled floodwaters to pass freely. Consequently, most of the flow of the river during the flood of 1914 was forced west over higher ground and into Los Angeles Harbor via Dominguez Creek. One channel in Los Angeles Harbor was rendered unnavigable when floodwaters deposited silt to a depth of eighteen feet. Another channel, newly dredged to a depth of twenty feet, was only two to four feet deep after the flood. Harbor officials said it would cost at least $580,000 to restore the port, which had seen its trade volume increase 800 percent since the federal government had agreed to erect a breakwater and the city of Los Angeles had annexed the surrounding area, promising to spend $10 million on port improvements. "The damage to the reputation of the harbor," said one engineer after the flood, "cannot be computed."[90]

Although floods were certainly nothing new in Southern California, the flood of 1914 clearly demonstrated to even the most skeptical that something had to be done to prevent the Los Angeles River from regularly overflowing its banks and occasionally carving entirely new courses across the increasingly developed landscape. Much of the city of Los Angeles by this time was reasonably well protected by railroad-constructed levees, but coordinated flood protections north and south of the city were nonexistent. The river, meanwhile, had become more dangerous because of changes made by humans, and the rapid growth of the region meant that the risk to life and property was greater than ever before. Los Angeles was fast becoming a sprawling metropolis and an industrial giant, which meant that even small storms now did more damage than the great floods of years past. Each new building and highway that was built, furthermore, increased the potential for flooding by reducing the area available to absorb rainfall and runoff, so as Southern California expanded, the flood danger grew with it. No longer the chief source of water for the largest city in the region, with most if its natural supply intercepted before it even reached its channel and its dry bed filling up with trash, the Los Angeles River was now merely an occasional hazard that had to be controlled.

Fifty-one Miles of Concrete

THE LOS ANGELES RIVER TODAY HAS WHAT IS PROBABLY the most extensive system of controls for a river of its size in the world.[1] The flood of February 1914 was the catalyst for the creation of the flood control program that led to these changes. County officials built dams and other facilities in the mountains to slow runoff and catch debris. Rivers and streams were straightened, deepened, and widened to prevent flooding and to keep water courses in place. Floodwaters were redirected from the harbor area to prevent future damage to the developing ports. But local taxpayers were unwilling to provide enough money to complete the planned projects, so after two disastrous floods in the 1930s the U.S. government took over the flood control program. The Army Corps of Engineers built five giant flood control dams in the San Fernando and San Gabriel Valleys to regulate runoff during storms. It increased controls by using reinforced concrete to line stream channels that had been protected only by wire fence or loose stones. By 1960, the federal government had created the fifty-one-mile storm drain that is still flatteringly called the Los Angeles River.

To understand why a coordinated, regional system of flood control became such a necessity after the flood of 1914, it is first useful to step back and examine the nature of flood control work all across Los Angeles County until that time. As was demonstrated by the story of initial levee building in the city of Los Angeles, early flood control efforts were haphazard and unscientific. This was even more true outside Los Angeles. Two early efforts at flood protection near the river's mouth are especially striking. After the flood of 1862 forced water from the Los Angeles River toward the infant port at Wilmington, Phineas Banning, who had founded the town five years before, hired five thousand Indians to build a dike with sacks of earth to turn the water back toward Long Beach. Much later, when those changes had caused the river to shift so far east that it threatened the approach to a railroad bridge between Long Beach and Terminal Island, the railroad simply dammed the mouth of the river with brush and rock to force its waters west.[2]

Changes made elsewhere may not have been as extreme, but they were no less selfish in their intentions or significant in their ultimate consequences. Railroads, which had caused so many problems by building trestle bridges in the beds of the rivers and streams, added to the flood danger by erecting dikes upstream from their bridges to force waterways through openings that were considerably more narrow than their natural floodplains. Farmers and ranchers, meanwhile, often used boulders and trees to redirect shifting stream courses away from their own land, thus increasing the flood risk nearby. Vineyard owner Jean Louis Vignes, for example, used brush and wood to turn the river east a few years after the flood of 1825, reclaiming a grove of willows that had been submerged when that flood had changed the course of the river. Some farmers drove rows of wood piles into stream banks and connected the piles with wire fence to prevent flood-borne debris from cutting new channels across their land. Others planted willows, cottonwoods, and gum trees beside streams to slow bank erosion.[3]

There was little coordination of effort, and much of the work was in direct conflict. Neighbors became enemies. Farmers were occasionally forced to guard their levees with rifles. An El Monte man reported in 1914 that he had once hired fifty men to erect a three-hundred-foot dike to prevent the San Gabriel River from flooding his property. During the flood of 1889, however, property owners across the river tore down the dike and redirected floodwaters away from their properties, causing the river to inundate his land and wash away his home. Such reports were not uncommon. "Many times I have gone up the river, taking a few Indians with me to move a few boulders about and get the water going the way we wanted it," recalled another farmer in 1914. "By placing a double row of boulders across the stream, it would raise the water level enough to throw the water over the other way. Of course, it brought opposition, for people on the other side did not want the water either. It finally became serious, and when a man wanted his work to stand, it was necessary to stay with it, armed with a double-barreled shotgun."[4]

Flood protection work at Los Angeles, while more effective than the piecemeal efforts attempted elsewhere, also proved the futility of using a localized approach to combat what was essentially a regional problem. The city's levees had been blamed for flooding south of Los Angeles in 1889, which had caused the river to shift its course two miles east. When a subsequent, though less severe, storm in January 1890 again caused flooding south of the city, a property owner whose land was inundated sued the Southern California Railway, claiming that negligence by the railroad in building the levee on the west side of the river had caused flooding that "destroyed" nine hundred acres of her land. The plaintiff, Arcadia De Baker, contended that the railroad, by building its levee more than a mile beyond the point stipulated in its agreement with the city, had altered the natural flow of the river, forcing its waters east. The Los Angeles County Superior Court found in favor of De Baker, but the California Supreme Court, on appeal, overturned the lower court's ruling, saying that the city of Los Angeles had the "duty" and "power" to build a levee to protect the city and that the railroad, acting on behalf of the city, could not be held liable "for mere errors of judgment" in the way the levee was built.[5]

Such incidents, along with the increasing damages caused by floods as development spread across Southern California, made clear that nothing less than a countywide program for controlling the flood risk would ever be truly effective. It is not known when Los Angeles County officials first considered the development of a flood control program of their own, but the contents of a brittle, dusty notebook on the shelves of a county technical library—field notes kept by a road engineer in April 1874—suggest that the county realized the need for flood control long before the region was extensively settled or the first coordinated improvements were made. Handwritten notes mention a proposal for the construction of an eight-foot-high, forty-foot-wide dam to prevent flooding near the present location of El Monte.[6]

Floods in 1889 prompted the first far-reaching proposals for flood control. Soon after the floods, the Los Angeles County Board of Supervisors hired a group of three engineers to make recommendations for curbing the flood risk. Surveys were conducted on the Los Angeles River south of the city limits, the Rio Hondo, and the entire length of the San Gabriel River. In 1894, the Board of Engineers issued a report on the control of forty-seven miles of waterways. Their proposals included a recommendation that the Los Angeles River be widened by as much as three hundred feet. In June 1902, meanwhile, Congress approved a harbor improvement project that included a proposal for the construction of a 6,360-foot-long dike to deflect floodwaters from the Los Angeles River away from the port at San Pedro. Interest in such projects waned, however, during the dry cycle that followed the repeated floods of the 1880s. County-funded proposals were shelved, and U.S. Army engineers decided that a dike was no longer needed to protect Los Angeles Harbor. Periodic dredging of the harbor, they believed, was enough to maintain minimum channel depths for navigation and would be cheaper than construction of the dike.[7]

The overflow of the San Gabriel River during a storm in March 1911 awakened fears. Gravel extraction companies had removed so much of the river's bed near Duarte that nearly all the flow of the San Gabriel had been forced back into its former channel, now the Rio Hondo, and the increased flow washed away bridges and destroyed valuable farmland during the flood. Studies conducted two years later showed that more than 90 percent of the water carried by the upper San Gabriel flowed west through the Rio Hondo and reached the ocean via the Los Angeles River at San Pedro Bay. Little water flowed in the main channel of the San Gabriel River below Whittier Narrows. After the 1911 flood, county supervisors were "bombarded with petitions for relief," and they created the San Antonio protection district in response, spending $105,880 to strengthen the channel of the Rio Hondo by constructing a series of pile dikes reinforced with barbed wire. An additional $188,370 was spent by five other local protection districts in particularly flood-prone sections of the county, but work was still fragmentary. As one official noted, "the effort to enlist the whole river population in a common scheme for the betterment of these flood conditions resulted in failure."[8]

Supervisors hired a former Santa Fe Railroad engineer named Frank H. Olmsted to coordinate the improvements on the Rio Hondo and later to prepare a comprehensive plan for the control of the San Gabriel River. Warning that "year by year the annual waste occasioned by not controlling the river will be more and more inexcusable and expensive," Olmsted in his report of October 1913 proposed $1.5 million in additional work. He recommended that spreading basins be established where the San Gabriel leaves the mountains to allow some of the floodwaters to percolate into the ground and replenish underground aquifers. He suggested, moreover, that the banks of the San Gabriel be reinforced and that the stream channels be kept clear of brush and rubbish. Finally, he proposed that the Rio Hondo be diverted into an artificial canal that would carry its flow south to the San Gabriel and ultimately Alamitos Bay, thus significantly reducing the amount of water destined for the lower Los Angeles River and the port at San Pedro. Acknowledging that his findings were preliminary and that more detailed investigations were necessary, Olmsted nevertheless insisted that the San Gabriel River could "be controlled so as to do no appreciable damage." More remarkable in light of what was to follow was his statement that "the work required is not prohibitive so far as the expense is concerned."[9]

Creating a County Flood Control Program

The flood of February 1914 demonstrated that even Olmsted's proposals—the most comprehensive recommended to that point—were grossly inadequate (fig. 5.1). As catastrophic as the flood had been, officials estimated that it was only the third or fourth largest flood in

Los Angeles County since California had become a state. Floods in 1862, 1884, and 1889 are all believed to have been greater. A U.S. government meteorologist, in fact, remarked in April 1914 that the floods of 1884 "make the last storm appear inconsequential."[10] William Mulholland, superintendent of the Los Angeles city water department, who had come to Los Angeles in 1877 and had witnessed all the great floods of the boom years, claimed that a flood in 1889 had been even greater, calling it the "highest and most violent flood" he had ever seen. Engineers used observations of peak flows during the 1889 floods to estimate that the flood discharge of the Los Angeles River during those storms had been 65 percent greater than it was in February 1914. Maximum discharge on the San Gabriel River in 1889 was estimated to have been 77 percent greater than in 1914.[11]

FIG. 5.1. The most extensive flood control proposals made for Los Angeles County before the 1914 flood would have done nothing to prevent this house from toppling into the Arroyo Seco. Its banks gave way as waters poured down the normally dry channel during the flood. Used with permission, Los Angeles Public Library/Security Pacific Collection.

Within days of the 1914 flood, new proposals for controlling the flood risk began to be promoted. Los Angeles District Attorney John D. Fredericks, a Republican candidate for governor that year, recommended that the county appoint a committee of engineers to investigate possible solutions. He also proposed, in a variation on an idea suggested for the Rio Hondo a year earlier by engineer Frank H. Olmsted, that the Los Angeles River be diverted into an artificial channel that would carry its entire flow in a straight line southeast from Vernon to the San Gabriel River and on to Alamitos Bay, thus eliminating the flood risk south of Los Angeles and preventing future silting of the harbor. Such a plan might sound outlandish today but, in a city that had just built a 233-mile aqueduct to augment its water supply, anything seemed possible. "The aqueduct had its inception in proven needs," Fredericks said in explaining his idea. "Now we have a storm-water bugbear."[12]

On 27 February 1914, as concerned citizens crowded its meeting room, the Los Angeles County Board of Supervisors agreed to form a board of engineers like the one Fredericks had recommended. The board was formally created a month later, and in April five engineers, one from each supervisorial district, were appointed. Supervisors also appealed to Congress and the California legislature for help. Realizing that they would need more money for the types of projects envisioned than the existing county budget could supply and aware that current laws did not give the county the legal authority necessary to implement a comprehensive flood control program, supervisors also created an advisory group called the Los Angeles County Flood Control Association to help draft flood control legislation. The group included representatives from various county departments, city governments, business interests, and civic organizations. As it turned out, three competing flood control conventions were held for the purpose of drafting legislation to be considered by state lawmakers.[13]

The chief obstacle to reaching consensus on a flood control bill was a difference in opinion on the way the work should be funded. Some favored the creation of assessment districts, which would tax only those in areas where work was to be done. This method was favored by the Los Angeles City Council and the Los Angeles Chamber of Commerce, not surprisingly, since city taxpayers had already spent considerable money on the construction of levees and were understandably reluctant to spend more to help outlying districts do what they had already done. Others, however, preferred a uniform assessment for all taxpayers throughout the flood-prone area. This approach eventually gained the approval of legislators. According to A. W. Fry, an auditor for the Los Angeles Trust and Savings Bank and a champion of the uniform assessment approach, "It seemed clear to me at the outset that forming storm protection districts down toward the sea would do no good, since the floods rise many miles away in the mountains."[14]

The flood control bill was approved by the legislature and signed by Gov. Hiram W. Johnson on 12 June 1915. It took effect two months later and created the Los Angeles County Flood Control District, giving the agency taxing powers and placing it under the direction of the Board of Supervisors. The district's boundaries encompassed 2,760 square miles, all but the northern quarter of the county. The largely unpopulated desert areas north of the San Gabriel Mountains were not included. The bill's authors decided to make the district less than countywide in area to sidestep a state constitutional requirement that a two-thirds majority must approve the sale of county bonds. The approval of district bonds requires only a simple majority. This would prove key, as only one of the bond issues that funded initial flood control work was backed by two-thirds of the electorate.[15]

As politicians, business leaders, and others wrangled over the details of the flood control bill, the Board of Engineers had begun to examine the technical aspects of flood control. They hired eighty to one hundred laborers to conduct detailed topographic surveys of the flood-prone areas, and most of the lowlands were mapped with two- and five-foot contours. Public meetings were held every Monday for the purpose of obtaining community input. Officials also canvassed the county, interviewing hundreds of longtime residents to gain a better understanding of past floods and the unpredictable nature of the region's waterways.[16] The board made its first tentative proposals in June 1914. It recommended that a series of low dams be built on mountain tributary streams to slow runoff, an approach borrowed from German and Swiss engineers working in the mountains of central Europe. The board also proposed that several large basins be excavated at the mouths of mountain canyons so some of the storm waters could be retained to replenish underground aquifers, an idea first suggested locally a year earlier by Olmsted (who was a member of the board). They recommended that the channels of lowland rivers and streams be straightened and lined with levees and that wire fence be erected in front of the levees to prevent debris-laden floodwaters from eroding the artificial embankments.[17]

Many of those interviewed who had witnessed the great floods of decades past, however, expressed skepticism that such floods could be prevented and that the rivers could be controlled. One man, who had ridden in a rowboat from Long Beach to Wilmington when the river had overflowed, said, "I have seen some pretty good ones, and if

you can tell me how you can put a body of water nearly two miles wide
. . . into an eighty foot channel and only six or eight feet deep, then
that beats me."[18] Some, such as William Mulholland, questioned the
intelligence and even the necessity of constructing large flood control
works. "To build dams for reservoirs in the mountains to hold water
back would be too expensive for the amount of good it would do,"
Mulholland said, adding that "the present channel of the Los Angeles
River is ample to carry away the water." Former California Gov. H. F.
Gage, who lived beside the San Gabriel River, said, "It's all rubbish
what they propose to do. The people should take care of the river."[19]

S. B. Reeve, a civil engineer and city surveyor, insisted that the flood
problem would be best addressed by the simple building of levees that
would force the river to dig a deeper channel for itself. The large projects that had been suggested in the days after the flood, he believed,
would be a waste of money. "It would not be much trouble to get a few
of the old timers together and make up a map of the old flooded district, and make plans whereby the river could be readily controlled,"
he said. "But the way the proposition is being handled only makes sal-
aries for some engineers."[20] Still others were critical of how long it
was taking for the first substantive flood control work to begin. "What
the people want is some action," said a resident of Compton. "I went
up and talked to [County Supervisor W. E.] Hinshaw about protection
here at my place. He said that they could do nothing. Then I asked if
he could not protect the country roads where they were threatened,
but I could get nothing out of him. A man from the road department
was down here. [He] had a lot of expensive ideas, but [they were] prin-
cipally hot air. The supervisors can find ways of appropriating money
for entertaining a lot of people . . . but try to do something for the citizens of the county who deserve attention, who are poor and need
some help—that is out of the question."[21]

There was also serious division within the Board of Engineers, so
much so that, in July 1915, as the board prepared its final recommendations, one of the engineers, James W. Reagan of Long Beach, announced that he would not sign the board's final report. Reagan was
critical of his colleagues, disagreeing most strongly with a proposal
for protecting the harbor area that had been recommended by U.S.
Army engineers engaged in port improvements and endorsed by the
rest of the flood control board. The plan called for the construction of
a massive dike north of Long Beach to divert the flow of the Los Angeles River into a leveed channel that would carry its waters six miles
down the coast to Alamitos Bay. Reagan argued that the dike would
create a new flood risk because a settling basin would form behind it,
allowing the deposition of silt that could later block the free flow of

water. He also thought that the project was too expensive. Faced with Reagan's continued refusal to sign the board's recommendations, the Board of Supervisors finally agreed to publish the recommendations of the majority of the board with a minority report written by Reagan. Both reports were published in August 1915.[22]

The report of the majority proposed $16.5 million in improvements that were projected to take five years to complete. Proposals emphasized upstream controls, calling for the construction of five dams in the mountains, basins for the spreading of floodwaters at the mouths of five canyons, channel rectification, and the reforestation of mountain slopes. Levees were to be built in places on the lowland rivers and streams. Some of the levees were to be as much as fifteen feet wide at the top—nearly twice as wide as many levees on the Mississippi River—to provide increased protection against erosion. Stream channels were to be dug deeper where necessary to increase their carrying capacity. Funds for improvements were to be divided relatively equally among the coastal plain, the San Gabriel Valley, and the mountains. Plans for the San Fernando Valley, still relatively rural in the initial years after the opening of the Los Angeles–Owens River Aqueduct, were less extensive. Settlement there was largely restricted to the southeastern portion of the valley, around Glendale and Burbank.[23]

A quarter of the estimated costs, $3.9 million, were for improvements to the Los Angeles River. A completely new channel for the river was to be excavated in the western San Fernando Valley. The meandering gullies that carried storm water to the river in that area were so shallow and poorly defined that engineers said it would be necessary to construct a channel "in its entirety" from Encino west for seven miles. They recommended that the first mile of the new channel be a covered conduit. Farther downstream, levees were to be constructed along seventeen miles of the river. Some were to be lined with rock riprap or concrete. Willows were to be planted where possible on top of the levees, but in other areas, the engineers said, the levees might be used as highways "for the benefit of the neighborhood." Although willows and other trees placed on stream banks were thought to be helpful for keeping waterways in place, vegetation growing in the river channel was believed to have the opposite effect. As a result, several thousand dollars had already been spent to remove brush from the river in the Glendale Narrows, and continued clearing of its channel in this area was recommended.[24]

The most significant changes proposed for the river were for the part of its course south of Los Angeles. Near Vernon, the river was to be returned to the channel it had occupied before the flood of 1889, thus eliminating a "dangerous curve" south of the Los Angeles city limits and another right angle bend at Laguna (see plan A in fig. 5.3). This change would have rerouted the river in an almost straight line southeast to its junction with the Rio Hondo, cutting one and a quarter miles off its length in the process. The most dramatic modification of the river would have been its diversion away from the harbor into an eleven-mile-long artificial channel that would have wound southeast around Long Beach en route to Alamitos Bay. If these two changes would have been implemented, the river's course between Los Angeles and the sea would have been almost entirely new. The majority report also proposed the construction of a series of small sills, or ridges, across the river through downtown Los Angeles to reduce the amount of sediment carried by the river. Sand and gravel caught behind the ridges, the report said, could be periodically dredged for use by local builders.[25]

Even in 1915, the high price of real estate in Southern California inhibited flood control planning. Because the Los Angeles River was not considered a navigable stream, most of its channel was privately owned and, therefore, had to be purchased before work could be done. The cost of land along the river south of Los Angeles precluded engineers from giving the river a wide berth. "Land is here so valuable that it is advisable to keep the right of way as narrow as possible," wrote Charles T. Leeds, a member of the board. The confining of the river into a relatively narrow channel would increase the velocity and erosive power of floodwaters, which meant that levees would need extra protection. The majority report recommended that levees constructed between the city limits and the Rio Hondo be reinforced with a continuous covering of rock riprap or cement. The price of real estate, officials said, also made the construction of a reservoir impractical at the only site on the coastal plain where the development of a large reservoir was physically possible—the marshy lowlands around Laguna.[26]

Formulating Plans for the First Flood Control Bond Issue

Despite strong opposition, the Board of Supervisors in August 1915 appointed James W. Reagan (fig. 5.2), the most vocal and controversial member of the engineering board, to draw up specific flood control plans. The fifty-one-year-old Kansas native,[27] a former Southern Pacific Railroad engineer, had a reputation for being stubborn and hot tempered and, as a member of the board, had disagreed with many of the proposals of his colleagues, insisting that more emphasis should be placed on projects outside the mountains, such as the realignment of stream channels and the building of levees. He questioned the effectiveness of a scheme proposed by the rest of the board to build numerous small dams in the mountains. Reagan had also recommended a different route for the diversion of the Los Angeles River, proposing that it be redirected in an "almost straight route" southeast from a Southern Pacific bridge near the present boundary of Maywood and Bell to Alamitos Bay. This alternative, he said, was not only safer but also less expensive than the plan endorsed by army engineers and the majority of the board.[28]

FIG. 5.2. James W. Reagan, controversial first chief engineer of the Los Angeles County Flood Control District. Used with permission, Department of Special Collections, University Research Library, University of California, Los Angeles.

Supervisors were bitterly divided over the appointment of Reagan, which was approved by a 3-2 vote after an acrimonious debate. On 31 August the *Examiner* described the session at which Reagan was hired as "one of the most heated" of the year. "It started rather stormily and ended in a hurricane." Supervisors F. E. Woodley and R. W. Pridham charged that Reagan was unfit for the job and had failed in his duty as a member of the Board of Engineers, claiming his report contained mostly criticism and no plan of action. They also argued that Reagan's opposition to the port protection plan promoted by army engineers could threaten the project. Reagan's supporters, meanwhile, compared the engineer to such respected contemporary figures as Abraham Lincoln, Ulysses S. Grant, and William Mulholland. The opposition of Woodley and Pridham, though, was not based solely on their dislike of Reagan. They also insisted that an engineer was not needed exclusively to coordinate flood control work, saying the work could be satisfactorily handled by existing departments, such as the county surveyor. They advocated, moreover, that if a flood control engineer was to be hired, that person should be hired under civil service rules rather than be appointed by supervisors. Such arguments resurfaced five months later when the Board of Supervisors, again by a 3-2 margin, officially created the office of the county flood control engineer and named Reagan as chief engineer.[29]

A flood in January 1916 emphasized the need for immediate action. Losses were greatest around San Diego, but Los Angeles County suffered $775,238 in damages, mostly from the destruction of highways and bridges and the washing away of agricultural lands. The Los Angeles River again broke through its banks near Vernon, creating a new channel one hundred yards to the south and forcing fifty families from their homes. At least two houses were washed into the river. Farther downstream, floodwaters from the river joined with the outflow from the Rio Hondo to inundate the low-lying areas of northwest Long Beach. The river in flood was a quarter of a mile wide at Willow Street. Forty families were driven from their homes, seventy employees of a woolen mill were marooned for two days, and the keeper of the city dog pound was stranded in his cottage. Residents in the area had to resort to small boats for transportation. Much of the overflow wound up in Long Beach Harbor, where it deposited so much silt that an ocean-bound steamer was grounded. It took four tugboats to pull it free.[30]

Officials later calculated that floodwaters from the river had dumped three million cubic yards of silt into Los Angeles and Long Beach Harbors. Residents, meanwhile, were growing impatient with the lack of progress that had been made on flood control work in the two years since the disastrous floods of 1914. One homeowner, driven from his home by floodwaters south of Los Angeles, was indignant in a letter to county supervisors. "You are cordially invited to come out and see the result of the way you have handled the flood question the last two years," he wrote. "Thirty homes are abandoned here on the Cudahy Ranch tonight on account of the Los Angeles River running wild over the country while the river bed is almost dry. The Vernon-Downey Boulevard is impassable, keeping me from tending my business. My home is flooded, making it untenable. Don't you think it's time for doing something other than hiring high-priced engineers?"[31] Others, tired of waiting for the government to act, contracted for work themselves. The owner of a property just south of the Los Angeles city limits—the same property that had been damaged in a flood in 1890, prompting its owner to sue the Southern California Railway—published an invitation for bids for construction of a levee nearly two miles in length on the east side of the river.[32]

James Reagan opened the office of the Los Angeles County Engineer in March 1916 with a staff of three. Surveys were begun on the Los Angeles River from its junction with the Rio Hondo to Dominguez Hills, the proposed location of the federal government's diversion dike, to determine the best course for the river. In July 1916, Congress appropriated $500,000 for the construction of the dike and the diversion channel on the condition that the county supply all land required and maintain the project after its completion. Despite Reagan's earlier objections, the diversion of the river north of Long Beach was central to his first detailed plan for flood control, submitted to the Board of Supervisors in December 1916. The report proposed a scaled-down program that included $4.3 million in work. Nearly a third of that, $1.3 million, was for diversion of the river away from the harbor, the economic importance of which had risen considerably since the opening of the Panama Canal two years before. Silting of the harbor had by this time begun to threaten navigation even in nonflood years. The army's plan was to build a 3-1/2-mile-long earthen dike across a gap between Dominguez Hills and the low hills east of the river. The river was to be diverted two miles north of the dike into a new channel, which would carry its waters to Alamitos Bay.[33]

U.S. government and county engineers had initially considered five alternatives for protecting the harbor area. Officials could periodically dredge the harbor. They could shift the river mouth to the then-smaller Long Beach Harbor. They could cut a new channel for the river between the two harbors or east of Long Beach Harbor. Or they could divert the river away from the harbor area entirely. The last approach was judged to be the cheapest. Three diversion routes were proposed (fig. 5.3). The so-called Dominguez diversion, later approved, was plan A. Plan B proposed to divert the river north of its meeting with the Rio Hondo in a straight line southeast to Alamitos Bay (a route similar to the one suggested by Reagan in 1915). Plan C recommended that the river be diverted near Vernon to the San Gabriel River, on a route that would have taken it just south of Downey. The Dominguez diversion was the most expensive of the three alternatives but was chosen because it was considered the safest and most effective.[34]

Reagan also proposed $350,000 in work on the Los Angeles River between the city and the diversion point. He recommended that the "tortuous" channel of the river be significantly straightened and confined between levees, protected by railroad track and rock riprap. The river corridor was to be widened gradually to eight hundred feet near Compton. Bank protection was also planned for the San Gabriel River, the Rio Hondo, and several tributary streams. The proposed projects were not limited to lowland rivers and streams, however. No doubt realizing that, to build support for his plan, he had to gain the approval of critics who demanded greater upstream controls, Reagan also proposed significant work in the mountains. Large dams were to be constructed on Pacoima Creek, on the Arroyo Seco, and in San Dimas Canyon. Smaller dams, known as *check dams*, were to be built in seventeen mountain canyons.[35] Check dams are small dams built at multiple locations in a single steep channel. They are designed to create a series of steps, thus lowering the grade of the channel and slowing the velocity of runoff.

The plan to divert the river to Alamitos Bay proved controversial, however. Owners of a proposed marina and residential development in the area, now the Long Beach suburb of Naples, charged that the increased flow of water into the bay from the diversion canal would destroy their property. In an attempt to allay their fears, federal government engineers proposed an alternate route for the channel that would have shifted it slightly west, away from the development site. But concern over the effect of the plan at Alamitos Bay was not the only problem standing in the way of the project. Land developers and business leaders south of the diversion point claimed that shifting the course of the river would reduce the volume of water percolating into

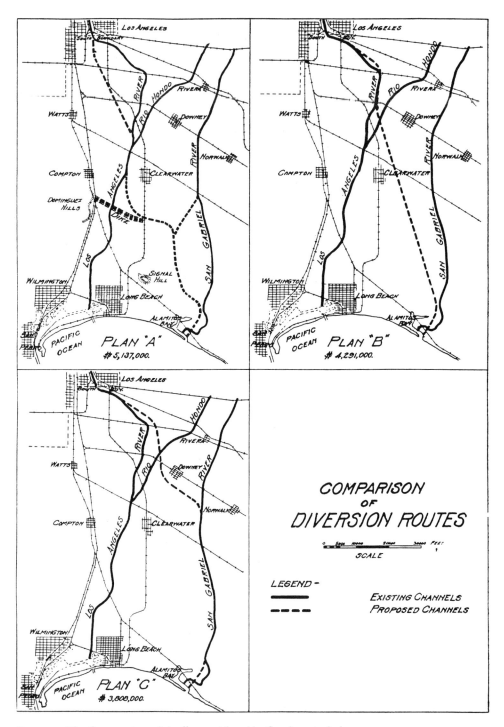

FIG. 5.3. The three routes originally considered by flood control planners for the diversion of the Los Angeles River away from the harbor area. Reprinted from Los Angeles County Board of Engineers, Flood Control, *Report of the Board of Engineers, Flood Control, to the Board of Supervisors, Los Angeles County, California* (Los Angeles, 1915), 222.

the aquifers from which they drew their domestic and irrigation supplies. Farmers and businesses in and around Compton, moreover, feared that the river would back up behind the dike and flood their community. County engineers and federal government officials denied these claims, but when threatened lawsuits seemed certain to delay construction, the project was scrapped and a less radical alternative for diverting the river away from the harbor was implemented.[36]

Federal and local officials decided to adopt an earlier proposal to divert the river directly south at Dominguez into a leveed channel that would empty into the ocean between Long Beach Harbor and downtown Long Beach. The plan called for the widening and raising of an existing Pacific Electric Railway embankment to serve as a dike between the Dominguez Hills and the hills east of the river. Two levees would then be built from the east end of the dike directly south through the city of Long Beach to the Pacific Ocean, confining the river in a new channel 566 feet wide and 14 feet deep.[37] A U.S. government engineer explained the change in the diversion route: "Though everybody in the harbor district would have liked to be entirely rid of the river, it was realized by many of them that it would not be in keeping with the Golden Rule nor even the Silver Rule, to impose the objectionable river on the weaker neighbor, especially when there was room for it at home." A few years later, the same engineer was more succinct in his explanation in a letter to his former boss. "We are not allowed," he wrote, "to put our unruly dog into our neighbor's yard instead of our own."[38]

Reagan included the new diversion proposal in a revised set of recommendations he submitted to the Board of Supervisors in January 1917. The revised plans were immediately approved by supervisors and became the basis for the first county flood control bond issue, which was placed on the ballot for the following month. The new plans recommended $4.5 million in work, a slight increase over earlier proposals. One quarter of the costs were for the harbor diversion, but only minor work was planned for the rest of the river. The amount of money earmarked for river projects, in fact, had been reduced from Reagan's proposals of a month before. No work was planned for the channel upstream from Tujunga Wash; between Tujunga Wash and the Arroyo Seco, the only work proposed was the clearing of brush and other vegetation from the river channel. The new plans also recommended that the river south of Los Angeles be lined with pile fence instead of levees. A double row of wood piles, faced with hog wire, was to be driven along both sides of the river (fig. 5.4). Brush was to be placed between the wire fences. Engineers referred to this method of channel rectification as *river training*. The pile dikes were intended to confine the river to a narrow course, forcing it to dig a deeper channel for itself.[39]

But the bond issue also proved contentious. Two prominent business groups, the Los Angeles Chamber of Commerce and the Hollywood Board of Trade, had strongly opposed the appointment of Reagan and continued to call for his ouster. When the county approved the chief engineer's proposals, the Chamber of Commerce, in tandem with the Los Angeles City Council and the progressive Municipal League, appointed three engineers to review the plans: Charles T. Leeds, a former army civilian engineer; John H. Quinton, who had been a consultant for the city water department; and S. A. Jubb, acting harbor engineer for the city of Los Angeles. Leeds had been a member, with Reagan, of the Board of Engineers appointed by the county after the flood of 1914. He was the author of the portion of the majority report, attacked by Reagan, that had recommended the Dominguez diversion.[40]

Perhaps not surprisingly, given the past antipathy between Leeds and Reagan, the three engineers delivered a scathing attack on the county's plans, calling the work proposed "entirely inadequate and largely of a temporary character." They further charged that the costs of many of the projects had been underestimated, that not enough work was planned for the mountains and foothills, and that the proposed methods for controlling the Los Angeles River and other lowland waterways were insufficient. "We cannot approve the plan of carrying the floodwaters of the Los Angeles River when it might be 800 feet wide, six or eight feet deep, and rushing along at a velocity of ten feet per second between walls composed of piles and hog wire," they wrote. Implementation of the Reagan plans, they warned, would mean "certain failure" and would discourage future flood control efforts. "To start wrong," they wrote, "is worse than to not start at all."[41]

Armed with the engineers' report, the Municipal League and the Chamber of Commerce urged the Board of Supervisors without success to postpone the bond referendum until a more satisfactory plan could be devised. Joining those organizations opposing Reagan's plans were Los Angeles Mayor Frederick T. Woodman, Supervisor Woodley, the Hollywood Board of Trade, and the Los Angeles Times. Others, meanwhile, advocated rejection of the bond issue on nonengineering grounds. The fact that flood control district employees were exempted from civil service provisions was again an issue. Debate over the most equitable method of assessment for flood control work, which had nearly thwarted passage of flood control legislation, also resurfaced. Many still opposed the districtwide assessment approach, believing that taxpayers should pay in proportion to the benefits they

FIG. 5.4. An example of the pile-and-wire-fence protection recommended for the Los Angeles River in the proposals for the 1917 bond issue and later erected along stream courses throughout Southern California. Engineers referred to this method of flood control as "river training" because the brush-lined fencing was intended to confine the river to a narrow course and force it to dig a deeper channel for itself. *Los Angeles Examiner* photograph. Used with permission, Department of Special Collections, University of Southern California Library/Hearst Newspaper Collection.

received.[42] One of the most visible opponents of the assessment plan was the *Times*, the largest newspaper in Southern California, which wrote in an editorial on the morning of the election, "The flood bond proposition to be voted on today reminds us forcibly of the unctuous gentleman, in the forepart of Rabelais, who believed it perfectly ethical to rob Peter to pay Paul."[43]

Organized backers of the bond issue, meanwhile, hitched their hopes for success to concern over the future of Los Angeles Harbor, which advertisements trumpeted as "our greatest public asset," and to emotional appeals for the well-being of the "humble home-builder."

A four-page broadsheet (fig. 5.5) published on the eve of the election by an organization called the Flood Control Campaign Committee included a dozen photos depicting the devastation of earlier floods—a home washed into the river, the waterlogged belongings of a family sitting in front of their house, ruined bridges and highways, a giant gas tank beside the Los Angeles River that was kept from toppling into floodwaters by "the heroic work of hundreds of men." One photo that showed a house undermined by floodwaters carried the caption: "We are all responsible for this man's loss." An advertisement published in the *Los Angeles Times* urging approval of the bond issue, meanwhile, claimed support for the referendum from thirty-six major trade organizations and municipalities, including most of the cities downstream from Los Angeles.[44]

FIG. 5.5. Front page of a promotional newspaper published to build support for the 1917 flood control bond election.

Perhaps helped by rain showers that started two days before the election and continued all the while polls were open, the bond issue was narrowly approved by voters, although the margin was so slim that for several days newspapers reported that the initiative had been defeated. When all the ballots were finally counted and the various appeals were sorted out, however, 34,346 voters had voted in favor of the bonds and 34,295 had voted against them—a margin of 51 votes. Opposition was greatest in Los Angeles, which figured to benefit least from the planned improvements. Support was strongest in the downstream cities. In Long Beach, which had been inundated by the river in the floods of 1914 and 1916 and would profit considerably from harbor improvements, the bonds carried by a 15-1 margin.[45]

Flood Control Construction Begins

Construction on the flood control projects approved in the 1917 bond issue did not start immediately, however, because the federal government suspended the sale of bonds after U.S. entrance into World War I. Permission was not granted for the issuance of the bonds until May 1918, and no money was actually collected from their sale until October of that year. Construction commenced soon after, and by 1921 the single most important project, the diversion of the Los Angeles River away from the harbor—called the raison d'être of flood control in Los Angeles County by one scholar—was completed (fig. 5.6).[46] The river's mouth was shifted one mile east, where a rock jetty extending into the ocean was built to prevent silt from accumulating at the entrance to Long Beach Harbor. The total cost of the project was $3.3 million, with the federal government and Los Angeles County each paying about half.[47]

Elsewhere, river channels were straightened, and some forty-five thousand piles were driven along their banks and connected with wire fencing to keep them in place. Stream channels were excavated with mule-drawn shovels to give them greater carrying capacity. In places, entirely new channels were dug to remove large, winding bends in stream courses. Hundreds of carloads of rock were used to strengthen the banks of the Los Angeles River where it turns sharply southeast in Vernon. Three large dams, meanwhile, were built in the foothills to help regulate runoff from the mountains. The only one built in the Los Angeles River system was Devil's Gate Dam (fig. 5.7), constructed on the Arroyo Seco above the Rose Bowl in northwestern Pasadena. More than thirty-eight hundred check dams were constructed in sixty-six mountain canyons.[48]

With much of the initial work completed, voters in May 1924 were asked to approve a second bond issue to provide an additional $35.3

FIG. 5.6. Rock-lined levee constructed as part of a project to shift the mouth of the Los Angeles River one mile to the east to prevent deposition of silt in the harbor area. Courtesy, Stephen Callis. Used with permission.

million for flood control improvements. By this time, Reagan had learned that, to assure more widespread support for his proposals, he had to become more politically adept and balance his own beliefs about what needed to be done with the desires of others. The strongest criticism of the first stage of flood control work was that too little money had been spent on projects in the mountains, the source of most of the runoff in the settled portions of Los Angeles County. Concurrent with that belief was the opinion that, in water-starved Southern California, more of the floodwaters should be captured so they could be used, rather than allowing them to be flushed to the sea. Although the original Board of Engineers had determined a decade before that no suitable site existed in lowland Los Angeles County for a large reservoir that could serve the dual purpose of flood control and water conservation, such sites did exist in the mountains and foothills.

The flood control program recommended by Reagan in the plans put forth for the bond issue of 1924 relied heavily on upstream approaches to flood control and, as such, represented a remarkable reversal in strategy for a man who less than a decade before had doubted the merits of such methods. "To place one's faith in conservation alone as a panacea for all flood difficulties," he had written in 1915, "would more than likely result disastrously to the lower district." The new plans, however, seemed to advocate just such an approach. Reagan proposed the construction of nine large dams and reservoirs in the mountains, with a combined storage capacity of 290,233 acre feet.

He proposed almost no additional work on the Los Angeles River, then still largely uncontrolled in the San Fernando Valley and through much of the Glendale Narrows. Little new channel work, in fact, was recommended anywhere in the county, even though a preliminary report had said that pile fences erected along stream channels, considered to be temporary protections, would be "very badly decayed" within seven years. More than 95 percent of the money allocated in the plan was for projects in the mountains. In sharp contrast to his earlier view, Reagan now believed that improvements to lowland waterways would not be needed once the mountain projects were completed. The dams and reservoirs, he said, "should nearly remove the necessity of flood control."[49]

The cornerstone of the new approach was to be a massive 425-foot-high concrete dam to be built across San Gabriel Canyon, north of Glendora in the San Gabriel Mountains, called by one newspaper the

FIG. 5.7. Devil's Gate Dam, built on the Arroyo Seco in Pasadena in 1920, was the first large dam built to regulate runoff in the area tributary to the Los Angeles River. Used with permission, Los Angeles Public Library/Security Pacific Collection.

"Grand Canyon of Southern California."[50] First proposed in 1921, the San Gabriel Dam would have been the largest dam in the world at the time. It was expected to cost $25 million to construct and was intended to provide storage for 240,000 acre feet of water. The dam would have reduced the flood potential on the San Gabriel River and, by limiting the flow into the Rio Hondo, would also have lessened the risk on the lower Los Angeles River, transforming it, in the words of one newspaper, "from a raging torrent in flood time to a babbling brook from year end to year end."[51] Reagan claimed that the dams would not only prevent floods but also boost the region's water supply by enabling the slow release of water into rivers and streams, where it could percolate into aquifers:

> Very little consideration is being given by the sub-dividers to the providing of the county in the near future with an adequate and vitally necessary supply of water . . . The depletion of the underground water supply in Los Angeles County is extremely alarming. The present plan of running this very much needed floodwater away to the sea as quickly as possible, in order that the rancher in the lower thirty-five miles of the district may be protected, should be discontinued as quickly as possible.[52]

The new approach brought a corresponding increase in support for Reagan's plans. Many of the groups that had so vehemently opposed his earlier proposals and had even called for his removal from office now backed the new bond issue. The Los Angeles Chamber of Commerce publicly endorsed the referendum. The *Los Angeles Times* applauded it as a "forward-looking program" in an editorial. "County flood control bonds should be authorized because they provide means to accomplish the double purpose of conserving much-needed water and of preventing floods."[53] In fact, there seems to have been almost no significant opposition to the plan. Whereas the 1917 bond issue had squeaked by at the ballot box, the new referendum won in a landslide, with 70 percent of district voters approving the bonds.

As construction was getting under way in the mountains, however, there was a simmering discontent in the city of Los Angeles and the San Fernando Valley, much of which by this time had been absorbed by the city. After the opening of the Los Angeles–Owens River Aqueduct, Los Angeles had annexed more than 188 square miles of the San Fernando Valley. The new water provided by the aqueduct encouraged residential development throughout the area and helped Los Angeles to surpass San Francisco as the most populous city in California. Between 1920 and 1925, the population of the city doubled to more than a million as the growth of the movie industry, major discoveries of oil, and the new ease with which people could travel cross-country spurred the last great real estate boom in the region. The peak of the boom came in 1923, when 11,608 acres in Los Angeles were sub-divided and 1,057 tracts were put on the market. Much of the new growth occurred north of the original city limits in San Fernando Valley suburbs like Canoga Park, Van Nuys, North Hollywood, and Studio City. Glendale and Burbank, independent municipalities, were also growing rapidly. By 1930, more than 100,000 people lived in the San Fernando Valley.[54]

Despite the growth north of downtown Los Angeles, the only flood control work planned for the San Fernando Valley in the 1924 bond issue was of a temporary nature. Small earthen embankments protected by fence and rock were to be placed along the main channels of Tujunga Wash. These were intended to provide protection until dams planned for Big Tujunga Creek and Pacoima Creek could be completed. Piles connected by wire fencing were the only protections planned along Verdugo Wash, which flows through the city of Glendale before emptying into the Los Angeles River opposite Griffith Park. Some worried that too little was being done. "I have seen such a storm, that if the like occurs again, the mud will flow down the chimneys of Van Nuys," said William Mulholland. The Finance Committee of the Los Angeles City Council, meanwhile, recommended a few months before the bond election that the city hire an engineer and begin its own flood control program. Echoing the warnings of J. J. Warner in the 1880s, another man cautioned that numerous homes built on the west side of the Los Angeles River in the Glendale Narrows faced grave danger from floods. "Hundreds of innocent people," he said, "are being led into this danger zone and sold homes being told that it is perfectly safe, Los Angeles just having voted millions for flood control."[55]

San Fernando Valley residents began to push for greater local improvements, but the original flood control act prevented the county from spending money raised though the sale of bonds on projects not included in original proposals. A new bond issue could not be placed before voters, moreover, unless state law was changed to permit a bond election to be called before all the money from a previous issue was spent. That statute was changed, however, in 1925. Pressure from valley interests was instrumental in convincing county officials to then place yet another bond issue on the ballot the following year. The new initiative proposed $26.9 million in work, emphasizing downstream controls and mountain projects designed to better protect the San Fernando Valley. Seven million dollars was to be spent to expand plans for a dam to be built on Big Tujunga Creek, the biggest source of runoff north of Los Angeles. A series of smaller structures, known as *de-*

bris basins, designed to intercept rocks and trees washed from the mountains during storms, were to be constructed in the foothills above several valley communities. Verdugo Wash was to be lined with concrete for two miles where it passed through the center of Glendale. More than $3.1 million in work was proposed for the Los Angeles River. A more definite channel was to be dug for the river in the western San Fernando Valley. From Burbank to Compton Creek, the river was to be straightened and confined between levees, some of them reinforced with rock riprap.[56]

As it turned out, the great dam planned for San Gabriel Canyon, upon which all other plans were based, was never built, and the county's flood control program began to unravel as a result. The project first began to be questioned after George W. Goethals, hired as a consultant by the Board of Supervisors, reported in October 1924 that the conservation claims made in promoting the project could not be supported by existing data. Others, meanwhile, began to challenge the need for such a large and expensive dam. After all, the Los Angeles–Owens River Aqueduct, considered one of the great engineering feats in the world at the time, had been built for $500,000 less. In January 1925, the Municipal League, long critical of Reagan, began promoting a plan to build a smaller dam, two miles downstream from the proposed site, that it claimed would not only provide the desired protection from floods but also save $10 million. Concerns about the safety of the dam site were also raised. Faced with mounting criticism, the Board of Supervisors hired a team of engineers and geologists to review the project. They delivered a favorable report, but this did little to dissuade the project's critics. The Municipal League and the Los Angeles chapter of the American Association of Engineers suggested that the board's consultants were biased. A grand jury, meanwhile, threatened to investigate the Flood Control District on charges of inefficiency brought by the Municipal League. The controversy became so contentious that a Municipal League official accused Reagan of assaulting the group's secretary when the official visited the chief engineer's office to examine a map. All of this happened in the months leading up to the November 1926 bond election.[57]

Perhaps not surprisingly, given such a prelude, the bond issue was defeated by a 7 percent margin, highlighting the growing disenchantment of voters with the flood control program. But the outcome could not be blamed solely on the San Gabriel Dam controversy. Defeat of the flood control bonds was part of a general voter revolt against bonds, which led to the defeat of every bond issue on the ballot except one (a $250,000 hospital bond). In all, $48.5 million in city and county bonds were rejected. The new flood control referendum may have simply come too soon after the $35.3 million in bonds approved two years before. The unwillingness of voters to support still greater flood control expenditures may also have reflected the fact that most Southern Californians—in 1926, just as in 1884—had never witnessed one of the great floods they were being asked to pay to prevent. In a region where newcomers still outnumbered natives, the flood risk was still unproven to many. The last significant flood had been in 1916, and the three winters before the bond election were unusually dry.[58] "Most of the residents of this county have no conception of the size and destructive force of a capital flood," a clearly bitter Flood Control District engineer wrote a few years later. "They read of floods on the Ohio and Mississippi and smugly congratulate themselves that they live in a dry climate. They are blind to the danger on their own doorstep."[59]

Five months after the defeat of the bond measure and a week following the release of a report by an independent board of engineers that was strongly critical of the San Gabriel Dam project, James W. Reagan resigned as chief engineer. Reagan's departure was inevitable, even if he hadn't left of his own accord, because a new supervisor who had campaigned against him was elected in the same election in which the bonds were defeated. The new supervisor seemed certain to shift the balance of power on the board in favor of Reagan's removal. Already, two of five supervisors had called for his ouster. Battles over the San Gabriel Dam project, meanwhile, went on for years. The project, decried in a handbill circulated at the time as "a monument to gross ignorance and incompetence," was eventually abandoned as unsafe after a rock slide in 1929.[60] By that time, $3 million had been spent. Investigations into wrongdoing by county officials in connection with the project continued, and in 1930 a grand jury, while declining to bring charges against Reagan or other district officials, strongly criticized the agency for failing to make adequate plans, ignoring sound engineering advice, and providing generally shoddy administration. Subsequent investigations uncovered even greater irregularities. In 1933, Sidney T. Graves, a member of the Board of Supervisors from 1926 to 1930 and a former state legislator, was sent to prison for accepting an $80,000 bribe from one of the contractors on the project.[61]

The San Gabriel Dam fiasco so damaged the reputation of the county flood control program that it undermined progress on improvements for years and fundamentally altered the nature of future work. The county would never again build a large concrete dam. District voters would not approve another flood control bond issue for twenty-eight years. Flood control planning was forced to become reactive rather than proactive. Newcomers, however, continued to stream into Southern California. More than two million people moved to Los Angeles County during the first three decades of the twentieth century, transforming it from a largely agricultural region with a population about equal to that of present-day Abilene, Texas, into a major metropolitan area. By 1930, development had begun to encroach upon the Los Angeles River from its source to the sea. Many once-rural sections of the San Fernando Valley were covered with homes. Van Nuys and North Hollywood each had more than 10,000 residents. Burbank, new home of Warner Bros. Pictures, had a population of more than 16,000. Glendale had been transformed in twenty years from a small town with fewer than 3,000 residents into a burgeoning city that was home to more than 60,000 people. Residential development had also begun to move into the foothills above Glendale and Pasadena.[62]

South of Los Angeles the situation was much the same. Many of the working class suburbs built along the Los Angeles River owe their origins to the boom years of the 1920s. Providing small but affordable homes for blue collar employees in nearby industrial plants, towns like Maywood, Bell, South Gate, and Lynwood came into existence virtually overnight; by 1930, more than 100,000 people lived in communities between Los Angeles and Long Beach. Long Beach, meanwhile, had emerged as the second largest city in the county, stimulated by the growth of its harbor, the discovery of oil, and its development as a navy town. It had more than 140,000 residents by 1930. As development spread all across Southern California, the flood control program designed in the wake of the 1914 flood proved inadequate. Flood control planners lacked the resources of private developers and did not have the legal authority to prevent homes from being built in flood-prone areas. The result was that flood control construction simply could not keep pace with the growth of the metropolis. This created an environment ripe for disaster.

Struggling to Keep Up

The end of James W. Reagan's twelve-year stint as chief engineer of the Flood Control District marked a significant change in direction for the agency. Under Reagan's leadership, management of the district had been autocratic and improvements often haphazard. Work had seldom followed a coordinated plan, and the distribution of projects had seemed oriented more toward gaining widespread support for bond referendums than toward creating a unified system of flood protection. Projects had often been approved before detailed surveys had even been conducted, and planned improvements had sometimes been forgotten once bonds had been passed by voters. Harold E.

Hedger, an engineer who had begun working for the Flood Control District in 1919 and who was later head of the agency, described the typical procedure:

> A decision would be made by the chief engineer that a dam was needed in one canyon or another, that protection work was needed at another point, and a survey party would go out and take some topography. Then the chief engineer or perhaps the chief designer in the office would decide how high the dam should be, not based on record hydrology, but just on what the physical aspects of the ground would seem to indicate. And the result was that the works that were installed were not interrelated at all, but were constructed generally at the point of greatest need.[63]

E. C. Eaton, a former state engineer hired two months before Reagan's departure as his top assistant, was named the new chief engineer. Tight-lipped where his predecessor had been boisterous, Eaton reorganized the department and gave greater authority to his subordinates. Over the next four years, he coordinated development of the first truly comprehensive plan for flood control in Los Angeles County, a model that became the basis for all future flood control construction. The plan, proposed in 1931 and adopted by the Board of Supervisors soon after, recommended $33 million for immediate work and outlined an ambitious program of future improvements. It called for the construction of flood protections on one hundred miles of stream channels, the building of dams and flood control basins capable of regulating 76,800 acre feet of runoff, the development of 1,500 acres of new spreading grounds, and the placing of debris basins in canyons throughout the mountains.[64]

At the time, fewer than twenty-one miles of the Los Angeles River, less than half its present length, had been controlled by what were considered permanent flood control works—levees reinforced by rock riprap or cement. About fifteen miles were lined with temporary protections, typically pile-and-wire fence. Gaps in levees undermined existing protections, while in the San Fernando Valley the river remained completely uncontrolled. Development had increased so much that some areas flooded even in years with below-normal rainfall (fig. 5.8). Flooding became so common that schools in some parts of the valley sent children home as soon as it started to rain. In all of Los Angeles County, just sixty miles of streams, 12 percent of the total, were leveed, while 40 percent of the bridges that crossed them were considered inadequate to allow floodwaters to pass freely. Only 33 percent of the mountain watershed was regulated by flood control devices. "No chain is stronger than the weakest link," Eaton cautioned. "While portions of these channels are adequately protected with permanent works, the many gaps and lack of continuity of the whole system renders much of this work ineffective."[65]

Officials estimated that, despite the work completed thus far, three hundred square miles of Los Angeles County were still subject to overflow, nearly as large an area as had been threatened before flood control work began. The flood-prone area had not diminished significantly in size because new development only aggravated the flood potential. Each new house, shopping center, industrial plant, parking lot, and street reduced the amount of ground surface available to absorb precipitation, thus heightening runoff and increasing the volume of water destined for the rivers and streams. Federal government engineers later calculated that an average single family home renders 23 percent of the lot on which it sits impervious. A typical apartment house covers about 53 percent of the ground surface. In commercial districts, as much as 95 percent of the ground is covered with buildings and pavement and is, therefore, unavailable to absorb runoff.[66] The recollections of Harold Hedger give some idea of the effect of development on the amount of water carried by area streams during storms. "I can remember the first time I saw Ballona Creek," he recalled in 1968. "In 1920, I could jump across it at many points even

FIG. 5.8. Scenes like this one became increasingly common even in normal winter rains as flood control construction failed to keep pace with urban development. *Los Angeles Examiner* photograph. Used with permission, Department of Special Collections, University of Southern California Library/Hearst Newspaper Collection.

when there was a pretty good storm going. Now, today, with that area all built up, the homes and streets and supermarkets and things of this sort, a quarter-inch of rain will produce a stream that will be a hundred feet wide and several feet deep."[67]

With Southern California rapidly losing its once-rural character, the economic significance of flood control also became increasingly important. The total assessed value of property in Los Angeles County increased 2,600 percent between 1914 and 1931. A flood 50 percent larger than the one in 1914, officials warned, could cause $100 million in damage.[68] Such a flood would have again rendered Long Beach an island. One-third of the San Fernando Valley would have been inundated. Downtown Los Angeles east of Alameda Street would have been under water. Floodwaters threatened to reopen former channels of the Los Angeles River through Huntington Park, Watts, and other working class communities south of Los Angeles. Compton would have been especially hard hit. South of Downey, floodwaters from the county's three major rivers would have joined to create a waterway more than six miles wide.[69]

The comprehensive plan called for the immediate construction of permanent flood protections along nearly eleven miles of the Los Angeles River. Levees reinforced by riprap or concrete were to be built along the river from the south end of Griffith Park to the Arroyo Seco, a distance of 4.5 miles. Another six miles of levees were to be built south of Los Angeles to close gaps in the existing levee system in Vernon, South Gate, and north Long Beach. These changes would have given the river reinforced levees from near Glendale all the way to the river's mouth at Long Beach. To accommodate heightened runoff in the western San Fernando Valley, meanwhile, the comprehensive plan recommended that an entirely new channel for the river, fifty feet wide and five feet deep, be dug from Owensmouth Avenue in Canoga Park 6.75 miles downstream to Havenhurst Avenue in Encino.[70]

Conservation was also integral to the comprehensive plan. Three new flood control dams were proposed for the San Gabriel Mountains. Another fifteen hundred acres of spreading grounds were to be built to allow some of the floodwaters to percolate into aquifers. In addition, two large flood control reservoirs were planned for the lowlands—one at the intersection of the San Gabriel River and the Rio Hondo, a point known as the Whittier Narrows, and another at Nigger Slough, the marshy area between the Dominguez Hills and the port at San Pedro. Dozens of check dams and debris basins were to be built in the mountains and foothills to slow runoff and debris. Eaton claimed that the new facilities, by slowing runoff and allowing it to percolate underground, would conserve enough water to satisfy the domestic water needs of 450,000 people. "The combined problems of flood control and conservation can be solved by the use of subsurface reservoirs at a fraction of the cost of surface storage," he wrote.[71]

A lack of funds, however, delayed the implementation of Eaton's plan. Just $1.4 million remained from the sale of bonds approved in 1917 and 1924, and the public mood toward flood control projects in the wake of the San Gabriel Dam debacle meant certain defeat for any new ballot initiatives. An application to the Federal Emergency Administration of Public Works in 1933 requesting $34.7 million in grants and loans was rejected.[72] With little money, only minor improvements could be made. Flood control construction ground nearly to a halt. New work amounted to little more than the plugging of holes in existing levees and the digging of deeper stream channels. In 1931, four miles of reinforced levees and another thirteen miles of temporary channel protections were erected. The following year, state funds paid for the construction of levees along the Los Angeles River between Fletcher Drive and the Arroyo Seco. In addition, several gaps in the levee system south of downtown Los Angeles were filled in. The river's channel in the San Fernando Valley was extended farther west through the excavation of a "training channel," but this channel was smaller and shorter than the one proposed in the comprehensive plan and was still too small to provide adequate drainage. The flood control system remained fragmentary and insufficient to protect the growing metropolitan area. As late as December 1933, 86 percent of stream channels in the district were still without levees or other permanent protections.[73]

The flood danger had become especially acute in the foothills above Glendale, which, over the previous decade, had been increasingly developed for homes. Subdivision of La Cañada Valley, which sits between the San Gabriel and Verdugo Mountains, had begun in the late eighteenth century, but population growth was greatest between 1923 and 1930. Communities like Montrose, Tujunga, Sunland, and La Crescenta were built in the worst possible locations—at the foot of steep mountain canyons that disgorge onto a high valley that had itself been carved out by water and rock pouring from mountain slopes for thousands of years. As elsewhere in Southern California, though, would-be developers paid little attention to the risk. Electricity came to La Cañada Valley in 1912, and Montrose and Tujunga were laid out the following year. Montrose got its own newspaper in 1922, and the next year a school and a post office were opened. Streetcar tracks were extended from Glendale to Montrose in 1924. In 1925, Tujunga was incorporated and Verdugo City was founded on ten acres west of Montrose. Residential development intensified in the west end of the valley in 1926 when two areas around Sunland, first settled in 1900, approved annexation to the city of Los Angeles, thus assuring their future water supply, always the biggest shortcoming in the foothills. As development spread, flood control planners watched warily, knowing that, unless something was done, catastrophe was inevitable. The bond issue of 1926 had proposed that debris basins be built in the mountains above La Cañada Valley and that channels be excavated to carry storm waters away from developed areas, but that referendum had been defeated.[74]

Minutes after midnight on New Year's Day 1934, just such a catastrophe occurred. Following three days of heavy rain, a wall of water, mud, and rocks twenty feet high tore through La Cañada Valley, killing at least forty-nine people, destroying 198 homes, and causing $6.1 million in damage ($73.4 million in current figures). Four hundred more homes were rendered uninhabitable. The destruction was so complete that, three years later, forty-five persons were still listed as missing, their bodies never found.[75] Two months before the flood, brush fires had burned a 7-1/2-square-mile area of the mountains above Montrose and La Crescenta, leaving soils unprotected and heightening the threat of erosion as the rainy season approached. Light rain had begun to fall on the afternoon of 30 December 1933 and had increased in intensity the following day until about midnight, when the mud-covered hills reached their saturation point and gave way. Mud poured down canyons, gathering momentum and volume as it descended and sweeping up rocks and trees in its path, before roaring like a tidal wave over the streets and homes of Montrose. The power of the moving mass was so great that twelve people who had sought refuge in an American Legion hall that was being used as a Red Cross evacuation site were killed when rocks ripped through the building's walls (fig. 5.9). The Los Angeles Times described the destruction as "worse than war."[76]

The deluge was brief but devastating. In just thirteen minutes, more than 600,000 cubic yards of mud and other debris—enough to fill 240 Olympic-size swimming pools to the brim—was deposited in the Montrose area. Eight hundred automobiles were buried in the sludge. Boulders weighing several tons were carried more than a mile. A giant boulder, six feet in diameter and weighing fifty-nine tons, was found on Foothill Boulevard. Floodwaters poured out of La Cañada Valley down Verdugo Creek, through the city of Glendale, and into the Los Angeles River. Flooding occurred all over Los Angeles County. Rainfall records were established at many locations, with Los Angeles receiving 7.4 inches of rain in twenty-four hours, a new high. Families in Reseda and Canoga Park were marooned, as the new suburbs were

FIG. 5.9. The American Legion hall in Montrose, where a dozen people were killed when a wall of water, mud, and rocks tore through the building during a sudden flood on New Year's Day 1934. *Los Angeles Examiner* photograph. Used with permission, Department of Special Collections, University of Southern California Library/Hearst Newspaper Collection.

incapable of absorbing the sudden runoff. More than a thousand houses were inundated in Venice and along Ballona Creek. A break in a levee on the Los Angeles River north of Long Beach allowed flood-waters to spread over several nearby farms.[77] But the damage else-where was slight compared to the desolation in the foothills. In a mo-ment of booster-driven irony, the *Los Angeles Times* remarked in a supplement published in the same issue in which it reported the news of the flood that "no place on earth offers greater security to life and greater freedom from natural disasters than Southern California."[78]

Although the worst flooding did not occur on the Los Angeles River, the flood of New Year's Day 1934 is nonetheless important to the history of the river because it focused national attention on the flood problem in Southern California and, as a result, helped shape the future direction of flood control efforts. Legendary folk singer Woody Guthrie wrote a song about the flood in which he blamed the devastation on "the wild Los Angeles River," although in truth most of the damage was caused by what scientists call *debris flows*, not streams in flood. "A cloudburst hit the mountains; it swept away our homes," he sang. "A hundred souls was taken in that fatal New Year's flood. A million hearts was grieving for the dear ones that they loved."[79]

In the days after the tragedy, Chief Engineer Eaton blamed the disaster on the defeat of the 1926 bond issue, which would have provided $2.4 million for flood control construction in the area where damages were greatest. "In no case where permanent types of protection work were installed was serious damaged experienced," he said.[80] Eaton soon became the chief target of public wrath as a result of his comments and the continued failure of the county to provide adequate flood protection. A local organization made up of two thousand engineers urged the Board of Supervisors to appoint an independent committee to "make a complete review" of the operations and plans of the Flood Control District.[81] Others called for Eaton's removal. Already linked to lingering legal battles over the San Gabriel Dam, the chief engineer resigned in August 1934.[82] S. M. Fisher, a surveyor in the Flood Control District office, was appointed as Eaton's temporary replacement until a more exhaustive search could be conducted.

That fall, a desperate Los Angeles County Board of Supervisors placed a $26.3 million bond issue on the ballot to fund emergency improvements in the foothills and numerous other projects similar to those that had been rejected by voters eight years before. Twelve debris basins were to be built above La Cañada Valley. Concrete channels were proposed to carry water from the debris basins to Verdugo Creek and on to the Los Angeles River. This time, $1.3 million in work was recommended for the river, which still had levees along less than half its length. Major projects were also planned for the San Gabriel River, Ballona Creek, Compton Creek, and the area around Westwood. But, with a decade of flood control failures still fresh in the minds of voters and the nation sinking into the worst economic depression in its history, the measure was defeated by a 4 percent margin. "Confidence in the Flood Control District," commented John Anson Ford, elected to the Board of Supervisors that year, "was badly shaken."[83]

The Federal Government Takes Over

With no money to pursue its comprehensive plan and with local taxpayers unwilling to support new flood control spending, county officials turned to the federal government for help. They requested $19.3 million in assistance under the Emergency Relief Appropriation Act, a Depression-era recovery program created by Congress. The district's comprehensive plan had been refined and expanded; it now proposed sixty-four separate projects carrying an ultimate price tag of $99.9 million. A presidential committee had endorsed the comprehensive plan three months after the disastrous flood of 1934. The latest version of the plan called for new flood control work on the entire length of the Los Angeles River. It recommended that a much larger channel be excavated for the river in the western San Fernando Valley and that the river channel be lined with concrete from Canoga Park to North Hollywood. Between North Hollywood and Fletcher Drive, the river was to be confined between levees, also lined with concrete. Near Elysian Park, the river was to be widened and its waters carried in a box-shaped, concrete channel to increase the river's capacity. South of downtown, four remaining gaps in the levee system were to be closed. For the first time, a flood control dam and reservoir were also envisioned for the main channel of the river. It was to be built in Van Nuys to regulate increasing runoff in the western half of the San Fernando Valley. The total cost for all of the Los Angeles River projects was estimated at $15 million.[84]

In July 1935, President Franklin D. Roosevelt approved an allocation of $13.9 million in Works Progress Administration (WPA) funds to finance fourteen of the most pressing projects in the comprehensive plan. The county was to provide $3.5 million for the purchase of land needed for the projects. Work was placed under the supervision of the U.S. Army Corps of Engineers and was to be carried out by unemployed local laborers on WPA relief rolls. The vast majority of WPA relief funds were designated for channel improvements and the construction of debris basins on the Los Angeles River and its tributaries. That same month, Congress authorized a preliminary examination of the Los Angeles and San Gabriel Rivers and their tributaries, the first step toward creating a more comprehensive, federally funded flood control program.[85]

Work began in August 1935 when U.S. Army Major Theodore Wyman and several military assistants were ordered to Los Angeles to review plans. By October, construction was under way and the work force had been expanded from fifteen people to two thousand. A second emergency appropriation providing an additional $3 million was made in 1936. The Los Angeles River was deepened, widened, and confined between concrete banks from Lankershim Boulevard in North Hollywood to Elysian Park, a distance of 11.5 miles. Channel capacity near Griffith Park was increased by more than 2,700 percent, from 2,500 to 71,600 cubic feet per second. Levees, reinforced by rock riprap, were built along 2.5 miles of the river south of Los Angeles. Debris basins and new drainage channels were constructed in five canyons in the Los Angeles River watershed and one in the Rio Hondo system. Debris basin construction took on a new importance in flood control planning after the flood of 1934 (fig. 5.10). Significant flood control work was also done on Verdugo Wash, Compton Creek, and Ballona Creek. In the first twelve months of construction, more than $20 million in federal and local funds were spent and nearly seventeen thousand people were employed. Ninety-five percent of them were local workers on WPA relief rolls.[86]

Congress significantly expanded the flood control duties of the U.S. Army Corps of Engineers with passage of the Flood Control Act of 1936. The act gave the agency sole responsibility for providing flood control on the nation's rivers and streams and authorized fifty flood control projects nationwide. More money was allocated for work in Los Angeles County than for projects anywhere else in the nation.[87] An additional $70 million was provided for county projects, almost one-quarter of all federal expenditures for flood control under the act. Nearly all of that money was to be spent for projects on the Los Angeles River and its tributaries, causing the chairman of the House Committee on Flood Control to express bemusement that such a large share of the federal flood control budget was to be spent on "a stream which is dry sometimes."[88] Congress also authorized the Department of Agriculture to conduct surveys to determine what might be done in the mountains and rural areas to limit the flood risk, but most of the funding for projects in Los Angeles County over the next two decades was allocated to the Corps of Engineers. Proposals by the U.S. Forest

FIG. 5.10. The construction of debris basins, like this one in Blanchard Canyon, a tributary of Verdugo Wash, became much more central to flood control planning in Los Angeles County after the 1934 flood. The metal tower in the center allows storm waters to pass into flood control channels while mud, rocks, and other materials are retained in the basin. Photograph by the author, 1997.

Service and the Soil Conservation Service for work in the upper water-shed of the Los Angeles River—designed to combat the flood problem where it begins by planting trees, improving fire protection, and con-structing minor flood control works on mountain streams—never re-ceived adequate funding to be fully implemented.[89]

Local government officials, business leaders, and private citizens who spoke in March 1936 at public hearings about the federal govern-ment's flood control program were uniformly supportive of the army's efforts. Even those organizations that had been most critical of the county's program welcomed federal involvement. One man, com-menting on the perceived lack of success of local flood control work, said, "So far we have spent millions of dollars and haven't gotten any-where."[90] Another blamed the lack of progress on the engineers who had been in charge. "If you build a bridge out of two-by-fours and ask an elephant to walk across," said an engineer from Monrovia, "you don't condemn the bridge, you condemn the men that built it." From this perspective, the U.S. government was seen as a white knight arriv-ing just in the nick of time. The same man from Monrovia said, "I am pleased that, at the present time, the army has moved into Southern California," Pausing, he added. "I am not so sure that I don't wish they had arrived about twenty years ago." His last comment was greeted with laughter, followed by uproarious applause.[91]

Initial federal government work was based on the county's com-prehensive plan, but army engineers soon discovered that the designs were inadequate. "In many cases, the [county's] plans were not based on accurate surveys and the design discharges were less than those customarily used by the United States Engineer Department," ex-plained a federal government hydraulic engineer.[92] In December 1936, Army Major Wyman submitted his own recommendations for control-ling the Los Angeles River. He completed a general plan for the San Gabriel River and the Rio Hondo in February 1938. These plans em-phasized a three-pronged approach. Debris basins were to be built at the mouths of mountain canyons to collect the mud and rock that washed from hillsides during storms and to prevent debris from clog-ging waterways. Large flood control basins were to be constructed on the major rivers and their tributary streams to regulate stream flow during storms. The stream channels themselves were to be deepened, widened, and lined with levees or concrete to enable floodwaters to be transported to the ocean as quickly as possible.[93]

Plans called for the Los Angeles River to be confined between con-crete banks from North Hollywood to the Rio Hondo. Between Lank-ershim Boulevard and Burbank Western Wash, a distance of 3.5 miles, the river was to be carried in a rectangular channel constructed entirely of reinforced concrete. From Burbank Western Wash to Elysian Park, a distance of just over eight miles, the river was to be given sloped banks and paved with concrete and grouted rock, but its bottom was to remain unlined. The existing river channel and the available right of way were so narrow where the river passes Elysian Park that the river through this section was to be confined in an entirely concrete channel with vertical walls as much as thirty-one feet tall. South of the Arroyo Seco, these walls were to give way gradually to sloped banks, but the river's channel was to remain entirely concrete all the way to Vernon. From Soto Street in Vernon to the Rio Hondo, the river's banks were to be paved with stone or concrete. Two large flood control basins were planned for the Los Angeles River watershed and a third was proposed. Sepulveda Flood Control Basin was to be built on the main channel of the river in Van Nuys, and Hansen Dam was to be constructed on Tujunga Wash. Flood control basins were also planned for the upper San Gabriel River and Whittier Narrows.[94]

Federal flood control engineers had little choice but to confine the Los Angeles River to a relatively narrow channel, a fraction of the width of its natural floodplain, because of the nature of existing development and the high price of real estate along its course. Zoning regulations that would allow planners to prevent building on flood-prone lands did not yet exist. A Los Angeles city engineer proposed in 1927 that subdivision be prohibited on lands threatened by floods, but a development-minded city council, ever-cognizant that each new home and business would increase its tax base, took no action on the suggestion.[95] After the flood of 1934, an official of the Los Angeles Regional Planning Commission made a similar proposal. "You can stop a man from selling rotten fruit, but he still has the right to sell rotten real estate," said C. D. Clark, a subdivision engineer for the planning body. "As things stand now, there is nothing to prevent a man from selling property in the middle of a wash that gets flooded every year. When a subdivision plan is submitted and perhaps turned down by the engineering, health and other county departments and by us, the owners can still sell it." The development of laws to regulate building on flood-prone lands was apparently slowed by concerns that such statutes might not hold up in court.[96]

Government planners, consequently, were largely powerless in their efforts to stem the tide of new construction beside the river. By the time the federal government took over the flood control program, homes and businesses had been built close to its channel along much of its length. Even in those areas where urban development had not yet reached the river, most of the land near its course had already been subdivided for such uses. In many places, the presence of farms along the river disguised the fact that plans were already in place for the construction of residential developments, shopping centers, or other commercial enterprises on the sites. This made the purchase of such land for flood control work prohibitively expensive. Thus, after army engineers revised the county's plans and required stream channels to be larger than originally proposed, one of the chief expenses of the Los Angeles County Flood Control District became the acquisition of real estate along the river. Under its agreement with the federal government, the county was required to furnish all land needed for flood control projects. "It has been a tremendously expensive thing to go down the channels and buy rights-of-way, widening the channel," said H. G. Legg, chairman of the Board of Supervisors' Flood Control Committee, in a hearing before Congress.[97]

Detailed land use maps of Los Angeles County produced in part with WPA funds between 1933 and 1939 demonstrate why federal flood control engineers were so limited in what they could do.[98] Even as early as 1937, when much of the San Fernando Valley was surveyed, more than three-quarters of the land on both sides of the river as far west as Sepulveda Boulevard in Van Nuys had been subdivided for residences. Roughly a fifth of those lots were already occupied by homes. Farther downstream, the percentage of riverfront property that had been subdivided increased to 100 percent, and around Studio City houses occupied as many as half the lots on some blocks. As the decade progressed, more and more of the home lots near the river were built upon, and the residences that had been constructed were occupied. Between 1930 and 1940, in fact, the residential population doubled and even tripled in many of the cities and communities along the river in the San Fernando Valley. By 1940, more than 200,000 people lived there.[99]

As the residential population rose, commercial development also increased to serve the growing population. Ventura Boulevard, then the primary east-west highway through the San Fernando Valley, also became its first major commercial thoroughfare. It begins to follow the south bank of the river closely near Coldwater Canyon Avenue in Sherman Oaks. By 1937, businesses were starting to encroach on the river in this area. Nearly half the lots on the north side of Ventura Boulevard, adjacent to the river, were occupied by stores and other businesses. The sound stages and executive offices of Republic Pictures, formed two years before, sat on a large lot south of the river, east of Radford Avenue (now home to CBS Studios). Perhaps indicative of how insignificant the river was culturally, a detailed guidebook to the Los Angeles area produced in the 1930s, which includes a driving tour along Ventura Boulevard and features a side trip that crosses the river at Van Nuys Boulevard, never even mentions the river in its description of sites along the route.[100]

Increasingly in the 1930s, the riverfront in the eastern San Fernando Valley became synonymous with the motion picture industry, as studios that had outgrown their facilities over the hill in Hollywood sought larger tracts of land on which to develop sound stages and outdoor movie sets. Universal City, home to Universal Pictures, founded on more than 800 acres at the head of Cahuenga Pass in 1915, stretched for more than a mile on the south side of the river. In 1929, Warner Bros. Pictures relocated to Burbank and, by 1935, it occupied 188 acres on the north side of the river, cater-corner to Universal City (fig. 5.11). Soon after, Walt Disney would also outgrow its Hollywood facilities and purchase property near the river. It bought fifty-one acres on Buena Vista Street in Burbank in 1938. Its studios, located 300 yards north of the river, were completed in 1940. The same guidebook that ignored the river farther upstream likewise made no mention of its presence in detailed descriptions of the major studios that backed up to its banks.[101]

The character of land use along the river in the 1930s was much the same for the rest of its length. Here and there undeveloped tracts still existed. In places, farmland that had not yet been subdivided bordered the river. But all along its course, open tracts alternated with residential development. Factories and warehouses sat next to farms. Undisturbed land that might have otherwise enabled the river to have been given a wider berth was separated from its channel by railroad and utility lines. These facts alone made it difficult for flood control engineers to consider more imaginative strategies for preventing floods. The dynamics of stream flow in the semiarid region also made it imprudent to allow the river to meander relatively freely on one part of its course while restricting it to a narrow channel elsewhere. Such an irregular design would have caused sediment to collect in the more open sections. Over time, that sediment would have built up and could have eventually blocked the river's flow, forcing it to again cut a new course to the sea—but now over valuable property.

Griffith Park, for example, would seem to have offered ample opportunity for the river to be kept in a quasi-natural state. The largest urban park in the nation, it was founded in 1896 where the river turns south at the eastern terminus of the Santa Monica Mountains. Even as late as 1934, when WPA workers surveyed this area, much of the land opposite the northeastern corner of the park on the east side of the river was vacant. But farther downstream, the small homes of the Atwater Village neighborhood occupied most of the east bank of the

FIG. 5.11. The Los Angeles River, its channel still largely uncontrolled, adjacent to the studios of Warner Bros. Pictures in Burbank in the 1930s. Several buildings on the Warner Bros. complex were destroyed when the river overflowed in this area in March 1938. The back lot of Universal Pictures is in the foreground. The Verdugo Mountains rise above Burbank. Used with permission, Los Angeles Public Library/Security Pacific Collection.

river. The course of the river became even more constricted near Elysian Park. The freight yards of the Southern Pacific Railroad extended for more than two miles along its eastern shore. Light industry and residences lined the west side. The narrowing of its channel as the river passed Elysian Park put these areas in grave danger from flooding.[102]

The most serious bottleneck on the river occurred through downtown Los Angeles. The riverfront east of the central business district was almost entirely built up by this time (fig. 5.12). Railroad tracks and power lines hugged both sides of the river. Large gas tanks also sat next to its channel. Freight yards, warehouses, and factories occupied most of the land west of the river. There was some open land to the east, but here, too, transportation lines and scattered industrial sites prevented the river channel from being widened significantly. The numerous bridges that crossed the river through this section also complicated matters (fig. 5.13). Sixteen railroad and highway bridges crossed the river in the five miles between Elysian Park and Soto Street in Vernon. Although the trestle bridges that had posed such a problem in earlier floods had long since been replaced by span structures, bridge piers and abutments nevertheless hindered the free flow of floodwaters. "The limited right of way and numerous highway and railroad bridge crossings have created a problem of the first magnitude," said a U.S. government engineer. Development through downtown so restricted the channel of the river, in fact, that one or more large flood control basins had to be built in the San Fernando Valley. It was simply not economically feasible, engineers explained, to construct a channel capable of containing the peak flow of the river through this section unless such facilities were built farther upstream.[103]

The riverfront remained largely industrial through Vernon. Stockyards, slaughterhouses, chemical and steel plants, salvage yards, and oil tanks lined the river course after it left Los Angeles. Many of the workers in those plants lived south of Vernon in riverside communities like Maywood, Bell, Cudahy, South Gate, Compton, and an unincorporated area east of the river (present-day Bell Gardens) derisively known as "Billy Goat Acres," so called because of the large number of Dust Bowl migrants who settled there during the Depression.[104] Residential neighborhoods lined the river from Maywood to its confluence with the Rio Hondo. It is important to remember, too, when considering the constraints under which flood control engineers operated, that the industrial areas and working class cities south of Los Angeles had been built in what had been, until 1889, the river's channel. This was the area where the river had historically been most erratic (see fig. 4.5). The river turned nearly ninety degrees southeast after leaving Los Angeles and, if its channel was not tightly controlled here, the river might return to its former course.

South of the Rio Hondo, land use along the Los Angeles River was a checkerboard of small farms, residential subdivisions, industry, and power line rights of way all the way to Long Beach. Still, many of the more permanent developments had been built close enough to the river to force it into a relatively narrow course. Homes and residential lots again predominated in north Long Beach. Farther downstream,

FIG. 5.12. The riverfront through downtown Los Angeles was heavily built up by 1932, when this photograph was taken. Railyards, railroad tracks, utility lines, and industry lined the river from Elysian Park south to Vernon. This view looks west across the river toward the Civic Center. The tall, white building *left of center* is Los Angeles City Hall. The river is shown from the Southern Pacific Railroad crossing south of Main Street to Fourth Street. Used with permission, Los Angeles Public Library/Security Pacific Collection.

oil tanks, fish canneries, warehouses, manufacturing plants, and other port-related developments lined the river's artificial channel above its mouth, completed in 1921. Long Beach, in the years since, had become the fifth largest city in California, thanks to oil, the navy, and its port (and, to some degree, tourism). As land use patterns along the river from the San Fernando Valley to the Pacific Ocean in the 1930s clearly demonstrated, the time had long since passed in which the river may have been allowed to flow relatively unhindered through a wider, more natural floodplain.

The Flood of March 1938

Federal flood control work had barely begun when the Los Angeles area was hit in March 1938 by the most damaging flood in its history, a week-long deluge that demonstrated the need for even greater controls than had first been conceived. Rain began to fall on 27 February and intensified two days later, when two frontal systems combined off the coast to form a broad frontal zone. By 3 March, some areas in the San Gabriel Mountains had received more than 32 inches of rain, nearly as much as they usually receive in an entire year. Los Angeles got 6.3 inches of rain in twenty-four hours, the second highest such total in its history. As in most great floods in Los Angeles, the ground was already saturated when the storm began—rain had fallen regu-

FIG. 5.13. The narrowing of the right of way of the Los Angeles River as it passed by Elysian Park and the numerous railroad and highway bridges that crossed its channel in this area created a bottleneck, which heightened the flood risk and ultimately required that several large flood control basins be built in the San Fernando Valley. Used with permission, Water Resources Center Archives, University of California, Berkeley/W. L. Huber Collection.

larly during the first half of February—so runoff was intense. The flood discharge on the Los Angeles River was the greatest on record, more than twice its peak in 1914. The peak flow of the river at Long Beach was 99,100 cubic feet per second, greater than the average flow of the Mississippi River near St. Louis. In the area drained by the river, 31,511 acres were flooded (fig. 5.14) and forty-five people died; damages totaled more than $17 million. In all of Los Angeles County, 108,000 acres were inundated, eighty-seven people were killed, and property damage exceeded $78 million ($888.8 million in current figures).[105] A *Los Angeles Times* reporter, who viewed the destruction from an airplane, remarked: "From 3,000 feet, a scene unfolds that groundlings can never grasp. Disaster, gutted farmlands, ruined roads, shattered communications, wrecked railroad lines—all leap into sharp-etched reality from that altitude." Rupert Hughes, who set the climactic scenes of his novel *City of Angels* in the midst of the flood, wrote, "It was as if the Pacific had moved in to take back its ancient bed."[106]

The most extensive flooding in Los Angeles County occurred in the San Fernando Valley, which alone experienced $12.4 million in damage. The Los Angeles River overflowed large areas west of Encino, where a channel had been excavated for the river a few years before. This channel was too small to accommodate increased runoff caused by rapid residential development in the area, and its banks had remained unprotected despite repeated recommendations for their improvement. Flooding was even more widespread downstream. The Van Nuys section of Los Angeles was completely isolated for several days when all approaching bridges were either flooded or destroyed. Construction had begun on two huge flood control basins that might have prevented such flooding—one on Tujunga Wash and another on the upper Los Angeles River—but both were still years from completion. A third flood control basin planned for Pacoima Wash had not yet been approved. The reservoirs behind all fourteen county-built flood control dams, meanwhile, were filled to overflowing, and many were clogged with debris. Inflow behind a dam on Big Tujunga Creek was four times its capacity. With the dams unable to hold back any more water, floodwaters poured toward Pacoima Wash and Tujunga Wash. The channels of those two streams were lined at the time only with insubstantial pile-and-wire fence, so floodwaters quickly spread over the landscape.[107]

Destruction from the flood was dramatic throughout Los Angeles County. Five people were thrown to their deaths in North Hollywood when the Lankershim Boulevard bridge over the Los Angeles River collapsed. Ten more drowned in Long Beach when a wooden pedes-

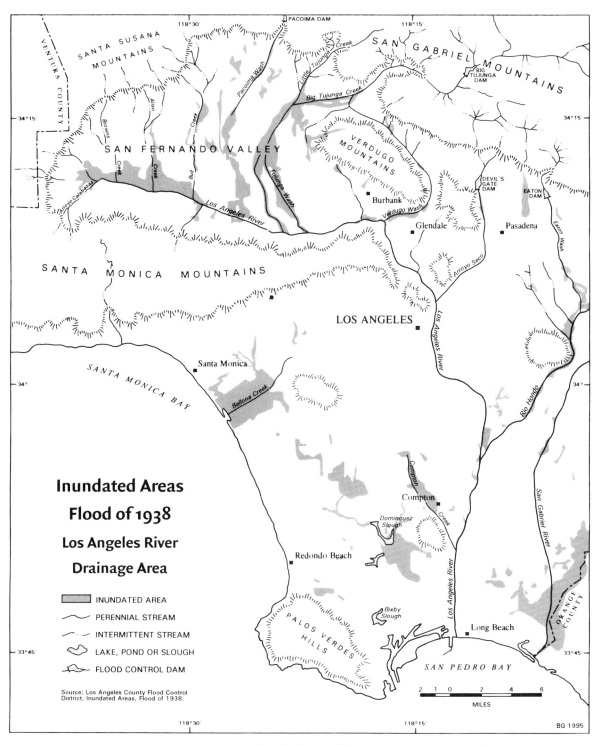

Inundated Areas

Flood of 1938

Los Angeles River

Drainage Area

INUNDATED AREA
PERENNIAL STREAM
INTERMITTENT STREAM
LAKE, POND OR SLOUGH
FLOOD CONTROL DAM

Source: Los Angeles County Flood Control
District, Inundated Areas, Flood of 1938.

MILES

BG 1995

FIG. 5.14. During the flood of March 1938, 108,000 acres in Los Angeles County were inundated, eighty-seven people were killed, and more than $78 million in property damage was experienced. This was the most damaging flood in Los Angeles history. Map by the author.

trian bridge just upstream from the river's mouth gave way. Raging waters cut wide new bends for the river on the north side of Griffith Park, washing away huge sections of two major highways (fig. 5.15). Numerous buildings were destroyed at Warner Bros. Pictures. Houses were floated from their foundations, and some washed into the river. Sewage lines ruptured, threatening public health. Near downtown Los Angeles, thirty thousand board feet of lumber, to be used in the construction of a bridge to the new Union Station, was swept into the river and carried to the sea, much of it later washing up on beaches near the river's mouth. A gas main underneath the Ninth Street bridge was ruptured by raging floodwaters, and its fumes were ignited by a passing railroad car. The resulting explosion sent flames shooting in the air, and for a brief time the river actually looked like it was on fire. Throughout the county, ninety-one railroad and highway bridges were destroyed or badly damaged, some of them twisted nearly beyond recognition (fig. 5.16). A three-hundred-foot-long Southern Pacific bridge near Elysian Park, built in 1903, was ripped apart, in the words of one newspaper, as if "constructed of flimsy kindling sticks." Uncounted miles of railroad tracks and automobile roads were also damaged.[108]

While the flood of 1938 showed how much work still had to be done, it also proved the value of improvements made thus far. "Large as it is, the damage is so much less than it would have been but for our magnificent system of flood-control dams," commented the *Times* in an editorial on 4 March. "People who have grumbled at the enormous cost of our flood-protection works might profitably compare it with the cost of what would have certainly happened here Wednesday but for those sturdy guardians of the Los Angeles basin." There was little flooding from the Los Angeles River south of the Arroyo Seco. By this time, the river channel had been confined most of the way from Los Angeles to the sea between levees protected by riprap or cement, with only minor gaps in the levee system still under construction. Some flooding did occur along the river near its junction with the Rio Hondo, which still had only temporary protection on one side of its channel. The most extensive flooding on the coastal plain occurred where flood control work had not yet begun—near Cerritos and Coyote Creeks and in the low-lying areas between Inglewood and Carson. In addition, major flooding occurred along Ballona Creek, where rapid residential and commercial development had heightened runoff into the stream channel. The area the Gabrielino had called *pwinukipar* was again "full of water."[109]

Flooding also supplied valuable insight into what types of improvements provided the greatest protection. Although levees protected by

FIG. 5.15. Floodwaters from the Los Angeles River washed away parts of Victory Boulevard and Riverside Drive on the north side of Griffith Park during the big flood of 1938. Courtesy, U.S. Army Corps of Engineers, Los Angeles District.

FIG. 5.16. This steel railroad bridge over the Los Angeles River near downtown Los Angeles was destroyed by raging waters during the flood of 1938. Courtesy, U.S. Army Corps of Engineers, Los Angeles District.

riprap prevented major flooding in places, many were seriously eroded by floodwaters. Some failed altogether. Los Angeles city engineers calculated that 39 percent of the stone revetments along the Los Angeles River were undermined. There were also extensive failures of levees protected by Gunite, a concrete material sprayed on in a thin layer (fig. 5.17). The lack of protection on channel floors, meanwhile, allowed floodwaters to seep up behind levee protections and in some cases carry them away. The only type of channel that held even in the most extreme conditions was that constructed entirely of reinforced concrete.[110] "Originally, the comprehensive plan was based on unlined channels in the lower Los Angeles River and the lower San Gabriel," recalled Harold Hedger, the Flood Control District's chief engineer from 1938 to 1959. "But we quickly agreed with the Corps that the certainty of [being able to confine] flood flows to an unlined channel with flows of the magnitude involved and the velocities they attained was unrealistic, and there would be no assurance that bank protection would remain in place."[111]

FIG. 5.17. Numerous banks along the Los Angeles River that had been protected by a concrete material called Gunite were undermined during the flood of 1938. The street visible in the upper left is Riverside Drive, near Elysian Park. Used with permission, Department of Special Collections, University of Southern California Library/Hearst Newspaper Collection.

Building a "Water Freeway"

New plans drawn up in the two years after the flood drew heavily on the experience of 1938. Using data obtained from the flood, engineers recalculated the volume and intensity of runoff that could be expected during the maximum storm the system was designed to contain and revised existing plans accordingly (fig. 5.18).[112] Reinforced concrete channels, with paved banks and bottoms, became the preferred form of protection for rivers and streams. Bridges were to be raised and strengthened. Channel capacities were to be enlarged in places. The Los Angeles River, for example, was to be widened over earlier plans by as much as thirteen feet south of Los Angeles. The volume of water that could be released from flood control reservoirs was also to be increased. Plans for Sepulveda Flood Control Basin were revised to enable the dam to release 9 percent more water during storm surges.[113]

The first Los Angeles River projects paid for by the federal government and built under the direction of the U.S. Army Corps of Engineers were completed a few months after the flood. Work was finished in October 1938 on three projects to lower the river's bed twenty feet, widen its channel, and pave its banks for a little over four miles upstream from Elysian Park. Three months later, construction was completed on the first segment of what would eventually be a continuous trapezoidal concrete channel to carry the river from Elysian Park to Long Beach. The first segment was built where the river straddles the boundary between Los Angeles and Vernon, long one of the most volatile stretches of its course. This was the point at which the river had broken through its banks in 1889 and cut a new channel two miles to the east. By May 1939, construction had also been finished on five miles of concrete-lined channel where the river winds along the edge of Griffith Park. This section includes the portion of the river where floodwaters in 1938 had washed away parts of two major highways. The most expensive single project on the river, Sepulveda Flood Control Basin (fig. 5.19), was completed in December 1941 at a cost of $6.7 million. Formed by an earth-filled dam 2.9 miles long and rising 57 feet above the riverbed, it has a storage capacity of 16,700 acre feet. Hansen Dam, built to regulate runoff from Tujunga Wash, had been completed a year before.[114]

After the flood of 1938, army engineers also began to develop a more elaborate long-term plan for flood control in Los Angeles County. In 1941, they submitted to Congress a greatly expanded general plan that called for $268.2 million in federal spending, including $185.6 million for projects not yet approved. Engineers now recognized that much more extensive construction would need to be

FIG. 5.18. Edward Koehn (*left*), chief of flood control design for the Los Angeles district of the U.S. Army Corps of Engineers, explains hydraulic action in a plywood model of proposed channel improvements for the Los Angeles River near the outlet of Tujunga Wash. Used with permission, Los Angeles Public Library/Herald-Examiner Collection.

done on tributary streams to slow runoff to the more populated districts. Nearly two-thirds of the proposed new spending was for projects outside the county's four principal rivers. The new general plan called for $71.8 million in additional flood control work in the watershed of the Los Angeles River, more than half of which was designated for work on tributary streams. Just under $35 million was to be spent on the river itself. The river was to be channelized for its entire length and its channel paved, partially or completely, everywhere except in Sepulveda Flood Control Basin.

Congress endorsed the army's new expanded plan for flood control in Los Angeles County and provided an additional $25 million for immediate work when it approved the Flood Control Act of 1941. The Los Angeles County Drainage Area Project, as the project became known, was the basis for all future construction. Throughout Los Angeles County, flood control work was to be done on 278 miles of main and tributary channels. Three more large flood control basins were to be constructed. Debris basins were to be excavated at the mouths of

FIG. 5.19. *Top:* The Los Angeles River as it passes through Sepulveda Dam, constructed to regulate peak flows on the river in the San Fernando Valley. Completed in 1941, it was the single most expensive flood control project on the river. *Bottom:* Although flood control is often blamed for turning the river into an eyesore, the spillway on the downstream side of Sepulveda Dam shows that flood control projects can also be visually striking. Photographs by the author, 1997.

thirty-three mountain canyons. More than three hundred bridges were to be built. The general plan called for a total of $139.1 million to be spent on the Los Angeles River and its tributaries. Flood control projects on the river were finally receiving the major injection of capital that had long been sought. Such expenditures were now considered a matter of national importance because Los Angeles had become the third largest metropolitan area in the nation. In the days leading up to U.S. entrance into World War II, the city's strategic location on the Pacific Coast, its emergence as an important defense industry center with the rise of the aircraft industry, and the growing stature of its ports probably also figured prominently in the minds of congressional representatives who voted in favor of the massive program of improvements. Between 1944 and 1958, Congress would authorize an additional $146.5 million for Los Angeles County flood control projects.[115]

Soon, construction crews were transforming the river from Canoga Park all the way to the sea (figs. 5.20-5.23). The last trees were removed from its banks, and vegetation was cleared from its channel. Fortresslike walls rose where willows had once stood. Steam shovels lowered the river's bed and straightened its course. A smooth layer of concrete was applied atop its sandy bottom. Powerful floodlights enabled construction to continue twenty-four hours a day, five days a week. Work slowed during World War II, but between 1947 and 1955 eighteen separate construction projects were begun on the river. The river was a nearly perpetual construction zone throughout the 1950s. Two-thirds of its present channel was built during that time. The last section of the river channel to be finished was a one-mile stretch between Los Feliz Boulevard and Hyperion Avenue, near Griffith Park. Originally constructed twenty years before but reconfigured to increase the strength of its banks, it was completed on 6 November 1959.[116] Shortly before the project's completion, an official of the U.S. Army Corps of Engineers, while noting that early Spanish explorers "would never recognize the Los Angeles River as it is at this writing," proudly proclaimed that its newly paved channel would be a "water freeway" from its beginning near the Chatsworth hills to its mouth at San Pedro Bay.[117] The comparison is especially apt in automobile-obsessed Southern California because water traveling in the complex network of flood control channels today may actually make better time than cars traveling on the region's congested highways. It has been said that a single drop of rain falling high in the San Gabriel Mountains can now reach the sea in less than sixty minutes. Storm-fed runoff in the Los Angeles River reaches speeds as high as forty-five miles an hour.[118]

FIG. 5.20. Private construction crews under contract to the U.S. Army Corps of Engineers work in the river channel south of Olympic Boulevard in Los Angeles in 1939. The Olympic Boulevard bridge is visible in the distance. Courtesy, U.S. Army Corps of Engineers, Los Angeles District.

FIG. 5.21. Piles of Portland cement await use in paving the bed of the Los Angeles River. Spotlights mounted on poles visible on the *right* enabled work to continue around the clock. Used with permission, The Huntington Library, San Marino, California.

FIG. 5.22. Workers pour concrete in the bed of the Los Angeles River during flood control construction in 1938. Used with permission, The Huntington Library, San Marino, California.

The U.S. Army Corps of Engineers program of flood control in Los Angeles County remains the biggest public works project that agency has ever undertaken west of the Mississippi River, and the numbers associated with Los Angeles River projects still sound astonishing. By the time construction was completed, fourteen private contractors in thirty-one separate contracts with the government had moved twenty million cubic yards of earth (roughly 800,000 dump truck loads worth). They mixed 3.5 million barrels of cement, placed 147 million pounds of reinforced steel, and set 460,000 tons of stone. All told,

FIG. 5.23. Completed channel of the Los Angeles River at Olympic Boulevard in 1940. The extent to which the channel was deepened by federal flood control projects can be seen by comparing the height of bridge supports in this photograph with those in figure 3.9. Courtesy, U.S. Army Corps of Engineers, Los Angeles District.

construction projects on the main channel of the river, with their price tags increased from original projections by inflation, cost $116.7 million. Unfortunately, it is not possible to calculate what the same flood control work would now cost because the money was spent over many years. The Los Angeles River watershed today is protected by three major flood control reservoirs, debris basins at the mouths of mountain canyons, and countless smaller structures in the mountains (fig. 5.24). Channels have been enlarged and reinforced on 47.9 miles of the river and 53.2 miles of its tributary streams.[119]

Flood control projects significantly altered not only the character of the Los Angeles River but also its course to the sea (fig. 5.25). The straightening of the river removed its many sharp bends and eliminated its divided channels. The port diversion, completed in 1921, had shifted the last four miles of the river one mile to the east. Subsequent construction even gave the river a new beginning. The river now officially begins where Bell Creek and Arroyo Calabasas end in the far western San Fernando Valley, just east of the football field at Canoga Park High School. Here, two narrow concrete conduits, dry most of the year, converge to form the river (fig. 5.26). Before subdivisions engulfed the San Fernando Valley, the river did not exist this far west. On a 1903 U.S. Geological Survey map of the area, the river originates southeast of a Southern Pacific Railroad station at Encino. The Los Angeles County Flood Control District added nearly seven miles to the beginning of the river in the 1930s when it excavated a "training" channel between Havenhurst Avenue and Owensmouth Avenue to accommodate increasing runoff from the new suburban development in the area. This channel was enlarged as runoff in the area escalated. Most of the other "streams" in this area are also artificial—designed by engineers, created by steam shovels, confirmed by reinforced steel and concrete. Such channels would have been imperceptible before settlement concentrated runoff, which led to gullying and the gradual formation of new drainage courses.[120]

The impact of flood control projects on the river can be even better seen by examining a single, short stretch of the river. Before flood control projects enlarged its channel and straightened its course, the river wiggled this way and that as it wound around Griffith Park. Farther west in the San Fernando Valley, the river flowed in a general easterly direction, but near Burbank it turned sharply north, then east for a half mile, then sharply south. The only remnant of this horseshoe bend today is a gentle curve where the river meets Burbank Western Wash. The former course of the river can be readily discerned on modern maps in the boundary of Griffith Park, which juts sharply north near Forest Lawn Drive. The Los Angeles Equestrian Center is located within the park on the north side of the river on land that, before flood control projects eliminated the horseshoe bend, would have been south of its channel. On the eastern side of Griffith Park, the river meandered back and forth before it was channelized, its course as sinuous as an uncoiling snake. The river channel through this section is now as straight as the freeway that roars beside it.[121] A researcher at UCLA in 1982 attempted to assess quantitatively the effect that flood control projects have had on the river's channel near Griffith Park. Using U.S. Geological Survey maps and aerial photographs,

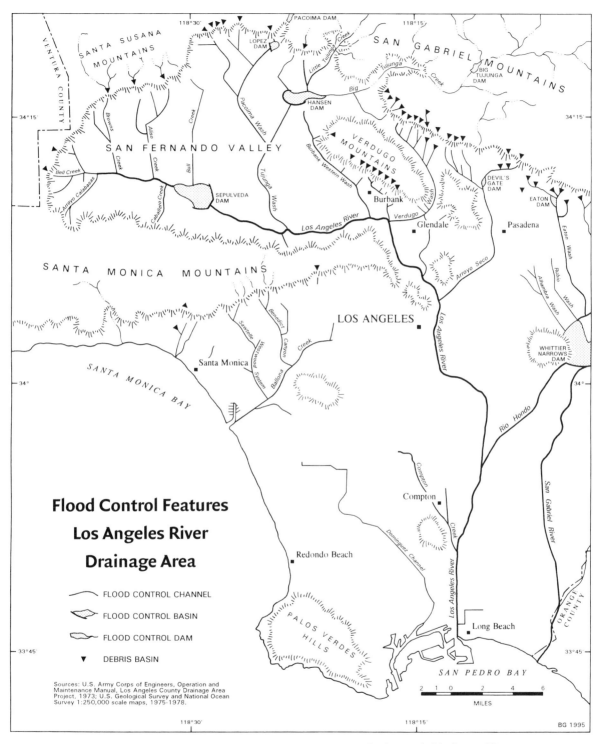

FIG. 5.24. The Los Angeles River today has probably the world's most extensive system of controls for a river of its size. Flood control channels, dams, and basins are shown; locations of debris basins are indicated by *small triangles.* Map by the author.

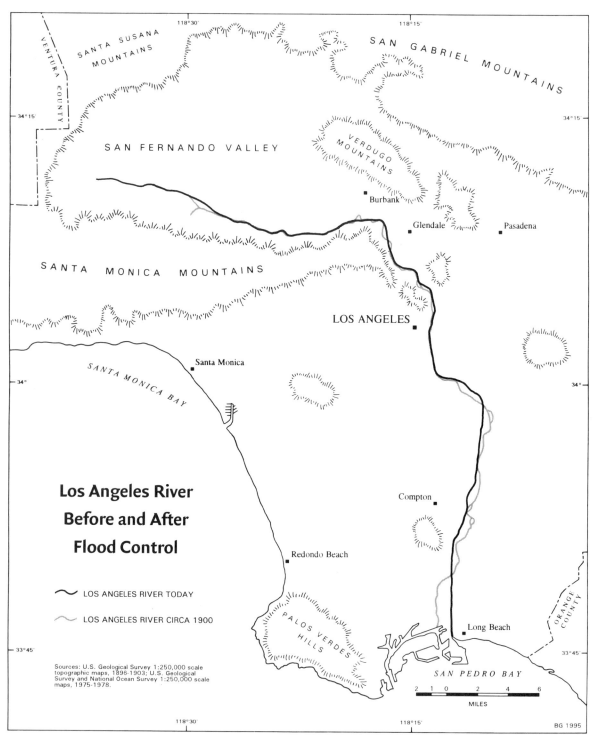

Los Angeles River Before and After Flood Control

LOS ANGELES RIVER TODAY

LOS ANGELES RIVER CIRCA 1900

Sources: U.S. Geological Survey 1:250,000 scale
topographic maps, 1896-1903; U.S. Geological
Survey and National Ocean Survey 1:250,000 scale
maps, 1975-1978.

VENTURA COUNTY

SANTA SUSANA MOUNTAINS

SAN GABRIEL MOUNTAINS

34°15'

SAN FERNANDO VALLEY

VERDUGO MOUNTAINS

Burbank

Glendale

Pasadena

SANTA MONICA MOUNTAINS

LOS ANGELES

Santa Monica

SANTA MONICA BAY

34°

Compton

Redondo Beach

PALOS VERDES HILLS

Long Beach

ORANGE COUNTY

33°45'

SAN PEDRO BAY

2 1 0   2   4   6
MILES

118°30'

118°15'

BG 1995

FIG. 5.25. Flood control projects significantly altered the course of the Los
Angeles River. The river's course circa 1900 is shown by the *lighter line*; the
Los Angeles River today is the *dark line*. Map by the author.

FIG. 5.26. On modern maps, the Los Angeles River begins where Arroyo Calabasas (*left*) and Bell Creek end in Canoga Park, about seven miles west of where the river rose to the surface before urban development and flood control projects redefined the hydrology of the San Fernando Valley. *Top:* The beginning of the river as it appeared in the mid-1950s, before the paving of its channel. Even these relatively natural-looking channels are artificial, however, first excavated by county flood control workers in the 1930s. *Bottom:* The same location today. Construction on this segment of the river was completed in 1958. *Top:* Photograph by Clement Padick. Reprinted from Padick, "Control and Conservation of Natural Runoff Water in the San Fernando Valley, California" (master's thesis, University of California, Los Angeles, 1956), figure 8. *Bottom:* Photograph by the author, 1995.

he calculated that channelization had reduced the length of the river between Tujunga Wash and Glendale Boulevard by 28 percent. In 1903, the river between those two points had been 11.3 miles long. After flood control construction on this section of the river was completed, the length of the river between the same two points was just 8.1 miles. The average depth of the river, which in 1903 had been four to six feet, had increased to seventeen feet. The average width of its channel, which had varied from 70 to 140 feet in 1903, had been increased to 260 feet by the time the last flood control projects were finished.[122]

The remainder of the Los Angeles County Drainage Area Project was completed in 1970. Army engineers had naively figured, when the system was first designed, that Los Angeles County had already attained its "ultimate urban, industrial and agricultural development"; as the population continued to grow, the general plan had to be gradually expanded.[123] By the time work was completed, new channels had been constructed on 100 miles of the Los Angeles and San Gabriel Rivers, the Rio Hondo, and Ballona Creek, plus 370 miles of tributary channels. Five major flood control basins, with a combined capacity of 110,441 acre feet, had been constructed in the San Fernando and San Gabriel Valleys. Fifteen smaller flood control dams and 129 debris basins had been built in the mountains and foothills.[124] The total cost of all projects was just over $1 billion. Government officials in 1992 estimated that the system, by that time, had prevented $3.6 billion in damages.[125] Flood control projects also increased the area that could safely be built upon. "Without the presence of the flood control system," commented Harold E. Hedger, the county's chief flood control engineer from 1938 to 1959, "eighty percent of the intense development within the county could not have taken place."[126] Although such a statement cannot be explicitly proven, one cannot deny the importance of flood control to the urbanization of Southern California.

The greatest test of the flood control system came in 1969, with construction 99 percent complete, when the Los Angeles area was hit by a series of record-breaking storms during the first two months of the year. Rain fell almost continuously for nine days in the last half of January, with Los Angeles receiving 13.3 inches of rain during the storms, the greatest amount of rain received in the city during a nine-day period since a U.S. Weather Bureau station had been established there in 1884. Rainfall was even more intense at higher elevations. The total rainfall in the San Gabriel Mountains north of Mount Wilson was over forty-five inches. Debris basins at the foot of mountain canyons were inundated with two million cubic yards of debris. Seven debris basins were filled completely. The Los Angeles River at Long Beach had a record flow of 102,000 cubic feet per second despite upstream regulation of its flow. Engineers calculated, based on historical rainfall data, that a storm of such intensity could only be expected once every 150 years.[127]

Though damage was great in many newly developed foothill areas not yet protected by flood control projects, improvements on the Los Angeles River and other lowland waterways held strong. No flooding was reported on any of the channels constructed by the U.S. Army Corps of Engineers. The only damage caused by the Los Angeles River was the cost of removing debris deposited by it on beaches near its mouth. Officials estimated that flood control projects prevented more than $1 billion in damages during the flood. They also boasted that dams, debris basins, and spreading grounds had enabled the county to conserve 320,000 acre feet of water from the storms. Nevertheless, although improvements had proven effective, continued development increased the flood danger elsewhere. Mudslides and debris flows in the foothills caused $31 million in damages and led to seventy-three deaths.[128] Newer subdivisions above Glendale and Azusa were especially hard hit. The previous summer, four forest fires had burned 22,103 acres in the mountains, leaving soil unprotected and subject to increased erosion.[129]

Floods in 1969 demonstrated that, despite the more than $1 billion that had been spent on flood control projects in Los Angeles County, construction had still failed to keep pace with growth. The population of the county had more than tripled since federal flood control work had begun. By this time most of the area south of the San Gabriel and Santa Susana Mountains was completely built up. Residential development had spread well beyond all projections, most dangerously into still more foothill areas threatened by forest fires, mudslides, and unregulated runoff. Expansion of the county storm drain system into these newly developed areas would eventually cost an additional $1 billion.[130] In the years to come, urban development would continue to heighten runoff into Southern California's rivers, streams, and storm drains. As parking lots, roads, subdivisions, and commercial developments covered more and more of the ground surface, flood control improvements made to the Los Angeles River would once more prove inadequate. Flood control projects made much of the new development possible, but by doing so they assured that the work already done would never be enough.

THE LOS ANGELES RIVER TODAY IS LIKE A SCAR ON THE landscape, a faint reminder of what it used to be. Its once wandering and twisting course is now regular and straight. Where the river was little more than a nameless gully wandering through shifting sands, its channel has been lengthened, deepened, and widened. Where its tree-covered banks were naturally only a few feet tall, it now has concrete walls as much as thirty-three feet high. Farther downstream, where the river was historically so indistinct that it was not even shown on maps, it now flows in a massive channel as wide as a football field is long. Because of the erratic nature of streamflows in the semiarid region and the erodibility of the mountain-derived soils, the river has been encased in concrete for nearly its entire length. It has concrete banks on 94 percent of its course and a completely concrete channel, with paved bed and sides, for three-quarters of its fifty-one miles. The river has been allowed to remain at least partially unlined in only three places—as it passes through Sepulveda Flood Control Basin and in two areas where the level of the water table prevents its bottom from being paved.

Adding to the river's unnatural appearance is the fact that most of its meager year-round flow is carried along much of its course in a narrow, low-flow channel, sometimes only eight feet across, built down the center of the river's wide bed. Engineers equipped the river with such a feature to prolong the life of its artificial channel. Even concrete is impermanent, but restricting the flow of water to one part of the channel can slow the gradual eating away of the concrete surface by the movement of water and the growth of vegetation. Water in the low-flow channel moves too fast to allow significant growth of algae or the accumulation of silt, in which larger plants can take root. The visual impact of confining the river's dry season flow to a fraction of the width of its channel is great. Because the river was designed to accommodate flood discharges as much as twenty thousand times its natural summertime flow, what you see when you look at the river most of the year is a broad swath of dry cement, which looks like nothing so much as a deserted freeway. This is especially true south of downtown Los Angeles, where the river's bed is as much as 510 feet wide.[1]

Guarded by chain link fence and barbed wire and bordered along large parts of its course by freeways and industry, the concrete river is ugly and forbidding. It is a frequent dumping ground, and its paved shores provide a giant canvas for graffiti. Thousands of miles of storm drains empty along its banks, spilling out an intermittent stream of fluorescent, green-black slime. Homes and businesses built along its course turn their backs to its channel, hiding its view behind cinder block walls or ivy-covered fences. Access to its channel is technically illegal along much of its length—to protect the county against liability in case of drownings during storms (fig. 6.1)—but these laws do little to keep out vagrants, gangs, and others.[2] Homeless people live in cardboard shacks built atop the river's banks, bathing and washing their clothes in its contaminated water (fig. 6.2).[3] Drug users shoot up beneath river bridges. Gang members gather on the river's shores at night, leaving behind their spray paint cans and empty forty-ounce beer bottles. Gun shots occasionally ring out from the darkened channel. The isolation of the river makes it a magnet for crime. Properties along its banks are susceptible to burglary. The river is so deserted in places that in the mid-1980s a series of rapes was committed in its channel by a man who, according to police, posed as a law enforcement or immigration officer, handcuffed his victims, and drove them to the river. Police dubbed the man the "Los Angeles River Rapist." Eerie at times in its emptiness, its concrete shores littered with broken glass and trash, certain parts of the river can seem as ominous as a dark alley at midnight. "I wouldn't go down there without a gun," said one riverfront resident in 1985. "At night, I wouldn't go down there at all." Even as environmentalists were advocating the revitalization of the river in the 1990s, some residents living beside its course near Griffith Park were demanding that government officials erect more substantial fences along its banks to keep people out.[4]

Forsaken for so long and fenced off from the communities to which it helped to give life, the river is now primarily a flood control channel and a conduit for urban waste. Although occasionally a member of a local environmental group will canoe the river after a winter rain, with requisite permission from county officials, about the only boat you're likely to see on the river is a plastic banana boat like the ones used by Dairy Queen, washed into the river from city streets. Because its channel is the destination for whatever finds its way into county storm drains, what Los Angeles sprays on its lawns, discards on its sidewalks, and pours into its gutters—whether toxic or just

FIG. 6.1. Access to the channel of the Los Angeles River is technically illegal along much of its course, punishable by a $500 fine or six months in jail, to protect the county from liability in case of drownings. Such laws are rarely enforced, however. Fences and streamside industry, nevertheless, make reaching the river difficult in many areas. Photograph by the author, 1995.

FIG. 6.2. Laundry day on the river near the Fourth Street bridge in downtown Los Angeles. Homeless people who live along the river's banks often wash their clothes and bath in its channel. Photograph by Stephen Callis. Used with permission.

plain trashy—often winds up in the river. More common than fish or plants where steelhead and sycamores once flourished are beer cans, plastic milk jugs, and Styrofoam cups by the truckload. Although the added water discharged into the river from wastewater treatment plants has increased the amount of vegetation growing on sand bars in its few soft-bottom stretches, the islands of willows and weeds also trap much of the floating trash, thus assuring that, even in those places where the river suggests its former character, human garbage mars the scene.

Even more noticeable than the cups and cans is the strange cargo of other refuse, too heavy to float; washed into the river during major storms or simply dumped from dead-end streets or bridges, it lodges on sand bars or behind clumps of vegetation in the river channel (fig. 6.3). Shopping carts are especially abundant. Old tires, worn-out couches, plastic tricycles, paint cans, and pickup truckloads of over-flowing trash bags are also typical. "We find anything that will fit down a storm drain down there—from dead bodies to countless types of chemicals," reported an official of the county Department of Public Works. "It doesn't happen every day, but sooner or later it all shows up."[5] During a recent two-day cleanup of the river sponsored by a local environmental group, two volunteers pulled a Jacuzzi from its channel in the Glendale Narrows. Other exotic items removed from the river included a VCR, a camper shell, a telephone, a putter, a moped, a five-foot-tall child's basketball goal, a Christmas tree still in its stand, and an American flag.[6] In the early 1990s, a Toyota Corolla turned up in the river channel near Elysian Park. It was never removed and became so covered with silt and sand that a few years later it was no longer visible beneath the vegetation that had sprouted from the sediment.

If the aesthetic influence of urbanization and flood control on the river has been astounding, the ecological consequences have been even more profound. The Natural History Museum of Los Angeles County in 1993 conducted a comprehensive study of plant and animal life along the river, which confirmed in detail what even the untrained observer might suspect. The study reported that the river was almost completely devoid of plant and animal life except in three sections of its course where its bottom had been left unpaved. Even algae was un-common where the river was completely concrete. Six of seven fish species that were native to the river have been eliminated. Four of six varieties of frogs, seven species of snake, and the only native turtle, the western pond turtle, have also disappeared. Although bird life is still relatively abundant, at least four bird species once found along the river, including the yellow-billed cuckoo and Swainson's hawk,

Chuck Wilson with the largest refrigerator taken from L. A. River

FIG. 6.3. *Top:* "The shopping cart," says hydrologist Peter Goodwin, "is the indicator species of the urban stream." These carts were discarded in the Los Angeles River in the San Fernando Valley. *Bottom:* Cartoon by John Callahan makes fun of the strange cargo sometimes carried by the river. *Top:* Photograph by the author, 1995. *Bottom:* Courtesy, John Callahan/Levin Represents. Used with permission.

have been completely extirpated. Water quality in the river is so bad that the only aquatic gastropod—a type of mollusk that includes snails—that still flourishes in the river survives because it is able to breathe air (even the heavily polluted Southern California variety).[7] "We have done horrible, obscene, unconscionable things to the wildlife of the Los Angeles watershed," commented Kimball Garrett, an ornithologist at the museum.[8]

A few elderly and longtime Los Angeles residents can still remember the river when it was bordered by a dense growth of willows and shrubs, when fish still swam its waters, and when its course was natural enough to allow youngsters to live out Tom Sawyer fantasies in an increasingly urbanized Southern California. Even in the twentieth century, long after its channel through downtown Los Angeles had become a dumping ground and its transformation by construction crews had begun, the river retained some of its native charms. The marshes and ponds formed by the river overflow were popular hunting grounds. Boy scout troops camped by the river in Long Beach. Kids built small dams with tree limbs and rocks across the shallow channel to create pools deep enough to dive into. They cut watercress from the river bank, selling it door to door for a nickel a bunch. Sometimes, when the water was deep enough, they built rafts and floated downstream, sleeping overnight on islands in the braided channel.[9] "We skinny-dipped in the pools, caught crawdads by the dozen and boiled them in an old tin can filled with river water and dash of vinegar," recalled one old-timer who grew up beside the river south of Los Angeles.[10]

Because riverfront development came later in the San Fernando Valley than it had elsewhere, the river there kept its natural character longer (fig. 6.4). Even as steam shovels were remaking its channel elsewhere, the river in places like Sherman Oaks, Studio City, and North Hollywood still looked like the shaded stream it had once been all along its course. "We'd dam up the L.A. River at Coldwater (Canyon Avenue)," remembered one valley resident. "We had a swimming hole called the John T. Die swimming hole. There were a bunch of trees, and we had a diving spot off the branches that went out over the water." Wildlife was also still present along the river, and large fish were occasionally pulled from its channel. One women said she saw a bear on the riverbank in North Hollywood in the 1930s. A twenty-five-inch steelhead trout was caught in the river near Glendale in January 1940 (fig. 6.5). "The river was a place of adventure," remembers Catherine Mulholland, granddaughter of Los Angeles's most famous engineer, who was born in 1923 and spent her summers with relatives in Studio City. "I remember pretending to be explorers.

We collected pollywogs. There were lizards, little horn toads, and other animal life." Others who grew up in the San Fernando Valley before the federal government took over the flood control program have similar recollections. "We smoked cornsilk and caught crawdads and got ourselves all stuck up with nettles," said one such resident. "Boy, that L.A. River—before they paved it, it was kind of a jungle down there."[11]

Flood control projects helped destroy once and for all the extensive willow-cottonwood forest that had supported a rich wildlife habitat along the river (fig. 6.6). The deepening and straightening of stream channels helped drain the remaining marshes, which had been home to myriad waterfowl. The paving of the river prevented the creation of pools along its banks, which had provided refuge to fish during heavy runoff. As a result, most fish are now washed to the sea before they grow to more than a few inches in size. Once the river's gravel bottom was replaced by concrete, fish like the steelhead and Pacific lamprey, which had spawned in the river, no longer had any place to bury their eggs. Flood control projects also increased the speed of water flowing in the river, making it impossible for species that require a slow flow, such as the unarmored threespine stickleback, to survive. The tiny stickleback, once one of the most abundant fishes in the lowlands of the Los Angeles Basin, is now listed as an endangered species by the federal government. The most common fish in the river today are small, nonnative species such as minnows and goldfish, many of them no doubt descendants of household pets, and mosquitofish, widely introduced by insect abatement programs. The only native fish still found in the main channel of the river, the arroyo chub, are limited in number. Occasional arroyo chub have been taken from the river in Sepulveda Flood Control Basin.

Channelization and the removal of vegetation also significantly reduced bird populations along the river. Many of the breeding birds that once lived in the area built their nests in the willows, cottonwoods, and sycamores that were once abundant in the floodplain forest. The destruction of this important habitat led to the elimination of such bird species as the yellow-billed cuckoo and Bell's vireo. The paving of the river's banks destroyed a favorite breeding spot for other birds, including the barn owl and the bank swallow, which built their nests in the river's earthen banks. Larger mammals, meanwhile, stopped visiting the river because it contained few fish big enough to eat and because its treeless floodplain no longer provided cover for the rodents and other smaller animals they hunted. Large mammals were driven still farther away as settlement spread. The last known grizzly bear in the watershed of the Los Angeles River was trapped and shot in

FIG. 6.4. The Los Angeles River at Tujunga Avenue in Studio City, September 1932. Courtesy, Stephen Callis. Used with permission.

FIG. 6.5. Twenty-five-inch steelhead trout caught in the river near Glendale in January 1940. Courtesy, family of Dr. Charles L. Hogue.

FIG. 6.6. The Los Angeles River about three hundred feet downstream from Buena Vista Street in Burbank about 1900 (*top*) and in 1997 (*bottom*). The contrast between these two views illustrates the effect of flood control projects on the character of the river and adjacent lands. The trees that grow to the *right* of the river in 1997 are not remnants of the dense riparian forest visible in 1990, but were planted along the nearby Ventura Freeway to reduce traffic noise in residential neighborhoods. *Top:* Used with permission, Water Resources Center Archives, University of California, Berkeley/Joseph Barlow Lippincott Collection. *Bottom:* Photograph by the author, 1997

1916 in Tujunga Canyon in the San Gabriel Mountains. Where deer, foxes, mountain lions, and bears once roamed, the only mammals that remain are a few scattered raccoons, skunks, squirrels, rats, and mice—ubiquitous species biologists call *generalists*.[12]

The river is perhaps best known these days as a filming location for motion pictures and the advertising industry. Giant, mutant ants are discovered in its concrete channel in the 1954 science fiction classic *Them!* A recent national magazine advertisement for a line of Nike hiking boots used the industrialized river to turn the idea of a wilderness adventure on its head. "Test how rugged it is in the Los Angeles River," said the ad in two-inch type above a photograph of climbers scaling the river's vertical walls. Because the river's smooth bed looks so much like a highway, it has been especially popular as a locale for filming race scenes and high-speed chases. In the movie version of *Grease*, for example, John Travolta drag races a member of a rival gang down the river's concrete channel, while a concerned Olivia Newton-John watches from its banks. In *Terminator 2*, a motorcycle-riding Arnold Schwarzenegger is chased up the river channel by an alien made of liquid metal driving a tractor-trailer. Even on film, the river has been the subject of ridicule. At one point in *Them!*, FBI agents are interviewing an old drunk in the county hospital who claims to have seen the monster insects in the riverbed. He pauses after making this declaration and then remarks about the river: "I seen it once when it had water in it!" These days, the river's less traditional uses are many. Metropolitan Transportation Authority bus drivers learn to back up in the riverbed, and Toyota test drives new cars there. Pilots have made emergency landings in its channel. Skateboarders find its endless paved slopes to be the ultimate playground.[13]

As these images suggest, there may not be another river anywhere that has been as thoroughly transformed by humans as the Los Angeles River. Once a beautiful stream, wandering peacefully amid willows and wild grapes, the river gradually became more important as a water source. As the region grew, its unpredictable nature proved too much of a hazard for it to be allowed to flow as it once had. Deprived of its surface flow and kept in place by concrete, much of its true course is now hidden by houses, factories, parking lots, and streets. The river as it now exists has almost nothing in common with the stream the Gabrielino hunted beside or that Father Juan Crespí so eloquently described. It bears little resemblance to the ample stream that nurtured a young Los Angeles or charmed an immigrant William Mulholland. It has been so degraded by humans that in 1995 the national conservation group American Rivers, seeking to build opposition to a new plan to increase flood protections along its channel, called it the most endangered urban waterway in the United States. In the preface to the report in which the group made that claim, Charles Kuralt, the late CBS-TV commentator, said that the Los Angeles River "symboliz[es] all the ills of America's urban rivers."[14]

Vestiges of the River's Past

Somehow in this desecrated landscape, however, a highly modified riparian ecosystem has managed to reemerge in the three sections of the river that are not entirely encased in concrete, particularly since the volume of treated wastewater discharged into the river was increased in 1984. Discharges of wastewater have more than doubled the volume of water carried by the river during summer months, and the increased year-round flow has nourished the growth of riparian trees and water-loving shrubs in Sepulveda Basin, near Griffith Park, and above the river's mouth, creating what ornithologist Kimball Garrett has called "habitat by mistake."[15] In places, the Los Angeles River now acts and even looks like a river, however artificial its course and unnatural the source of its flow. Willows and cottonwoods grow on sand bars created by the winter runoff. Bulrushes and giant reeds wave in the wind beside the river's banks. Snowy egret and great blue heron sun themselves in midstream, drawn by the six-inch crawfish that scour the river bottom. Sandpipers scurry along concrete shores in search of food. Dozens of other bird species also visit the river, and a few have even returned to its channel to breed. These views have inspired environmentalists to wonder what a restored river might look like and have stimulated the development of an increasingly potent movement to revitalize its course.

The river has an earthen channel for just under three miles as it passes through Sepulveda Flood Control Basin, which doubles as a recreation area except during severe storms. This is the only portion of the river's course where its channel is not constructed at least partially of concrete. The river's channel was left entirely unlined to enable maximum absorption of floodwaters. Because the river here runs through the center of a large, open area that is intended to flood during major storms, moreover, it poses no threat to structures. Flowing peacefully between willows and large shrubs, the river in Sepulveda Basin looks surprisingly natural, and the landscape along its banks suggests what the floodplain forest on its lower course may have once looked like (fig. 6.7). Vegetation grows so thick beside the river that it is almost impossible in places to navigate a path to its shore. Ducks move slowly along. Now and then a snake will poke its head above the water. Dozens of tiny fish dart quickly away at the slightest disturbance. This is one of the few spots in Southern California where a bird

FIG. 6.7. Mulefat, saltbush, and common reed grass line the Los Angeles River in Sepulveda Flood Control Basin, the only place where the river's channel is not constructed at least partly of concrete. Photograph by the author, 1995.

called the blue grosbeak breeds. Several hundred Canada geese spend winters in the area.[16] Even here, however, the river's natural appearance is deceiving. Its channel through Sepulveda Basin is also artificial, created by flood control projects in the 1940s. Plastic bags and other trash lodged high in the streamside bushes, caught in the branches when the basin has been allowed to fill with water during storms, provide a hint of the basin's true purpose.

The river has a soft bottom inside concrete banks for six miles through the Glendale Narrows. The water table through this section is too close to the surface to allow the river bottom to be paved. The underground ridge that forces water in the natural reservoir beneath the San Fernando Valley above ground, creating the river, is sometimes just forty feet below the surface here. If the river bottom were covered with concrete, the pressure that forces the water upward would also cause it to break through and destroy the pavement. As a result, the river bottom between Burbank Western Wash and a point two thousand feet north of the Arroyo Seco is lined with cobblestone.[17] This area is sometimes known as Frogtown, a nickname applied when the sounds of bullfrogs still filled the air. (The name has since been adopted by a local street gang, whose graffiti cover the river's banks.) A greater variety of plant and animal life is found along this section of the river than anywhere else on its course, despite the fact that it is bordered on the west by the noisy Golden State Freeway and on the east by railroad yards and industry.

The cobblestone bottom supports dense vegetation (fig. 6.8). Willow, sycamore, and pepper trees, along with nonnative species like bamboo, mulberry, and eucalyptus, grow in midstream. Grasses and herbs thrive in the murky, marshlike pools that have formed behind sand bars. Horse trails follow the river from the several stables on the east side of its channel, and a low-water crossing upstream from Los Feliz Boulevard allows riders to cross the river and reach Griffith Park through a tunnel beneath the freeway. This is the section of the river that is most revered by environmentalists (fig. 6.9). It is not hard to understand why. Willows grow forty to fifty feet tall. Egrets and herons stand motionless for long stretches, as if meditating. Vegetation is so lush in places that, as mallard and cinnamon teal float amid the reeds (fig. 6.10), it is almost possible to imagine that you have left Los Angeles and are standing beside a real river, one that exists according to the dictates of nature, not the mathematics of flood control engineers.

Birds are especially abundant here. Kimball Garrett of the Natural History Museum of Los Angeles County counted 116 different bird species, including 102 native species, in weekly surveys conducted for one year along a 0.8-mile stretch of the river. Among the most common were red-winged blackbird, house finch, rock dove, and mallard. At least 13 species were found to nest along the river channel. They included cinnamon teal, pied-billed grebe, American coot, black phoebe, barn swallow, and the common yellowthroat.[18] Flocks of as many as twenty thousand birds of a variety known as Vaux's swift have been seen foraging along the vegetated riverbed in spring and fall, drawn by the flying insects that hatch at those times of year. A few species have proven especially adaptive to changes made to the river by flood control projects. The northern rough-winged swallow, for example, nests in holes and drain pipes along the river's paved banks.[19] One of the more conspicuous forms of wildlife here, though not native, are the large crawfish that inch along the river's edge where the water is motionless behind sand bars. Groups of teen-agers are often seen crouching on the shore, buckets in hand, trying to catch them. Crawfish shells litter the concrete shores, left by the herons and egrets that feed on the crustaceans. Catfish as large as a foot long have also been caught in the river in this area.

The river has a cobble-and-earth bottom for a little over two and a half miles above its mouth in Long Beach, where its bed is likewise coincident with the water table. The river bottom here was also left unpaved because the percolating river water helps retard the infiltration of salt water into area ground water basins. The soft bottom has en-

FIG. 6.8. The Los Angeles River as it flows beneath the Sunnynook footbridge near Griffith Park. This is one of three areas where the river is not entirely encased in concrete. Because the soft bottom supports dense riparian vegetation that is home to myriad bird species, this part of the river has been the focus of revitalization efforts. Photograph by Ford Lowcock. Used with permission.

couraged the build-up of silt in the river channel south of Willow Street, and a ten- to fifteen-foot-wide riparian corridor has been allowed to develop (the county periodically clears one side of the channel so vegetation does not interfere with storm flows). This corridor supports cattails, rushes, and willows, along with weedy species such as castor bean. Clumps of sunflowers also rise from sand bars. South of Anaheim Street, seawater mixes with freshwater in the river channel. County flood control officials persist in calling this section of the river the *tidal prism*, but in 1994 environmentalists were successful in persuading the Regional Water Quality Board to officially designate this section of the river as an *estuary*. Fisherman dot the river shore near its mouth on weekend afternoons (fig. 6.11). Halibut, sand bass, and other salt-water fish are caught in the river near Queensway Bay in Long Beach. Mussels are also sometimes harvested from the river channel. Nearby, black-crowned night herons nest in ficus trees at an abandoned naval station.[20]

The soft-bottom section of the river in Long Beach supports the largest concentration of shore birds in coastal Los Angeles County. As many as ten thousand migratory shore birds have been spotted here in a single day. A half-dozen species of sandpiper are most common, but several rare bird visitors have also been spotted, including the reddish egret, the American golden plover, the white-faced ibis, and the predatory peregrine falcon, a federally listed endangered species. Bird

FIG. 6.9. The Los Angeles River looks so natural in parts of the Glendale Narrows that canoeists occasionally paddle its waters (with requisite permission from flood control officials). Photograph by Dennis Livzey, Outline. Used with permission.

watchers frequent this stretch, particularly between July and October, when migrating birds are most abundant. Shore birds, especially the common snipe, are also found farther upstream, where shallow water during dry months leaves mats of algae on the pavement that are attractive to birds." "This area has become a sanctuary for some interesting wildlife species," noted biologist Gordon A. Reetz. "It is remarkable that wildlife utilize this habitat to the extent they do."[22]

The Birth of a Movement

Shocked by the river's appearance along most of its course but charmed by the trees and bird life that flourish in its three soft-bottom sections, Lewis MacAdams was the first person in fifty years to promote the idea that the Los Angeles River could be something more than a drainage ditch. A native of Texas, he had been educated at Princeton and the State University of New York at Buffalo before relocating about 1970 to the "hippie" town of Bolinas in northern California. There he wrote poetry, dug ditches for the local water district, became immersed in town politics, and got his first taste of the water wars that would so influence his future activism when he participated in a successful protest to stop the U.S. Army Corps of Engineers from building a sewer system that would have discharged the town's liquid wastes into the ocean. Later, MacAdams was elected to the board of the Bolinas Public Utility District, the town's water supplier, which acted as the de facto local government in the unincorporated community. As a member of the board, he worked to limit development by declaring a moratorium on new water hookups. He also ran the poetry center at San Francisco State University for four years.

In 1980, not long after his marriage had fallen apart, MacAdams somewhat reluctantly moved to Los Angeles ("I thought everyone there wore white shoes," he later joked). He had begun writing a movie script with the musician Boz Scaggs, a friend from high school in Dallas, and had also become friends with the German film director Wim Wenders, so, "like every other schmo," MacAdams said, he moved to Hollywood to try his hand at screenplays. He arrived with only twenty dollars to his name, however, and had to resort to less glamorous gigs. He began writing for the Venice-based bimonthly magazine *Wet* (he later became its editor) and also worked, when necessary, as a laborer. He had gotten a job as part of the federal government's Comprehensive Employment and Training Act (CETA) program and was helping to renovate a loft in the industrial district east of downtown Los Angeles when he saw the river for the first time. "I'd never seen anything like it," he said. "I was stunned." Such a reaction to the river was hardly unique, but with MacAdams's longtime interest

FIG. 6.10. Ducks swim in the Los Angeles River in the Glendale Narrows. More than one hundred bird species have been sighted in this area. Photograph by the author, 1997.

FIG. 6.11. A couple from Carson fishes in the river near its mouth in Long Beach. Photograph by Stephen Callis. Used with permission.

in water issues, the derelict stream made a lasting impression. "I knew from the very first time I saw it that I would have some involvement with it," he said.[23]

MacAdams did not act on that initial impulse about the river for another five years. He continued to be active in the poetry community and began to do occasional performance art pieces as well. After the demise of *Wet*, he wrote for a variety of local publications. In 1985, he was asked to contribute an article to a special issue about the problems of Los Angeles that was being planned by a local alternative weekly, the *Reader*. About the same time, the Museum of Contemporary Art asked him to participate in a series of shows it was planning by Los Angeles performance artists. With the characteristic shrewdness of an artist and writer living from paycheck to paycheck, MacAdams decided to make the river the focus of both the article and the performance. It was the performance art piece that was the seed from which a fledgling movement to green the river took root. The environmental group Friends of the Los Angeles River was born, although its beginnings were anything but favorable.

The first part of what MacAdams calls the performance was not a performance in the public sense. It was just MacAdams and three of his friends, sculptor Pat Patterson, gallery owner Roger Wong, and architect Fred Fischer. They met one morning at an old dairy on Vignes Street and proceeded over the First Street bridge, where they used a pair of wire cutters to cut a hole in the fence along the river. "We clambered down the concrete walls and into the concrete channel," MacAdams wrote years later. "We felt like we were exploring the moon." They walked upstream past railroad yards, warehouses, factories, and the old Los Angeles city jail to the river's confluence with the Arroyo Seco, passing the point where Captain Gaspar de Portolá had led the first Spanish land expedition to Southern California across the river in 1769. The scene MacAdams and his friends encountered that summer day could not have been more different than the one described by Father Juan Crespí more than two hundred years before. Yet, amid the tumult and rubbish, MacAdams saw hope. "The air around us was in an unholy din," he later wrote. "A Southern Pacific freight train rumbled up the tracks on one bank. A Santa Fe freight rumbled down the tracks on the other. Traffic on two freeway bridges and the Riverside Drive bridge roared by. The odor was industrial. The scene was a latter-day urban hell. We asked the river if we could speak for it in the human realm. We didn't hear it say no, and that was how Friends of the Los Angeles River began."[24]

In September 1985, MacAdams, Patterson, and Wong staged the second part of the performance, a mixed-media event at the Wallenboyd Theater in downtown Los Angeles. They called it *Friends of the Los Angeles River*. Patterson built a fifteen-foot totem pole made out of driftwood hauled from the river. MacAdams painted his body green, dressed up in a white suit, delivered a monologue in the guise of William Mulholland, and then did a series of animal impressions. The performance also included video, film, and slides and concluded with a question-and-answer session about how the river could be revived. MacAdams called it "the first act of a forty-year artwork to bring the Los Angeles River back to life through a combination of art, politics, and magic."[25] The performance, however, was a bust. "Everybody hated it," he said. "People just didn't get it." The theater's managers were so disgusted that they threatened to withhold payment. MacAdams's girlfriend left him over it. The *Los Angeles Times*, in reviewing the show, wondered if it was all a joke. "With friends like MacAdams," the paper remarked, "the river needs no enemies."[26]

Undeterred, MacAdams took some of the money he was eventually paid for the performance and got bumper stickers with the name "Friends of the Los Angeles River" printed on them. Even if his first attempt to convince the public of the merits of restoring the river had been a failure, he was nevertheless able to persuade a group of two dozen or so friends and acquaintances to take another walk along the river a few weeks later. Many of them carried homemade signs. Someone made a cassette tape of industrial music and reggae to provide a soundtrack for the excursion. This time, MacAdams and his compatriots made it farther upstream, walking beyond the Arroyo Seco and reaching the point of the river where its bed turns from concrete to cobblestone, thus allowing vegetation to grow in the channel. "The contrast was amazing," MacAdams says. "We got there right as the sun was going down. It was really beautiful." Friends of the Los Angeles River was formally incorporated as a nonprofit organization the next year and, since then, has grown to become one of the most visible and outspoken environmental organizations in Southern California.

About the same time Friends of the Los Angeles River was forming, others were also beginning to notice the river. In October 1985, a *Los Angeles Times* feature writer embarked on a journey to travel all the way up the river from its mouth in search of its source, in an often tongue-in-cheek attempt to emulate the expeditions of storybook explorers tracing the origins of such legendary rivers as the Amazon or the Nile. The writer, Dick Roraback, decided to make the trip when he realized that, after living in Los Angeles for ten years, he knew nothing about the river that passed through the city. Roraback had grown up beside the Hudson River, lived for eighteen years along the Seine, and resided for shorter periods on the Nile and the Yukon. He was embarrassed to admit that, though he had driven over the Los Angeles River, by his own estimate, more than fifteen thousand times, he did not remember ever actually seeing it. He began his journey by the *Queen Mary* in Long Beach and, walking or bicycling upstream, did not end his search until three months later (at least in print) in the Simi Hills of Ventura County, where a few raindrops produced a puddle that ran down a hill and into Bell Creek (and, one can assume, eventually wound up in the river). Along the way, he talked to fishermen, kids playing in the river's concrete channel, and people who lived or worked nearby. He kept copious notes of the sights he saw and maintained an inventory of the sundry objects he found in the river. He even composed a song or two to pass the time. Roraback reported his "findings" in an eleven-part series published in the *Times* between October 1985 and January 1986.[27]

Roraback would have been the first to admit he was no David Livingstone or Meriwether Lewis, but the Los Angeles River he encountered was not the Nile or the Columbia, as his account of his first day on the river soon made clear. "A spent package of Dorito Chips drifts by," he wrote, "then a three-legged stool, remarkably intact. Next an empty container of Montebello Original L.I. Iced Tea cocktail. Finally a dead mouse."[28] In his next dispatch, he said of the river, "a mere mile or so north of its mouth, it narrows to a stream, then a creek, and finally a joke."[29] Like MacAdams, Roraback was plainly appalled by what he saw, but his series was not a call to arms. He did not resolve to fight for the river's future or to organize on its behalf, and, at times, the river seemed to serve primarily as a foil for the author's wit. Still, the series was extremely popular and opened the eyes of more than a few Angelenos to the river in their midst. Roraback received more than five hundred letters in response to the series.[30] Readers wrote that they woke up in eager anticipation of the explorer's next dispatch. Old-timers reminisced in print of the river of yore. MacAdams, too, wrote a letter, chiding Roraback for his "gently mocking tone" but sending him a Friends of the Los Angeles River bumper sticker (which Roraback immediately affixed to his Toyota).[31] The series also proved influential. The grim portrait Roraback painted helped Friends of the Los Angeles River to become more than an art project. Many people who later became active in the group first became truly aware of the river through Roraback's articles. MacAdams, in fact, has commented that the series "had repercussions far beyond the writer's intent."[32]

A third person who would prove important in efforts to revitalize the river was just arriving in Los Angeles about the time that Roraback was reaching Glendale on his trip upstream. Dilara El-Assaad, an agricultural engineer and landscape architect, moved to Southern California in November 1985 from Beirut, Lebanon, to be nearer her sister and brother after their father died. El-Assaad had not seen Roraback's series nor did she know about the nascent efforts to create Friends of the Los Angeles River when she first noticed its concrete channel. She had enrolled in the graduate program in landscape architecture at the University of Southern California and was taking an orientation tour of downtown Los Angeles when she saw the river for the first time. "I thought it was beautiful," she later recalled.[33] To El-Assaad, the engineer, there was majesty even in the concrete—in the smooth lines of the river's channel, in its functionality, in the grandeur of its bridges. As a landscape architect, however, she was drawn to the river for its potential. Here was a ribbon of open space, largely unused and inaccessible, running from one end of Los Angeles to the other. As a newcomer, El-Assaad had been discouraged by the lack of parkland and green space in her new home. She found the endless freeways, subdivisions, and shopping centers suffocating. "When I came here I was scared of this country," she said. "I saw this density here, all these streets, all this concrete. All the time, I was driving. Then all of a sudden I saw this huge open space. It took my breath away."[34]

Ignoring the ridicule of her fellow students, El-Assaad set out to create a broad plan for reincorporating the river back into the lives of Southern Californians. Every project she worked on in graduate school was oriented to that goal, and the culmination of those efforts was her master's thesis, completed in 1988, which was entitled "Redefining the Role of the L.A. River in the Urban Landscape of Southern California." In it, she proposed that trees be planted on both sides of the river from Sepulveda Flood Control Basin in Van Nuys to the river's mouth in Long Beach, not only to break the monotony of the urban landscape, but also to utilize the ability of trees to absorb carbon dioxide as a means of cleaning the region's notoriously filthy air. She recommended that four major nodes for human use be created along this greenway—a park that could act also as a detention basin during storms on the site of the Taylor Yard railroad facility in the Glendale Narrows, a linear parkway that could replace some of the railroad tracks through downtown Los Angeles, an agricultural demonstration farm in north Long Beach, and another park at the river's mouth. She even proposed that inflatable dams be used to keep water in the river during dry months. El-Assaad also suggested that a master plan be created to coordinate riverfront development all along its course.[35]

Though El-Assaad's thesis was not published, the influence of her proposals has nevertheless been significant. She was a keynote speaker at an early conference on the revitalization of the river. She has been asked to speak about her ideas by U.S. Congressman Xavier

Becerra and state Assemblyman Richard Katz. She has given presentations on her proposals to the state Commission of Parks and Recreation, the city of Los Angeles planning and public works commissions, and a conference sponsored by the American Society of Landscape Architects. As a planner for the city of Los Angeles in 1992, she helped draft the planning department's official response to a new U.S. Army Corps of Engineers flood control proposal for the river. A master plan like the one she suggested was eventually created, and she was part of the team that developed it. Now a transportation planner for the Southern California Association of Governments, El-Assaad continues to be active in planning for the river's future.

In the years since Lewis MacAdams first clambered down the river's concrete banks, Dick Roraback hiked its channel in search of its source, and Dilara El-Assaad developed her plan to turn it into a greenway, interest in revitalizing the Los Angeles River has increased dramatically. Environmentalists are now calling for removal of some of the river's concrete bed and the return of the river to a more natural state. They envision a waterway again lined with willows and cottonwoods, reeds and cattails, and dream of a day when steelhead will return to the river and its waters will once more be safe to drink. Leading the movement has been Friends of the Los Angeles River (FoLAR). Through its efforts to turn the river into a greenway and its opposition to a variety of proposals that would further degrade its channel, FoLAR has built an influential constituency and helped to increase awareness of the river locally as well as nationally. The group now has a paid executive director, publishes a quarterly newsletter, claims a membership of fifteen hundred people, and has drawn thousands to its annual river cleanups. It has also helped stage three conferences about the future of the river, has produced flood control proposals of its own to counter new government plans, and has taken the county to court over a new project to build flood walls along part of its channel. "When the yellow-billed cuckoo is singing in the sycamores," says MacAdams, "our work will be done."[36]

The new interest in the river has also drawn the attention of a diverse range of other organizations, individuals, and government agencies, both locally and nationally. A dizzying array of proposals for the river have been formally studied, and even more have been suggested. National organizations such as American Rivers, the Trust for Public Land, and the Sierra Club and local groups like Heal the Bay and North-East Trees have become involved. Government agencies like the National Park Service, the California State Coastal Conservancy, and the state Mountains Recreation and Conservation Authority are working on river projects. Even the two agencies that have sometimes been seen as enemies by those most interested in restoring the river, the U.S. Army Corps of Engineers and the county Department of Public Works (successor to the Los Angeles County Flood Control District), have produced plans to open the riverside to human uses. Media coverage of river topics has also increased considerably. And though progress on efforts to revitalize the river has lagged far behind all the talk—the river itself looks much as it did in 1985—an increasing amount of money is being directed to projects along its banks. Bike paths and parks are being built, trees are being planted, and much more work is forthcoming.

The heightened awareness of the Los Angeles River also reflects larger trends. National and global efforts to improve urban rivers have intensified with the implementation of more stringent water quality regulations, the general decline of riverside industry, and the blossoming of the environmental movement in the years since the first Earth Day in 1970. In Denver, for example, the area along the once trash-strewn South Platte River, upon which the city was founded in 1859, has been transformed into a greenway that includes hiking and biking trails, parks, boat chutes, and an amphitheater. In San Jose, California, which (like Los Angeles) was founded as an agricultural village beside a year-round stream by the government of Spain, local government agencies are joining with the U.S. Army Corps of Engineers to build the Guadalupe River Park. The $138-million project is designed not only to protect the city from floods but also to create a 2.6-mile linear park with a 10-mile network of trails. One of the biggest urban river success stories has been in Chicago, where a $3.7 billion project to reduce discharges of raw sewage into the Chicago River has improved water quality so much that the number of fish species living in the river has quadrupled. A local group, the Friends of the Chicago River, has even begun staging swimming races in the once heavily polluted waterway. That group also sponsors regular river hikes, canoe trips, and cruises on the river and helped draft the city's first river protection ordinance, which regulates new development on the riverfront.[37] In two decades, the image of the Chicago River has changed so thoroughly that the *Chicago Tribune* recently observed that the river is "about to challenge Chicago's lakefront and the Loop for the heart and soul of the city."[38]

The number of riverfront renewal projects that have been undertaken worldwide is staggering. Much of the work has been made possible by the abandonment of riverfront industrial sites and the growing recognition that highways and railroads have cut off cities from what in so many cases was their reason for being. In Cincinnati, for instance, city officials spent $22 million to turn the site of an old scrap yard into a twenty-two-acre park that includes a tree-lined promenade along the Ohio River, a five-thousand-seat pavilion, and a four-mile-long historic trail that connects the Ohio and Kentucky riverfronts. In Portland, Oregon, a busy expressway along the Willamette River was demolished and replaced with a 1.2-mile-long park that is anchored on one end by a mixture of shops, restaurants, residences, and a marina and on the other by a Japanese-American historical plaza. Declining industrial cities such as Detroit and Cleveland, meanwhile, have pinned their hopes for urban renewal in part on riverfront development. Riverside parks, trails, and greenways are being created in cities as diverse as Buffalo; Chattanooga, Tennessee; Saskatoon, Saskatchewan; and Tokyo.[39]

Many urban river revitalization projects in North America owe a considerable debt to the oldest and most famous such development anywhere, the Paseo del Rio, or River Walk, in San Antonio, Texas. First conceived in 1929 to combat an Army Corps of Engineers plan to eliminate a horseshoe bend in the San Antonio River where it passes through that city's downtown, the original 1 1\2-mile-long Paseo Del Rio was completed as a Works Progress Administration project in 1941. Workers built walkways on both sides of the river, erected twenty-one bridges, planted banana trees, and constructed an open-air theater with its stage on one side of the narrow river and an amphitheater carved from the bank on the other. The walkway, however, was neglected until the 1960s, when city officials sponsored a bond issue to renovate it and began actively to encourage businesses to reorient themselves to the river. The Paseo del Rio is now the center of San Antonio's tourism industry. Lengthened by artificial extensions in 1968 and 1988, its well-shaded walkways are lined with restaurants, shops, coffee bars, and hotels. Water taxis take tourists up and down its now 2.8-mile length. An annual river parade, a mariachi festival, and a month-long Christmas celebration are among the regular activities along the river walk.[40] Friends of the Los Angeles River founder Lewis MacAdams has suggested that a San Antonio–like river walk be developed north of downtown Los Angeles by digging an artificial channel from the river through the abandoned railroad yards north of Chinatown. Responding to that suggestion, a group of architects and planners in early 1998 developed a more detailed proposal for creating just such an attraction along the historic route of the Zanja Madre, the irrigation ditch that helped give birth to Los Angeles.[41]

The Early Efforts to Green the River

Proposals to revitalize the Los Angeles River have not only drawn on successful projects in San Antonio, Denver, and elsewhere but have also been inspired by earlier river beautification efforts in Southern

California. Although none of the earlier proposals to improve the Los Angeles River made it beyond the planning stage, in light of the new interest in the river—and a growing curiosity about the earlier plans— it is worth taking a final step back in time to examine the nature of these proposals, to try to determine why they failed, to analyze what the proposals and their failure might tell us about human attitudes toward the river, and to ascertain whether earlier experiences provide any lessons for those now working to resurrect the river.

Although proposals to establish a system of scenic parkways, like those that had been built in New York, Chicago, and Boston by renowned landscape architects Frederick Law Olmsted and Calvert Vaux, were made in Los Angeles as early as the 1890s, the first such proposal largely ignored the river. Los Angeles City Engineer Henry Dockweiler in 1897 proposed the construction of a circular, seventeen-mile, tree-lined boulevard connecting five city parks—East Lake (now Lincoln), Hollenbeck, Westlake (now MacArthur), Echo, and Elysian—and recommended that additional parkways be built to Santa Monica, up Vermont Avenue to Griffith Park, and through the Arroyo Seco. The circular drive would have crossed the river about where North Broadway traverses it today, but otherwise none of the parkways would have involved the river.[42] That the river was, for the most part, left out of Dockweiler's proposals may reflect a growing attitude that the river had few aesthetic benefits.

The first specific proposals for the beautification of the river were those of Dana Bartlett, the Maine-born and Iowa-raised minister who moved to Los Angeles in 1896 and founded the Bethlehem Institute, which provided baths, counseling, and social services to the working poor. Convinced that Los Angeles could avoid the poverty and crowded conditions of other urban areas, he wrote a book in 1907 called *The Better City*, in which he urged his fellow citizens to plan for the future. Influenced by the City Beautiful movement, which was sweeping city planning nationwide at the time, Bartlett called for the creation of riverside parks and promenades and proposed that a great civic center be built over the river in downtown Los Angeles. "The river along its entire length can be made into a line of beauty," he wrote. "Think of what value to the city this river might become if placed under a special commission empowered to carry out a definite plan for its reclamation from base uses."[43]

Bartlett's specific proposals were ambitious, though some sound naive when considered nearly a century later. He suggested, for instance, that the riverbed from Elysian Park to First Street be cleared of all rubbish and undergrowth and that "the sand hills" (its levees?) be leveled, "thus making, during nine months of the year," when rain was not swelling the river from bank to bank, it is assumed, "an extensive playground for the children of the congested districts." Such a plan overlooked the danger of turning a riverbed into a playground in a region where sudden showers sometimes fall outside the rainy season and streams can turn to torrents even when the sun is shining, because of runoff from mountain storms. It is worth noting, too, that Bartlett made his proposals during an extended dry period. The last great flood in Los Angeles had occurred in 1889, seven years before his arrival in the city. Bartlett also proposed that landscaped boulevards be developed on both sides of the river, ornamental bridges be built across its channel, and factories and warehouses along its banks "be hidden behind a wealth of climbing vines and roses." He proposed that a civic center—with halls for lectures and entertainment, meeting rooms, public baths, a gymnasium, and steps leading to the riverbed playground—be built on piers in the river. "Treated according to such a plan," he said, "the river bed may add much to the making of the City Beautiful."[44]

Charles Mulford Robinson, a journalist, publicist, and poet from Rochester, New York, was one of the fathers of the City Beautiful movement, and it was he who first used the phrase in a planning context when he wrote a series of articles published in the *Atlantic Monthly* in 1899. The rise of the City Beautiful coincided with a growing interest in artistic city planning that developed after the World's Columbian Exposition, held in Chicago in 1893. The new attention paid to urban aesthetics led to the creation of citizens' organizations concerned with beautification issues in several eastern cities before the turn of the century and the Municipal Art Commission in Los Angeles in 1903. That group was primarily interested, at first, in the cleaning of streets, the planting of trees, and the installation of street lights but was eventually given the responsibility for approving all designs for municipal buildings. In 1906, it proposed that an expert be hired to create a plan for the beautification of Los Angeles and, the following year, the city council approved the commission's recommendation that Robinson, who had just completed plans for Denver and Honolulu, be hired. He arrived in Los Angeles the second week of November and presented his recommendations less than three weeks later. His report was published in 1909 under the title *The City Beautiful*.[45]

Robinson proposed a sweeping program of improvements, including the construction of a large civic center, a railway station, a library and art gallery, two new parks in the business district, and a parkway system that was to reach in every direction from the city center. He also proposed numerous small-scale improvements, including the planting of trees, the elimination of fences, the beautification of schoolyards and playgrounds, and the creation of small parks at major street intersections.[46] He even went so far as to recommend that streetlights be dusted nightly. But the ever-optimistic Robinson was clearly bewildered by what to do about the river. "The river presents a very serious problem, and one which cannot be solved with entire aesthetic satisfaction," he wrote. "A river bed that for the most of the year is dry and that has on both of its banks a railroad is not an attractive object." Consequently, he made few recommendations for the river channel. He suggested only that it be cleared of rubbish, that the removal of sand from the riverbed by construction crews "be organized on a business-like basis," and that the river's banks be planted with willows and cottonwoods. He also proposed that all existing bridges over the river, which he said were "about as ugly as they can be," be replaced by "handsome structures." Although Robinson proposed the development of more than a dozen parkways in Los Angeles, including one in the Arroyo Seco, none was planned with the river as its focus.[47]

Few of the specific recommendations of Robinson, however, were ever implemented. The city did eventually develop its civic center on the site he recommended. His suggestion that the bridges over the river be replaced, furthermore, laid the groundwork for the construction of ten architecturally significant bridges between 1910 and 1933 (fig. 6.12).[48] But in Los Angeles, as elsewhere, his plans—though influential—were too grandiose ever to receive widespread support. Robinson also displayed an arrogant disregard for the fiscal limitations of local government, which helped to assure that most of his recommendations would never be carried out. In his Los Angeles plans, he refused to supply cost estimates for any of his proposals and seemed almost insulted that such estimates might be expected, saying only, "I assumed that Los Angeles was big enough and rich enough, and brave enough, and had enough confidence in itself to do what was necessary." City Beautiful proponents nationwide were often criticized as pretentious and impractical. Although Robinson produced twenty-five planning reports like that for Los Angeles, he never, according to historian William H. Wilson, "achieved much City Beautiful construction through the urban political process."[49] Even his relatively modest proposals for the river channel seem to have been ignored, as evidenced by the river's continued use as a dump (even by city officials) and by the number and nature of other proposals for beautifying the river made over the next twenty-five years.

Though Robinson's specific plans produced little actual work, they did beget still more proposals. In 1910, Superintendent of Parks Frank Shearer proposed that a thirty-five-mile-long scenic drive be built to connect Griffith Park and Elysian Park. This was the first such pro-

FIG. 6.12. The Macy Street bridge, constructed in 1926, was one of ten architecturally significant bridges built over the Los Angeles River between 1910 and 1933. Used with permission, Los Angeles Public Library/Security Pacific Collection.

posal seriously to involve the river, though the potential use of the riverside as a connecting route between the two parks was ignored. Instead, the parks were to be linked by a scenic drive winding along the crest of the hills that form the more elevated parts of the present-day Echo Park and Silver Lake neighborhoods, passing by Silver Lake Reservoir, around which two thousand trees had been planted. Seven miles of the drive were to be in Griffith Park. In the northeast corner of the park, the drive was to follow the river, winding through the extensive groves of willow and cottonwood that still spread on both sides of its banks in that area. "From this point the drive is shady, crossing and recrossing the river," said a newspaper report. "Here also a number of picnic sites can be developed." From Griffith Park, the drive was to run west to Cahuenga Pass and south to Hollywood, returning to Los Angeles via Sunset Boulevard. At least the park portion of the drive seems to have been built. Later that year, nine miles of "good road" were completed in the park and four "rustic bridges" were built over the Los Angeles River.[50]

A year later, the Los Angeles Board of Park Commissioners proposed an even more extensive network of parkways and scenic boulevards (fig. 6.13). The centerpiece of the system was to be a parkway through the Arroyo Seco to connect Los Angeles with the Angeles National Forest above Pasadena. Plans were also drawn up for a Silver Lake Parkway, which was to run southwest from Silver Lake Reservoir for more than three miles. Several major streets, meanwhile, were to be turned into tree-lined boulevards to create a system of scenic drives connecting all of the city's parks. In proposing the system of parkways, Joseph B. Lippincott, a local engineer and member of the parks

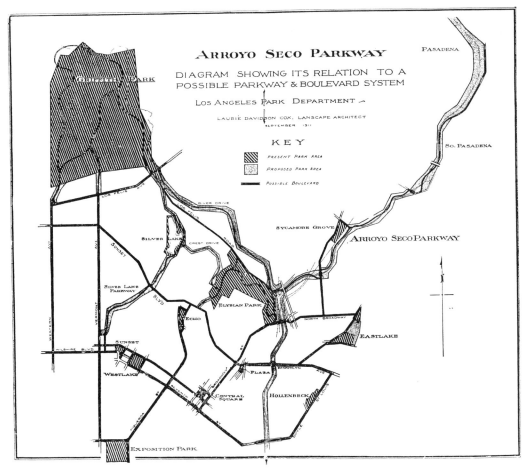

FIG. 6.13. The Los Angeles Board of Park Commissioners in 1911 proposed the development of an extensive system of parkways and tree-lined boulevards in Los Angeles, including the creation of a park and "river drive" along the Los Angeles River between Griffith Park (*top left*) and Elysian Park (*center*). The *diagonal hatching* shows park area in 1911, the *shading* shows proposed park areas, and the *heavy lines* show possible boulevards. Reprinted from Los Angeles Park Commission, *Silver Lake Parkway* (Los Angeles, 1912), 6–7.

board (the same Lippincott who was key to development of the Los Angeles–Owens River Aqueduct and who would help draft the first comprehensive flood control plans for Los Angeles County), touted the benefits of similar systems that had been developed in Chicago, Kansas City, and Minneapolis, insisting that parks and other recreation areas were "morally and physically elevating." He chastised Los Angeles for not being more aggressive in the development of parks and scenic drives, complaining that the park board had too little power and too small a budget. "If Los Angeles is to become a serious contender for a place among the beautiful cities of America," he said, "there must be a great awakening by her citizens to the necessity of the creation of an adequate system of parks, parkways and boulevards."[51]

The only definite plan for the river was part of the plan for the Arroyo Seco Parkway. The parkway was to begin at Elysian Park, and the land along the river in that area was to be acquired and planted with trees, "screening out from the park and parkway the numerous railroad tracks and views of the commercial districts," according to Laurie Davidson Cox, the landscape architect who drew up specific plans. In addition, the wooden bridge that crossed the river at Buena Vista Street (now North Broadway) was to be replaced with a "magnificent" concrete span. A map of the proposed parkway and boulevard system also shows a continuous park on both sides of the river between Griffith Park and Elysian Park, through which a "river drive" winds back and forth across the river, crossing its channel five times. Though no specific plans for this parkway seem to have been developed, Cox said in his report that, "if the treatment of the river [near Elysian Park] is carried out, nothing would be more logical than at some time to continue this treatment on a larger scale with parkway drives and walks north along the river to Griffith Park."[52]

Although the Arroyo Seco Parkway was eventually developed in a much altered form (and without the river embellishments), the rest of the plan stands as but one more missed opportunity of the sort that fill the archives of planning departments. Nevertheless, some of the difficulties encountered by park officials in their efforts to implement the plan could provide valuable instruction to modern-day planners because they are the same problems that could hinder the development of a continuous greenway along the Los Angeles River. A major obstacle in development of the Arroyo Seco Parkway, for example, was the fact that the proposed route passed through three cities and parts of unincorporated Los Angeles County, which made organization of a unified plan more complex and difficult. Frustration over efforts to get the project under way, in fact, prompted Lippincott in 1912 to propose the creation of a metropolitan parks commission, such as those that existed in Boston and Chicago, to coordinate park development throughout the region. No such organization was ever created, however, and the multitude of government agencies that today have jurisdiction over the channel of the Los Angeles River, and the land adjacent to it, has complicated river renewal efforts. The river passes through thirteen different cities in its fifty-one miles. At least thirty-six different government entities have some authority or responsibility over the river channel. Recognizing that the fragmentary nature of governance along the river could undermine proposals for revitalizing its course, state Senator Tom Hayden in 1998 introduced a bill into the California legislature that would have created a Los Angeles and San Gabriel Rivers Conservancy to oversee planning for the two waterways, but that bill was voted down in an Assembly committee amid opposition from numerous cities and agencies that saw their authority threatened.[53]

The failure of Los Angeles to create the Silver Lake Parkway, meanwhile, demonstrated the difficulty of creating linear park systems, a problem that modern planners are rediscovering as they try to develop projects along the Los Angeles River. More traditionally shaped parks, depending on their size, may require the acquisition of only a few parcels of land, but linear developments, even short ones, often pass through hundreds of properties, which makes the acquisition of real estate for such projects not only more complicated but sometimes more expensive. In June 1914, Los Angeles Mayor Henry R. Rose recommended that the Silver Lake Parkway project be abandoned because of the difficulty of acquiring land along the route. Already $573,000 had been spent. "The condemnation proceedings to acquire rights of way for the connection of Silver Lake with Wilshire Boulevard will be a long time in litigation," he said. Current efforts to create a bike path along the west side of the Los Angeles River between Griffith Park and Elysian Park face similar problems. One 2.6-mile segment of the proposed bikeway passes through sixty-six privately owned parcels.[54]

"A Window into a Lost Future"

The single biggest proposal for the beautification of the Los Angeles River and the one that has received the greatest attention from modern-day activists and planners was made in 1930 as part of a comprehensive plan for park development in Los Angeles County created by Frederick Law Olmsted Jr. and Harland Bartholomew, two of the most respected urban designers of their day. The son of America's most famous park builder, Olmsted had earlier developed the plans for Palos Verdes Estates, an exclusive Los Angeles suburb, and New York's Forest Hills. Bartholomew had laid out the innovative Los Angeles commercial district of Westwood Village. Together they had also produced master plans for Los Angeles County's highways and a state park system. They were hired by a citizens' committee on parks organized in 1927 by the Los Angeles Chamber of Commerce to survey the parks, playgrounds, and beaches of the metropolitan area and produce a plan for their improvement.[55]

Like Joseph B. Lippincott and others before them, Olmsted and Bartholomew were dismayed at the deficiency of parks and other recreational facilities in the region. The city of Los Angeles, they reported, had set aside less than 2 percent of its total land area for parks, a smaller amount than Boston, Chicago, San Francisco, or any of the other major cities to which they compared it.[56] Throughout the region, the situation was even more alarming, with barely 0.5 percent of the land area south of the mountains devoted to parkland.[57] Los Angeles was especially lacking, they pointed out, in neighborhood facilities (the city had fewer parks under five acres than St. Louis or Minneapolis) and parkways (the region still had no scenic drives that could rightly be called by that name, they said). Southern California, they warned, was rapidly losing its most valuable assets—its beaches, its mountain vistas, its tree-lined drives. In the rush of private development, too little land had been reserved for public use. "The Los Angeles region probably has greater future need for parks," they wrote, "than any other community of its size."[58]

Olmsted and Bartholomew recommended a massive program of improvements they said would cost $230.1 million to implement and take forty to fifty years to complete. They proposed, as Lippincott had years before, that a regional park district be established to oversee the development of such a program. Their specific plans called for public beach frontage to be more than doubled. They recommended the creation of a far-reaching system of regional parks and interconnecting parkways that, when completed, would encompass 71,000 acres—7.5 percent of the land south of the mountains. They also proposed that another 92,000 acres of parkland be established in outlying areas. The heart of the program was the system of parkways, which was reminiscent of Frederick Law Olmsted's "Emerald Necklace" that rings Boston. In all, 214 miles of parkways, reaching to every corner of the county, were proposed. These were to be "real parks" and, though they were to include roads for auto travel, would have "nothing in common with the 'boulevards' as that term is generally used." Rather, Olmsted and Bartholomew explained, such parkways should be wide enough and with sufficient plantings of trees (fig. 6.14) to produce "a sense of spaciousness and seclusion." Many of them were to be built along stream courses and were intended not only to provide added parkland and reduce traffic congestion, but also to lower the flood risk by taking flood-prone land out of circulation. As part of this approach, they recommended that regulations be established to prevent building on floodplains. "The combination of parks with flood-control necessities is frequently possible," they wrote. "Wherever practiced it . . . will yield a double return on the investment."[59]

Olmsted and Bartholomew recommended that parkways be established along 17.6 miles of the Los Angeles River—from Tujunga Wash to Elysian Park and from the river's confluence with the Rio Hondo to north Long Beach. The river parkway in the San Fernando Valley was to connect with a parkway proposed for the crest of the Santa Monica Mountains and two others that would extend up stream courses to the San Gabriel Mountains. The parkway proposed for the river south of Los Angeles, meanwhile, was to form one segment of a forty-mile-long greenway that would stretch from the foothills above Azusa all the way to Orange County. By acquiring wide strips of land along the river, they said, the natural character of the stream course could be preserved while keeping development far enough away from its channel to reduce the need for more traditional flood control work. North

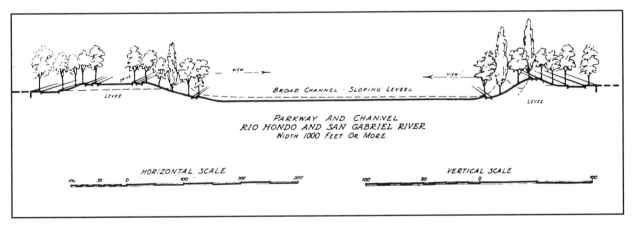

FIG. 6.14. Frederick Law Olmsted Jr. and Harland Bartholomew in 1930 proposed the development of a far-reaching system of parkways as part of a $230.1 million parks plan for Los Angeles County. Many of these parkways were to be built along stream courses, including the course of the Los Angeles River. This sketch shows a cross-section of a typical river parkway as envisioned by Olmsted and Bartholomew. Reprinted from Olmsted Brothers and Bartholomew and Associates, *Parks, Playgrounds, and Beaches for the Los Angeles Region*, report submitted to the Citizens' Committee on Parks, Playgrounds, and Beaches (Los Angeles: Citizens' Committee, 1930), plate 48.

of Elysian Park, they recommended that a right of way 400 to 1,500 feet wide be acquired along the river, three to seven times wider than its present channel, with the parkway following its south bank. Downstream from the Rio Hondo, they recommended that a corridor 1,000 to 1,500 feet wide be acquired. Like modern-day environmentalists, Olmsted and Bartholomew envisioned a river channel lined with willows, cottonwoods, sycamores, and wild grapes. "The most serious question in any plan of improvement," they said, "will necessarily be that of providing satisfactory and effective revetments or other forms of river control without seriously injuring the landscape value of the river bed."[60]

Multifaceted in its objectives and bold in both magnitude and approach, the Olmsted-Bartholomew plan, nevertheless, "sunk like a stone after being printed," in the words of one historian.[61] It was unsuccessful for some of the same reasons that earlier efforts to create parks and beautify Los Angeles had failed—it was overly ambitious and dependent for its execution on a regional parks agency that did not exist. The huge $230.1 million price tag was seven times the entire budget of the city of Los Angeles in 1930. Even before the release of the report, one member of the citizens' committee that sponsored it commented, "I am going to say now at the outset that I think it is very, very difficult to have this plan adopted." Even John Treanor, chairman of the citizens' committee, when he outlined the nature of the plan to the Chamber of Commerce's Board of Directors, admitted, "The public of Los Angeles is undoubtedly unprepared to countenance large schemes for park development at the present time." The creation of new parks was seen by many in the rapidly growing region as less essential than the building of highways, the development of adequate water resources, and other more basic improvements. The steady expansion of the infrastructure had already pushed both city and county to near their legal limits of bonded indebtedness. Some Chamber leaders may have also been scared off by the plan's recommendation for the creation of a metropolitan parks agency that would have had far-reaching powers, even its own police force. "It is terrifying if you come down to look at it with the powers given," said one member of the Chamber's Board of Directors. Another called it "a radical measure."[62]

The plan was also doomed by the timing of its release. Olmsted and Bartholomew submitted their report in March 1930, five months after the crash of the stock market that signaled the beginning of the Great Depression. Within a year, 20 percent of the work force in Los Angeles would be unemployed. The assessed value of property in the city would fall by one-third in four years, seriously reducing tax revenues that might fund such improvements and making government officials

understandably reluctant to pursue a program that would take perhaps another 100,000 acres off property tax rolls. Los Angeles Mayor
John C. Porter, in fact, recommended in 1931 that the city abandon all
public improvement projects to lighten the burden on taxpayers. Government employment relief projects provided some money for park
improvements during the Depression, but most of these expenditures
were geared toward labor-intensive projects that did not require large
outlays for land or materials. More than half the costs in the Olmsted-
Bartholomew plan were for real estate acquisition.[63]

In the desperate days before World War II, the lofty recommendations of Olmsted and Bartholomew were largely ignored. The Los Angeles Chamber of Commerce, which had funded the study, distanced
itself from the plan. Though it had originally intended to print several
thousand copies of the recommendations, once the contents were
known the Chamber decided to print only 200, just enough to distribute to the 162 members of the citizens' committee that had called
for its development. So few copies were published, in fact, that the
Chamber of Commerce was unable even to provide the five members
of the Los Angeles Board of Park Commissioners, the most important
parks agency in the region, with their own copies. Indicative of the in-
difference with which the plan was received, the park board ordered
the single copy it was given to be filed, without discussion. Ten years
after the plan's publication, the head of the city's Department of Recreation remarked that "the progress since 1930 toward the attainment
of the objectives set by that report has been negligible." It was not until after the war that Los Angeles voters were prepared to approve significant expenditures for new parks.[64] By that time, continued urban
development had rendered many of the Olmsted-Bartholomew proposals impractical, and an active federal government flood control
program had eliminated any hope of establishing parkways along the
Los Angeles River.

Ironically, the proposals of Olmsted and Bartholomew have received more attention recently than they did when they were first
made. Mike Davis, the most quoted commentator about late twentieth-century Los Angeles, has called them "a window into a lost future." They are frequently cited by those interested in creating a modern-day greenway along the river,[65] and there are even plans to
republish the report.[66] Environmentalists today point to the plan as an
example of what should have been done with the river. They are quick
to condemn flood control engineers as short-sighted, unimaginative,
and even corrupt. But they rarely consider the constraints under which
the engineers operated or the tenor of the times. The United States
was in the midst of the worst economic depression in its history when

most of the flood control system was designed. The need for protection was widespread, and the floods of 1934 and 1938 had made clear that the work could not wait. The acquisition of wide strips of land along the river for parkways might have reduced the need for structural flood control work, but it would not have eliminated the need altogether and probably would have increased the cost of flood control because of the high price of real estate in Southern California. As early as 1915, county officials had determined that the river would have to be confined to a narrow channel south of Los Angeles because land was prohibitively expensive.[67] The Olmsted-Bartholomew recommendations, moreover, were not true flood control proposals. Although they did address the flood problem, they lacked the technical support that might have prompted government engineers to pay attention. The proposals were never mentioned in any of the reports of the Los Angeles County Flood Control District or federal government flood control engineers.[68]

It is important to remember, too, that the river had been so transformed by development along its banks and diversions of its surface flow that, even before the first extensive flood control projects were begun, it was rarely viewed as an asset or a thing of beauty, as something to be saved. Rather, it was an occasional hazard that had to be controlled. Significant environmental concern about the river is a modern phenomenon. The content of hundreds of interviews conducted by county flood control officials after the flood of 1914, along with testimony given at a public hearing held by federal government flood control engineers in 1936, suggests that residents then had little concern for the natural character of the region's rivers and streams.[69] Most opposition to flood control efforts was based on differences of opinion about the best method for reducing the flood risk and the most equitable means for financing the work. Aesthetics do not seem to have been an issue. Harold E. Hedger, chief engineer of the Flood Control District until 1959, later commented that the only environmental concern considered in flood control planning was whether stream channels should be left open or covered completely like sewers.[70]

Flood control officials, it must also be emphasized, were not landscape architects or park builders. Their responsibilities were legally limited, as is illustrated by an exchange of letters in 1933 between the director of the Los Angeles County Regional Planning Commission and the chief engineer of the Flood Control District. Charles H. Diggs, director of the planning board, wrote Chief Engineer E. C. Eaton recommending that trees be planted along flood control channels. Eaton replied that "we are wholeheartedly in accord with any project to enhance the appearance of our barren stream channels, but are prohibited from expending our funds for such a project unless it has a distinct flood control value."[71] Such beautification proposals also sometimes masked their true motivation. Diggs saw the planting of trees along flood control channels not as a way to enhance the beauty of the region's rivers and streams, but as a means for "screening off unsightly portions" and "enhancing the value of adjacent property."

Over the years, other proposals for beautifying the river and creating parkways along its banks were made, but as flood control construction intensified and the popularity of the automobile grew, the nature of such proposals began to reflect new priorities. In 1933, for example, the Los Angeles Board of Park Commissioners approved a general beautification scheme for the river at the urging of the Los Angeles Chamber of Commerce. Several other city departments also became involved, and Flood Control District officials even approved the plan's implementation.[72] The importance of the project was tied to the development of a new passenger railroad terminal on Alameda Street. Many of the tracks leading to the new station were to pass directly along the river, and city officials and business leaders feared that, unless something was done to enhance its appearance, the view of the river would give travelers a bad first impression of the city. In urging the city council in 1934 to approve the project, Los Angeles Mayor Frank L. Shaw said, "The Los Angeles River has long been an eyesore in our city and with the construction of the new Union Railway Station now getting under way, I believe it would be greatly to the city's advantage if the beautification of the river bed could be carried forward to realization."[73]

The details of the plan were far different from the sort of improvements Olmsted and Bartholomew had suggested, however. Flood control was clearly seen as the first priority. The river channel was to be straightened and its banks were to be built up and lined with rock riprap. A roadway was to be constructed on each side of the river, but a drawing of the plan indicates that these roads were to be only ten feet wide (fig. 6.15). Each was labeled on the drawing, moreover, as a "service road," hardly a "parkway" of the type Olmsted and Bartholomew had envisioned. Trees were to be planted on both sides of the river from Elysian Park to the south city limits, but only at the top of the river's levees, between the riprapped banks and the service road. A drawing of the "proposed landscape treatment" of the river shows a small stream running through a straight and wide channel, confined between uniform banks topped by a single row of trees (some of which look to be palms, hardly the native trees of the floodplain forest).[74] Even this modest proposal, however, does not seem to have been implemented, perhaps because city officials were unable to obtain adequate funding during the depression years, but also probably because flood control strategies for the river were significantly modified after the arrival of the U.S. Army Corps of Engineers on the scene in 1935.

The very idea of what constituted a parkway also began to change as traffic congestion in the region increased. In 1939, the Transportation Engineering Board of the city of Los Angeles proposed the development of a comprehensive "parkway" system that was to include a "Riverside Parkway" to be built on the west side of the Los Angeles River from downtown Los Angeles to Burbank.[75] Closer examination of the plan, however, reveals that, by this time, the term *parkway* had come to mean nothing more than a landscaped expressway—more highway than park—designed to accommodate seventy-five thousand cars a day at speeds of up to sixty miles an hour. The 1939 "parkway" plan, in fact, became the blueprint for the region's freeway system. The first freeway constructed in Los Angeles, the Pasadena Freeway, was an outgrowth of a proposal first suggested in 1897 to create a parkway through the Arroyo Seco. That freeway was originally called the Arroyo Seco Parkway. The Golden State Freeway follows a route very similar to that first proposed for the Riverside Parkway.

FIG. 6.15. Conceptual drawing of a beautification plan proposed for the Los Angeles River in 1933, showing proposed landscaping and service roads. Like the other proposals for the enhancement of the river channel made in the first half of the twentieth century, it was never implemented. Reprinted from Los Angeles Board of Park Commissioners, *Annual Report* (Los Angeles, 1933), 24.

As flood control projects straightened, deepened, and widened the river channel and eventually covered its sandy bed with concrete, the river itself began to resemble a roadway, and its potential as such was recognized both officially and unofficially. Hot rodders found that its uninterrupted channel was an ideal place to race their cars (fig. 6.16). Even government officials began to wonder whether the river's usually dry bed would make a good highway. One of the earliest proposals to use the channel of the river as an automobile route was actually made by Frederick Law Olmsted Jr. and Harland Bartholomew, six years before they developed their parks plan calling for the building of parkways along the river. They suggested, as part of a street plan for Los Angeles prepared for a countywide traffic commission, that a "river truck speedway" be constructed directly in the riverbed through downtown Los Angeles. "It would be submerged by flood waters so rarely and for such short periods as not materially to impair its usefulness," they wrote.[76] Many similar proposals have been made over the years. During World War II, for instance, city planners suggested that the riverbed might be used as a corridor for transporting defense materials. The potential of using the river channel as a transportation route was also studied in 1943, 1949, 1972, 1976, and 1979.[77]

One such proposal helped galvanize modern-day interest in restoration of the river. State Assemblyman Richard Katz in 1989 suggested using the river as a truck route and automobile expressway during dry months to ease traffic on local freeways. To Katz, a Democrat from suburban Sylmar, the freeway-like bed of the river represented a relatively inexpensive way to prevent permanent gridlock. The infrastructure was already in place. It was barely being used. And it provided a continuous route from the San Fernando Valley to Long Beach. Amid the chuckles that came in response to his suggestion, Katz wrote an opinion piece in a local newspaper that was headlined, "What's so silly about a bargain freeway?" "I am the first to admit that the idea is unconventional," he wrote. "Still, the transportation crisis in Los Angeles is so severe that we can't afford to overlook any potential solution just because it hasn't been tried."[78]

It is easy to imagine what could have inspired such a scheme in a metropolitan area where 3:00 A.M. traffic jams are not unheard of. Indeed, it's unlikely Katz was the first daydreaming commuter, stuck in traffic on the Ventura, Golden State, or Long Beach freeway, who gazed over at the empty river channel that parallels those highways and wondered, "What if?" Katz's plan also included components designed to appease environmentalists. Trees were to be planted to create a greenbelt along the river's banks. Bikeways and parks were also to be built. Desperate for ideas on how to alleviate the region's

FIG. 6.16. As the Los Angeles River was paved by flood control projects, it began to look more like a roadway than a river and was perceived as such. In this photograph from the 1950s, police officers break up a teen-age drag race scene in the riverbed near downtown Los Angeles. *Los Angeles Examiner* photograph. Used with permission, Department of Special Collections, University of Southern California Library/Hearst Newspaper Collections.

legendary traffic congestion, the Los Angeles County Transportation Commission provided $100,000 to study the proposal. Preliminary investigations indicated that a river expressway could reduce congestion on two local freeways by 20 percent. The idea faded from consideration, however, amid ridicule and opposition from federal and local officials who said it would undermine flood protection.[79]

New Hope for the River

Nothing has helped to build support for efforts to revitalize the river more than new threats to its future. Until the controversy over the Katz proposal, Friends of the Los Angeles River had been a small, little-known organization. But the group's vocal and uncompromising opposition to the plan attracted the attention of politicians, environmental groups, and others all over Southern California and even outside the region, and before long many other people began to take up the river's cause. Membership in the group grew considerably during the months when debate over the proposal was frequently in the news. The *Los Angeles Times* and the influential local alternative newspaper *LA Weekly* wrote major articles about revitalization efforts. National publications such as the *Wall Street Journal* and the *Christian Science Monitor* also published stories about the river. "The Katz proposal really got people thinking about the river," FoLAR founder Lewis MacAdams said later. "I have often said that Richard Katz was one of the best friends the Los Angeles River ever had."[80]

The new interest spurred the first significant official activity concerning possible river revitalization in years. Los Angeles Mayor Tom Bradley, upon his reelection in 1989, pledged to make the river one of the priorities of his fifth term, and in January 1990 he created the Los Angeles River Task Force to investigate what could be done.[81] The task force, while acknowledging the continued importance of flood control, recommended that the river's natural ecosystem be restored "wherever possible," that public access to the river be improved, and that bicycle and hiking routes be developed along its course. It proposed the establishment of a new government agency to coordinate river improvements and recommended that a master plan be produced for the river. It also suggested three demonstration projects— the development of a nature walk and recreational program in Sepulveda Basin, the construction of a bike path near Griffith Park, and the creation of a historic site along the river where the Portolá expedition first forded its channel in 1769.[82]

That same year, the Southern California Institute of Architecture put forth a far more ambitious—albeit less practical—plan for the river's restoration. It proposed that the river be declared a regional park and that a Los Angeles River Valley Authority, with far-reaching powers, be established to oversee flood control, water quality monitoring, water supply issues, and the regulation of development along the river. It recommended that the river's concrete channel be removed in places and that its banks be pushed back to allow for the regeneration of wetlands. It advocated the planting of native trees not only atop the river's banks but in perforations on the sides of its concrete channel and on a series of low earth dams that it proposed be built in the riverbed to encourage greater percolation of its waters:

> In its present form, the river provides no benefit to the varied settlement along its course. The Los Angeles River is a deep scar through the heart of Los Angeles, legally unoccupiable and impassable, acting as a concave Berlin Wall in its separation of communities of different incomes and functions. Implicit in this uninhabited and paved state, however, is an uncommon opportunity; the river is the last remaining "wild" area in the city of Los Angeles, and its re-creation can be approached with few preconceptions.[83]

Soon, too, a variety of other agencies and organizations began to get involved. In May 1990, the Natural History Museum of Los Angeles County obtained a grant from the state Department of Fish and Game to survey the existing plant and animal life along the river. About the same time, the California legislature authorized the State Coastal Conservancy to conduct a study examining possible beneficial uses along its course. In 1991, Friends of the Los Angeles River and L.A. Beautiful, an organization that has been working on beautification issues in the city since 1949, sponsored a conference on the future of the river. The following year, at the request of Los Angeles City Councilman Mike Hernandez, the American Institute of Architects organized a design workshop to develop possible concepts for the redevelopment of the Taylor Yard, the Southern Pacific (now Union Pacific) switching and maintenance facility upstream from Elysian Park, which is gradually being phased out of operation. In November 1992, meanwhile, Los Angeles County voters approved Proposition A, providing $540 million for the development of parks and open space. These funds would provide the first money for actual projects along the river.[84]

Even the U.S. Army Corps of Engineers and the Los Angeles County Department of Public Works, the two agencies responsible for flood control in the region and generally resistant to suggestions that the river be opened to other uses, got in on the act. At the request of the city of Los Angeles, the Corps of Engineers conducted a preliminary study to investigate opportunities for environmental restoration, water conservation, and recreation along nineteen miles of the river north of downtown Los Angeles. It recommended more detailed studies of the possible development of a detention basin at the Taylor Yard, the restoration of wetlands and the creation of spreading grounds in the Griffith Park area, and the construction of a bikeway along the river from Sepulveda Basin to the Arroyo Seco. In the single biggest acknowledgment that efforts to green the river had received official recognition, the Los Angeles County Board of Supervisors in July 1991 directed the county Department of Public Works, along with two other departments, to coordinate development of a Los Angeles River Master Plan, acting on an idea proposed earlier by Mayor Bradley's river task force.[85]

Amid the newfound interest in the river, however, the U.S. Army Corps of Engineers announced its intention to embark on a huge new project to build concrete walls two to eight feet high atop levees along the last twelve miles of the river to increase flood protection. Continued urban development had heightened runoff so much, officials said, that the county's flood control system was no longer capable of containing the one-hundred-year flood it was designed to contain. The project, officially known as the Los Angeles County Drainage Area (LACDA) project, also called for walls to be built along nine miles of Compton Creek and the Rio Hondo, the widening of part of the Rio

Hondo channel, the armoring of the backs of river levees with a layer of grouted stone, and the raising of bridges to accommodate the parapet walls.[86] Not surprisingly, the plan immediately drew strong opposition from the increasingly diverse interests seeking to revitalize the river. The controversy that developed, like the reaction to the earlier proposal to turn its channel into a freeway, helped build support for efforts to improve the river.

Concern over whether the flood control system still provided adequate protection was first raised in February 1980, when debris from the river was found on the top of levees in Long Beach after a major storm, suggesting that the river may have come perilously close to overtopping its banks. Officials reported that the peak discharge of the river at Long Beach during the storm was a record 129,000 cubic feet per second, 26 percent greater than the previous high. Levees in Long Beach had been thought to provide better than one-hundred-year protection, but maximum stream flows in the 1980 storm were later calculated to be about equal to the level that could be expected in the type of storm that occurs once every forty years. Although some Long Beach residents claimed that data provided by stormflow gauges during the storm were inaccurate and suggested that photos showing debris atop levees may have been staged, the Corps of Engineers began a detailed study to determine whether the flood control system still provided satisfactory protection.[87]

Subsequent investigations revealed that flood controls on the Los Angeles River did not provide the desired one-hundred-year protection on about half its length. Levees were found to be especially inadequate on the last twelve miles of the river and on the Rio Hondo, where protection was less than the fifty-year level. Some stretches provided only twenty-five-year protection. Officials estimated that the type of flood that could be expected to occur once every one hundred years would inundate an eighty-two-square-mile area that is home to 500,000 people (fig. 6.17). Such a flood, they said, could cause $2.3 billion in damage. Losses would be greatest south of the Rio Hondo in communities like Downey, Compton, Bellflower, Lakewood, and Long Beach. Floodwaters would fill the corridors of Compton College. Carson Mall would be inundated by eight feet of water. At Jordan High School in Long Beach, floodwaters would be five feet deep. Flooding could also be expected near Griffith Park, in downtown Los Angeles, and along Tujunga Wash, but new flood control work was not proposed for those areas because floods would be less severe and the potential benefits could not justify the cost of construction.[88]

The flood control system became inadequate because no one had anticipated, when it was first conceived, that Los Angeles County

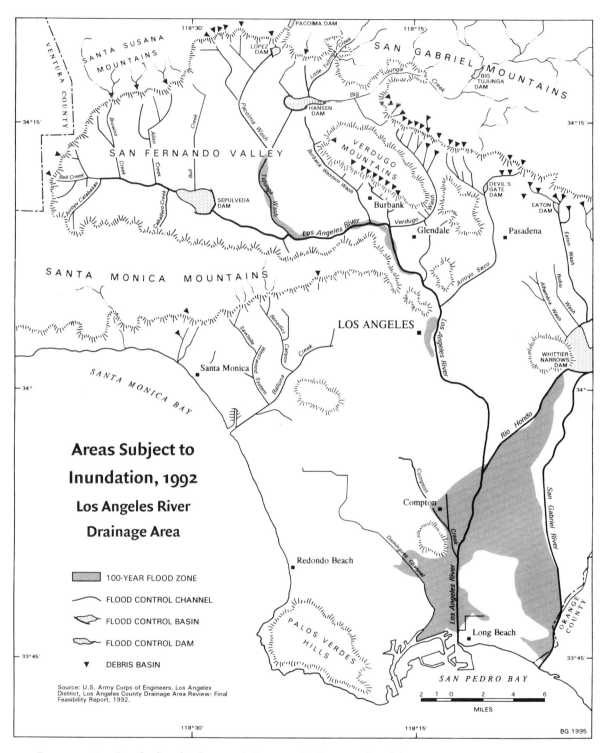

FIG. 6.17. Continued urban development in Los Angeles County reduced the effectiveness of existing flood protections so much that by 1992 an eighty-two-square-mile area was again subject to flooding. Map by the author.

would ever be as fully developed as it is today (fig. 6.18). "When the original river was designed, the assumption was made that the San Fernando Valley would still be half agriculture," explained Carl Blum, deputy director of the county Department of Public Works. "Because of the urban development that has taken place, the river is too small at the lower end."[89] A researcher at the University of California at Los Angeles in 1982 calculated that, between 1947 and 1979, urbanization of the watersheds of the Los Angeles and San Gabriel Rivers, including their mountainous portions, increased from 19.3 to 44.0 percent. Since so much of the once-porous ground had been covered by buildings and pavement, runoff had increased proportionately. One inch of precipitation during the period 1966–79 was found to have produced an average of 58 percent more runoff in the Los Angeles River than it had during the period 1949–65.[90] Construction of a comprehensive system of storm drains also increased the flow of water into the river. In addition, more sophisticated methods for estimating the frequency and magnitude of floods, plus fifty years of additional storm data, had shown that floods that were thought to occur once every one hundred years when the system was designed actually occur every fifty years.[91]

The need for improvements to the flood control system became even more pressing when the Federal Emergency Management Administration (FEMA) identified the eighty-two-square-mile flood-prone area as a "flood-hazard zone," a designation that imposes new construction requirements and requires residents and businesses in the area to buy flood insurance. Under FEMA regulations, new buildings would have to have been built higher than anticipated flood levels, up to fifteen feet above the ground in some areas. A study conducted by the University of Southern California Planning Institute found that such requirements would eventually cost the area 177,000 jobs and the loss of $30 billion in economic productivity. After protests from several cities brought support from members of Congress, FEMA agreed to establish a special zone for southeastern Los Angeles County that provides subsidized insurance and limits new building regulations—so long as progress on the planned improvements continues. In the meantime, height requirements for new construction were relaxed. New buildings are still required to be built above the ground, but never more than three feet above the surface.[92]

The plan to build walls on the last twelve miles of the river was vigorously opposed by environmentalists, led by Friends of the Los Angeles River. That group claimed the project would further degrade the "once-enchanted" river, increase urban blight, reduce property values, and waste "precious" water, while providing only short-term flood protection. FoLAR argued that the plan ignored the possible

FIG. 6.18. The persistent expansion of the built-up area and the building of new subdivisions, like this one in Sylmar on the north side of the San Fernando Valley, eventually caused flood control improvements on the Los Angeles River to become inadequate by reducing the ground surface available to absorb precipitation, which increases runoff into area rivers and streams. Photograph by Stephen Callis. Used with permission.

multiple uses of the river and failed to consider an integrated approach to flood control that would utilize several smaller projects, such as the construction of new detention basins, the widening of the river where possible, and more well-developed watershed management. The project was also criticized by state Senator Tom Hayden and Los Angeles Mayor Tom Bradley, who described it as "twenty-one miles of urban blight." The city of Los Angeles Planning Department's official response to a Corps of Engineers' environmental impact statement on the project said, "It is inconceivable that any advanced city in Europe could desire to build such a wall between itself and the river upon which it is situated."[93]

In January 1995, Friends of the Los Angeles River published two alternative proposals it claimed would not only provide one-hundred-year protection against floods, but also conserve water, improve water quality, and help restore the river to a more natural state. The first proposal recommended that gravel pits in the San Gabriel Valley be used

as storage basins during major storms and called for the rehabilita-
tion of Devil's Gate Dam, which had been shut down since structural
problems had been discovered after a 1972 earthquake. It also called
for the Los Angeles River to be widened and deepened south of Compton Creek to increase its capacity and suggested that a three-mile section of the river's concrete channel be removed to enable trees and
other vegetation to return to the river channel (fig. 6.19). The group
estimated the cost of the first proposal to be $368 million. The second
proposal recommended that the height of Whittier Narrows Dam be
raised five feet to provide additional storage and that peak flows normally discharged from the dam into the Rio Hondo be redirected into
the San Gabriel River. Like the first proposal, it called for the Los Angeles River to be widened for five miles above its mouth. FoLAR estimated the cost of the second proposal to be $105 million.[94]

U.S. Army Corps of Engineers officials questioned the feasibility
of the FoLAR plan and the reliability of the group's cost estimates.
LACDA project director Stuart H. Brehm III, furthermore, scoffed at
the suggestion that the river's concrete bed be removed, saying it

FIG. 6.19. Artist's interpretation of how the Los Angeles River might have
looked downstream from Compton Creek if a Friends of the Los Angeles
River proposal to widen the river and remove part of its concrete channel had
been implemented. Sketch by Dianne Herring. Courtesy, Friends of the Los Angeles
River.

would be "like reinventing the wheel." He also denied that the Corps of Engineers plan was environmentally damaging. "It's just a bunch of walls," he said.[95] Federal government officials pointed out that the three principal elements to the FoLAR proposals had already been considered during initial planning for the project but had been rejected as too expensive or insufficient to provide the necessary protection.[96] Corps engineers did not, however, consider using a combination of smaller projects, the approach employed in the FoLAR plan. Representatives of the Los Angeles County Department of Public Works, meanwhile, said that the FoLAR proposals lacked sufficient technical support to warrant serious consideration. Under the terms of its agreements with the federal government, the county was required to pay one-third of the project's costs. "There's a lot of information that is missing," said Diego Cadena, project manager for the county. "The calculations are not there. The assumptions are hard to verify. We look at this as just a concept."[97] Unconvinced that the new proposals would do the job and worried that further delays could threaten federal government funding for the project, the Los Angeles County Board of Supervisors in April 1995 approved the $312 million project by a 4-1 margin, clearing the way for construction to begin.[98]

Four weeks later, Friends of the Los Angeles River and two other local environmental groups, Heal the Bay and TreePeople, filed a lawsuit in Los Angeles County Superior Court seeking to halt the project. They charged that the county had violated state environmental regulations by failing to adequately consider alternative proposals. The suit was later joined by a dozen environmental groups, including American Rivers, the Sierra Club, and the Audubon Society. The plaintiffs had hoped to reach an out-of-court settlement with the county, but negotiations dragged on, and in February 1996 construction on the LACDA project began. Finally, in July 1996, a Superior Court judge ordered the Board of Supervisors to reconsider the project and reevaluate whether an environmental impact report produced to accompany plans met state standards. Project opponents claimed victory, but the victory proved limited. That August, supervisors reapproved the project, certifying the report as adequate. Their only concession to project opponents was that they agreed to spend $250,000 to hire an independent consultant to investigate alternative proposals and to fund a Los Angeles River Watershed Task Force to help in long-term planning. Construction on the project, meanwhile, continued without interruption. The final obstacle to continuation of the LACDA project was surmounted in August 1997 when the consultant, Orange County–based Simons, Li & Associates, recommended that the project be carried out as originally planned. The consultant concluded that none of the alternative proposals would assure adequate protection and said that even the best of those considered was more expensive and would take longer to complete than the Army Corps of Engineers plan.[99]

Local media portrayed the controversy over the project as a David versus Goliath struggle that could have far-reaching implications for Southern California. "The battle over flood control on the Los Angeles River is really a fight for its soul," read one headline.[100] The *Los Angeles Times*, which has called the river one of the city's "most glaring eyesores" and has consistently applauded proposals to revitalize its channel, opposed the project on its editorial page.[101] One editorial called the fight over the project a "Rorschach test of sorts for the future of this region."[102] But in the end, the immediate needs of flood control won out over the long-term interest in improving the river. Even lawmakers who were critical of the Army Corps of Engineers plan voted in favor of it, fearing that continued delays might prompt the federal government to withdraw its support for any project, thus forcing homeowners and businesses to buy costly flood insurance. "I hate it," said Supervisor Gloria Molina, an early supporter of efforts to green the river, who reluctantly cast her vote in favor of the plan. "I don't like it, but I have no choice."[103] The majority of the Board of Supervisors, meanwhile, expressed a desire to pursue more holistic watershed management approaches in future flood control planning.

Although the LACDA project is not expected to be completed until at least 2001, the walls along the Los Angeles River were finished by the end of 1997 (fig. 6.20). Fewer miles of walls were built than had originally been proposed because flood control officials discovered during the design stage that in many places they could raise levees instead.[104] The walls that were built, meanwhile, are not nearly as ugly as critics of the project claimed they would be—they certainly don't constitute "twenty-one miles of urban blight." If you didn't know any better, you might think that the walls were installed simply to keep bicyclists from tumbling down the river's steep banks. In no place do they stand more than four feet above the tops of levees. Even where taller walls were built, adjacent bike paths and access roads were raised to assure that the walls themselves would never be more than four feet above the land on the outside of the channel. Critics of the project were also able to get the county to add texture to the walls and to plant vines and other vegetation alongside to improve their appearance. Even Lewis MacAdams acknowledged that the walls were not so bad. "I always saw it as a symbolic issue," he said.[105]

FIG. 6.20. The controversy spurred by a U.S. Army Corps of Engineers project to construct concrete walls atop levees along the Los Angeles River—like this one near Pacific Coast Highway in Long Beach—helped to build support for efforts to revitalize its course. Photograph by the author, 1997.

Creating a Los Angeles River Greenway

If the controversy over the 1989 proposal to turn the Los Angeles River into a freeway put the river back on the map, the years of debate and legal wrangling over the LACDA project raised public consciousness about the river to a level unprecedented in its history. The river that for so long was easy to overlook is now difficult to escape. Open the *Los Angeles Times* or even the *New York Times* and you might find a story about it.[106] Turn on the radio and you could hear a commentary about the river on National Public Radio's *Morning Edition* or a debate about its future on a local talk show or call-in program.[107] Flip on the television and there it is again—on the nightly news, CBS-TV's *Sunday Morning*, or the cable Discovery Channel. All over Los Angeles are signs of the river's symbolic reemergence. There in the window of a neighborhood police station in Los Feliz is a poster promoting the greening of the river. Tacked to a telephone pole in Silver Lake is another poster, featuring a modernistic depiction of a man in the middle of the industrialized river, this one promoting an art sale to benefit Friends of the Los Angeles River.[108] Spanning the entrance to the city's new $300 million downtown transit center, built behind Union Station a mile west of the river, is a giant mural entitled "City of Dreams, River of History." Inside the entrance is a water sculpture modeled after the river. Bronze likenesses of trout, turtles, sycamore leaves, and other characteristic flora and fauna of the river have been embedded in the lobby floor.[109] The river, it seems, is everywhere.

Years ago, long after the river had been covered in concrete and fenced off from the neighborhoods and industrial districts along its banks, veteran Los Angeles newspaper columnist Jack Smith observed "the Los Angeles River is not the Seine, the Thames, the Danube nor the Tiber. It plays no great role in the social, commercial and cultural life of our city; as far as I know it has never inspired a line of poetry or song." But that, too, has clearly changed.[110] In recent years, the river has been the subject of photo and art exhibits at the Los Angeles Public Library, El Pueblo de Los Angeles Historical Monument, El Camino College, and several private galleries. A video about the river has been featured at the Museum of Contemporary Art and toured the nation as part of a traveling exhibition sponsored by the Smithsonian Institution. A local dance troupe even staged a performance called Mother Ditch right in the channel of the river, its dancers wearing rubber boots.[111] The river has also been immortalized in both poetry and song. Acclaimed poets Gary Snyder and Luis Rodriguez (not to mention Friends of the Los Angeles River founder Lewis MacAdams) have written poems about it.[112] A local singer who goes by the name of E received radio airplay for a song in which he laments his sorry life and compares himself to the river.[113] Emblematic of the river's more modern cultural significance, a Los Angeles high school teacher has created a "virtual" tour of the river on the world wide web.[114]

These days, moreover, seemingly everyone has a vision for the future of the river. More than 160 people from seventy different government agencies, private organizations, and companies participated in the development of the Los Angeles River Master Plan, completed in June 1996. Two consecutive Democratic candidates for mayor in Los Angeles have made the river a centerpiece of their campaigns.[115] A top aide to Republican Mayor Dick Riordan wants to turn the river into a quarter-mile-wide greenbelt through downtown Los Angeles, possibly using a series of low dams to keep water in it, whereas a prominent developer has actually suggested that the river be removed from its concrete channel and redirected on a meandering course through the business district and Exposition Park.

In an idea reminiscent of river revitalization projects in Portland, Oregon, and elsewhere, a professor at the University of Southern California has proposed that the railroad tracks on the east side of the river be shifted to the opposite bank to enable the development of a riverfront park.[116] Academics, in general, have taken to the river like egrets in search of crawdads. Several area colleges have offered courses and seminars on its possible restoration, and at least seven graduate theses about the river have been produced.[117] Countless planning workshops, conferences, and round-table discussions have also been held. In 1996, the American Society of Landscape Architects sponsored a design charette in conjunction with its national meeting in Los Angeles to seek plans for the river and produced a multimedia CD-ROM showcasing ideas developed by landscape architects from as far away as Iowa and Maine. Major corporations are also getting involved. Universal Studios, located on the south bank of the river in the San Fernando Valley, announced in 1998 its intention to open more than a mile of the riverfront to the public as part of a long-range plan. It hopes to convert the riverfront adjacent to its back lot into a linear park with pedestrian and bike trails and a "river interpretive center."[118]

The area along the river that offers the greatest opportunity for habitat restoration and recreational development and, thus, has been the continual subject of proposals and studies is the Taylor Yard, the huge railroad facility developed by the Southern Pacific in the 1920s upstream from Elysian Park. Beginning in 1973, the Southern Pacific began to shift its operations to a newer facility seventy miles to the east in Colton and, in 1992, it put most of the Taylor Yard up for sale. Forty acres were bought by the Metropolitan Transportation Authority, which built a maintenance shed for its Metrolink trains there, but the rest was taken over by the Union Pacific when it acquired the Southern Pacific in 1996. Most of the original facilities on the site have long since been abandoned, and the Union Pacific is eventually expected to sell most of the land. Because the remaining 180 acres constitutes the single largest piece of developable property along the river—and in central Los Angeles—the Taylor Yard figures prominently in all discussions about the river.

In addition to being the subject of a design workshop sponsored by the American Institute of Architects in 1992, the Taylor Yard was suggested that same year as a possible site for a detention basin by the U.S. Army Corps of Engineers. In 1994, an unlikely alliance between Friends of the Los Angeles River and the county Department of Public Works, with money provided by a grant from the state's urban streams restoration program, conducted a study to determine the feasibility of using the site as a multiobjective flood control and riparian restoration project. The study recommended a $214.4 million project to create a three-tiered development that would include wetlands, woodland areas with ponds and hiking trails, and an upland park area with athletic fields and other recreation facilities.[119]

Ideas for the redevelopment of the Taylor Yard also took center stage at a "River through Downtown" conference held at the Los Angeles Public Library in February 1998.[120] The new proposals took on a special urgency because just weeks before the conference it was reported that a Dallas developer had agreed to purchase a fifty-three-acre piece of the railyard and turn it into a business park catering to entertainment companies. Earlier, a Chicago developer had announced plans for a large retail project on a forty-acre parcel nearby. Already, Federal Express had developed a distribution facility on eleven acres of the site. Fearing that such projects could derail efforts to transform the Taylor Yard into a model for the restoration of the river, two state senators, Tom Hayden and Richard Polanco, along with leaders of Friends of the Los Angeles River, the Sierra Club, and the Santa Monica Mountains Conservancy, on the eve of the conference called for a moratorium on development at the site.[121]

The new proposals for the Taylor Yard, developed by a team of architects, planners, and designers during a three-day workshop sponsored by FoLAR and several other organizations, were similar to those that had already been made in that they recommended that the site be turned into a multi-use development, offering opportunities for stormwater retention, habitat restoration, recreation, and commercial development. Under the plan, the levee on the east side of the river would be removed for a short distance to allow water from the river to fill wetlands adjacent to its channel (fig. 6.21). Athletic fields, skateboard and dog parks, and agricultural sites would occupy slightly higher ground, though still within the floodplain. Those areas would act as a detention basin during storms, providing increased flood protection for downtown Los Angeles. Farther from the river and outside the detention basin, mixed-use commercial development would be encouraged. Support from elected officials like Hayden, Polanco, and Los Angeles City Councilman Mike Hernandez has given new weight to such ideas. Representatives of the California State Coastal Conservancy committed to spending $250,000 of 1996 Proposition A funds to pay for a feasibility study of a specific project on at least part of the site, if the Union Pacific would cooperate. FoLAR founder Lewis MacAdams, meanwhile, said that, as a result of the new attention, the railroad for the first time had shown a willingness to talk to environmental groups and others about the future of the railyard.[122]

Beyond the multitude of ideas, proposals, and studies, some actual progress has been made on river revitalization efforts. In 1994, a local tree-planting organization, NorthEast Trees, began planting trees and shrubs along service roads atop the river's concrete banks between Griffith Park and Elysian Park, one of three sections where the river

FIG. 6.21. Sketch showing how a railroad yard located along the Los Angeles River north of downtown might look if a multiobjective flood control and riparian restoration project were developed at the site. This view looks south toward Elysian Park and shows a proposed break in the levee on the east side of the river that would allow water from the river to fill wetlands along its banks. Recreational facilities and commercial enterprises would be developed farther from the river. Part of the site would be used as a detention basin during storms to better protect downtown Los Angeles from floods. Sketch by Jesse Im. Courtesy, Friends of the Los Angeles River.

has an unpaved bottom and, therefore, looks more like a river than it does on most of its course. Approximately two thousand sycamore, elderberry, cottonwood, and other native trees and five hundred native shrubs were to be planted on a 4.5-mile stretch of the river. The project, funded by a state Department of Transportation grant obtained by the Mountains Recreation and Conservation Authority (MRCA), a state agency that manages twenty-two parks in Los Angeles County, also paid for the construction of five "pocket" parks along the river between Fletcher Drive and Elysian Park (fig. 6.22). These tiny parks, smaller than a typical suburban backyard, contain benches, water fountains, and bike racks and will serve as rest areas when a planned bike path on the west side of the river is completed. NorthEast Trees has also begun work on a project to create a short greenway on the east side of the river in the Atwater Village neighborhood across from Griffith Park. Funded with money provided by Proposition A, the parks and open space bond issue approved by voters in 1992, the project will create pedestrian and equestrian trails along 1.3 miles of the river. Approximately one thousand native trees and shrubs will be planted.[123]

Proposition A money also helped pay for the development of a somewhat larger park along the river in the Glendale Narrows. In July 1995, the Santa Monica Mountains Conservancy, a state agency that is closely allied with the MRCA, dedicated the Elysian Valley Gateway Park on one-third of an acre on the west side of the river, just downstream from where the Glendale Freeway crosses its channel (fig. 6.23). Developed on the site of two abandoned houses across from a machine shop in a working class Hispanic neighborhood, the little park with the big name has picnic tables, a sandbox, and several large trees and offers access to the river through a gated chain link fence. The location was chosen because it is adjacent to one of the river's three soft-bottom sections. Although the spot is hardly idyllic—it sits

FIG. 6.22. One of five pocket parks created by NorthEast Trees and the Mountains Recreation and Conservation Authority on the west side of the river in the Glendale Narrows. Maintenance sheds for the Metropolitan Transportation Authority's Metrolink commuter rail line are located across the river from the park, which sits just upstream from the Figueroa Street bridge. Photograph by the author, 1997.

opposite noisy Taylor Yard and the river's concrete banks are littered with broken glass—the river through this area does support lush vegetation and a diverse variety of birds. The park was given its rather lofty name because its creators believed that it would become the first segment of what they called the Los Angeles River Greenway, a hoped-for fifty-one-mile corridor of parks and connecting trails. The cost of acquiring the land and developing the park, which was done with the help of a private organization called the Trust for Public Land, was about $350,000.[124]

The city of Los Angeles, meanwhile, has followed through on a proposal first made by Mayor Bradley's Los Angeles River Task Force to build a bikeway along the river. Construction began in July 1995 on the first phase of a planned seven-mile bikeway that will eventually run from the north side of Griffith Park to Elysian Park on the west side of the river. The first leg of the bikeway, a 3.2-mile segment from Riverside Drive, across from Burbank, to Los Feliz Boulevard, opened in July 1997 (fig. 6.24). It is the first lighted bike path in Los Angeles. Constructed primarily on land owned by the Los Angeles Department of Water and Power, it cost $800,000 to design and $1.8 million to build, whopping figures considering that the bike path is a mostly straight strip of asphalt twelve feet wide, with a yellow line painted

FIG. 6.23. Elysian Valley Gateway Park, developed in 1995 along the west side of the river, just downstream from the Glendale Freeway, by the Santa Monica Mountains Conservancy. Photograph by the author, 1997.

FIG. 6.24. Bicyclists ride on the first leg of a planned seven-mile-long bike path along the west side of the river in the city of Los Angeles. When completed, the bike path will run from the north side of Griffith Park to Elysian Park. Photograph by the author, 1997.

down the middle and a fence erected between the path and the river's sloping banks. The high cost of the bike path provides another lesson on the difficulty of creating riverside trails and other linear recreational facilities. Michelle Mowery, bicycle coordinator for the city of Los Angeles, blamed the excessive costs on administrative overhead incurred in securing agreements to use the land from the five federal, state, and local government agencies and one private company that have some authority over the right of way through which the bike path runs. "Quite honestly, this is not something anybody wanted to do," she said. "There are nine million uses along there. It required a huge number of agreements between agencies. I can't tell you what a tremendous amount of work it has been. It has been our most complicated bike project to date."[125]

The location of the first leg of the bike path is also far from perfect—only a chain link fence separates riders from the ten-lane Golden State Freeway—but the bikeway is, nevertheless, drawing new people to the river. The remainder of the bike path is expected to be completed by 2000, although work could be further complicated by the fact that private parties own part of the land over which the extensions will pass. The city also plans to build a short bike path, probably not more than a mile in length, along the river in front of the Taylor Yard to connect the communities east of the river, such as Glassell Park and Cypress Park, to the longer bikeway on the opposite side of its channel. The two bike paths will be connected by a bridge. Officials from a variety of government agencies are hopeful that additional bike paths can eventually be built farther upstream and through downtown Los Angeles to connect to a more rudimentary county-maintained bike path that follows the river from Vernon to the river's mouth. It was completed in 1977. The U.S. Army Corps of Engineers has talked about building bike paths along the river in the San Fernando Valley.[126]

Many more projects were also in the works, some funded with money from the 1992 bond issue, while others will be paid for out of funds provided by three subsequent bond referendums. Money from the 1992 county bonds was to be used to create a riverside park in the city of Maywood and four "outdoor classrooms" along the Los Angeles River and two tributary streams and to pay for improvements to the county-maintained bike path. In November 1996, voters approved a second Proposition A, which will provide at least $16.2 million for projects along the Los Angeles and San Gabriel Rivers and their tributaries. In that same election, state voters approved a water projects initiative, Proposition 204, that will provide $7 million for river projects in Los Angeles County. The MRCA was designated to coordinate planning for $12 million of the new Proposition A money and $5 million of the Proposition 204 funds. It planned to spend $5 million of that money to purchase part of Lawry's California Center on Avenue 26, upstream from the confluence of the Arroyo Seco and the river, and create a "river center," with a museum, offices for its river division and perhaps other organizations such as FoLAR, facilities for an environmental educational program for at-risk youths, and meeting space for community groups. It also planned to develop a larger riverside park on five acres one-quarter of a mile upstream from the Elysian Valley Gateway Park, possibly equipping it with a nursery to raise native plants for riverside plantings and to be used for educational programs with area schools. Also in November 1996, voters in the city of Los Angeles narrowly approved Measure K, a parks initiative that will provide $10 million for river improvements. City officials were expecting to develop some sort of linear park along the river in Sherman Oaks or Studio City, though specific plans still had to be developed.[127]

The nature of the projects that have thus far been completed and those that are now being contemplated highlights what would seem to be a subtle but fundamental shift in the focus of efforts to revitalize the river. In the beginning, Lewis MacAdams and Friends of the Los Angeles River talked of peeling back the concrete and restoring the river in such a way that trout would return to its waters and tall sycamores would again grow in midstream. Some, including MacAdams, still talk this way. But as interest in renewing the river has expanded and a more diverse range of people, agencies, and organizations have become involved, the priorities of revitalization efforts have taken on a decidedly more mainstream flavor. What began as a movement to restore the river has evolved into a campaign to embellish its edges. All the work done thus far has been done along the tops of the river's concrete banks or outside the fences that border its official right of way. All of the projects that are now being actively discussed—more parks and bike paths, San Antonio–like river walks, detention basins that could allow wetlands restoration—would likewise be undertaken entirely outside the river channel. Despite all the new attention that is being paid to the river and the money that is being directed to projects along its banks, the river itself remains unchanged.

The gradual shift in the focus of river revitalization efforts has also led to a divergence among the groups involved, though publicly, at least, they remain closely associated. MacAdams and FoLAR are the purists, emphasizing the restoration of the river itself and related issues such as watershed management, water conservation, and habitat restoration over the building of parks and bike paths. They are the most uncompromising in their approach. They are the people most likely to stand in front of bulldozers, confront construction crews, or file lawsuits. In the spirit of pioneering ecologist Edward Abbey, they are the monkeywrenchers. FoLAR has shown a willingness, nevertheless, to work with those whose primary interests have been in the development of riverside recreational facilities and to participate in activities that could be seen as diverting attention away from the group's original goals. "Building a constituency means working with as many people who are working in your general direction as possible," MacAdams explained. "The larger the constituency for the river, the better off we are. So the more people I can draw down to the river, by whatever means possible, is positive." Still, MacAdams sometimes grows impatient and perhaps a little resentful when FoLAR is asked to stay away from an important meeting because of its adversarial reputation or is not invited to a park dedication. "We tend to be in the position where everybody wants us to do the dirty work, then everybody else will come in and take the credit and compromise," he said. "What has happened is that all these other groups have taken on important issues which are much easier to deal with, leaving us with the hard stuff.

Everybody has more or less been willing to cede these issues of flood protection and water conservation in favor of getting permission to build parks."[128]

At the opposite end of the spectrum from MacAdams among those working to revitalize the river is Cynthia D'Agosta. A landscape architect, D'Agosta was rivers division chief for the Mountains Recreation and Conservation Authority, which, by virtue of the fact that it is responsible for administering $21 million in bond money that could be spent on river projects, has emerged as the most important government agency working on behalf of its renewal. The MRCA originally became involved with the river as part of a general plan to build parks and increase open space in the Los Angeles area. A native of northern California, D'Agosta received her master's degree in landscape architecture from Harvard in 1989, working on river projects throughout New England while in school. After she graduated, she took a job with a Laguna Beach landscape architecture firm but in 1992 left private practice to become a parks planner with the County of Los Angeles, where she was one of the principal planners involved in developing the Los Angeles River Master Plan. She left her job with the county in 1995 because, she said, once the master plan process was completed, the Department of Parks and Recreation "wanted to drop all participation in the river." She explained, "They are not in the mode of acquisition of new properties. They didn't see a role for themselves in river development." She worked as a consultant to the Trust for Public Land, the county Department of Public Works, and the Mountains Conservation Foundation before taking her position with the MRCA in June 1997.

Conciliatory where MacAdams is confrontational, diplomatic when he can be divisive, D'Agosta sees the revitalization of the river as an issue of "retrofitting" or "adaptive reuse" rather than of restoration. "The point is that we have an infrastructure system built into the rivers and streams, being the flood control system, that we cannot negate," she said. "Restoration by its definition is to restore to a natural state. We're not going to be able to do that. We cannot just go in and immediately tear out the concrete and begin again. The approach is to recognize the infrastructure we have and what we need, and begin to look at adapting that to the desires of the community today with regards to habitat and open space." To people like D'Agosta, the revitalization of the river is primarily a means to increase parkland and open space in congested Southern California and to reconnect the region's diverse cities and neighborhoods. This is a decidedly human-centered perspective.

D'Agosta sees the creation of parks and greenways along the river as the necessary first step of a very long process, a means of reacquainting a larger public with the river, but she says her ultimate goals are very similar to those of MacAdams. She envisions an uninterrupted trail, "lush, green and forested," running along the entire river course and a river channel that has a soft bottom and soft sides on a much greater part of its length. To make that vision a reality, it will first be necessary, she believes, to demonstrate on some of the river's tributaries that more imaginative approaches to flood control will, in fact, work. She hopes, for example, to persuade flood control officials to allow the MRCA to test two such projects on Tujunga Wash and Compton Creek using 1996 Proposition A funds. D'Agosta insists, moreover, that every new project along the river should include some element of habitat restoration—possibly a small wetland area in addition to more typical park amenities—to assure that each development has a real connection with the river. "The changes you can make are incremental and probably need to begin outside of the channel," she said. "Maybe ten years from now, we can look at massive changes within the channel. But we are going to have to get engineers to understand that this can happen."[129]

The contrasting viewpoints of MacAdams and D'Agosta about the Los Angeles River Master Plan typify the differences in their attitudes. MacAdams is sharply critical of it, while D'Agosta is cautiously optimistic. "This is something that [Supervisor] Gloria Molina demanded so county public works did it, begrudgingly," MacAdams said. "It was a way to show supervisors that they weren't just in charge of more concrete. They made sure that it had no weight. It's in no sense a master plan. It doesn't deal with any issues other than parkland. It doesn't deal with water conservation. It doesn't deal with flood control."[130] Even D'Agosta will admit that the massive document—five years in the making and 642 pages in length—is not really a master plan in the true sense. The county coordinated its development but, because it has no jurisdiction over the riverfront except for a small piece of land in the San Fernando Valley, it has no authority to implement the plan. The cities that border the river are not required to pay attention to it. The master plan, moreover, makes few definite recommendations and almost completely ignores the river itself. It is filled with ideas for bike paths, parks, and landscaping projects but, in many ways, is more of a master suggestion than a master plan. D'Agosta, nonetheless, believes that, because so many organizations and government agencies contributed to its development, the master plan has value simply "because of the level of communication it opened up." She added, "Even though it's not a document you can go to court with, the different planning commissions, city councils and people in decision making positions are looking at it as a document that should guide what happens along the river."[131]

River or Flood Control Channel?

Even in the altogether unnatural Los Angeles River, the sounds that rang through its concrete channel on the brisk November morning in 1997 were unusual. Adding to the roar of cars and tractor-trailers from the Golden State Freeway, which runs alongside the river just west of its channel, and the clanking of railroad cars shifting back and forth in the freight yards downstream on the opposite side was the whir of chainsaws and the scraping of bulldozers. In anticipation of the unusually heavy precipitation that had been forecast for the Los Angeles area in the coming winter because of strong El Niño conditions that had developed off the California coast, employees of the U.S. Army Corps of Engineers and the county Department of Public Works had begun to clear vegetation from the river's soft-bottom sections and a few other places where enough sediment had accumulated on its concrete bed to allow plants to take root.

County flood control officials said it was imperative that the vegetation be removed or at least cut back because the trees and shrubs that had grown up in the river reduced the capacity of its channel and, thus, undermined its ability to contain storm flows. Vegetation that washed down the river during storms, they warned, could also dam up behind bridge abutments and cause the river to overflow. The removal of vegetation from stream channels that are part of the county's flood control system was nothing new. "For years we cleaned them up every year or every other year," said Jim Noyes, chief deputy director of the Department of Public Works. "We just went out and did it."[132] But as concern for the environment grew in the 1970s and 1980s, new and more stringent regulations began to be implemented by the state and federal government to protect remaining habitat, and flood control officials became increasingly limited in what they could do. In the years leading up to the El Niño threat, for instance, county officials had been permitted to clear only one-half of the river channel in Long Beach each year. As the web of regulations became more dense, furthermore, flood control officials found it increasingly difficult to obtain the permits required to allow them to remove vegetation from stream channels.[133]

In the meantime, county officials claimed, vegetation had grown so thick in some portions of the Los Angeles River that channel capacity had been reduced by half. The threat of El Niño, which some climatologists predicted could result in twice the normal amount of rainfall in Los Angeles, raised the ante. County officials had been trying since 1995 to secure permits to clear brush from stream channels, but because of the increasingly complex permitting process those permits had still not been approved two years later. As the storm season approached, exasperated county officials appealed to Governor Pete Wilson and the state's two U.S. senators for help and even threatened to sue the U.S. Army Corps of Engineers, one of the agencies responsible for issuing the permits. Finally, in October 1997, over the strenuous objections of environmental groups and others, the Corps of Engineers granted the county an emergency permit, but one of the conditions of the permit was that the county would be required to create new habitat to make up for any that was destroyed.[134]

County employees, with help from the U.S. Army Corps of Engineers, began clearing vegetation from the river a few days later. River boosters continued to fight the action, arguing that the emergency permit allowed the agencies, in the words of Lewis MacAdams, to "permanently clear cut every living thing in the river—without public discussion." Friends of the Los Angeles River and others again threatened to file lawsuits. As the bulldozing got under way, state Sen. Tom Hayden, along with representatives from FoLAR and the Sierra Club, held a press conference within earshot of the heavy machinery to draw attention to what they claimed was an illegal activity. On two different occasions, MacAdams all by himself confronted Corps workers, once sloshing through the river in a leaky old pair of rain boots to chase after bulldozers scraping away sand bars on which plants had sprouted (fig. 6.25) and another time accosting a hard-hatted laborer chainsawing limbs from a willow tree. In a letter to the *Los Angeles Times*, MacAdams wrote, "By cynically whipping up El Niño hysteria, these two agencies are trying to regain the dominance they once had and recreate the sterile, concrete, dead channels they so deeply cherish." As the debate intensified, flood control officials backed off slightly, agreeing to leave some of the vegetation and to use handcutting methods rather than bulldozers in the soft-bottom sections of the river to allow root systems to remain. They also said that, where possible, they would remove nonnative species, such as the especially invasive bamboo, rather than willows and other native species. (Critics say this was not done.) Much of the vegetation in the river was saved, as a result, but huge amounts were destroyed. A frustrated MacAdams, weary from one more battle with the Corps and the county, commented, "It shows how far we have come, but how far we still have to go."[135]

The new controversy underscored the fact that, despite the progress made toward revitalizing the river, government flood control officials still refused to acknowledge it as anything but a flood control channel. In this light, an exchange that occurred between MacAdams and Noyes, chief deputy director of the county public works agency, as debate was heating up over the clearing of the channels, is especially telling. Representatives from several government agencies and environmental organizations had gathered in the offices of Los Angeles County Supervisor Zev Yaroslovsky to discuss the issue. At one point in describing what the county planned to do, Noyes referred to the river as the "flood control channel." MacAdams interrupted him and said, "You mean 'river.'" Noyes continued, but every time he used the phrase "flood control channel," MacAdams interrupted and interjected the word "river." This happened again and again, until, as MacAdams remembered it, "it got really ugly. He was just getting furious. I saw him a couple of days later and he wouldn't even speak to me."[136]

Such symbolic disagreements are important because they illustrate the gulf that still exists between those working for the river's renewal and the government agencies legally responsible for its maintenance. Federal and county flood control officials continue to assert complete

FIG. 6.25. A discouraged Lewis MacAdams, founder of Friends of the Los Angeles River, stands in the river as bulldozers clear vegetation from its channel in anticipation of heavy El Niño-driven rains, expected in the winter of 1997–98. Photograph by the author, 1997.

control over what goes on in the river's channel. They have slowly and reluctantly agreed to unlock the gates that kept the public out and have yielded some of the right of way along the river for bike paths and parks, but they draw the line at the top of the river's banks and have steadfastly refused to allow any project that might undermine the river's flood control function. They have even demanded that organizations planting trees along access roads install underground barriers to prevent tree roots from reaching the river's concrete banks, since the roots have the ability to work away at the concrete.[137] "Some people would like the water channels to become riparian corridors," said another public works official, Carl Blum, the agency's deputy director, "but that's not what the system is for."[138]

More than any other issue, the continuing debate over flood control will be pivotal in determining just how far efforts to revitalize the Los Angeles River will go. Elsewhere, urban riverfronts have been opened up to renewal in large part because of the decline of riverfront industry and the abandonment of the transportation facilities that had served those industries. As factories moved elsewhere and trucks replaced railroads and boats as conduits for commerce, rivers ceased to be an essential part of the cities through which they flowed. Such industrial restructuring has also occurred in Los Angeles, but the Los Angeles River remains important because it is the backbone of the region's flood control system. River boosters look to urban waterways in Chicago, Portland, San Antonio, and Denver and wonder why the Los Angeles River cannot be like those rivers—picturesque and lively, lined with shops and restaurants, recreational trails and marinas. But such dreams display a naïveté about the reasons why the Los Angeles River was encased in concrete in the first place. None of those rivers presents the potential danger to life and property of the usually meek and mild Los Angeles River. None of those cities has the peculiar combination of conditions that makes Los Angeles so naturally flood prone. None is surrounded so closely by such steep mountains, which concentrate and speed runoff. None has a climate that produces such extremes of precipitation as to make it so difficult to keep rivers in place.

The needs of flood control have also shaped public perceptions of the river, which have been so negative for so long that they could in the end be more difficult to overcome than the dictates of flood control engineers. To many in Southern California, not just flood control officials, the river remains chiefly a flood control channel, a blighted concrete ditch too ugly to care about. This is particularly true in downstream cities, where the flood risk is greatest and the river is most unsightly. Although efforts to revitalize the river have increased public

FIG. 6.26. How do you make people care about a river that looks so little like one? That is one of the biggest challenges facing those trying to build support for efforts to revitalize the Los Angeles River, shown here in North Hollywood. Photograph by the author, 1995.

awareness of it, they have done little to alter this view. Even as a new park was being announced for the riverfront in Maywood, one nearby resident remarked about the river, "Why would anyone want to go down there?"[139] No number of parks and bike paths will change the fact that, on much of its course for most of the year, the river carries little water in its huge concrete channel. The nature of stream flow in Southern California necessitated that the river be given a deep, wide bed even though it is dry a great deal of the time. Other urban rivers, such as the Chicago River or even such storied waterways as the Seine, are also lined with concrete, but those rivers are filled with water, bank to bank, year-round. The perceptual difference is striking. On the majority of its course, it is very hard to imagine the Los Angeles River as something more than it is (fig. 6.26).

It could even be argued that the Los Angeles River is no longer a river at all, that it is already dead, and that efforts to restore it are really attempts, as one writer remarked, to create "the perfect simulation of a 'natural river,'" to remake it yet again, although this time in a more pleasing image.[140] Even if environmentalists are one day successful in having part of its concrete channel removed, will what remains be any more the Los Angeles River than what exists today, so long as its channel is artificial and its source is treated sewage? Millions of people now live where the river once wandered. That alone assures that the river's paved banks will remain and that water in the subterranean reservoir that was its historic source will be pumped to the surface before it can reach the river. In a sense, new efforts to revitalize the river are like the campaign promise of the long-forgotten politician who wanted to paint the river's concrete channel blue to make it look more like a river. What will happen to the Los Angeles River? It has never been more impossible to say. Only a fool would bet on its future. But a few years ago, only a fool would have cared.

Notes

Introduction

1. Laurel Marcus, "Watershed Restoration: An Idea Whose Time Has Come—Again," *California WaterfrontAge*, spring 1988, 16.

2. Christopher Kroll, "What River? Changing Views of the River," *California Coast & Ocean*, summer 1993, 32.

3. Jack Smith, "Vacation Worries," *Los Angeles Times*, 15 September 1985; Patt Morrison, commentary, *Morning Edition*, National Public Radio, 3 May 1995.

CHAPTER 1   *The River as It Once Was*

1. Los Angeles County Board of Engineers, Flood Control (hereafter LAC-BEFC), *Report of the Board of Engineers, Flood Control to the Board of Supervisors, Los Angeles County, California* (Los Angeles, 1915), 205.

2. J. J. Warner, Benjamin Hayes, and J. P. Widney, *An Historical Sketch of Los Angeles County, California, from the Spanish Occupancy, by the Founding of the Mission San Gabriel Archangel, September 8, 1771, to July 4, 1876* (1876; reprint, Los Angeles: O. W. Smith, 1936), 18.

3. Juan Crespí, *A Description of Distant Roads: Original Journals of the First Spanish Expedition into California, 1769–1770*, trans. Alan K. Brown (forthcoming), revised journals, entry for 26 April 1770.

4. H. F. Raup, "Transformation of Southern California to a Cultivated Land," *Annals of the Association of American Geographers* 49, no. 3, pt. 2 (1959): 75; William R. Brownlie and Brent D. Taylor, *Sediment Management for Southern California Mountains, Coastal Plains and Shoreline. Pt. C, Coastal Sediment Delivery by Major Rivers in Southern California*, EQL Report 17-C (Pasadena: Environmental Quality Laboratory, California Institute of Technology, 1981); J. M. Guinn, "Exceptional Years: A History of California Floods and Drought," *Publications of the Historical Society of Southern California* 1, pt. 5 (1890): 38; George H. Cecil, "Flood Damage and Benefits from Flood Control," in *Comprehensive Plan for Flood Control and Conservation: Present Conditions and Immediate Needs* (Los Angeles: Los Angeles County Flood Control District, 1931), 52.

5. Bennie W. Troxel, "Geologic Guide No. 3: Los Angeles Basin," in *Geology of Southern California*, California Division of Mines Bulletin 170 (Sacramento, 1954), 1; A. O. Woodford et al., "Geology of the Los Angeles Basin," in ibid., 65; Brownlie and Taylor, *Sediment Management*, C229; J. W. Nelson et al., *Soil Survey of the Los Angeles Area, California* (Washington, 1919), 22.

6. Walter C. Mendenhall, *Development of Underground Waters in the Central Coastal Plain Region of Southern California*, Geological Survey Water-Supply and Irrigation Paper 138 (Washington, 1905), 21.

7. Warner, Hayes, and Widney, *Historical Sketch*, 18; LACBEFC, *Report of the Board of Engineers; House, Los Angeles and San Gabriel Rivers and Their Tributaries, and Ballona Creek, Calif.*, 76th Cong., 3d sess., 1940, H. Doc. 838, serial 10505.

8. Emma H. Adams, *To and Fro in Southern California with Sketches in Arizona and New Mexico* (Cincinnati, 1887), 67–68.

9. L. C. Holmes et al., *Soil Survey of the San Fernando Valley Area, California* (Washington, 1919), 5–8; Los Angeles Board of Public Service Commissioners, *Tenth Annual Report* (Los Angeles, 1911), 47–49.

10. An acre foot is the amount of water it would take to cover an acre to a depth of one foot. It is the most common unit of volume measurement in modern-day water resources management and is used to express the amount of water carried by streams and aqueducts and also the capacity of reservoirs. One acre foot is equivalent to 325,851 gallons, 43,560 cubic feet, or 1,233.5 cubic meters.

11. Upper Los Angeles River Area Watermaster, *Watermaster Service in the Upper Los Angeles River Area, Los Angeles County: 1992–93 Water Year* (Los Angeles, 1994), 2–14; California Department of Water Resources, *California Water: Looking to the Future*, Bulletin 160-87 (Sacramento: Resources Agency, 1987).

12. LACBEFC, *Report of the Board of Engineers*, 103.

13. House, *Los Angeles and San Gabriel Rivers*, 11–15; National Climatic Data Center, *Comparative Climatic Data for the United States through 1992* (Asheville, N.C., 1993), 89; Homer Aschmann, "The Evolution of a Wild Landscape and Its Persistence in Southern California," *Annals of the Association of American Geographers* 49, no. 3, pt. 2 (1959): 34.

14. L. C. Holmes et al., *Soil Survey of the San Fernando Valley Area, California* (Washington, 1919), 8; LACBEFC, *Report of the Board of Engineers*, 103.

15. E. C. Eaton, *Comprehensive Plan for Flood Control and Conservation: Present Conditions and Immediate Needs* (Los Angeles: Los Angeles County Flood Control District, 1931), 31; Crespí, *A Description of Distant Roads*, revised journals, entry for 5 August 1769; P. C. Remondino, *The Mediterranean Shores of America; Southern California: Its Climate, Physical and Meteorological Conditions* (Philadelphia, 1892).

16. Gordon R. Miller, "Los Angeles and the Owens River Aqueduct" (Ph.D. diss., Claremont Graduate School, 1977), 28; H. D. McGlashan and F. C. Ebert, *Surface Water Supply of the Pacific Slope of Southern California*, Geological Survey Water-Supply Paper 447 (Washington, 1921), 441.

17. Robert H. Becker, *Designs on the Land: Disenos of California Ranchos and Their Makers* (San Francisco: Book Club of California, 1969).

18. Walter C. Mendenhall, *Development of Underground Waters in the Eastern Coastal Plain Region of Southern California*, Geological Survey Water-Supply and Irrigation Paper 137 (Washington, 1905), 22; Mendenhall, *Underground Waters in the Central Coastal Plain*, 40–160.

19. Boyle Workman, *The City That Grew* (Los Angeles: Southland Publishing, 1935), 131.

20. Joseph W. Wolfskill, quoted in James W. Reagan, comp., "A Report on Floods, River Phenomena, and Rainfall in the Los Angeles Region, California," 1914–15 (Univ. Research Library, Univ. of California, Los Angeles, typescript), 37.

21. U.S. Geological Survey, 1:62,500-scale topographic quadrangle maps for Downey (1896), San Pedro (1896), Redondo (1896), Pasadena (1900), and Calabasas (1903); U.S. Geological Survey, 1:250,000-scale topographic maps, *Southern California Sheet No. 1* (1901) and *Southern California Sheet No. 3* (1901); Reagan, "Report on Floods," 91, 250, 345, 400, 413; James L. Stamps, ed., *The Historical Volume and Reference Works: Covering Artesia, Bellflower, Bell Gardens, Compton, Dairy Valley, Downey, Lynwood, Montebello, Norwalk, Paramount, South Gate* (Arlington, Calif.: Historical Publishers, 1965), 212.

22. Brownlie and Taylor, *Sediment Management*, C223–C225, C240.

23. California Division of Mines and Geology, *Planning Scenario for a Major Earthquake on the Newport-Inglewood Fault Zone*, Special Publication 99 (Sacramento, 1988), 23; Troxel, "Geologic Guide No. 3," 5; Walter C. Mendenhall, *Development of Underground Waters in the Western Coastal Plain Region of Southern California*, Geological Survey Water-Supply and Irrigation Paper 139 (Washington, 1905), 15; Michael Josselyn and Sarah Chamberlain, "History: The Way It Was," *California Coast & Ocean*, summer 1993, 22; Reagan, "Report on Floods," 61, 247–48.

24. Richard Dean Friesen, William Kelley Thomas, and Donald R. Patten, "The Mammals of Ballona," in *The Biota of the Ballona Region, Los Angeles County*, ed. Ralph W. Schreiber (Los Angeles: Los Angeles County Natural History Museum Foundation, 1981), M-1.

25. Bernice Eastman Johnston, *California's Gabrielino Indians* (Los Angeles: Southwest Museum, 1962), 78.

26. Mendenhall, *Underground Waters in the Western Coastal Plain*, 15; Ruth Emily Baugh, "The Geography of the Los Angeles Water Supply" (Ph.D. diss., Clark Univ., 1929), 57, 60; Reagan, "Report on Floods," 335.

27. Henry P. Silka, *San Pedro: A Pictorial History* (San Pedro, Calif.: San Pedro Bay Historical Society, 1984), 31.

28. David Edward Hughes, recollections, 29 November 1937, folder 40, David Edward Hughes Papers, Water Resources Center Archives, Univ. of California, Berkeley.

29. Major R. R. Raymond, quoted in House, *Los Angeles and Long Beach Harbors, Cal.*, 64th Cong., 1st sess., 1916, H. Doc. 462, serial 6976, 23.

30. Eaton, *Comprehensive Plan*, 9; James W. Reagan, "Report of J. W. Reagan . . . upon the Control of Flood Waters in This District by the Correction of Rivers, Diversion and Care of Washes, Building of Dikes and Dams for Storage and Conservation Purposes, Safeguarding Public Highways and Private Property, and the Protection of Harbors," 20 December 1916 (Los Angeles County De-

partment of Public Works Technical Library, Alhambra, Calif., typescript), 20; Louis Mesmer, *Soil Survey of the Los Angeles Area, California* (Washington, 1904), 1275.

31. Reagan, "Report on Floods," 364.

32. William Hamilton Hall, *Irrigation in California [Southern]: The Field, Water-Supply, and Works, Organization and Operation in San Diego, San Bernardino, and Los Angeles Counties* (Sacramento: State Engineer of California, 1988), 369.

33. Kimball L. Garrett, ed., "The Biota of the Los Angeles River: An Overview of the Historical and Present Plant and Animal Life of the Los Angeles River Drainage" (Los Angeles: Natural History Museum of Los Angeles County, 1993, typescript), 6; Reagan, "Report on Floods," 284.

34. The tree stood at the foot of Aliso Street, which had been named for it. Though *aliso* is Spanish for "alder," the tree was actually a sycamore. It died and was cut down in the 1890s, when it was estimated to be four hundred years old. See Cecilia Rasmussen, "From Site of Ancient Tribal Tree, the City of Angels Grew," *Los Angeles Times*, 12 April 1997. See also Henry Winfred Splitter, "Los Angeles in the 1850's as Told by Early Newspapers," *Quarterly, Historical Society of Southern California* 31, no. 1/2 (1949): 114.

35. J. M. Bigelow, "Report on the Botany of the Expedition," in *Report of Explorations and Surveys to Ascertain the Most Practicable and Economical Route for a Railroad from the Mississippi River to the Pacific Ocean*, vol. 4, 33d Cong., 2d sess., 1856, S. Exec. Doc. 78, 16.

36. Johnston, *California's Gabrielino Indians*, 80, 117; Reagan, "Report on Floods," 37, 177, 359, 363; A. W. Whipple, *Report of Explorations for a Railway Route near the Thirty-fifth Parallel of North Latitude from the Mississippi River to the Pacific Ocean*, 33d Cong., 2d sess., 1857, S. Exec. Doc. 78, 136.

37. Quoted in Edwin A. Beilharz, *Felipe de Neve: First Governor of California* (San Francisco: California Historical Society, 1971), 100.

38. Aschmann, "Evolution of a Wild Landscape," 36.

39. House, *Los Angeles and San Gabriel Rivers*, 11.

40. George H. Bixby, quoted in Reagan, "Report on Floods," 363–64.

41. Garrett, "Biota of the Los Angeles River," 4–9.

42. Philip A. Munz and David D. Keck, *A California Flora* (Berkeley and Los Angeles: Univ. of California Press, 1959), 12; Herbert L. Mason, *A Flora of the Marshes of California* (Berkeley and Los Angeles: Univ. of California Press, 1957), 10; Allan A. Schoenherr, *A Natural History of California*, California Natural History Guide 56 (Berkeley and Los Angeles: Univ. of California Press, 1992), 526–37; E. H. Myers, quoted in Reagan, "Report on Floods," 357.

43. Herbert Eugene Bolton, ed., *Fray Juan Crespi: Missionary Explorer of the Pacific Coast* (1927; reprint, New York: AMS Press, 1971), 148; Edwin Bryant, *What I Saw in California* (1846; reprint, Santa Ana, Calif.: Fine Arts Press, 1936), 393; Lewis H. Height Jr., "Settlement Patterns of the San Fernando Valley, Southern California" (master's thesis, Univ. of California, Los Angeles, 1953), 17; Theodore S. Van Dyke, *Southern California: Its Valleys, Hills, and Streams; Its Animals,*

Birds, and Fishes; Its Gardens, Farms, and Climate (New York, 1886), 16; Homer Aschmann, "Man's Impact on the Southern California Flora," in *Symposium Proceedings: Plant Communities of Southern California*, California Native Plant Society Special Publication 2 (Berkeley, 1976), 43.

44. Charles Franklin Carter, trans., "Duhaut-Cilly's Account of California in the Years 1827–28," *California Historical Society Quarterly* 8, no. 3 (1929): 246.

45. Frank M. Keffer, *History of the San Fernando Valley* (Glendale, Calif.: Stillman Printing, 1934), 73.

46. Garrett, "Biota of the Los Angeles River," 7–8; Schoenherr, *Natural History of California*, 329, 338; Reagan, "Report on Floods," 256; Ted L. Hanes, "Vegetation of the Santa Ana River and Some Flood Control Implications," in *California Riparian Systems: Ecology, Conservation and Production Management*, ed. Richard E. Warner and Kathleen M. Hendrix (Berkeley and Los Angeles: Univ. of California Press, 1984), 883–84.

47. Reagan, "Report on Floods," 413; Garrett, "Biota of the Los Angeles River," 7; Bolton, *Fray Juan Crespi*, 151; M. Violet Gray and James M. Greaves, "Riparian Forest as Habitat for the Least Bell's Vireo," in *California Riparian Systems: Ecology, Conservation, and Production Management*, ed. Richard E. Warner and Kathleen M. Hendrix (Berkeley and Los Angeles: Univ. of California Press, 1984), 606; Height, "Settlement Patterns," 17; Aschmann, "Evolution of a Wild Landscape," 37.

48. Crespí, *A Description of Distant Roads*, revised journals, entry for 26 April 1770.

49. Linda J. Barkley, "Mammals of the Los Angeles River Basin," in Garrett, "Biota of the Los Angeles River," G-1; Kimball L. Garrett, "The Avifauna of the Los Angeles River: An Historical Overview and Current Analysis," in Garrett, "Biota of the Los Angeles River," F-3, F-4, F-32, F-34; Schoenherr, *Natural History of California*, 526–37; Keffer, *History of San Fernando Valley*, 16; Reagan, "Report on Floods," 179, 359; Johnston, *California's Gabrielino Indians*, 33; Camm C. Swift and Jeffrey Seigel, "The Past and Present Freshwater Fish Fauna of the Los Angeles River," in Garrett, "Biota of the Los Angeles River," D-1; J. Albert Wilson, *History of Los Angeles County, California* (Oakland, Calif., 1880), 14; Ludwig Louis Salvator, *Los Angeles in the Sunny Seventies*, trans. Marguerite Eyer Wilbur (Los Angeles: Bruce McCallister/Jake Zeitlin, 1929), 25; Gladys Lillian Brandt, "The San Fernando Valley: A Study in Changing Adjustment between Its Economic Life and Its Natural Environment" (master's thesis, Univ. of Chicago, 1928), 6; Crespí, *A Description of Distant Roads*, revised journals, entry for 5 August 1769.

50. Garrett, "Avifauna of the Los Angeles River."

51. Swift and Seigel, "Freshwater Fish Fauna," D-1, D-2; Schoenherr, *Natural History of California*, 593–94, 611–15.

52. Johnston, *California's Gabrielino Indians*, 32–33, 80.

53. Lowell John Bean and Charles R. Smith, "Gabrielino," in *Handbook of North American Indians*, vol. 8 (Washington: Smithsonian Institution, 1978), 540; William McCawley, *The First Angelinos: The Gabrielino Indians of Los Angeles* (Ban-

ning, Calif.: Malki Museum Press/Ballena Press, 1996), 2; Johnston, *California's Gabrielino Indians*, 4.

54. Bean and Smith, "Gabrielino," 548.

55. Robert F. Heizer, ed., *The Indians of Los Angeles County: Hugo Reid's Letters of 1852*, Southwest Museum Papers 21 (Los Angeles: Southwest Museum, 1968), 9.

56. McCawley, *First Angelinos*, 9–10.

57. Bean and Smith, "Gabrielino," 538.

58. A. L. Kroeber, *Handbook of Indians of California*, Bureau of American Ethnology Bulletin 78 (Washington, 1925), 625. Indian groups speaking Shoshonean languages occupied about a third of present-day California.

59. Ibid., 621, 631; McCawley, *First Angelinos*, 10–11.

60. Aschmann, "Evolution of a Wild Landscape," 49.

61. Bean and Smith, "Gabrielino," 539; Johnston, *California's Gabrielino Indians*, 80; Reagan, "Report on Floods," 411.

62. Bolton, *Fray Juan Crespi*, 147.

63. The village of Yangna apparently survived at its original location at least fifty years after the founding of Los Angeles. A census conducted in 1830 reported that there were 962 people living in the village, though by this time 4 out of 5 residents were non-Indian and the settlement, in the words of Gabrielino scholar William McCawley, "may have resembled a refugee camp more than a community." In 1836, pressure from Los Angeles residents forced relocation of the village to near the present intersection of Commercial and Alameda Streets. It lasted only ten years at that site. In June 1845, in response to escalating complaints that Indians were bathing in the city's irrigation ditches, the settlement was relocated to the east side of the river. See McCawley, *First Angelinos*, 202.

64. Bean and Smith, "Gabrielino," 540; John R. Swanton, *The Indian Tribes of North America*, Bureau of American Ethnology Bulletin 145 (Washington, 1952), 491; Johnston, *California's Gabrielino Indians*, 122.

65. Juan Crespí, *A Description of Distant Roads*, field draft, entries for 5–6 August 1769.

66. McCawley, *First Angelinos*, 38.

67. Johnston, *California's Gabrielino Indians*, 123; Stamps, *Historical Volume*, 227; Heizer, *Indians of Los Angeles County*, 9; McCawley, *First Angelinos*, 66; Bean and Smith, "Gabrielino," 544.

68. Crespí, *A Description of Distant Roads*, revised journals, entry for 5 August 1769; Ruth Underhill, *Indians of Southern California*, Sherman Pamphlets 2 (Washington: Education Division, Office of Indian Affairs, 1941), 15–17; Bruce Miller, *The Gabrielino* (Los Osis, Calif.: Sand River Press, 1991), 78.

69. E. O. C. Ord, *The City of Angels and the City of the Saints, or a Trip to Los Angeles and San Bernardino in 1856* (San Marino, Calif.: Huntington Library, 1978), 5.

70. McCawley, *First Angelinos*, 129–30; Underhill, *Indians of Southern California*, 17; Heizer, *Indians of Los Angeles County*, 22–23; B. Miller, *The Gabrielino*, 77; Edwin F. Walker, *Indians of Southern California*, Southwest Museum Leaflets 10 (Los Angeles: Southwest Museum, 1949), 7; Johnston, *California's Gabrielino Indians*, 33.

71. Heizer, *Indians of Los Angeles County*, 21–22; Bean and Smith, "Gabrielino," 546; Hubert Howe Bancroft, *Wild Tribes*, vol. 1 of *The Native Races of the Pacific States* (New York, 1875), 405–6; Johnston, *California's Gabrielino Indians*, 33; B. Miller, *The Gabrielino*, 79.

72. Walker, *Indians of Southern California*, 5; McCawley, *First Angelinos*, 29; Heizer, *Indians of Los Angeles County*, 21; Alexander Forbes, *California: A History of Upper and Lower California* (1839; reprint, New York: Arno Press, 1973), 191; Kroeber, *Handbook of Indians of California*, 630.

73. Underhill, *Indians of Southern California*, 28, 34; B. Miller, *The Gabrielino*, 81, 91; Johnston, *California's Gabrielino Indians*, 29, 72–73; Bean and Smith, "Gabrielino," 542.

74. Heizer, *Indians of Los Angeles County*, 32, 36.

75. McCawley, *First Angelinos*, 11.

76. Donna Preble, *Yamino-Kwiti: Boy Runner of Siba* (Caldwell, Idaho: Caxton Printers, 1948), 62–65; see also Heizer, *Indians of Los Angeles County*, 54.

77. Howard J. Nelson, *The Los Angeles Metropolis* (Dubuque, Iowa: Kendall/Hunt, 1983), 126–27; James D. Hart, *A Companion to California* (Berkeley and Los Angeles: Univ. of California Press, 1987), 69, 397–98; Bolton, *Fray Juan Crespí*, xvii–xxii; Raymund F. Wood, "Juan Crespí: The Man Who Named Los Angeles," *Southern California Quarterly* 53, no. 3 (1971): 204–9.

78. Wood, "Juan Crespí," 209.

79. There are three known extant versions of Crespí's diaries. For years, it was assumed that the journals transmitted by Francisco Palou in his "Noticias de la Nueva California," published in Spanish in 1857 and translated into English by Herbert E. Bolton in 1926, were a mostly verbatim transcript of Crespí's journals. Two earlier versions of the journals, however, were discovered in the 1940s in archives in Mexico and Rome and have since proved to have been written in the author's own hand. These originals reveal that Palou significantly shortened and altered the original Crespí manuscripts, replacing portions of the text with the accounts of the army engineer Costansó and supplementing those with his own contributions. Alan K. Brown, an emeritus professor of English at Ohio State University, who has transcribed and translated the two more recently discovered Crespí texts, believes that Crespí wrote entries in camp, compiling them every few days from field notes (which no longer seem to exist) and that many pages of the manuscript uncovered in Mexico were actually written during the expedition. The Rome manuscript, in contrast, is a substantially rewritten version, completed by Crespí himself no later than 1771. Confusing passages from the draft manuscript have been clarified, new information has been added, and the text in general is more readable, although some interesting details have been left out.

The differences between the Palou version of the diaries and the two more recently uncovered manuscripts are astounding. The most noticeable difference is the length. The Mexico and Rome manuscripts are about the same length, roughly sixty thousand words for the journey from San Diego to San Francisco and back. The Palou version is 40 percent shorter, about thirty-five thousand words. In translation, the entry in the Palou version for 2 August 1769, the day the expedition first encountered the Los Angeles River, is 298 words. The Mexico and Rome versions are both more than one thousand words. If the changes made by Palou were simply a matter of shortening and refining, perhaps they might be more easily overlooked. Alas, much was lost in the process. Professor Brown, who has been been critical of Palou for replacing Crespí's "crotchety and detailed account" with an "excessively businesslike, prosy and over-general style," nevertheless has pointed out that both Palou and Junípero Serra—Crespí and Palou's superior—eventually came to prefer the unaltered original texts, which afterward fell into a nearly two-centuries-long oblivion. For a more complete discussion of the Crespí journals, see Brown's "The Various Journals of Juan Crespí," *Americas* 21, no. 4 (1965): 375–98. Professor Brown has been kind enough to share with the author his translations of the Mexico "field draft" and the revised Rome text for the portion of Crespí's journals that covers present Los Angeles County. Brown's complete translations of the Crespí diaries are to be published in book form as *A Description of Distant Roads: Original Journals of the First Spanish Expedition into California, 1769–1770*.

80. Crespí, *A Description of Distant Roads*, field draft, entry for 1 August 1769.

81. Ibid., revised journals, entry for 2 August 1769.

82. Ibid., field draft, entry for 2 August 1769.

83. Ibid., revised journals, entry for 2 August 1769.

84. Ibid.

85. Ibid., field draft, entry for 2 August 1769.

86. Ibid., revised journals, entry for 2 August 1769. On a second trip north in 1770, Crespí, crossing the river for a third time, remarked, "It would not be necessary to toil a great deal in order to irrigate a great amount upon its large plain."

87. Ibid., entry for 3 August 1769.

88. Ibid., field draft, entry for 3 August 1769.

89. Ibid., revised journals, entry for 3 August 1769.

90. Frederick J. Teggert, ed., *The Portola Expedition of 1769–1770: Diary of Miguel Costansó*, Publications of the Academy of Pacific Coast History 2, no. 4 (Berkeley, 1911), 21.

91. Bolton, *Fray Juan Crespí*, 147.

CHAPTER 2   *Sustenance for the Young Pueblo*

1. Missions were established at San Diego in 1769, at Monterey in 1770, near King City (San Antonio de Padua) and at San Gabriel in 1771, at San Luis

Obispo in 1772, at San Francisco and San Juan Capistrano in 1776, and at Santa Clara in 1777. Presidios were established at San Diego in 1769, Monterey in 1770, and San Francisco in 1776.

2. William Hamilton Hall, *Irrigation in California [Southern]: The Field, Water-Supply, and Works, Organization and Operation in San Diego, San Bernardino, and Los Angeles Counties* (Sacramento, 1888), 558; Edwin A. Beilharz, *Felipe de Neve, First Governor of California* (San Francisco: California Historical Society, 1971), 98–101; J. M. Guinn, *A History of California and an Extended History of Los Angeles and Environs* (Los Angeles, 1915), 73.

3. Felipe de Neve to Antonio Bucareli y Ursúa, 7 July 1777. Excerpted in John and Laree Caughey, *Los Angeles: Biography of a City* (Berkeley and Los Angeles: Univ. of California Press, 1977), 64.

4. Ibid., 65.

5. Beilharz, *Felipe de Neve*, 97–103; de Neve to Bucareli.

6. Beilharz, *Felipe de Neve*, 104–5.

7. Felipe de Neve, "Translation of Portion of Order of Governor Felipe de Neve for Founding of Los Angeles," *Annual Publications, Historical Society of Southern California* 15, pt. 2 (1933): 154.

8. Jonathan Garst, "A Geographical Study of the Los Angeles Region of Southern California" (Ph.D. diss., Edinburgh Univ., 1931), 137–38.

9. Beilharz, *Felipe de Neve*, 107–9.

10. Zephyrin Engelhardt, *San Gabriel Mission and the Beginnings of Los Angeles* (San Gabriel, Calif.: Mission San Gabriel, 1927), 51–52. Even those who remained were a motley bunch. None of the men apparently could sign his name. None figured significantly in the development of Los Angeles. None had a great enough effect even to have a street or other public place named for him. "Poor in purse, poor in blood, poorer in the sterner qualities of character, they left no impress on the city they founded," remarked J. M. Guinn, an early historian of Los Angeles. See Guinn, *Extended History of Los Angeles*, 76. Engelhardt, historian of the San Gabriel Mission, suggested that they were such a lowly lot that Governor de Neve refused to participate in formal ceremonies for the founding of the pueblo because "he was ashamed to figure in a scene with the colonists such as they were."

11. Guinn, *Extended History of Los Angeles*, 75; Hubert Howe Bancroft, *California Pastoral, 1769–1848* (San Francisco, 1888), 250.

12. The original pueblo boundaries extended from what is now Hoover Street on the west to Indiana Avenue on the east and from Fountain Avenue on the north to the line of Exposition Boulevard on the south.

13. Ruth Emily Baugh, "Site of Early Los Angeles," *Economic Geography* 18 (1942): 91; J. Gregg Layne, *Annals of Los Angeles: From the Arrival of the First White Men to the Civil War, 1769–1861*, California Historical Society Special Publication 9 (San Francisco, 1935), 7; Beilharz, *Felipe de Neve*, 108; Ruth Emily Baugh, "The Geography of the Los Angeles Water Supply" (Ph.D. diss., Clark Univ., 1929), 13.

14. *An Illustrated History of Southern California* (Chicago, 1890), 730; Sarah Bixby Smith, *Adobe Days* (Cedar Rapids, Iowa: Torch Press, 1925), 90; Baugh, "Site of Early Los Angeles," 90–93; Guinn, *Extended History of Los Angeles*, 391; James W. Reagan, comp., "A Report on Floods, River Phenomena and Rainfall in the Los Angeles Region, California," 1914–15 (Univ. Research Library, Univ. of California, Los Angeles, typescript), 32.

15. Howard J. Nelson, *The Los Angeles Metropolis* (Dubuque, Iowa: Kendall/ Hunt, 1983), 133; Boyle Workman, *The City That Grew* (Los Angeles: Southland Publishing, 1935), 1.

16. Quoted in Engelhardt, *San Gabriel Mission*, 63. Drunken Indians were often forced to labor in the fields of the colonists or to help maintain the city's irrigation ditches. According to Horace Bell, who settled in Los Angeles in 1852 and wrote about the early days under American rule in an 1881 memoir, *Reminiscences of a Ranger, or Early Times in Southern California*, "After sundown, the pompous marshal . . . would drive and drag the herd [of Indians] to a big corral in the rear of Downey Block, where they would sleep away their intoxication, and in the morning they would be exposed for sale. They would be sold for a week, and bought up by the vineyard men and others at prices ranging from one to three dollars, one third of which was to be paid to the peon at the end of the week. [This] would invariably be paid in *aguardiente* (a type of brandy), and the Indian would be made happy until the following Monday morning. Los Angeles had its slave mart, as well as New Orleans and Constantinople—only the slave at Los Angeles was sold 52 times a year as long as he lived. Thousands of honest, useful people were absolutely destroyed in this way."

17. Hubert Howe Bancroft, *History of California* (San Francisco, 1885), 1:461, 1:660, 2:350; Alexander Forbes, *California: A History of Upper and Lower California* (1839; reprint, New York: Arno Press, 1973), 260–66; Marguerite Eyer Wilbur, trans. and ed., *Duflot de Mofras' Travels on the Pacific Coast* (Santa Ana, Calif.: Fine Arts Press, 1937), 186; J. Gregg Layne, "Water and Power for a Great City: A History of the Department of Water & Power of the City of Los Angeles, to December 1950," 1952 (Special Collections Department, Univ. Research Library, Univ. of California, Los Angeles), 2.

18. Charles Franklin Carter, trans., "Duhaut-Cilly's Account of California in the Years 1827–28," *California Historical Society Quarterly* 8, no. 3 (1929): 246.

19. Baugh, "Los Angeles Water Supply," 15; Bancroft, *History of California*, 1:460; Layne, *Annals of Los Angeles*, 9; Guinn, *Extended History of Los Angeles*, 255; Nelson, *Los Angeles Metropolis*, 137.

20. Irving McKee, "The Beginnings of California Winegrowing," *Quarterly, Historical Society of Southern California* 30, no. 1 (1948): 63; Bancroft, *History of California*, 2:350; J. A. Wilson, *History of Los Angeles County, California* (Oakland, Calif., 1880), 64.

21. McKee, "Beginnings of California Winegrowing," 63; Nelson, *Los Angeles Metropolis*, 163.

22. Carter, "Duhaut-Cilly's Account," 246.

23. A French scholar, Léonce Jore, suggested that Vignes may have been drawn to Los Angeles by the presence of a friend and former traveling companion, Father Bachelot, a Franciscan priest who had been assigned to the pueblo church. See Jore, "Jean Louis Vignes of Bordeaux, Pioneer of California Viticulture," trans. L. Jay Oliva, *Southern California Quarterly* 45, no. 4 (1963): 296.

24. Quoted in William Heath Davis, *Sixty Years in California: A History of Events and Life in California* (San Francisco, 1889), 170.

25. Cleve E. Kindall, "Southern Vineyards: The Economic Significance of the Wine Industry in the Development of Los Angeles, 1831–1870," *Historical Society of Southern California Quarterly* 41, no. 1 (1959): 29–31; Wilbur, *Duflot de Mofras' Travels*, 185. The barrel never reached the king. It was destroyed by fire in a warehouse on the docks of Hamburg, Germany.

26. Edwin Bryant, *What I Saw in California* (1846; reprint, Santa Ana, Calif.: Fine Arts Press, 1936), 400–401; W. H. Emory, *Notes of a Military Reconnaissance, from Fort Leavenworth, in Missouri, to San Diego, in California, Including Parts of the Arkansas, Del Norte, and Gila Rivers*, 30th Cong., 1st sess., 1846, S. Exec. Doc. 7, 122.

27. McKee, "Beginnings of California Winegrowing," 63–66; Nelson, *Los Angeles Metropolis*, 163; Thomas Antisell, "Geologic Report," in *Report of Explorations and Surveys to Ascertain the Most Practicable and Economical Route for a Railroad from the Mississippi River to the Pacific Ocean*, 33d Cong., 2d sess., 1856, S. Exec. Doc. 78, vol. 7, pt. 2, 82; Kindall, "Southern Vineyards," 33; John S. Hittel, *The Resources of California, Comprising Agriculture, Mining, Geography, Climate, Commerce, Etc., Etc., and the Past and Future Development of the State* (San Francisco, 1863), 205; Wilbur, *Duflot de Mofras' Travels*, 185.

28. Guernsey County, Ohio, was second, producing about twenty thousand gallons.

29. Layne, "Water and Power," 23; Davis, *Sixty Years in California*, 171; Baugh, "Los Angeles Water Supply," 24; Guinn, *Extended History of Los Angeles*, 251; McKee, "Beginnings of California Winegrowing," 68; H. D. Barrows, "Water for Domestic Purposes versus Water for Irrigation," *Annual Publications, Historical Society of Southern California* 8 (1911): 208; Mrs. A. S. C. Forbes, "Los Angeles When It Was 'The City of Vines,'" *Annual Publications, Historical Society of Southern California* 15, no. 2/3 (1932): 337; Iris Higbie Wilson, *William Wolfskill, 1798–1866: Frontier Trapper to California Ranchero* (Glendale, Calif.: Arthur H. Clark, 1965), 168.

30. William P. Blake, "Geologic Report," in *Report of Explorations and Surveys to Ascertain the Most Practicable and Economical Route for a Railroad from the Mississippi River to the Pacific Ocean*, 33d Cong., 2nd sess., 1857, S. Exec. Doc. 78, vol. 5, pt. 2, 77–78.

31. Perkins, Stern & Co., *Catalogue of California Wines with Statistics of Vines Planted, Description of Varieties, Comments of the Press, &c.* (Boston, 1863), California ephemera F13-11, Henry E. Huntington Library, San Marino, Calif.; Antisell, "Geologic Report," 81–82; J. J. Warner, Benjamin Hayes, and J. P. Widney, *An Historical Sketch of Los Angeles County, California, from the Spanish Occupancy, by*

the Founding of the Mission San Gabriel Archangel, September 7, 1771, to July 4, 1876 (1876; reprint, Los Angeles: O. W. Smith, 1936); Iris Engstrand, "Early Southern California Viticulture, 1830–1865," in A Southern California Historical Anthology, ed. Doyce B. Nunis Jr. (Los Angeles: Historical Society of Southern California, 1984), 124–26; I. H. Wilson, William Wolfskill, 57, 91.

32. Wolfskill was honored at the 1856 California State Fair for having the best vineyards in the state. See I. H. Wilson, William Wolfskill, 156.

33. In 1872, the New England Agricultural Society awarded Keller a medal for the best exhibition of native wine. Box 5, folder 22, Matthew Keller Collection, Huntington Library.

34. Perkins, Stern, Catalogue of California Wines, 4.

35. Kindall, "Southern Vineyards," 34–35; newspaper quoted in Perkins, Stern, Catalogue of California Wines, 9; Harris Newmark, Sixty Years in Southern California, 1853–1913 (New York, 1916), 398; Nelson, Los Angeles Metropolis, 163–73.

36. Blake, "Geologic Report," 77.

37. Guinn, Extended History of Los Angeles, 201; J. A. Wilson, History of Los Angeles County, 63; I. H. Wilson, William Wolfskill, 150.

38. Guinn, Extended History of Los Angeles, 298.

39. Barrows, "Water for Domestic Purposes," 208; I. H. Wilson, William Wolfskill, 150–51, 176; Guinn, Extended History of Los Angeles, 298; Hittel, Resources of California, 192; Clifford M. Zierer, "The Citrus Fruit Industry of the Los Angeles Basin," Economic Geography 10 (1934): 53–73.

40. J. A. Wilson, History of Los Angeles County, 61–62; James Clark, "An Emigrant in the Fifties," Quarterly, Historical Society of Southern California 19, no. 3–4 (1937): 112; Bryant, What I Saw in California, 394; Illustrated History, 763; Bancroft, History of California, 2:111; William A. Spalding, History and Reminiscences, Los Angeles City and County, California (Los Angeles: J. R. Finnell & Sons, 1931), 91; Layne, Annals of Los Angeles, 10; Warner, Hayes, and Widney, Historical Sketch, 76; Guinn, Extended History of Los Angeles, 293–95; Antisell, "Geologic Report," 81.

41. Barrows, "Water for Domestic Purposes," 209; Layne, "Water and Power," 8.

42. Blake, "Geologic Report," 77.

43. Robert Glass Cleland, The Cattle on a Thousand Hills: Southern California, 1850–1880 (San Marino, Calif.: Huntington Library, 1951), 174; Newmark, Sixty Years in Southern California, 117; Hittel, Resources of California, 166; A. W. Whipple, Report of Explorations for a Railway Route near the Thirty-fifth Parallel of North Latitude from the Mississippi River to the Pacific Ocean, 33d Cong., 2d sess., 1857, S. Exec. Doc. 78, 135; Titus Fey Cronise, The Natural Wealth of California (San Francisco, 1868), 105; Clark, "An Emigrant of the Fifties," 112; J. E. Proctor, quoted in Reagan, "Report on Floods," 147; Bryant, What I Saw in California, 394; Illustrated History, 763.

44. E. O. C. Ord, "Report to Major E. R. S. Canby," in Report of the Secretary of War, 31st Cong., 1st sess., 1850, S. Exec. Doc. 4, 126–27.

45. E. O. C. Ord, *The City of Angels and the City of Saints, or a Trip to Los Angeles and San Bernardino in 1856* (San Marino, Calif.: Huntington Library, 1978), 9.

46. Hittel, *Resources of California*, 408.

47. For a more complete discussion of the changes due to Los Angeles's transformation from a Spanish pueblo and Mexican *ciudad* to an American town, see Robert M. Fogelson, *The Fragmented Metropolis: Los Angeles, 1850–1930* (Cambridge: Harvard Univ. Press, 1967), 24–32.

48. Hittel, *Resources of California*, 407; W. W. Robinson, *Los Angeles from the Days of the Pueblo: A Brief History and Guide to the Plaza Area* (San Francisco: Chronicle Books, 1981), 64; Newmark, *Sixty Years in Southern California*, 30, 62.

49. E. O. C. Ord and W. Hutton, "Plan de la Ciudad de Los Angeles," tracing made from the original, 1849, Huntington Library.

50. Hall, *Irrigation in California [Southern]*, 569; Baugh, "Los Angeles Water Supply," 127.

51. It is unclear exactly when the river became known as the Los Angeles River. The change was probably gradual. An 1837 map of the Rancho San Antonio, south of Los Angeles, refers to the channel south of the city as the "Arroyo del Pueblo." A French visitor to the city in 1841 wrote that "the village is situated on the banks of the Porciúncula, or Los Angeles River." The first known application of the name *Los Angeles River* on a map was on an 1852 U.S. Land Office map. For a detailed examination of the history of the names of the major rivers of Southern California, see J. N. Bowman, "The Names of the Los Angeles and San Gabriel Rivers," *Quarterly, Historical Society of Southern California* 29, no. 2 (1947): 93–99.

52. Newmark, *Sixty Years in Southern California*, 198.

53. Built by Abel Stearns and bought in 1883 by Jacob Lowe and Herman Levi, the Capitol Milling Company is believed to be the oldest surviving commercial enterprise in Los Angeles.

54. Don J. Kinsey, *The Romance of Water and Power* (Los Angeles: Department of Water and Power, 1926), 7; W. W. Robinson, "Story of Ord's Survey: As Disclosed by the Los Angeles Archives," *Quarterly, Historical Society of Southern California* 19, no. 3/4 (1937): 125.

55. Guinn, *Extended History of Los Angeles*, 255, 391; Vincent Ostrom, *Water and Politics: A Study of Water Policies and Administration in the Development of Los Angeles* (Los Angeles: Haynes Foundation, 1953), 30, 37; Bancroft, *California Pastoral*, 355.

56. "Water Overseer Ruled Early L.A.," *Los Angeles Times*, 26 February 1951; Layne, "Water and Power," 18; Ostrom, *Water and Politics*, 38; Los Angeles Common Council, Minutes, 11 September 1866, Los Angeles City Archives.

57. Los Angeles Common Council, Minutes, 24 May 1855, 16 July 1861; Newmark, *Sixty Years in Southern California*, 210, 220; Workman, *City That Grew*, 77–79; Elisabeth Mathieu Spriggs, "The History of the Domestic Water Supply of Los Angeles" (master's thesis, Univ. of Southern California, 1931), 17; Ludwig Louis Salvator, *Los Angeles in the Sunny Seventies*, trans. Marguerite Eyer Wilbur (Los Angeles: Bruce McCallister/Jake Zeitlin, 1929), 138.

58. Freemont Rider, ed., *Rider's California: A Guide-book for Travelers* (New York: Macmillan, 1925), 438.

59. *Los Angeles Star*, 27 August 1870; Hittel, *Resources of California*, 407; Salvator, *Sunny Seventies*, 54; Los Angeles Common Council, Minutes, 7 December 1857; Hall, *Irrigation in California [Southern]*, 551, 566

60. Gordon R. Miller, "Los Angeles and the Owens River Aqueduct" (Ph.D. diss., Claremont Graduate School, 1977), 5; Ostrom, *Water and Politics*, 38; Newmark, *Sixty Years in Southern California*, 125; Guinn, *Extended History of Los Angeles*, 191, 297.

61. *Los Angeles Star*, 17 May 1851, 12 February 1859; Bell, *Reminiscences of a Ranger*, 31.

62. "Water Overseer Ruled Early L.A."; G. R. Miller, "Owens River Aqueduct," 4–7; Spriggs, "Domestic Water Supply," 18; Warner, Hayes, and Widney, *Historical Sketch*, 127; Ana Begue Packman, *Leather Dollars: Short Stories of Pueblo Los Angeles* (Los Angeles: Times-Mirror Press, 1932), 18.

63. W. W. Robinson, "The Indians of Los Angeles: As Revealed by the Los Angeles City Archives," *Quarterly, Historical Society of Southern California* 20, no. 4 (1938): 158; Guinn, *Extended History of Los Angeles*, 271; "Water Overseer Ruled Early L.A."

64. *Los Angeles Star*, 8 April 1868; Los Angeles Common Council, Minutes, 4 March 1875; Fogelson, *Fragmented Metropolis*, 33–34.

65. Newmark, *Sixty Years in Southern California*, 116; Guinn, *Extended History of Los Angeles*, 391; Kinsey, *Romance of Water and Power*, 7.

66. Guinn, *Extended History of Los Angeles*, 391.

67. *Los Angeles Star*, 28 May 1853; Thomas Brooks, *Notes on Los Angeles Water Supply* (Los Angeles: Bureau of Water Works and Supply, 1938).

68. Brooks, *Notes*; Newmark, *Sixty Years in Southern California*, 211; Workman, *City That Grew*, 77; Spriggs, "Domestic Water Supply," 25; G. R. Miller, "Owens River Aqueduct," 8.

69. *Los Angeles Star*, 23 July 1859, 21 August 1860; George W. Gift to Damien Marchessault, 15 June 1860, HM 16555, Huntington Library; J. A. Wilson, *History of Los Angeles County*, 117, 151; Brooks, *Los Angeles Water Supply*; Guinn, *Extended History of Los Angeles*, 392.

70. *Brief History of the Los Angeles City Water Works* (Los Angeles, 1897), 6; Workman, *City That Grew*, 81–83; Brooks, *Los Angeles Water Supply*; Smith, *Adobe Days*, 142; Newmark, *Sixty Years in Southern California*, 292, 518; Nelson, *Los Angeles Metropolis*, 147.

71. Fogelson, *Fragmented Metropolis*, 39; Newmark, *Sixty Years in Southern California*, 366; Ostrom, *Water and Politics*, 41–42; Baugh, "Los Angeles Water Supply," 132.

72. Guinn, *Extended History of Los Angeles*, 392–93.

73. *Los Angeles Star*, 13 June 1868.

74. Guinn, *Extended History of Los Angeles*, 393.

75. Crystal Springs Drive in Griffith Park is the only evidence today of the one-time existence of these springs. The former site of the springs is now criss-crossed by Interstate 5 and the various freeway access ramps around Los Feliz Boulevard.

76. *Los Angeles Daily News,* 12 January 1869; *Los Angeles Star,* 23 July 1870; Brooks, *Los Angeles Water Supply;* J. A. Wilson, *History of Los Angeles County.* The dam no longer exists. Its former site is in the small section of Elysian Park that sits between the Pasadena Freeway and North Broadway.

77. Guinn, *Extended History of Los Angeles,* 394–95; Spalding, *History and Reminiscences,* 173; Warner, Hayes, and Widney, *Historical Sketch,* 128.

78. J. A. Wilson, *History of Los Angeles County,* 118; Ostrom, *Water and Politics,* 38; Workman, *City That Grew,* 78; Nelson, *Los Angeles Metropolis,* 264; Layne, "Water and Power," 25.

79. Hall, *Irrigation in California* [Southern], 537, 548–49, 566–67; quotation in Guinn, *Extended History of Los Angeles,* 300.

80. Hall, *Irrigation in California* [Southern], 557, 565–67.

81. Harry C. Carr, "Los Angeles Twenty Years Ago," in *From Pueblo to City* (Los Angeles, 1910), 7; Emma H. Adams, *To and Fro in Southern California with Sketches in Arizona and New Mexico* (Cincinnati, 1887), 69; Karl Baedeker, *The United States with an Excursion into Mexico* (Leipzig, Germany, 1893), 446.

82. Hall, *Irrigation in California* [Southern].

83. Ibid., 541.

84. Layne, "Water and Power," 20, 23.

85. Hall, *Irrigation in California* [Southern], 535–45.

86. Ibid., 550–53.

87. Ibid., 565.

88. Workman, *City That Grew,* 23; J. M. Guinn, "Los Angeles in the Later Sixties and Early Seventies," *Publications of the Historical Society of Southern California* 4 (1893): 64; Spalding, *History and Reminiscences,* 251; Ben C. Truman, *Semi-tropical California: Its Climate, Healthfulness, Productiveness, and Scenery; Its Magnificent Stretches of Vineyards and Groves of Semi-tropical Fruits, Etc., Etc., Etc.* (San Francisco, 1874), 107.

89. Los Angeles County once stretched from the Tehachapi Mountains on the north to San Juan Capistrano on the south and east all the way to the Colorado River, the boundary between California and Arizona. In 1853, the eastern portion of the county became San Bernardino County; in 1866, the northern part became Kern County; and in 1889, the southern part became Orange County.

90. H. F. Raup, "Transformation of Southern California to a Cultivated Land," *Annals of the Association of American Geographers* 49, no. 3, pt. 2 (1959): 64; Baugh, "Los Angeles Water Supply," 28; Cleland, *Cattle on a Thousand Hills,* 138; Guinn, *Extended History of Los Angeles,* 247; Agatha Fredericks, "Development of Irrigation in California" (master's thesis, Univ. of Southern California, 1928), 116.

91. Robert Cameron Gillingham, *The Rancho San Pedro: The Story of a Famous Rancho in Los Angeles County and of Its Owners, the Dominguez Family* (Los Angeles: Cole-Holmquist Press, 1961), 230; Raup, "Transformation of Southern California," 67; California State Engineering Department, *Detail Irrigation Map, Compton, Downey, Los Angeles, and Santa Monica sheets* (Sacramento, 1888).

92. Remi A. Nadeau, "Wheat Ruled the Valley," *Westways*, April 1963, 20; Paul A. Ewing, *The Agricultural Situation in the San Fernando Valley, California* (Washington: Department of Agriculture, 1939), 376; Hall, *Irrigation in California* [Southern], 516–34; Lewis H. Height Jr., "Settlement Patterns of the San Fernando Valley, California" (master's thesis, Univ. of California, Los Angeles, 1953), 66–68.

93. Salvator, *Sunny Seventies*, 141–42.

94. "The Los Angeles River," *Los Angeles Times*, 11 February 1882.

CHAPTER 3   *Draining the River Dry*

1. Glenn S. Dumke, *The Boom of the Eighties in Southern California* (San Marino, Calif.: Huntington Library, 1944), 4, 29; J. M. Guinn, *A History of California and an Extended History of Los Angeles and Environs* (Los Angeles, 1915), 254; Gordon R. Miller, "Los Angeles and the Owens River Aqueduct" (Ph.D. diss., Claremont Graduate School, 1977), 29.

2. John E. Welsh, "Reminiscences of California," 3 January 1911, HM 16371, Henry E. Huntington Library, San Marino, Calif.

3. Charles D. Clark, "Land Subdivision," in *Los Angeles: Preface to a Master Plan*, ed. George W. Robbins and L. Deming Tilton, Pacific Southwest Academy Publication 19 (Los Angeles: Ward Ritchie Press, 1941), 162.

4. For a representative view, see C. P. Heininger, *Album of Los Angeles and Vicinity* (San Francisco, 1888).

5. Bureau of the Census, *Twelfth Census of the United States, Taken in the Year 1900, Population, Part 1* (Washington, 1901).

6. John William Crandell, "Visions of Forgotten Angels: The Evolution of Downtown Los Angeles, 1830–1910" (master's thesis, Univ. of California, Los Angeles, 1990), 25; Howard J. Nelson, *The Los Angeles Metropolis* (Dubuque, Iowa: Kendall/Hunt, 1983), 156; Dumke, *Boom of the Eighties*, 47, 56–57; William Hamilton Hall, *Irrigation in California* [Southern]: *The Field, Water-Supply, and Works, Organization, and Operation in San Diego, San Bernardino, and Los Angeles Counties* (Sacramento, 1888), 556–57.

7. Guinn, *Extended History of Los Angeles*, 298.

8. Homer Aschmann, "Man's Impact on the Southern California Flora," in *Symposium Proceedings: Plant Communities of Southern California*, California Native Plant Society Special Publication 2 (Berkeley, 1976), 44; Guinn, *Extended History of Los Angeles*, 263, 362; C. S. Compton and J. H. Dockweiler, "Topographical Map of Los Angeles River Showing Said Stream between the Buena Vista Street Bridge in the City of Los Angeles and Main Tejunga [sic] Wash," 1897,

four sheets, Los Angeles Department of Water and Power; Hall, *Irrigation in California [Southern]*, 555–57.

9. Los Angeles Board of Water Commissioners (LABWC), *Annual Report*, 1902, 4, 24; William Mulholland, "A Brief Historical Sketch of the Growth of the Los Angeles City Water Department," *Public Service*, June 1920; Thomas Brooks, *Notes on Los Angeles Water Supply* (Los Angeles: Bureau of Water Works and Supply, 1938); Los Angeles City Water Company advertisement in Southern California Bureau of Information, *Southern California: An Authentic Description of Its Natural Features, Resources, and Prospects* (Los Angeles, 1892), 79.

10. Brooks, *Los Angeles Water Supply*; Mulholland, "Historical Sketch"; Vincent Ostrom, *Water and Politics: A Study of Water Policies and Administration in the Development of Los Angeles* (Los Angeles: Haynes Foundation, 1953), 39–40; Elisabeth Mathieu Spriggs, "The History of the Domestic Water Supply of Los Angeles" (master's thesis, Univ. of Southern California, 1931), 17.

11. Los Angeles City Council, Minutes, 9 April 1894, Los Angeles City Archives.

12. "Report of Water Overseer," 3 December 1894, 21 June 1897, Los Angeles City Archives; "Report of the Water Overseer, 1899," Los Angeles City Archives; Fred Eaton, "Annual Report of the Mayor, 1900," Los Angeles City Archives; Edward M. Boggs, "A Study of Water Rights on the Los Angeles River, California," in *Report of Irrigation Investigations in California*, Department of Agriculture Office of Experiment Stations Bulletin 100 (Washington, 1901), 345; Los Angeles City Council, Minutes, 11 April 1900.

13. Ostrom, *Water and Politics*, 40; Los Angeles City Council, Minutes, 28 June 1897, 25 June 1898, 28 May 1900, 25 November 1901, 13 April 1903.

14. Boggs, "Water Rights," 344, 349; H. D. Barrows, "Water for Domestic Purposes versus Water for Irrigation," *Annual Publications, Historical Society of Southern California* 8 (1911): 209.

15. Barrows, "Water for Domestic Purposes," 208–9.

16. C. P. Dorland, "The Los Angeles River: Its History and Ownership," *Publications of the Historical Society of Southern California* 3 (1893): 32–33; *Los Angeles v. San Fernando et al.*, 14 C.3d (1975), 233.

17. W. W. Robinson, "The Rancho Story of San Fernando Valley," *Historical Society of Southern California Quarterly* 38, no. 3 (1956): 225; Guinn, *Extended History of Los Angeles*, 396.

18. *The Statutes of California, Passed at the Twentieth Session of the Legislature, 1873–1874* (Sacramento, 1874), 633.

19. *Feliz v. Los Angeles*, 58 Cal. (1881), 73; Mike Eberts, *Griffith Park: A Centennial History* (Los Angeles: Historical Society of Southern California, 1996), 26–27.

20. *Feliz v. Los Angeles*, 80. The three decisions were *Lux v. Haggin* (1886), *Vernon Irrigation Co. v. Los Angeles* (1895), and *Los Angeles v. Pomeroy* (1899). For a more complete discussion of the history of litigation over the city's rights to the water in the river, see Norris Hundley Jr., *The Great Thirst: Californians and Water, 1770s–1990s* (Berkeley and Los Angeles: Univ. of California Press, 1992).

21. *Vernon Irrigation Co. v. Los Angeles*, 106 Cal. (1895), 237; Hundley, *Great Thirst*, 135.

22. Hundley, *Great Thirst*, 134–35; Ostrom, *Water and Politics*, 32.

23. *Los Angeles v. San Fernando et al.*, 217, 232, 246.

24. R. E. McDonnell, *Rates, Revenues, and Results of Municipal Ownership of Water Works in the U.S.* (Los Angeles: Burns-McDonnell-Smith Engineering, 1932). The percentage of publicly owned water systems nationwide increased from 42.9 percent in 1890 to 52.9 percent in 1896 and to 70 percent by 1924.

25. The water company's rates were a key reason many Los Angeles residents favored a return of the water system to municipal control. The *Los Angeles Times* reported in 1899 that families in Los Angeles paid an average of $15.00 a year for water service. Rates in many eastern cities with municipal water service were lower. In Hartford, Connecticut, families paid an average of $5.00 a year for water; in Cleveland, $5.50; Cincinnati, $6.50; and Buffalo, $8.00. Among the cities discussed in the article, only Oakland (which, like Los Angeles, received its water from a private company) had higher rates. Oakland families paid an average of $16.00 a year. See "The Water Question," *Los Angeles Times*, 18 August 1899.

26. "Our Water Supply," *Los Angeles Evening Express*, 14 March 1892; William A. Spalding, *History and Reminiscences, Los Angeles City and County, California* (Los Angeles: J. R. Finnell & Sons, 1931), 335; William L. Kahrl, *Water and Power: The Conflict over Los Angeles' Water Supply in the Owens Valley* (Berkeley and Los Angeles: Univ. of California Press, 1982), 15, 23; LABWC, *Annual Report*, 1902, 4.

27. "Report of the Water Committee," *Los Angeles Herald*, 26 December 1893.

28. "City Engineer's Water Report," *Los Angeles Evening Express*, 26 July 1897; "The Water Company's Offer," *Los Angeles Herald*, 28 July 1897; *Pasadena News*, 26 July 1897.

29. "Citizens Plan a Coup," *San Francisco Call*, 16 October 1897; "Water," *Los Angeles Evening Express*, 3 January 1898; "The Plant Is of No Value to Anybody," *San Francisco Call*, 23 January 1898.

30. G. R. Miller, "Owens River Aqueduct," 20.

31. "Mayor Eaton's Last Broadside," *Los Angeles Times*, 7 January 1901; *Los Angeles v. Pomeroy*, 124 Calif. (1899), 597.

32. Brooks, *Los Angeles Water Supply*; Los Angeles Department of Water and Power, *Water and Power Facts* (Los Angeles, 1993), 11; Ostrom, *Water and Politics*, 47–48.

33. Mulholland's cabin was located near the present intersection of Riverside Drive and Los Feliz Boulevard. A fountain dedicated to Mulholland now occupies the approximate site.

34. Spriggs, "Domestic Water Supply," 57.

35. "Last Spike in Deal Closed," *Los Angeles Times*, 29 July 1905.

36. Kahrl, *Water and Power*, 23–24.

37. Ostrom, *Water and Politics*, 47–48; LABWC, *Annual Report*, 1902; *Los An-*

geles Directory Co., *Los Angeles City Directory* (Los Angeles, 1902); Bureau of the Census, *Thirteenth Census of the United States, Taken in the Year 1910*, vol. 1, *Population* (Washington, 1913).

38. Harry Carr, *Los Angeles: City of Dreams* (New York: D. Appleton-Century, 1935), 145; G. Wharton James, *Picturesque Southern California* (Pasadena, 1898), 29.

39. Although stream flow and reservoir capacity are often expressed today in acre feet or cubic feet per second, the gallon was the more common unit of measurement in the early twentieth century. To provide consistency and to enable more easy comparison, therefore, all water supply data in chapters 2 and 3, which are primarily concerned with the river as a water source, are expressed in gallons. One gallon is equivalent to 0.13 cubic foot. One acre foot is equivalent to 325,851 gallons. One cubic foot per second is equivalent to 646,317 gallons per day.

40. Alfred Dougas Flinn, Robert Spurr Weston, and Clinton Lathrop Bogert, *Waterworks Handbook* (New York, 1916), 414, 545. Consumption in cities that were extensively metered was generally under 100 gallons per person a day. In 1906, for example, per capita consumption in Boston was 91 gallons a day. Other cities in the East and Midwest had similar rates of consumption: Per capita daily water use in Cleveland was 96 gallons; Hartford, Connecticut, 62; Milwaukee, 89; and Yonkers, New York, 83.

41. Los Angeles Board of Public Service Commissioners (LABPSC), *Complete Report on the Construction of the Los Angeles Aqueduct* (Los Angeles, 1916), 35; LABWC, *Annual Report*, 1902; Brooks, *Los Angeles Water Supply.*

42. Joseph Barlow Lippincott to Frank H. Olmsted, 18 December 1899, in "Annual Report of the City Engineer," Los Angeles City Archives.

43. H. B. Lynch, *Rainfall and Stream Run-off in Southern California since 1769* (Los Angeles: Metropolitan Water District of Southern California, 1931), 23; LABPSC, *Complete Report*, plate 22; Cary McWilliams, *Southern California: An Island on the Land* (Salt Lake City: Peregrine Smith, 1983), 197; Joseph Barlow Lippincott, *California Hydrography*, Geological Survey Water-Supply and Irrigation Paper 81 (Washington, 1903), 123; William Mulholland and Lippincott & Parker, Consulting Engineers, *Report on Water Supply* (Los Angeles: Board of Water Commissioners, 1906), 33; LABWC, *Annual Report*, 1903, 1904.

44. By 1911, the only remnant of the extensive network of irrigation ditches was a cement conduit along the west side of Figueroa Street, south of Washington Boulevard, the former channel of Zanja No. 8-R. See Barrows, "Water for Domestic Purposes," 209. The walls of Zanja No. 8-R were still visible as late as the 1930s. By then, though, they had been filled with dirt and planted with hedges, their former use no longer immediately apparent. See "Old Zanja on Figueroa," *Los Angeles Times*, 30 January 1939. Today, the only reminder of the extensive network of irrigation ditches is strictly symbolic. A few feet of the former path of the Zanja Madre is marked by a line of bricks on Olvera Street, the block-long *mercado* that is part of the city-owned El Pueblo de Los Angeles Historic Monument.

45. Los Angeles Department of Water and Power (LADWP), *Data on Available Water Supply and Future Requirements of the City of Los Angeles and the Metropolitan Area* (Los Angeles, 1928), 44; Brooks, *Los Angeles Water Supply*; "Water Overseer Ruled Early L.A.," *Los Angeles Times*, 26 February 1951; J. Gregg Layne, "Water and Power for a Great City: A History of the Department of Water & Power of the City of Los Angeles to December 1950," 1952 (Special Collections Department, Univ. of California, Los Angeles), 25, 77; LABWC, *Annual Report*, 1904, 13.

46. Brooks, *Los Angeles Water Supply*; Homer Hamlin, *Underflow Tests in the Drainage Basin of the Los Angeles River*, Geological Survey Water-Supply and Irrigation Paper 112 (Washington, 1905), 39; O. W. Peterson, "The Measurement of Underflow at Huron Street Section, Los Angeles River, Cal.," April 1904, Water Resources Center Archives, Univ. of California, Berkeley; LABWC, *Annual Report*, 1910, 11–14.

47. Mulholland, "Historical Sketch"; Brooks, *Los Angeles Water Supply*; LABWC, *Annual Report*, 1906, 15; 1910, 10.

48. Los Angeles Directory Co., *Los Angeles City Directory*, 1902–1906 (Los Angeles); LADWP, *Available Water Supply*; LABWC, *Annual Report*, 1902, 1905, 1906, 1910; Mulholland and Lippincott & Parker, *Report on Water Supply*, 21; LABPSC, *Complete Report*, 35, 43.

49. LABWC, *Annual Report*, 1903, 10–11, 15.

50. LABWC, *Annual Report*, 1904, 23.

51. LABWC, *Annual Report*, 1902, 29.

52. LABPSC, *Complete Report*, 36–44; "Mountain Supply," *Los Angeles Record*, 28 February 1898; Kahrl, *Water and Power*, 49; Walter C. Mendenhall, *Development of Underground Waters in the Eastern Coastal Plain Region of Southern California*, Geological Survey Water-Supply and Irrigation Paper 137 (Washington, 1905), 22.

53. Kahrl, *Water and Power*, 47, 49.

54. LABPSC, *Complete Report*, 47–51; LABWC, *Annual Report*, 1905, 7; Nelson, *Los Angeles Metropolis*, 77–78.

55. LADWP, *Water and Power Facts*.

56. See, esp., Kahrl, *Water and Power*; Abraham Hoffman, *Vision or Villainy: Origins of the Owens Valley–Los Angeles Water Controversy* (College Station: Texas A&M Univ. Press, 1981); and G. R. Miller, "Owens River Aqueduct." Kahrl, who has mounted the strongest critique of the city's tactics, occasionally stumbles in his analysis. In attempting to prove that the city repeatedly revised streamflow data in its reports, he cited a 1928 Department of Water and Power publication as evidence that the city had raised its streamflow estimates for the drought years once the controversy had subsided. The figures Kahrl quoted from the 1928 report, however, are for mean annual domestic consumption, not streamflow, as he contended. See Kahrl, *Water and Power*, 472, and LADWP, *Available Water Supply*, 44.

57. Los Angeles Directory Co., *Los Angeles City Directory*, 1913 (Los Angeles); Los Angeles Board of Public Service Commissioners (LABPSC), *Annual Report*, 1913, 17; Kahrl, *Water and Power*, 86.

58. For a more detailed discussion of the early rivalry between Los Angeles and San Diego, see Robert M. Fogelson, *The Fragmented Metropolis: Los Angeles, 1850–1930* (Cambridge: Harvard Univ. Press, 1967), 43–62.

59. H. F. Raup, "Transformation of Southern California to a Cultivated Land," *Annals of the Association of American Geographers* 49, no. 3, pt. 2 (1959): 65; Bureau of the Census, *Ninth Census*, vol. 1, *The Statistics of the Population of the United States* (Washington, 1872), 90; Fogelson, *Fragmented Metropolis*, 108–17; Nelson, *Los Angeles Metropolis*, 180–81.

60. *Vernon Irrigation Co. v. Los Angeles*, 106 Cal. (1895), 237.

61. Arthur C. Davis, "Territorial Growth of the City of Los Angeles, California," 1934 (Doheny Library, Univ. of Southern California, Los Angeles); Ostrom, *Water and Politics*, 144–48.

62. *Los Angeles v. Pomeroy*, 124 Calif. (1899), 597; *Los Angeles v. Hunter, Los Angeles v. Buffington*, 156 Cal. (1909), 607.

63. Ostrom, *Water and Politics*, 144–48; Davis, "Territorial Growth."

64. Los Angeles today encompasses 469 square miles, but it is no longer the largest city in area in the nation. That distinction belongs to Anchorage, Alaska, which has a land area of 1,698 square miles. The largest city in the continental United States is Jacksonville, Florida, the municipal limits of which spread over 759 square miles. See Bureau of the Census, *Statistical Abstract of the United States, 1995* (Washington, 1995), 44–46.

65. *Los Angeles v. San Fernando et al.*, 199; "Case Closed, at Long Last, in Water Dispute," *Los Angeles Times*, 28 January 1979; John F. Mann, "Pueblo Water Rights of the City of Los Angeles," *California Geology*, December 1976, 270; Timothy Egan, "One Juror Smiled; Then They Knew," *New York Times*, 4 October 1995, national edition.

66. Upper Los Angeles River Area Watermaster (ULARAW), *Watermaster Service in the Upper Los Angeles River Area, Los Angeles County: 1992–93 Water Year* (Los Angeles, 1994), 1–3; Melvin L. Blevins and John F. Mann, "Management of Upper Los Angeles River Area (ULARA) Ground Water Contamination," in *Are California's Ground Water Resources Sustainable?* proceedings of the Ground Water Conference, Water Resources Center Report 84 (Sacramento: Center for Water and Wildland Resources, 1994), 115.

67. Charles D. Warner, *Our Italy* (New York, 1891); Jimmie Rodgers, "Blue Yodel No. 4 (California Blues)," on *Never No Mo' Blues: Jimmie Rodgers Memorial Album* (RCA Records LP AHM1-1232).

68. Meg Perry, "A Historical Analysis of Land Use Transitions Occurring in the Los Angeles River/Alameda Street Sector of Downtown Los Angeles" (master's thesis, California State Univ., Los Angeles, 1995), 41.

69. Charles J. Fisher, "The Influence of the Railroad on Industrial Development in Los Angeles," in *Cruising Industrial Los Angeles* (Los Angeles: Los Angeles Conservancy, 1997), 8–9; Boyle Workman, *The City That Grew* (Los Angeles: Southland Publishing, 1935), 231; Fogelson, *Fragmented Metropolis*, 138–39; Perry, "Los Angeles River/Alameda Street Sector," 65–66, 88–89; Har-

ris Newmark, *Sixty Years in Southern California, 1853–1913* (New York, 1916), 601.

70. Pro Bono Publica, "A Wholesale Misdemeanor," *Los Angeles Times*, 6 December 1887.

71. "Los Angeles Discharge," *Los Angeles Times*, 24 July 1889; "The Sewer Problem—What Should Be Done," *Los Angeles Times*, 25 July 1889.

72. Fogelson, *Fragmented Metropolis*, 33–34; Los Angeles City Council, Minutes, 12 August 1896, 21 September 1903.

73. T. F. Osborn to Los Angeles City Council, 23 November 1904, Los Angeles City Council Petitions 1904, Communication 1347, Los Angeles City Archives.

74. Los Angeles City Council, Minutes, 12 December 1903; Los Angeles City Ordinance 21780 (New Series), 31 January 1911; Bart Wheeler, "In a Hobo Jungle," *Los Angeles Times*, 12 April 1931, Sunday magazine; Woody Guthrie, "Los Angeles New Year's Flood," on disc 3 of *Library of Congress Recordings* (Rounder Records CD 1041/2/3).

75. Los Angeles City Council, Minutes, 27 April 1896, 11 November 1901, 3 August 1903, 18 November 1907.

76. Los Angeles City Council, Minutes, 13 February 1912.

77. James W. Reagan to Los Angeles City Council, 7 October 1920, Los Angeles City Council Petitions 1920, Communication 2606, Los Angeles City Archives; Los Angeles Board of Public Works to Los Angeles City Council, 18 October 1920, Los Angeles City Council Petitions 1920; Los Angeles City Council, Resolution, 20 October 1925, Los Angeles City Council Petitions 1925, Communication 6420, Los Angeles City Archives.

78. Dana W. Bartlett, *The Better City: A Sociological Study of the Modern City* (Los Angeles, 1907), 32–33; Charles Mulford Robinson, *The City Beautiful: Report of the Municipal Art Commission for the City of Los Angeles* (Los Angeles, 1909), 3; Olmsted Brothers and Bartholomew and Associates, *Parks, Playgrounds, and Beaches for the Los Angeles Region*, report submitted to the Citizens' Committee on Parks, Playgrounds, and Beaches (Los Angeles: Citizens' Committee, 1930), 125–30.

79. Frank L. Shaw to Los Angeles City Council, Los Angeles City Council Minutes, 26 March 1934.

80. *From Pueblo to City, 1849–1910* (Los Angeles, 1910), 66.

81. Los Angeles City Council, Minutes, 13 February 1912.

82. Los Angeles Department of Water and Power, *Statistical Reports*, 1965. The Department of Water and Power stopped providing statistics on the river supply after 1965, instead including the river in a broader category for total local supply.

83. LABPSC, *Annual Report*, 1911, 9; Layne, "Water and Power," 185.

84. Paul A. Ewing, *The Agricultural Situation in the San Fernando Valley, California* (Washington: Department of Agriculture, 1939), 39–44; Fogelson, *Fragmented Metropolis*, 104; Clement Padick, "Control and Conservation of Natural Runoff Water in the San Fernando Valley, California" (master's thesis, Univ. of Cal-

ifornia, Los Angeles, 1956), 82; Bureau of the Census, *Fifteenth Census of the United States: 1930, Population*, vol. 1, *Number and Distribution of Inhabitants* (Washington, 1931).

85. LABPSC, *Annual Report*, 1916, 11; 1917, 11.

86. LABPSC, *Annual Report*, 1917, 10–11; 1918, 12; 1920, 17; 1921–25; 1930, 10–11.

87. Los Angeles Conservancy, *Cruising Industrial Los Angeles* (Los Angeles, 1997), 14, 24, 29; Perry, "Los Angeles River/Alameda Street Sector," 89–91; Fogelson, *Fragmented Metropolis*, 128–29; Nelson, *Los Angeles Metropolis*, 185; Works Projects Administration, Writers' Program, Southern California, *Los Angeles: A Guide to the City and Its Environs* (New York: Hastings House, 1941), 165–67; Central Manufacturing District, *Central Manufacturing District and Los Angeles Junction Railway, Los Angeles, California, Showing Rail and Harbor Connections, Traffic Roads, Residential and Industrial Areas*, map (Los Angeles, 1932).

88. Los Angeles River Pollution Committee (LARPC), *Progress Report, Los Angeles River Pollution Committee, for the Period May 1948–April 1949* (Los Angeles, 1949).

89. D. B. Willets, "Los Angeles River: Waterway or Wasteway" (paper presented at a meeting of the Pollution Committee of the California Section, American Water Works Association, Pasadena, Calif., 29 October 1952).

90. LARPC, *Progress Report, May 1948–April 1949*, 11.

91. Willets, "Waterway or Wasteway"; California Division of Water Resources, *Investigation of Los Angeles River* (Sacramento, 1952), 40, 73.

92. California Department of Water Resources, *Quality of Surface Waters in California, 1958*, Bulletin 65-58 (Sacramento, 1960), 27; California Regional Water Pollution Control Board No. 4, *Fourteenth Progress Report, Los Angeles River Pollution Committee, October 1, 1960 through September 30, 1961* (Los Angeles, [1962?]), 8; California Department of Water Resources, *Quality of Surface Waters in California, 1962*, Bulletin 65-62 (Sacramento, 1965), 14; California Department of Water Resources, *Watermaster Service in the Upper Los Angeles River Area, Los Angeles County, for Period October 1, 1968, through September 30, 1969* (Sacramento, 1970), 16.

93. ULARAW, *Watermaster Service in the Upper Los Angeles River Area, Los Angeles County, Relevant Data, 1968–69 through 1992–93* (Los Angeles, 1995), 2–28; Environmental Protection Agency (EPA), *San Fernando Valley Superfund Sites*, Region IX Fact Sheet 12 (San Francisco, 1993), 1; Blevins and Mann, "Upper Los Angeles River Area," 117.

94. EPA, *Superfund Sites*, 3; Melvin L. Blevins, telephone conversation with the author, 10 March 1995; ULARAW, *Watermaster Service, Relevant Data*.

95. Rich A. Nagle, telephone conversations with the author, 16 September 1997, 7 July 1998.

96. ULARAW, *Watermaster Service, 1992–93 Water Year*, Appendix C.

97. Ibid.; ULARAW, *Watermaster Service, Relevant Data*, 2–37; Eric Slater, "Another Hazard on the Links," *Los Angeles Times*, 10 August 1994; "Los Angeles River Virtual Tour," world wide web site created by Kurt Ballash, Jeffer-

son High School, Los Angeles (http://www.lalc.k12.ca.us/target/units/river/riverweb.html).

98. Los Angeles Department of Water and Power, *Headworks Pilot Recharge Project: Water Quality Investigation* (Los Angeles, 1993), 1; Myron Levin, "L.A. River Study May Give Water 2nd Chance," *Los Angeles Times*, 20 June 1991; Nagle, telephone conversation with the author, 16 September 1997.

CHAPTER 4   *A Stream That Could Not Be Trusted*

1. This assertion has been made again and again. See, e.g., U.S. Engineer Office, *Los Angeles County Drainage Area Flood Control* (Los Angeles, 1939), 1; House, *Survey Report for Los Angeles River Watershed*, 77th Cong., 1st sess., 1941, H. Doc. 426, serial 10599, 18; Richard E. Bigger, *Flood Control in Metropolitan Los Angeles*, Univ. of California Publications in Political Science, vol. 6 (Berkeley and Los Angeles: Univ. of California Press, 1959), 2; James G. Jobes, quoted in Anthony F. Turhollow, *A History of the Los Angeles District, U.S. Army Corps of Engineers, 1898–1965* (Los Angeles: Army Engineer District, 1975), 145; William L. Kahrl, ed., *The California Water Atlas* (Sacramento: State of California, 1979), 75.

2. House, *Los Angeles and San Gabriel Rivers and Their Tributaries, and Ballona Creek, Calif.*, 76th Cong., 3d sess., 1940, H. Doc. 838, serial 10505, 25–26.

3. Herbert Eugene Bolton, ed., *Fray Juan Crespi: Missionary Explorer of the Pacific Coast* (1927; reprint, New York: AMS Press, 1971), 147, 270; H. B. Lynch, *Rainfall and Stream Run-off in Southern California since 1769* (Los Angeles: Metropolitan Water District of Southern California, 1931), 31.

4. House, *Los Angeles and San Gabriel Rivers*, 11; House, Committee on Flood Control, *Comprehensive Flood Control Plans: Hearings before the Committee on Flood Control*, 75th Cong., 3d sess., 1940, 18 March 1940 to 9 April 1940; Los Angeles County Board of Engineers, Flood Control (LACBEFC), *Report of the Board of Engineers, Flood Control to the Board of Supervisors, Los Angeles County, California* (Los Angeles, 1915), 3; Howard J. Nelson, *The Los Angeles Metropolis* (Dubuque, Iowa: Kendall/Hunt, 1983), 92.

5. Harold C. Troxell, *Floods of March 1938 in Southern California*, Geological Survey Water-Supply Paper 844 (Washington, 1942), 331.

6. William Hamilton Hall, *Irrigation in California [Southern]: The Fields, Water-Supply, and Works, Organization, and Operation in San Diego, San Bernardino, and Los Angeles Counties* (Sacramento, 1888), 386.

7. Bigger, *Flood Control*, 7.

8. John McPhee's essay "Los Angeles against the Mountains" remains the most captivating elucidation of this phenomenon. See McPhee, *The Control of Nature* (New York: Farrar Straus Giroux, 1989).

9. U.S. Engineer Office, *Los Angeles County Drainage Area Flood Control*, 9; House, *Los Angeles and San Gabriel Rivers*, 12; U.S. Engineer Office, *Flood Control in the Los Angeles County Drainage Area* (Los Angeles, 1938), 1–2.

10. LACBEFC, *Map of a Portion of Los Angeles County* (Los Angeles, 1915).

11. LACBEFC, *Report of the Board of Engineers*, 103.

12. House, *Los Angeles and San Gabriel Rivers*, 11–15, 25–26.

13. Ibid., 11–15, 25; LACBEFC, *Report of the Board of Engineers*, 102–4.

14. LACBEFC, *Report of the Board of Engineers*, 114–15; James W. Reagan, comp., "A Report on Floods, River Phenomena and Rainfall in the Los Angeles Region, California," 1914–15 (Univ. Research Library, Univ. of California, Los Angeles, typescript), 405.

15. Reagan, "Report on Floods," 42.

16. Hubert Howe Bancroft, *California Pastoral, 1769–1848* (San Francisco, 1888), 252.

17. LACBEFC, *Report of the Board of Engineers*, 205; Ralph Iredale, *Air Rights: An Exploration of Their Possible Use in the Construction of New Communities and Facilities in Los Angeles, with Particular Reference to the Los Angeles River* (n.p., 1974); Robert Cameron Gillingham, *The Rancho San Pedro: The Story of a Famous Rancho in Los Angeles County and Its Owners, the Dominguez Family* (Los Angeles: Cole-Holmquist Press, 1961), 231.

18. Reagan, "Report on Floods," 25, 96.

19. Ibid, 9, 43; D. Henderson, quoted in ibid., 61.

20. Juan Crespí, *A Description of Distant Roads: Original Journals of the First Spanish Expedition into California, 1769–1770*, trans. Alan K. Brown (forthcoming), revised journals, entry for 2 August 1769; Herbert Eugene Bolton, ed., *Anza's California Expeditions*, vol. 4, *Font's Complete Diary* (New York: Russell & Russell, 1966), 245.

21. Walter C. Mendenhall, *Development of Underground Waters in the Central Coastal Plain Region of Southern California*, Geological Survey Water-Supply and Irrigation Paper 138 (Washington), plate 1.

22. William A. Spalding, *History and Reminiscences, Los Angeles City and County, California* (Los Angeles: J. R. Finnell & Sons, 1931), 91; J. Gregg Layne, *Annals of Los Angeles: From the Arrival of the First White Men to the Civil War, 1769–1861*, California Historical Society Special Publication 9 (San Francisco, 1935), 12; J. M. Guinn, "Exceptional Years: A History of California Floods and Drought," *Publications of the Historical Society of Southern California* 1, pt. 5 (1890): 33; J. M. Guinn, "Story of a Plaza," *Publications of the Historical Society of Southern California* 4 (1899): 247; Reagan, "Report on Floods," 95.

23. Don Jose del Carmen Lugo, "Life of a Rancher," trans. Thomas Savage, *Quarterly, Historical Society of Southern California* 32, no. 3 (1950): 190–91.

24. J. J. Warner, Benjamin Hayes, and J. P. Widney, *An Historical Sketch of Los Angeles County, California, from the Spanish Occupancy, by the Founding of the Mission San Gabriel Archangel, September 8, 1771 to July 4, 1876* (1876; reprint, Los Angeles: O. W. Smith, 1936), 17–18.

25. Thomas ap C. Jones, *Visit to Los Angeles in 1843* (1858; reprint, Los Angeles: Cole-Holmquist Press, 1960), 11–12.

26. Thomas Antisell, "Geologic Report," in *Report of Explorations and Surveys to*

Ascertain the Most Practicable and Economical Route for a Railroad from the Mississippi River to the Pacific Ocean, 33d Cong., 2d sess., 1856, S. Exec. Doc. 78, vol. 7, pt. 2, 80.

27. California State Engineering Department, *Detail Irrigation Map*, Compton, Downey, and Los Angeles sheets (Sacramento, 1888)

28. Thomas Gregory, quoted in Reagan, "Report on Floods," 154.

29. Frank H. Olmsted, "Reports of Messrs. Olmsted and Gillelen," in *Los Angeles and Long Beach Harbors, Cal.*, 64th Cong., 1st sess., 1916, H. Doc. 462, serial 6976, 12; LACBEFC, *Report of the Board of Engineers*, 205; U.S. Geological Survey, *Downey Sheet*, topographic quadrangle map, scale, 1:62,500 (Washington, 1896).

30. Gillingham, *Rancho San Pedro*, 44, 156; Rancho Los Cerritos, *Rancho Los Cerritos* (Long Beach, Calif., n.d.).

31. David Edward Hughes, "Memorandum No. 7," 24 March 1915, folder 55, Hughes Papers, Water Resources Center Archives, Univ. of California, Berkeley.

32. Reagan, "Report on Floods," 19, 42, 89; House, *Los Angeles and Long Beach Harbors, Cal.*, 64th Cong., 1st sess., 1916, H. Doc. 463, serial 6976, 90; LACBEFC, *Report of the Board of Engineers*, 209; Los Angeles and Salt Lake Railroad, "Map of the Los Angeles River from the Los Angeles City Limits to the Pacific Ocean," 1919, History and Genealogy Department, Los Angeles Public Library, Central Library; James W. Reagan, "Report of J. W. Reagan . . . upon the Control of Flood Waters in This District by the Correction of Rivers, Diversion and Care of Washes, Building of Dikes and Dams for Storage and Conservation Purposes, Safeguarding Public Highways and Private Property, and Protection of Harbors," 20 December 1916 (Los Angeles County Department of Public Works Technical Library, Alhambra, Calif., typescript).

33. Spalding, *History and Reminiscences*, 126; Carl W. Stover and Jerry L. Coffman, *Seismicity of the United States, 1568–1989 (Revised)*, Geological Survey Professional Paper 1527 (Washington, 1993), 102.

34. Harris Newmark, *Sixty Years in Southern California, 1853–1913* (New York, 1916), 257–58.

35. J. M. Guinn, *A History of California and an Extended History of Los Angeles and Environs* (Los Angeles, 1915), 289; Guinn, "Exceptional Years," 35; Newmark, *Sixty Years in Southern California*, 289. The Common Council in 1854 had approved a petition from several citizens allowing them to build a footbridge over the river and charge a five-cent toll, but there is no indication that the bridge was ever built. Los Angeles Common Council, Minutes, 10 April 1854, Los Angeles City Archives.

36. Guinn, "Exceptional Years," 36.

37. William H. Brewer, *Up and Down California in 1860–1864*, 2d ed., ed. Francis P. Farquhar (Berkeley and Los Angeles: Univ. of California Press, 1949), 30; Newmark, *Sixty Years in Southern California*, 170.

38. Reagan, "Report on Floods," 411; Warner, Hayes, and Widney, *Historical*

Sketch, 97; Newmark, *Sixty Years in Southern California*, 291; Brewer, *Up and Down California*, 80; Guinn, "Exceptional Years," 36.

39. Quoted in W. A. Sadler, "The Great Flood of January 22, 1862," *San Bernardino County Museum Association Quarterly* 39, no. 1 (1992): 49.

40. Benjamin Hayes, *Pioneer Notes from the Diaries of Judge Benjamin Hayes, 1849–1875* (Los Angeles: Marjorie Tisdale Wolcott, 1929), 270.

41. "City Improvements," *Los Angeles Star*, 25 January 1862.

42. Los Angeles Common Council, Minutes, 5 December 1865, 11 September 1866, 21 September 1866. The California Legislature in March 1868 approved establishment of the river tax, authorizing the city to levy a tax of not more than 0.25 percent on each $100 of taxable property for "improving the channel and banks of said river . . . for the protection of property on the banks." See *The Statutes of California, Passed at the Seventeenth Session of the Legislature, 1867–8* (Sacramento, 1868), 167.

43. *Los Angeles News*, 3 January 1868, quoted in Reagan, "Report on Floods," 306; Newmark, *Sixty Years in Southern California*, 412–13; Joseph S. O'Flaherty, *An End and a Beginning: The South Coast and Los Angeles, 1850–1887* (New York: Exposition Press, 1972), 143; Reagan, "Report on Floods," 248.

44. Olmsted, "Reports," 10–11; Warner, Hayes, and Widney, *Historical Sketch*, 18.

45. "The Topography of the City," *Daily Los Angeles Star*, 15 July 1870.

46. *Los Angeles Tribune*, 25 December 1889, quoted in Reagan, "Report on Floods," 14.

47. "Topography of the City."

48. *Los Angeles Star*, 3 September 1870; Los Angeles Common Council, Minutes, 22 December 1870.

49. Los Angeles Common Council, Minutes, 26 December 1872, 9 January 1873.

50. Reagan, "Report on Floods," 104, 361, 415, 428; Guinn, "Exceptional Years," 33; J. E. Proctor, quoted in Reagan, "Report on Floods," 147.

51. "Old Map Showing Zanja System," zanjas superimposed on H. J. Stevenson's 1876 "Map of the City of Los Angeles, California," photocopy, Los Angeles Department of Water and Power Library.

52. Reagan, "Report on Floods," 224, 329.

53. Quotation from House, *Los Angeles and Long Beach Harbors*, 78; on lowered riverbed, see LACBEFC, *Report of the Board of Engineers*, 225.

54. LACBEFC, *Report of the Board of Engineers*, 174; Reagan, "Report on Floods," 9, 45, 264, 315.

55. Newmark, *Sixty Years in Southern California*, 401; Meg Perry, "A Historical Analysis of Land Use Transitions Occurring in the Los Angeles River/Alameda Street Sector of Downtown Los Angeles" (master's thesis, California State Univ., Los Angeles, 1995), 33; "Old Map Showing Zanja System"; H. J. Steven-

son, *Map of the City of Los Angeles, California* (Los Angeles, 1884); Boyle Workman, *The City That Grew* (Los Angeles: Southland Publishing, 1935), 151, 182–83.

56. J. J. Warner, "A Warning," *Los Angeles Times*, 30 July 1882; J. J. Warner, letter to the editor, *Los Angeles Times*, 6 August 1882.

57. Southern California Directory Co., *Los Angeles City and County Directory for 1881–2* (Los Angeles, 1881).

58. Alfred Moore, letter to the editor, *Los Angeles Times*, 2 August 1882. To Moore's letter, Warner responded: "Floods are not, in modern times, preceded by Noah to warn the exposed of their danger; nor are they respecters of persons, but they come upon the defenseless mother, not infrequently in the dark, stormy hours of night, when, instead of fleeing away for safety, she is chained to the spot by the moans of her still more helpless children."

59. Lynch, *Rainfall and Stream Run-off*, 31; Ford A. Carpenter, "Flood Studies at Los Angeles," *Monthly Weather Review* 42, no. 6 (1914): 388; House, *Los Angeles and Long Beach Harbors*, 105.

60. The only bridge to survive the flood was the covered bridge built at Aliso Road in 1870. Ironically, that bridge would become, according to more than one newspaper, the city's "stand-by" during major storms. It survived the floods of 1884, 1886, and 1889. It is unclear why the covered bridge survived when so many other bridges on the river were destroyed. See "A Fierce Freshet: Los Angeles River on a Rampage," *Los Angeles Times*, 20 January 1886; "The 'Rain' of Terror: Continuation of Greatest Recorded Storm," *Los Angeles Evening Express*, 26 December 1889.

61. Troxell, *Floods of March 1938*, 391; Edwin Baxter, "Leaves from the History of the Last Decade, 1880–90," *Publications of the Historical Society of Southern California* 3 (1893): 76; Reagan, "Report on Floods," 68, 78, 97; N. B. Hodgkinson, "The Story of Flood Control in Los Angeles County," 1937 (Los Angeles County Department of Public Works Technical Library, Alhambra, Calif., typescript), 2; Lynch, *Rainfall and Stream Run-off*, 23; House, *Los Angeles and San Gabriel Rivers*, 27; Paul A. David and Peter Solar, "A Bicentenary Contribution to the History of the Cost of Living in America," *Research in Economic History* 2 (1977): 1–80; Bureau of Labor Statistics (BLS), "Consumer Price Index—All Urban Consumers," U.S. city average, all items, September 1997, BLS web site (http://stats.bls.gov); "Fierce Freshet"; William H. Quinn, Victor T. Neal, and Santiago E. Antunez de Mayola, "El Niño Occurrences over the Past Four and a Half Centuries," *Journal of Geophysical Research* 92, no. C13 (15 December 1987): 14,457.

62. Newmark, *Sixty Years in Southern California*, 541; Guinn, "Exceptional Years," 37; Reagan, "Report on Floods," 34.

63. Workman, *City That Grew*, 228.

64. Quoted in Reagan, "Report on Floods," 82–86.

65. "Fierce Freshet"; Reagan, "Report on Floods," 36; West Side, "Why Is This Thus?" *Los Angeles Times*, 16 January 1885.

66. "A Wreck: A Resurvey of the Flooded District," *Los Angeles Times*, 21 January 1886; "Fierce Freshet"; David and Solar, "Cost of Living in America"; BLS, "Consumer Price Index."

67. "A Wreck"; "The Last Flood," *Los Angeles Times*, 20 January 1886.

68. *De Baker v. Southern California Railway*, 106 Cal. (1895), 276–77; "First Annual Report of the City Engineer," 1 December 1889, Los Angeles City Archives; "Plan of Levee, West Side of Los Angeles River, from Macy Street to . . . below First Street," 1886, City of Los Angeles Bureau of Engineering.

69. "First Annual Report of the City Engineer."

70. Los Angeles Directory Co., *Maxwell's Los Angeles City Directory and Gazetteer of Southern California* (Los Angeles, 1894).

71. Guinn, *Extended History of Los Angeles*, 254.

72. "The Los Angeles River," *Los Angeles Evening Express*, 28 December 1889; LACBEFC, *Report of the Board of Engineers*, 205; California State Engineering Department, *Detail Irrigation Map*, Compton, Downey, and Los Angeles sheets (Sacramento, 1888); U.S. Geological Survey, 1:62,500-scale topographic quadrangle maps for Downey (1896), San Pedro (1896), and Redondo (1896).

73. Reagan, "Report on Floods," 15–18, 146, 427.

74. Cubic feet per second is a unit expressing the rate of discharge of water. It is the volume of water, in cubic feet, passing a reference point in one second. It is equivalent to 7.48 gallons per second, 448.83 gallons per minute, 646,317 gallons per day, or 1.98 acre feet per day.

75. LACBEFC, *Report of the Board of Engineers*, 146; H. Hawgood, "Memo on Re-occurrence of Floods of the Los Angeles River," 1914 (Los Angeles County Department of Public Works Technical Library, Alhambra, Calif., typescript); House, *Los Angeles and San Gabriel Rivers*, 27; David and Solar, "Cost of Living in America"; BLS, "Consumer Price Index."

76. LACBEFC, *Report of the Board of Engineers*, 370; "Third Annual Report of the City Engineer," 21 December 1891, Los Angeles City Archives; Los Angeles City Council, Minutes, 24 September 1900, 24 February 1903; Harry F. Stafford, "Plan of Rip-rap Levee for East Side of Los Angeles River, North of Buena Vista St. Bridge," 1903, City of Los Angeles Bureau of Engineering.

77. Carpenter, "Flood Studies at Los Angeles," 388; Lynch, *Rainfall and Stream Run-off*, 23.

78. Bureau of the Census, *Twelfth Census of the United States, Taken in the Year 1900, Population, Part 1* (Washington, 1901); Bureau of the Census, *Thirteenth Census of the United States, Taken in the Year 1910*, vol. 1, *Population* (Washington, 1913); Nelson, *Los Angeles Metropolis*, 267; Central Manufacturing District, *Central Manufacturing District and Los Angeles Junction Railway, Los Angeles, California, Showing Rail and Harbor Connections, Traffic Roads, Residential and Industrial Areas*, map (Los Angeles, 1932).

79. Marshall Stimson, *Fun, Fights, and Fiestas in Old Los Angeles: An Autobiography* (Los Angeles, 1966), 58.

80. Leonard Pitt and Dale Pitt, *Los Angeles A to Z: An Encyclopedia of the City and County* (Berkeley and Los Angeles: Univ. of California Press, 1997), 175; Bureau of the Census, *Fourteenth Census of the United States, Taken in the Year 1920,* vol. 1, *Population* (Washington, 1921); E. Caswell Perry, *Burbank: An Illustrated History* (Northridge, Calif.: Windsor Publications, 1987), 37.

81. Quinn, Neal, and de Mayola, "El Niño Occurrences," 14,452; James A. Ruffner and Frank E. Blair, eds., *The Weather Almanac* (Detroit: Gale Research, 1981), 94.

82. *Los Angeles Times,* 19 February 1914.

83. LACBEFC, *Report of the Board of Engineers,* 31; Carpenter, "Flood Studies at Los Angeles," 386; H. D. McGlashan and F. C. Eberts, *Surface Water Supply of the Pacific Slope of Southern California,* Geological Survey Water-Supply Paper 447 (Washington, 1921), 546; LACBEFC, *Provisional Report of Board of Engineers, Flood Control* (Los Angeles, 1914).

84. Harold E. Hedger, interviews by Daniel Simms, 17 May 1965, 19 May 1965, 8 July 1965, Oral History Program, Univ. of California, Los Angeles; "Survey Damage as Deluge Ceases and Rivers Recede," *Los Angeles Times,* 22 February 1914; "Half Million Pigeons Drowned or Homeless," *Los Angeles Times,* 22 February 1914; LACBEFC, *Provisional Report;* "Long Beach is an Island City," *Los Angeles Times,* 22 February 1914.

85. "Floods and Future," *Los Angeles Times,* 26 February 1914.

86. George H. Cecil, "Flood Damage and Benefits from Flood Control," in *Comprehensive Plan for Flood Control and Conservation: Present Conditions and Immediate Needs* (Los Angeles: Los Angeles County Flood Control District, 1931), 55; LACBEFC, *Provisional Report;* James W. Reagan, "Tentative Report to the Board of Supervisors of the Los Angeles County Flood Control District Outlining the Work Already Done and Future Needs of Flood Control and Conservation, with Tentative Estimates, Maps, Plans and Flood Pictures," 7 February 1924 (Los Angeles County Department of Public Works Technical Library, Alhambra, Calif., typescript), 2; House, *Los Angeles and Long Beach Harbors,* 105; David and Solar, "History of the Cost of Living in America"; BLS, "Consumer Price Index."

87. Nelson, *Los Angeles Metropolis,* 268; LACBEFC, *Portion of Los Angeles County;* U.S. Geological Survey, 1:62,500-scale topographic quadrangle maps for Downey (1896), San Pedro (1896), Redondo (1896), Pasadena (1900), and Calabasas (1903); LACBEFC, *Report of the Board of Engineers,* 335.

88. "Quick Action on Flood Problem Is Assured," *Los Angeles Times,* 28 February 1914.

89. LACBEFC, *Portion of Los Angeles County.*

90. House, *Los Angeles and Long Beach Harbors,* 23–34, 45, 89; Nelson, *Los Angeles Metropolis,* 227–29; Robert M. Fogelson, *The Fragmented Metropolis: Los Angeles, 1850–1930* (Cambridge: Harvard Univ. Press, 1967), 119.

CHAPTER 5   *Fifty-one Miles of Concrete*

1. William R. Brownlie and Brent D. Taylor, *Sediment Management for Southern California Mountains, Coastal Plains, and Shoreline,* pt. C, *Coastal Sediment Delivery by Major Rivers in Southern California,* EQL Report 17-C (Pasadena: Environmental Quality Laboratory, California Institute of Technology, 1981), C-231.

2. House, *Los Angeles and Long Beach Harbors, Cal.,* 64th Cong., 1st sess., 1916, H. Doc. 462, serial 6976, 45–46.

3. Hubert Howe Bancroft, *History of California* (San Francisco, 1885), 2:563; James W. Reagan, "A Report on Floods, River Phenomena, and Rainfall in the Los Angeles Region, California," 1914–15 (University Research Library, Los Angeles, typescript), 71, 112, 153; Harold E. Hedger, interviews by Daniel Simms, 17 May 1965, 19 May 1965, 8 July 1965 (Oral History Program, Univ. of California, Los Angeles), 8; Frank H. Olmsted, "Reports of Messrs. Olmsted and Gillelen," in House, *Los Angeles and Long Beach Harbors,* 11.

4. W. R. Dodson, quoted in Reagan, "Report on Floods," 230; George H. Peck, quoted in Reagan, "Report on Floods," 369.

5. *De Baker v. Southern California Railway,* 106 Cal (1895), 279, 283–84.

6. [E. T. Wright?], "Field Notes, April [1874]," handwritten notebook, Los Angeles County Department of Public Works Technical Library, Alhambra, Calif.

7. Los Angeles County Board of Engineers, Flood Control (LACBEFC), *Report of the Board of Engineers, Flood Control, to the Board of Supervisors, Los Angeles County, California* (Los Angeles, 1915), 2, 370; House, *Los Angeles and Long Beach Harbors,* 26, 48.

8. Olmsted, "Reports," 13.

9. Ibid., 10–13, 15.

10. LACBEFC, *Report of the Board of Engineers,* 275; Ford A. Carpenter, "Flood Studies at Los Angeles," *Monthly Weather Review* 42, no. 6 (1914): 385.

11. LACBEFC, *Report of the Board of Engineers,* 4, 144.

12. "Three Million Dollars Price of Safe Rivers," *Los Angeles Times,* 27 February 1914.

13. "Quick Action on Flood Problem Is Assured," *Los Angeles Times,* 28 February 1914; Richard Bigger, *Flood Control in Metropolitan Los Angeles,* University of California Publications in Political Science, vol. 6 (Berkeley and Los Angeles: Univ. of California Press, 1959), 12–13.

14. "Gov. Johnson Paves Way for Gigantic Engineering Project," *Los Angeles Tribune,* 20 June 1915.

15. Los Angeles County Flood Control District (LACFCD), *History, Function and Plans* (Los Angeles, 1955), 1; Bigger, *Flood Control,* 13.

16. Reagan, "Report on Floods."

17. LACBEFC, "First Monthly Report to the Los Angeles County Board of Supervisors," August 1914 (Los Angeles County Department of Public Works Technical Library, Alhambra, Calif., typescript); LACBEFC, *Provisional Report of*

Board of Engineers, Flood Control (Los Angeles, 1914); House, Los Angeles and Long Beach Harbors, 83; Bigger, Flood Control, 13.

18. Lafayette Saunders, quoted in Reagan, "Report on Floods," 89.

19. Mulholland quoted in ibid., 142; Gage quoted in ibid., 147.

20. Reagan, "Report on Floods," 44.

21. D. Henderson, quoted in ibid., 60–61.

22. "First Long Step Made toward Flood Control," Los Angeles Times, 28 July 1915; "Flood Control Experts Clash," Los Angeles Times, 15 August 1915.

23. LACBEFC, Report of the Board of Engineers, 27–28, 162, 194; Lewis H. Height Jr., "Settlement Patterns of the San Fernando Valley, Southern California" (master's thesis, Univ. of California, Los Angeles, 1953), 114.

24. LACBEFC, Report of the Board of Engineers, 12–13, 113–14; LACBEFC, Provisional Report.

25. LACBEFC, Report of the Board of Engineers, 223–25.

26. Ibid, 225, 322.

27. Coincidentally, two of five members of the board of engineers had Kansas roots. Like Reagan, Joseph B. Lippincott, who had also been instrumental in development of the Los Angeles–Owens River Aqueduct, had been educated at the University of Kansas.

28. LACBEFC, Report of the Board of Engineers, 223, 279–332; Harold E. Hedger, "History of Los Angeles County Flood Control District: Early Personages, Personnel, Activities, and Office Locations, 1917–1952," 1975 (Los Angeles County Department of Public Works Technical Library, Alhambra, Calif., typescript).

29. "Battle Begets Engineer Job," Los Angeles Times, 25 January 1916.

30. "River Overflows," Los Angeles Times, 15 January 1916; "Extensive Damage by Floods Everywhere," Los Angeles Times, 18 January 1916; H. D. McGlashan and F. C. Ebert, Southern California Floods of January 1916, U.S. Geological Survey Water-Supply Paper 426 (Washington, 1918), 27, 34–35; Edwin C. Kelton, "History of Past Floods, Coastal Streams of Southern California, 1811–1938, and List of Prior Reports on Floods, Precipitation, Need for Flood Control Improvements, Etc., Los Angeles and San Gabriel River Basins," 1939 (Water Resources Center Archives, Univ. of California, Berkeley, typescript), 11; James W. Reagan to Los Angeles County Board of Supervisors, 7 February 1916, Los Angeles County Department of Public Works Technical Library, Alhambra, Calif.; Army Chief of Engineers, Report of the Chief of Engineers, U.S. Army (Washington, 1916), 1538.

31. Adrian M. F. French to Los Angeles County Board of Supervisors, 17 January 1916, Los Angeles County Department of Public Works Technical Library, Alhambra, Calif.

32. "Levee Specifications for Title Insurance and Trust Company on Arcadia de Baker Estate near Hobart Station," 1915, folder 101-1, Joseph Barlow Lippincott Papers, Water Resources Center Archives, Univ. of California, Berkeley.

33. Los Angeles County Engineer, "Annual Report of the County Engineer for the Fiscal Year Ending June 30, 1916" (Los Angeles County Department of Public Works Technical Library, Alhambra, Calif., typescript); Charles T. Leeds, "Improvement of Rivers and Harbors in the Los Angeles, Cal., District," in *Report of the Chief of Engineers, U.S. Army* (Washington, 1917), 3263; Howard J. Nelson, *The Los Angeles Metropolis* (Dubuque, Iowa: Kendall/Hunt, 1983), 229; Charles T. Leeds and H. Hawgood to U.S. Board of Engineers for Rivers and Harbors, 27 August 1915, Los Angeles County Department of Public Works Technical Library, Alhambra, Calif.; LACBEFC, *Report of the Board of Engineers*, 11, 222.

34. LACBEFC, *Report of the Board of Engineers*, 217–24.

35. James W. Reagan, "Report of J. W. Reagan . . . upon the Control of Flood Waters in This District by the Correction of Rivers, Diversion and Care of Washes, Building of Dikes and Dams for Storage and Conservation Purposes, Safeguarding Public Highways and Private Property, and the Protection of Harbors," 20 December 1916 (Los Angeles County Department of Public Works Technical Library, Alhambra, Calif., typescript), 4, 6, 18B, 43, 47.

36. House, *Los Angeles and Long Beach Harbors*, 103, 111; House, Committee on Rivers and Harbors, *Los Angeles and Long Beach Harbors, Cal.*, 64th Cong., 2d sess., 1917, H. Doc. 9, 5–6; Leeds, "Improvement of Rivers and Harbors"; Leeds and Hawgood to Board of Engineers, 27 August 1915.

37. U.S. Engineer Office, "Request for Proposals for Constructing Silt Diversion Works near Los Angeles and Long Beach Harbors, California," 18 July 1919, file 59, David Edward Hughes Papers, Water Resources Center Archives, Univ. of California, Berkeley; House Committee, *Los Angeles and Long Beach Harbors, Cal.*

38. David Edward Hughes, "Reminiscences on Breaking Ground for Harbor Protection Work," 27 October 1919, Hughes Papers, typescript; Hughes to Col. M. M. Raymond, 3 October 1921, Hughes Papers.

39. James W. Reagan, *Report of J. W. Reagan . . . upon the Control of Flood Waters in This District by Correction of Rivers, Diversion and Care of Washes, Building of Dikes and Dams, Protecting Public Highways, Private Property, and Los Angeles and Long Beach Harbors* (Los Angeles, 1917), 5, 6, 32, 35.

40. "Deadlock in Flood Control Matters," *Los Angeles Times*, 25 March 1916, magazine; Municipal League of Los Angeles, *Important Statement on Flood Control* [Los Angeles, 1917].

41. J. H. Quinton, Charles T. Leeds, and S. A. Jubb, *Report of Board of Engineers on Flood Control* [Los Angeles?, 1917].

42. "Flood Control Election Is Opposed," *Los Angeles Herald*, 15 February 1917; "Supervisors Override Judgment of Experts," *Los Angeles Times*, 16 February 1917; "Voters Urged to Study Report against Bonds," *Los Angeles Times*, 17 February 1917; "Should We Vote These Flood Control Bonds?" *Los Angeles Times*, 18 February 1917.

43. "Today's Bond Election," *Los Angeles Times*, 20 February 1917.

44. Flood Control Campaign Committee, *Flood Control Advocate*, 20 February 1917, box 23, folder 8, Joseph Barlow Lippincott Papers, Water Resources Center Archives, Univ. of California, Berkeley; *Los Angeles Times*, 20 February 1917.

45. "More Rain," *Los Angeles Times*, 19 February 1917; "Rainstorm Continues in Southern California," *Los Angeles Times*, 21 February 1917; Bigger, *Flood Control*, 120, 163.

46. James W. Reagan, "Tentative Report to the Board of Supervisors of the Los Angeles County Flood Control District Outlining the Work Already Done and Future Needs of Flood Control and Conservation, with Tentative Estimates, Maps, Plans, and Flood Pictures," 7 February 1924 (Los Angeles County Department of Public Works Technical Library, Alhambra, Calif., typescript), 2; Bigger, *Flood Control*, 134.

47. House, *Los Angeles and San Gabriel Rivers and Their Tributaries, and Ballona Creek, Calif.*, 76th Cong., 3d sess., 1940, H. Doc. 838, serial 10505, 4; Bigger, *Flood Control*, 57. The shifting of the river channel did not completely eliminate disruptions to ocean traffic caused by silt carried from the river. As recently as 1995, the Army Corps of Engineers spent $2.5 million to remove debris deposited at the river's mouth. During a series of storms in January of that year, sand and silt washed down the river had nearly sealed off Queensway Landing, a small harbor at the river mouth that houses boats for excursions to Catalina Island and seasonal whale-watching tours. See Steve Eames, "Corps of Engineers to Dredge River Mouth," *Los Angeles Times*, 9 February 1995, Long Beach edition.

48. Reagan, "Tentative Report," 4; "For Full Water Conservation," *Los Angeles Times*, 29 January 1922; Stephen R. Van Wormer, "A History of Flood Control in the Los Angeles County Drainage Area," *Southern California Quarterly* 73, no. 1 (1991): 64.

49. LACBEFC, *Report of the Board of Engineers*, 331; Reagan, "Tentative Report," 6; James W. Reagan, *Report of J. W. Reagan . . . upon the Control of Flood Waters in This District by Correction of Rivers, Diversion and Care of Washes, Building of Dikes and Dams, Protecting Public Highways, Private Property, and Los Angeles and Long Beach Harbors* (Los Angeles, 1924), 5.

50. J. L. Mathews, "Grand Canyon of Southern California to Be Site of Greatest Dam in the World," *Los Angeles Times*, 4 May 1924.

51. "For Full Water Conservation."

52. Reagan, "Tentative Report," 6.

53. "Flood Issue Is Vital to Los Angeles," *Los Angeles Times*, 4 May 1924; "Forward-looking Program," *Los Angeles Times*, 5 May 1924.

54. Nelson, *Los Angeles Metropolis*, 187; Robert Fogelson, *The Fragmented Metropolis: Los Angeles, 1850–1930* (Cambridge: Harvard Univ. Press, 1967), 224–27; Clement Padick, "Control and Conservation of Natural Runoff Water in the San Fernando Valley, California" (master's thesis, Univ. of California, Los Angeles, 1956), 82; Bureau of the Census, *Census of Population: 1960*, vol. 1, *Charac-*

teristics of the Population, Part A, Number of Inhabitants (Washington, 1960), 6-18–6-22.

55. Reagan, *Report* (1924), 13–14; Mulholland quoted by Volney H. Craig in a letter to the Los Angeles City Council, 26 July 1923, Los Angeles City Council Petitions 1923, communication 3926, Los Angeles City Archives; Los Angeles City Council Finance Committee, Resolution, July 1923, Los Angeles City Council Petitions 1923; H. Gale Atwater to Los Angeles City Council, 8 September 1924, Los Angeles City Council Petitions 1924, communication 5848, Los Angeles City Archives.

56. Bigger, *Flood Control*, 124; James W. Reagan, *Report of J. W. Reagan . . . upon the Control and Conservation of Flood Waters in This District by Correction of Rivers, Diversion and Care of Washes, Building of Dikes and Dams, Protecting Public Highways, Private Property, and Los Angeles and Long Beach Harbors* (Los Angeles: Los Angeles County Flood Control District, 1926).

57. George W. Goethals, "Report on Flood Control Project," 4 October 1924, in scrapbook of E. B. Davey, Henry E. Huntington Library, San Marino, Calif.; Bigger, *Flood Control*, 125–26.

58. "People Rise Up to End Bonding," *Los Angeles Times*, 5 November 1926; H. B. Lynch, *Rainfall and Stream Run-off in Southern California since 1769* (Los Angeles: Metropolitan Water District of Southern California, 1931), 23.

59. N. B. Hodgkinson, "The Story of Flood Control in Los Angeles County," 1937 (Los Angeles County Department of Public Works Technical Library, Alhambra, Calif., typescript), 4.

60. "Reagan Gets Ready to Quit Post, Report," *Los Angeles Evening Express*, 9 November 1926; "A Notable Work," undated handbill, clipping book 8, Joseph Barlow Lippincott Papers, Water Resources Center Archives, Univ. of California, Berkeley; Bigger, *Flood Control*, 127–28. Two smaller, rock-fill dams were later built near the original dam site. See Van Wormer, "History of Flood Control," 80–81.

61. Van Wormer, "History of Flood Control," 27; Bigger, *Flood Control*, 128; "San Gabriel Dam Blame Fixed on Supervisors," *Los Angeles Times*, 7 November 1930; "Flood Control Wastage Scored by Grand Jury," *Los Angeles Times*, 13 January 1931; "Graves Guilty, Jury's Verdict," *Los Angeles Times*, 31 March 1933.

62. Padick, "Conservation of Natural Runoff," 82; Bureau of the Census, *Fifteenth Census of the United States: 1930, Population*, vol. 1, *Number and Distribution of Inhabitants* (Washington, 1931).

63. Hedger, interviews by Daniel Simms, 29.

64. Hedger, "History," 10; E. C. Eaton, *Comprehensive Plan for Flood Control and Conservation: Present Conditions and Immediate Needs* (Los Angeles: Los Angeles County Flood Control District, 1931); LACFCD, *Flood Control and Water Conservation . . . Vital to Los Angeles County* (Los Angeles, [1971?]).

65. Eaton, *Comprehensive Plan*, 11–13.

66. U.S. Engineer Office, *Los Angeles County Drainage Area Flood Control* (Los Angeles, 1939), 12–15.

67. Hedger, interviews by Daniel Simms, 43.

68. Eaton, *Comprehensive Plan*, 12, 17, 31, 49.

69. LACFCD, *Possible Overflow Areas during Flood 50% Greater than 1914, under Present Conditions*, map (Los Angeles, 1931).

70. Eaton, *Comprehensive Plan*, 31–34.

71. Ibid., 3.

72. Ibid., 42; Public Works Administration Board of Review, "Report by Board of Review to Federal Emergency Administration of Public Works on Application of Los Angeles County Flood Control District," 24 May 1934, in LACFCD, *Comprehensive Plan for Flood Control and Water Conservation, Assembled from Computations and Data Made Prior to February 18, 1935* (Los Angeles, 1935). Although the review board found that "many of the projects applied for are urgently needed" and said the comprehensive plan "appears to be a logical solution of the flood problem confronting the area," it denied the loan request on the grounds that the benefits from such a program would be primarily local and because of concern over inadequacies in the local flood control act and the proposed method of repayment.

73. LACFCD, *Annual Report, 1931–1933* (Los Angeles); LACFCD, *Comprehensive Plan*.

74. E. Caswell Perry and Carroll W. Parcher, *Glendale Area History* (Glendale, Calif.: Eric Schneirsohn/Xanadu Galleries, 1981), 146–47; Grace J. Oberbeck, *History of La Crescenta–La Cañada Valleys* (Montrose, Calif.: Ledger, 1938), 45, 57, 79; Leonard Pitt and Dale Pitt, *Los Angeles A to Z: An Encyclopedia of the City and County* (Berkeley and Los Angeles: Univ. of California Press, 1997), 245, 489; *Montrose, California: The First Eighty Years, 1913–1993* (Montrose, Calif.: Montrose–Verdugo City Chamber of Commerce, [1993?]), 37; Reagan, *Report* (1926), 7.

75. Harold C. Troxell and John Q. Peterson, *Flood in La Canada Valley, California, January 1, 1934*, U.S. Geological Survey Water-Supply Paper 796-C (Washington, 1937); Paul A. David and Peter Solar, "A Bicentenary Contribution to the History of the Cost of Living in America," *Research in Economic History* 2 (1977): 1–80; Bureau of Labor Statistics (BLS), "Consumer Price Index—All Urban Consumers," U.S. city average, all items, September 1997, BLS web site (http://stats.bls.gov).

76. Chapin Hall, "Desolation in Montrose Flood Area Appalling," *Los Angeles Times*, 5 January 1934.

77. Hedger, interviews by Daniel Simms, 34; Troxell and Peterson, *Flood in La Canada Valley*; "Thirty-seven on Death List in Record 8.27-Inch Deluge," *Los Angeles Times*, 2 January 1934; "Co-ordination of Flood Relief Efforts Sought," *Los Angeles Times*, 4 January 1934.

78. "Natural Disasters," *Los Angeles Times*, 2 January 1934.

79. Woody Guthrie, "Los Angeles New Year's Flood," on disc 3 of *Library of Congress Recordings* (Rounder Records CD 1041/2/3).

80. "Storm Lesson Pointed Out," *Los Angeles Times*, 6 January 1934; "County

Flood-Control Plan Would Prevent Recurrence of New Year's Disaster," *Los Angeles Times*, 7 January 1934; Reagan, *Report* (1926), 7.

81. Los Angeles Engineer Council of Founder Societies, "Report of Special Engineering Committee on Flood Control," February 1934, in Army Corps of Engineers, Los Angeles District, "Transcript of Hearing and Exhibits to Accompany Preliminary Examination Report, Flood Control, Los Angeles and San Gabriel Rivers and Their Tributaries, California," 31 March 1936, Los Angeles (Water Resources Center Archives, Univ. of California, Berkeley, typescript).

82. "Minuteers Demand Dismissal of Eaton as Flood Engineer," *Los Angeles Daily News*, 8 June 1934; "Eaton Quits Flood Post," *Los Angeles Times*, 1 September 1934.

83. S. M. Fisher, *Report of S. M. Fisher of the Los Angeles County Flood Control District on Control and Conservation of Flood, Storm, or Other Waste Waters of the District* (Los Angeles: Los Angeles County Flood Control District, 1934); Bigger, *Flood Control*, 163; C. H. Howell, "Data Requested by U.S. District Engineer's Office at Los Angeles for Report as Provided by Scott Bill," in Army Corps of Engineers, "Transcript of Hearing and Exhibits"; John Anson Ford, *Thirty Explosive Years in Los Angeles County* (San Marino, Calif.: Huntington Library, 1961), 99.

84. LACFCD, *Comprehensive Plan*; House, *Development of Rivers of the United States*, 73d Cong., 2d sess., 1934, H. Doc. 395.

85. Hodgkinson, "Story of Flood Control," 36; House, *Los Angeles and San Gabriel Rivers*, 21; House, *Preliminary Examination of San Gabriel and Los Angeles Rivers for Flood Control*, 74th Cong., 1st sess., 1935, H. Rep. 840, 1.

86. LACFCD, *Comprehensive Plan*; James G. Jobes, "The United States Engineer Department: Its Organization and Work in Southern California," paper presented to a meeting of the city and county executives of Los Angeles, [1936?]; Army Chief of Engineers, *Report of the Chief of Engineers, U.S. Army* (Washington, 1941), 1768; U.S. Engineer Office, *Flood Control in the Los Angeles District* (Los Angeles, 1939); House, *Los Angeles and San Gabriel Rivers*, 21.

87. *Flood Control Act of 1936*, U.S. Statutes at Large 49 (1936): 1750. The Flood Control Act of 1936 provided funds for flood control projects on almost every major waterway in the United States, including the Mississippi, Ohio, Arkansas, and Missouri Rivers.

88. House Committee on Flood Control, *Comprehensive Flood Control Plans: Hearings before the Committee on Flood Control*, 75th Cong., 3d sess., 30 March–19 April 1938; Rep. Will M. Whittington, D-Mississippi, quoted in ibid., 552. Whittington also said, "I know of no more favorable project that has been adopted for any community in the United States."

89. House, *Los Angeles and San Gabriel Rivers*, 32–33; Bigger, *Flood Control*, 16, 69, 107; Army Chief of Engineers, *Annual Report of the Chief of Engineers, U.S. Army* (Washington, 1960), 1521; Forest Service, *Los Angeles River Flood Prevention Project: Project Accomplishments and Recommendations for Completion of Program in Mountain and Foothill Areas* (Los Angeles: Angeles National Forest, 1961), 12.

90. Clarence Daugherty, quoted in Army Corps of Engineers, "Transcript of Hearing and Exhibits," 69.

91. Myron C. Burr, quoted in Army Corps of Engineers, "Transcript of Hearing and Exhibits," 130.

92. Jobes, "United States Engineer Department."

93. U.S. Engineer Office, *Los Angeles County Drainage Area Flood Control*, 3; C. T. Newton and Harold E. Hedger, "Los Angeles County Flood Control and Water Conservation," paper presented at a convention of the American Society of Civil Engineers, Waterways and Waterworks Division, Los Angeles, Calif., 9–13 February 1959.

94. U.S. Engineer Office, *Flood Control in the Los Angeles County Drainage Area* (Los Angeles, 1938); U.S. Engineer Office, *Los Angeles County Drainage Area Flood Control*.

95. John C. Shaw, quoted by Horace B. Ferris, secretary, Board of Public Works, City of Los Angeles, in a letter to Los Angeles City Council, 21 December 1927, Los Angeles City Council Petitions 1927, communication 11057, Los Angeles City Archives.

96. Clark quoted in "County Flood-Control Plan Would Prevent Recurrence"; Ralph B. Wertheimer, *Flood Plain Zoning: Possibilities and Legality with Special Reference to Los Angeles County, California* (Sacramento: California State Planning Board, 1942), 2.

97. House Committee, *Comprehensive Flood Control Plans*, 551.

98. Los Angeles County Regional Planning Commission, "Land Use Survey, County of Los Angeles," 1939, 16 vols. (Henry E. Huntington Library, San Marino, Calif.); Los Angeles Department of City Planning, "Land Use Survey, City of Los Angeles," 1939, 10 vols. (Henry E. Huntington Library, San Marino, Calif.). These maps represent a remarkable snapshot of the state of development in the Los Angeles metropolitan area before World War II. The two sets of maps fill twenty-six large volumes, each of which, when opened, covers a large table. There are more than 850 maps in all, produced at scales of 1:3,600 and 1:7,200, three times as large a scale as the most detailed maps of Los Angeles published by the U.S. government.

99. Padick, "Conservation of Natural Runoff," 82. Between 1930 and 1940, the population of San Fernando Valley riverfront communities increased as follows: Canoga Park, 35 percent; Reseda, 130 percent; Encino, 66 percent; Van Nuys, 80 percent; Sherman Oaks, 221 percent; Studio City, 256 percent; North Hollywood, 126 percent; Burbank, 106 percent; Glendale, 32 percent.

100. Works Projects Administration, Writers' Program, Southern California, *Los Angeles: A Guide to the City and Its Environs* (New York: Hastings House, 1941), 380–81.

101. Ibid., 380, 389–91; E. Caswell Perry, *Burbank: An Illustrated History* (Northridge, Calif.: Windsor Publications, 1987), 56.

102. Lloyd Aldrich, "Flood Control of Los Angeles River," 31 March 1936, in Army Corps of Engineers, "Transcript of Hearing and Exhibits."

103. U.S. Engineer Office, *Los Angeles County Drainage Area Flood Control*, 48, 92.

104. Pitt and Pitt, *Los Angeles A to Z*, 45.

105. M. F. Burke, *Flood of March 2, 1938* (Los Angeles: Los Angeles County Flood Control District, 1938), 6–9; Lawrence H. Daingerfield, "Southern California Rain and Flood, February 27 to March 4, 1938," *Monthly Weather Review* 66, no. 5 (1938): 139–43; Harold C. Troxell, *Floods of March 1938 in Southern California*, U.S. Geological Survey Water-Supply Paper 844 (Washington, 1942); Fritz Van der Leeden, Fred L. Troise, and David Keith Todd, *The Water Encyclopedia* (Chelsea, Mich.: Lewis Publishers, 1990), 128; David and Solar, "Cost of Living in America"; BLS, "Consumer Price Index."

106. *Los Angeles Times*, 4 March 1938; Rupert Hughes, *City of Angels* (New York: Charles Scribner's Sons, 1941), 324.

107. "Thirty Dead in Southland Floods," *Los Angeles Times*, 3 March 1938; "Sixty-two Known Storm Dead," *Los Angeles Times*, 4 March 1938; Paul A. Ewing, *The Agricultural Situation in San Fernando Valley, California* (Washington, 1939), 13; Burke, *Flood of March 2, 1938*; U.S. Engineer Office, *Report on Engineering Aspects, Flood of March 1938* (Los Angeles, 1938); American National Red Cross, *California Floods of 1938: Official Report of Relief Operations* (Washington, 1938), 8.

108. "New Rainstorm Hits Southland," *Los Angeles Times*, 2 March 1938; "Ten Hurled to Death When River Sweeps Away Bridge," "Several Feared Lost in River," "Torrent Splits Espee Bridge," "Gas Main, Severed by River Torrent, Explodes in Towering Mass of Flames," *Los Angeles Times*, 3 March 1938; "Any Driftwood Today? Long Beach Has Slight Surplus," *Long Beach Sun*, 4 March 1938; Jackson Mayers, *Burbank History* (Burbank, Calif.: James W. Anderson, 1975), 108; Roger G. Hatheway, *Historical and Architectural Evaluation, LACDA Feasibility Study, Bridges* (Los Angeles: Army Corps of Engineers, Los Angeles District, 1987), 15; U.S. Engineer Office, *Los Angeles County Drainage Area Flood Control*, 40; House Committee, *Comprehensive Flood Control Plans*, 541.

109. LACFCD, *Inundated Areas, Flood of March 2, 1938*, map (Los Angeles, 1938); U.S. Engineer Office, *Los Angeles County Drainage Area, California: Types of Channel Improvement Prior to Flood*, map (Los Angeles, 1938).

110. John Anson Ford, statement about flood control, 11 April 1938 (Los Angeles County Department of Public Works Technical Library, Alhambra, Calif., typescript); U.S. Engineer Office, *Report on Engineering Aspects*.

111. Hedger, interviews by Daniel Simms, 41.

112. The "design storm" engineers used to develop a comprehensive flood control system was a four-day storm in which rain fell continuously the first three days and reached its maximum intensity on the fourth day. Hydrologists have since calculated that this type of storm can be expected to occur about once every fifty years in Los Angeles. System designers in the 1930s were hampered in their analysis by the fact that historic rainfall records for the city went back only fifty-five years. See Army Corps of Engineers, *Los Angeles County Drainage Area Review: Final Feasibility Study, Interim Report, and Environmental Impact Statement, Revised* (Los Angeles, 1992), 51.

113. U.S. Engineer Office, *Flood Control in the Los Angeles County Drainage Area*; U.S. Engineer Office, *Los Angeles County Drainage Area Flood Control*.

114. Army Corps of Engineers, *Operation and Maintenance Manual, Los Angeles County Drainage Area* (Los Angeles, 1975); Army Corps of Engineers, "Data for Dams Constructed by the Corps of Engineers in the Los Angeles District," 1951 (Public Affairs Department, Army Corps of Engineers, Los Angeles District, typescript); Van Wormer, "History of Flood Control," 88.

115. House, *Los Angeles and San Gabriel Rivers*, 32–33; Army Chief of Engineers, *Annual Report* (1960), 1544.

116. Army Corps of Engineers, *Operation and Maintenance Manual*, A-29.

117. Lee R. Henning, "Concrete Lining for a River Channel," *Western Construction*, February 1958, 31.

118. "A River Doesn't Run through It," *Los Angeles Times*, 26 December 1994.

119. Ibid.; Army Chief of Engineers, *Annual Report* (1960), 1522, 1546–47.

120. LACBEFC, *Provisional Report*; Eaton, *Comprehensive Plan*, 31–32; LACFCD, *Comprehensive Plan*; U.S. Geological Survey, *Topography: Calabasas Quadrangle*, map, 1:62,500 scale (Washington, 1903).

121. U.S. Geological Survey, *Topography: Santa Monica Quadrangle*, map, 1:62,500 scale (Washington, 1902).

122. Douglas L. Holker, "Effects on the Los Angeles River Due to Urbanization," unpublished paper, Univ. of California, Los Angeles, 1982 (Water Resources Center Archives, Univ. of California, Berkeley, typescript).

123. U.S. Engineer Office, *Los Angeles County Drainage Area Flood Control*, 35.

124. The flood control system, as constructed by the Los Angeles County Flood Control District and the Army Corps of Engineers, also includes 225 concrete stream-bed stabilization dams, 33 storm water pumping plants with storm water detention facilities, 29 ground water recharge facilities, about 2,400 miles of local storm drains, and 97,000 catch basins and other inlets. See Woodward-Clyde Consultants, *Master Environmental Impact Report: Los Angeles County Drainage Area Project*, prepared for Los Angeles County Department of Public Works (Santa Ana, Calif.: Woodward-Clyde Consultants, 1994), S-1.

125. Army Corps of Engineers, *Los Angeles County Drainage Area Review*, 24–27; Army Corps of Engineers, *Project Notes: Los Angeles County Drainage Area Project (LACDA)* (Los Angeles, n.d.).

126. Stanley R. Steenbock, "And Keep Your Honors Safe . . . : A Brief Overview and Affectionate Farewell to the Los Angeles County Flood Control District, 1915–1985," 1985 (Los Angeles County Department of Public Works Technical Library, Alhambra, Calif., typescript), 38.

127. Army Corps of Engineers, *Report on Floods of January and February 1969 in Los Angeles County* (Los Angeles, 1969); Larry Simpson, *Storms of 1969: Summary Report* (Los Angeles: Los Angeles County Flood Control District, 1969); S. E. Rantz, *Urban Sprawl and Flooding in Southern California*, U.S. Geological Survey Circular 601-B (Washington, 1970), B9.

128. Sixteen persons drowned or were killed by mudslides; fifty-seven died in flood-related accidents.

129. "Flood Damage Report, February 26, 1969" (Public Affairs Department, Army Corps of Engineers, Los Angeles District, typescript); Simpson, *Storms of 1969*, 34.

130. Army Corps of Engineers, *Project Notes*; Rantz, *Urban Sprawl and Flooding*, B4.

CHAPTER 6   *Exhuming the River*

1. Army Corps of Engineers, *Operation and Maintenance Manual, Los Angeles County Drainage Area Project, California* (Los Angeles, 1975).

2. Even with the fences along its course and the prohibition against entering its channel, an average of six people drown in the river every winter. "A River Doesn't Run through It," *Los Angeles Times*, 26 December 1994.

3. Louis Sahagun, "L.A. River Offers Refuge for Homeless Immigrants," *Los Angeles Times*, 13 August 1990. The director of a skid row social service agency estimated that 150 immigrants lived along the downtown portion of the river in 1990, camping and cooking along its banks and bathing, washing clothes, and defecating in its channel.

4. Philip L. Fradkin, *The Seven States of California: A Natural and Human History* (New York: Henry Holt, 1995), 345; Marita Hernandez, "Man Held as 'River Rapist' Denies Guilt," *Los Angeles Times*, 12 January 1985; Larry Wickline, quoted in Dick Roraback, "Que Serra Serra along Friar Crespi's Porciuncula," *Los Angeles Times*, 14 November 1985.

5. Don Nichols, quoted in Sahagun, "L.A. River Offers Refuge."

6. "New Attendance Record at Central Locations of 8th Annual River Clean Up," *Current News*, spring/summer 1997, 1.

7. Kimball L. Garrett, ed., "The Biota of the Los Angeles River: An Overview of the Historical and Present Plant and Animal Life of the Los Angeles River Drainage," 1993 (Natural History Museum of Los Angeles County, Los Angeles, typescript), 5; Camm C. Swift and Jeffrey Seigel, "The Past and Present Freshwater Fish Fauna of the Los Angeles River," in Garrett, "Biota of the Los Angeles River," D-1; Robert L. Bezy, Cynthia A. Weber, and John W. Wright, "Reptiles and Amphibians of the Los Angeles River Basin," in ibid., E-2; Kimball L. Garrett, "The Avifauna of the Los Angeles River: An Historical Overview and Current Analysis," in ibid., F-3, F-4; C. Clifton Coney, "Freshwater Mollusca of the Los Angeles River: Past and Present Status and Distribution," in ibid., C-8.

8. Kimball L. Garrett, presentation to "Rethinking the River," conference, Long Beach, Calif., 12 November 1994.

9. Dick Roraback, "From Basin Camp, the Final Assault," *Los Angeles Times*, 30 January 1986.

10. Gene Lippert, "A Heck of a Treck," *Los Angeles Times*, 17 November 1985.

11. On swimming hole, Greenberg, quoted in Lawrence C. Jorgensen, *The San Fernando Valley: Past and Present* (Los Angeles: Pacific Rim Research, 1982), 169; on bear, Roraback, "From Basin Camp"; Catherine Mulholland, telephone

conversation with the author, 12 August 1997; Huffaker, quoted in Jorgensen, *San Fernando Valley*, 169.

12. Garrett, "Biota of the Los Angeles River," 6; Swift and Seigel, "Freshwater Fish Fauna," D-2, D-3, D-6; Phillis M. Faber, Ed Keller, Anne Sands, and Barbara M. Massey, *The Ecology of Riparian Habitats of the Southern California Coastal Region: A Community Profile*, U.S. Fish and Wildlife Service Biological Report 85 (7.27) (Washington: Fish and Wildlife Service, 1989), 63; Garrett, "Avifauna of the Los Angeles River," F-68; Linda J. Barkley, "Mammals of the Los Angeles River Basin," in Garrett, "Biota of the Los Angeles River," G-3, G-5.

13. "Test How Waterproof a Boot is in a Creek, Test How Rugged it is in the Los Angeles River," advertising for Nike "Air Khumbu Plus" boots, *Rolling Stone*, 25 August 1994; *Them!* prod. David Weisbart, 94 min., Warner Bros. Pictures, 1954, motion picture; *Grease*, prod. Robert Stigwood and Allan Carr, 110 min., Paramount Pictures, 1978, motion picture; *Terminator 2: Judgment Day*, prod. James Cameron, 135 min., Carolco Pictures, 1991, motion picture; Marc Ramirez, "Even Buildings Turn Their Faces Away from L.A.'s River," *Wall Street Journal*, 1 August 1989; Army Corps of Engineers, *Los Angeles County Drainage Area Review: Final Feasibility Study Interim Report and Environmental Impact Statement, Revised* (Los Angeles, 1992), 69; Scott Armstrong, "L.A. Ponders Future of Its 'River,'" *Christian Science Monitor*, 1 February 1990.

14. American Rivers, *North America's Most Endangered and Threatened Rivers of 1995* (Washington, 1995), preface, 10–11.

15. Kimball L. Garrett, "The Changing Biota of the Los Angeles River during the Twentieth Century," presentation to "Nature's Workshop: Environmental Change in Twentieth-Century Southern California," conference, California State University, Northridge, 20 September 1997.

16. Garrett, "Avifauna of the Los Angeles River," F-11.

17. Garrett, "Biota of the Los Angeles River," 5.

18. Garrett, presentation to "Rethinking the River" conference.

19. Garrett, "Avifauna of the Los Angeles River," F-42.

20. Gary D. Wallace, "Report on the Vascular Plants of the Los Angeles River," in Garrett, "Biota of the Los Angeles River," B-4; Woodward-Clyde Consultants, *Master Environmental Impact Report: Los Angeles County Drainage Area Project*, prepared for the Los Angeles County Department of Public Works (Santa Ana, Calif., 1994), 3–30; Douglas P. Shuit, "Nature Lessons," *Los Angeles Times*, 28 March 1997, San Fernando Valley edition; Dick Roraback, "Up a Lazy River, Seeking the Source," *Los Angeles Times*, 20 October 1985.

21. Christopher Kroll, "What River? Changing Views of the River," *California Coast & Ocean*, summer 1993, 33; Garrett, presentation to "Rethinking the River" conference; Garrett, "Avifauna of the Los Angeles River," F-8, F-9.

22. Gordon A. Reetz, "Flood Control and Wildlife Preservation in Los Angeles Water Projects," 1976 (Public Affairs Department, Army Corps of Engineers, Los Angeles District, typescript).

23. Lewis MacAdams, telephone conversation with the author, 21 November 1997.

24. Lewis MacAdams, "Restoring the Los Angeles River: A Forty-Year Art Project," *Whole Earth Review,* spring 1995, 64.

25. Don Shirley, "'WVIP' Tunes In the Look and Sounds of the 40s," *Los Angeles Times,* 27 September 1985.

26. MacAdams, telephone conversation, 21 November 1997; Shirley, "'WVIP' Tunes In."

27. *Los Angeles Times:* Dick Roraback, "Up a Lazy River, Seeking the Source," 20 October 1985; "The L.A. River Practices Its Own Trickle-down Theory," 27 October 1985; "Exploring the L.A. River: Small Tales from Along Lario Trail," 31 October 1985; "Scenes from the L.A. River: Exploring with Ants in His Pants," 3 November 1985; "Bridging the Gap on the L.A. River: With a Song in His Heart and a Yolk in His Shoe," 7 November 1985; "Que Serra Serra along Friar Crespi's Porciuncula," 14 November 1985; "Of Goats, Pans, Poetry, and an 'Airwolf' Episode: Explorer Takes the High Road to a TV Location on the River," 21 November 1985; "By the Filmic Shores of Burbank: Reflecting on the Muddy Banks of a Town of Tinsel," 28 November 1985; "Getting Closer and Closer, but That's Par for the Course," 8 December 1985; "Just a Trickle Away: It's Another Case of Double Dribble," 23 January 1986; "From Basin Camp, the Final Assault," 30 January 1986.

28. Roraback, "Up a Lazy River."

29. Roraback, "Trickle-down Theory."

30. Dick Roraback, telephone conversation with the author, 5 December 1997. Remembering the response to the series years later, Roraback said, "I was surprised and very pleased. I didn't know anybody ever thought about the river. There was a sort of latent nostalgia for something nobody had ever experienced."

31. Roraback, "From Basin Camp."

32. Lewis MacAdams, "In Search of L.A.'s Wild Side," review of *Sagebrush and Cappuccino: Confessions of an L.A. Naturalist* by David Wicinas, *California Coast & Ocean,* spring 1996, 38–39.

33. Dilara El-Assaad, presentation to "Visions of the Los Angeles River/Rivera Promenade," conference and exhibition, El Pueblo de Los Angeles Historical Monument, Los Angeles, 22 November 1997.

34. Dilara El-Assaad, telephone conversation with the author, 1 December 1997.

35. Dilara El-Assaad, "Redefining the Role of the L.A. River in the Urban Landscape of Southern California" (master's thesis, Univ. of Southern California, 1988), 44–57.

36. Bettina Boxall, "River Devotee Seeks a Revival," *Los Angeles Times,* 26 October 1989, Glendale edition.

37. David Salveson, "Urban River Revival," *Urban Land* 56, no. 6 (1997): 31–35;

Ann Breen and Dick Rigby, *Waterfronts: Cities Reclaim Their Edge* (New York: Mc-Graw-Hill, 1994), 198–200, 276; Joe Shoemaker, *Returning the Platte to the People* (Westminster, Colo.: Greenway Foundation/Tumbleweed Press, 1981); Scott Herhold, "River Park Faces Battles," *San Jose Mercury News*, 21 April 1996; Friends of the Chicago River, *Help Shape the Future of the Waterway That Shaped Chicago* (Chicago, n.d.); Patrick T. Reardon, "Healing Waters," *Chicago Tribune*, 30 August 1995.

38. Patrick T. Reardon, "River Sets New Course," *Chicago Tribune*, 27 August 1995.

39. Breen and Rigby, *Waterfronts*, 14, 189–90, 241–43; Ann Breen and Dick Rigby, *The New Waterfront: A Worldwide Urban Success Story* (New York: McGraw-Hill, 1996), 32–33, 66, 140; Carl Abbott, "Japanese-American Plaza," *Landscape Architecture* 81, no. 2 (1991): 38; James Ricci, "Detroit: Along the River," *Travel/Holiday*, August 1990, 22–25; "Friends of the Buffalo River," *CRUW News* 1, no. 2 (1997): 10; Charles E. Little, *Greenways for America* (Baltimore: Johns Hopkins Univ. Press, 1990), 141.

40. Ann Breen and Dick Rigby, "Sons of Riverwalk," *Planning* 54, no. 3 (1988): 26–30; Jan Jarboe, "Down by the Riverside," *Texas Monthly*, June 1994, 106–11; Ken Greenberg, "Tiendas Del Rio," *Landscape Architecture* 81, no. 2 (1991): 32–35.

41. Lewis MacAdams, interview by the author, Los Angeles, 24 October 1997; Friends of the Los Angeles River, Sierra Club, and Urban Resources Partnership, *The River through Downtown: Conference Program* (Los Angeles: n.p., 1998), 18–21.

42. Little, *Greenways for America*, 11; "Boulevard Routes," *Los Angeles Times*, 24 August 1897; "A Boulevard Project," *Los Angeles Times*, 3 September 1897.

43. Dana W. Bartlett, *The Better City: A Sociological Study of a Modern City* (Los Angeles, 1907), 32.

44. Ibid., 34.

45. William H. Wilson, *The City Beautiful Movement* (Baltimore: Johns Hopkins Univ. Press, 1989), 46, 87; Robert Howard Tracy, "John Parkinson and the Beaux-Arts City Beautiful Movement in Downtown Los Angeles, 1894–1935" (Ph.D. diss., Univ. of California, Los Angeles, 1982), 199–204; Charles Mulford Robinson, *The City Beautiful: Report of the Municipal Art Commission for the City of Los Angeles, California* (Los Angeles, 1909).

46. Fences enclosing properties, then as now, reflected the city's Spanish and Mexican heritage. This meant little to Robinson, who, in recommending their removal, wrote: "This is a relic of other days and, in its idea, of other lands." Robinson, *City Beautiful*, 8.

47. Robinson, *City Beautiful*, 2, 3. Robinson did propose a parkway for the Los Feliz Road, which follows roughly the present route of Riverside Drive. Despite its name, however, Riverside Drive typically runs at least a quarter-mile west of the river. Robinson recommended that the city acquire a broad strip of land on both sides of the road to ensure the "preservation of the beauty of the

drive, making possible such continuity of park effect that in driving from Elysian to Griffith, one will not be conscious that the park has been left."

48. Stephen D. Mikesell, "The Los Angeles River Bridges: A Study in the Bridge as a Civic Monument," *Southern California Quarterly* 68, no. 4 (1986): 374. The ten bridges are at Glendale Boulevard/Hyperion Avenue, Fletcher Drive, North Broadway, Macy Street, First Street, Fourth Street, Sixth Street, Seventh Street, Ninth Street, and Washington Boulevard.

49. Robinson, *City Beautiful*, 2; W. H. Wilson, *The City Beautiful Movement*, 4.

50. "Conversion of Griffith Park Is Planned," *Los Angeles Examiner*, 7 August 1910; "Automobile Roads in Griffith Park," *Los Angeles Herald*, 30 October 1910.

51. Joseph Barlow Lippincott, "Park Methods and Results: A Comparison of Los Angeles and Other Western Cities," *California Outlook*, 18 November 1911 (suppl.), 4–5; "Lippincott Asks for Widening of Vermont," unidentified newspaper clipping, 13 November 1912, Joseph Barlow Lippincott Papers, clipping book 5, Water Resources Center Archives, Univ. of California, Berkeley.

52. Laurie Davidson Cox, "The Arroyo Seco—a California Parkway," *California Outlook*, 18 November 1911, 11, 14.

53. "Commissioner Lippincott to Urge Body Similar to Those in Boston and Chicago," *Los Angeles Examiner*, 27 March 1912; Friends of Los Angeles River (FoLAR), *Proposed Flood Control Strategy for the Los Angeles and San Gabriel River Systems* (Los Angeles, 1995), v. For more information on the Hayden bill (SB 2010, 1998), see the state of California's legislative information world wide web page (http://www.leginfo.ca.gov).

54. Rose's comment in Los Angeles City Council, Minutes, 4 June 1914, Los Angeles City Archives; on number of private parcels, Michelle Mowery, telephone conversation with the author, 12 November 1997.

55. Olmsted Brothers and Bartholomew and Associates, *Parks, Playgrounds, and Beaches for the Los Angeles Region*, report submitted to the Citizens' Committee on Parks, Playgrounds and Beaches (Los Angeles: Citizens' Committee, 1930).

56. Ibid., 5, 32. To use parkland acreage as a percentage of total land area in comparing the park situation in Los Angeles with other metropolitan areas is somewhat misleading because Los Angeles was less densely populated than any other major city in North America at the time. In 1930, many parts of the city were still agricultural, particularly in the northern half of the San Fernando Valley. Los Angeles compared much more favorably if its park acreage was compared on a population basis. Of the ten cities to which Olmsted and Bartholomew compared Los Angeles, only Minneapolis and Kansas City had more parkland per 1,000 residents than did Los Angeles.

57. Mike Davis, "How Eden Lost Its Garden: A Political History of the Los Angeles Landscape," in *The City: Los Angeles and Urban Theory at the End of the Twentieth Century*, ed. Allen J. Scott and Edward J. Soja (Berkeley and Los Angeles: Univ. of California Press, 1996), 162.

58. Olmsted and Bartholomew, *Parks, Playgrounds, and Beaches*, 5.

59. Ibid., 13, 16.

60. Ibid., 124–25.

61. William L. Deverell, e-mail message to the author, 6 December 1997.

62. "Budget Work Starts," *Los Angeles Times*, 14 April 1930; Oscar Mueller and John Treanor quoted in William L. Deverell and Greg Hise, eds., *Planning, Nature, and the City* (Berkeley and Los Angeles: Univ. of California Press, forthcoming); Robert M. Fogelson, *The Fragmented Metropolis: Los Angeles, 1850–1930* (Cambridge: Harvard Univ. Press, 1967), 260; "People Rise Up to End Bonding," *Los Angeles Times*, 5 November 1926; members of the Board of Directors of the Chamber of Commerce quoted in William L. Deverell and Greg Hise, "Planning, Nature, and the City: The Olmsteds and the Urban West" (paper presented to the annual meeting of the Association of American Geographers, Boston, 27 March 1998). It is perhaps ironic to note, in light of the future treatment of the Los Angeles River, that Treanor was a wealthy cement company executive.

63. Leonard Leader, *Los Angeles and the Great Depression* (New York: Garland Publishing, 1991), 9, 28–29, 62, 77, 230. City voters in May 1931 approved the sale of $5 million in bonds for employment relief, including $1 million that was to be spent for park improvements. Eighty-three percent of the park funds were used to pay labor costs. Ninety percent of the money spent in Los Angeles by the Civil Works Administration, a federal government relief agency, was spent on wages.

64. Deverell and Hise, *Planning, Nature, and the City*; Los Angeles Board of Park Commissioners, Minutes, 27 March 1930, Los Angeles City Archives; George Hjelte, "Facilities for Recreation," in *Los Angeles: Preface to a Master Plan*, ed. George W. Robbins and L. Deming Tilton (Los Angeles: Pacific Southwest Academy, 1941), 220; George Hjelte, *The Development of a City's Public Recreation Service, 1904–1962* (Los Angeles: Public Service Publications, 1978), 41. Los Angeles voters in 1945 approved the sale of $39.5 million in bonds for parks, playgrounds, recreation centers, and beaches. At the time, this was believed to have been the largest municipal bond issue that had ever been approved anywhere for such purposes.

65. Davis, "How Eden Lost Its Garden," 164. See, e.g., Mike Davis, presentation to "Rethinking the River," conference, Long Beach, Calif., 12 November 1994; Greg Goldin and Mike Davis, "A River Runs through It: The Perils of Life in Los Angeles," *LA Weekly*, 3–9 February 1995, 25; Cynthia D'Agosta, "The Los Angeles River Greenway: Retrofitting an Historic Public Landmark," *Mountain Country*, May 1996, 8–10; Michael Lecesse, "A River Reborn: A Collaboration between the ASLA and the Trust for Public Land Brings Hope to the Los Angeles River Greenway," *Landscape Architecture* 86, no. 6 (1996): 38; Los Angeles County Department of Public Works et al., *Los Angeles River Master Plan* (Los Angeles, 1996), 312; Trust for Public Land et al., *The Los Angeles River Greenway*, poster (Los Angeles, 1996); Sean Woods, "Changing Perceptions of an Urban Waterway: The Los Angeles River," presentation to "Nature's Workshop: Environmental Change in Twentieth-Century Southern California," conference,

California State University, Northridge, 20 September 1997; Tom Hayden and Lewis MacAdams, "Flood Control by Riparian Rape," *Los Angeles Times,* 3 November 1997.

66. The report is scheduled to be republished in 1999 by the University of California Press with the title *Planning, Nature, and the City.* The new edition, edited by historians William L. Deverell and Greg Hise, will include introductory essays by Mike Davis, Marguerite Shaffer, and Terry Young, along with an interview with landscape architect Laurie Olin.

67. Los Angeles County Board of Engineers, Flood Control, *Report of the Board of Engineers, Flood Control, to the Board of Supervisors, Los Angeles County* (Los Angeles, 1915), 225.

68. Olmsted himself had written in 1909 that, despite the work of landscape architects and planners, engineers had left a far greater impress on the urban landscape. He said that, if those interested in more attractive urban design were ever to have a greater influence, they would have to involve engineers. Little seems to have changed in the two decades after he made that assertion, but part of the blame has to rest on the shoulders of designers like Olmsted, who too seldom realized that, to reach the engineers, they had to speak their language. See W. H. Wilson, *The City Beautiful Movement,* 288–89.

69. James W. Reagan, comp., "A Report on Floods, River Phenomena, and Rainfall in the Los Angeles Region, California," 1914–1915 (University Research Library, Univ. of California, Los Angeles, typescript); Army Corps of Engineers, Los Angeles District, "Transcript of Hearing and Exhibits to Accompany Preliminary Examination Report, Flood Control, Los Angeles and San Gabriel Rivers and Their Tributaries, California," 31 March 1936, Los Angeles (Water Resources Center Archives, Univ. of California, Berkeley, typescript).

70. Stanley R. Steenbock, "And Keep Your Honors Safe . . . : A Brief Overview and Affectionate Farewell to the Los Angeles County Flood Control District, 1915–1985," 1985 (Los Angeles County Department of Public Works Technical Library, Alhambra, Calif., typescript), 40.

71. Charles H. Diggs to E. C. Eaton, 5 December 1933; E. C. Eaton to Charles H. Diggs, 27 December 1933, Los Angeles County Department of Public Works Technical Library, Alhambra, Calif.

72. Minutes of special meeting, Los Angeles Board of Park Commissioners, 13 March 1933, Los Angeles City Archives; Robert M. Allen to Los Angeles City Council, 7 September 1934, Los Angeles City Council Petitions 1934, communication 5129, Los Angeles City Archives; Lloyd Aldrich to Robert M. Allen, 7 September 1934, Los Angeles City Council Petitions 1934, communication 5129.

73. Los Angeles City Council, Minutes, 26 March 1934, Los Angeles City Archives.

74. Ibid; Los Angeles Board of Park Commissioners, *Annual Report* (Los Angeles, 1933), 24.

75. Los Angeles Transportation Engineering Board, *A Transit Program for the Los Angeles Metropolitan Area* (Los Angeles, 1939); Richard Sachse, "Transit: The Movement of People," in *Los Angeles: Preface to a Master Plan*, ed. George W. Robbins and L. Deming Tilton (Los Angeles: Pacific Southwest Academy, 1941), 106.

76. Frederick Law Olmsted Jr., Harland Bartholomew, and Charles Henry Cheney, *A Major Traffic Street Plan for Los Angeles*, prepared for the Committee on Los Angeles Plan of Major Highways of the Traffic Commission of the City and County of Los Angeles (Los Angeles, 1924), 47.

77. James M. Danza, "Water Quality and Beneficial Use Investigation of the Los Angeles River: Prospects for Restored Beneficial Uses" (master's thesis, California State Univ., Fullerton, 1994), 20; Army Corps of Engineers, *The LACDA System Recreation Study* (Los Angeles, 1980), 5-14, 5-15; William L. Deverell, *The Mexican Problem and the Rise of Los Angeles* (Berkeley and Los Angeles: Univ. of California Press, forthcoming).

78. Richard Katz, "What's So Silly about a Bargain Freeway?" *Los Angeles Times*, 8 September 1989.

79. Ibid.; Erica Dermitzel, "The Los Angeles River: Its Past, Present, and Potential" (master's thesis, Univ. of California, Los Angeles, 1993), 11; California State Coastal Conservancy (CSCC), *Los Angeles River Park and Recreation Area Study* (Oakland, 1993), 33.

80. Boxall, "River Devotee Seeks a Revival"; Mike Davis, "The Los Angeles River: Lost and Found," *LA Weekly*, 1–7 September 1989, 18–23; Ramirez, "Even Buildings"; Armstrong, "L.A. Ponders Future"; MacAdams, telephone conversation, 21 November 1997.

81. Davis, "Los Angeles River," 20; Frederick M. Muir and Doug Smith, "Plan to Revitalize L.A. River Unveiled," *Los Angeles Times*, 19 January 1990.

82. Los Angeles River Task Force, *Report of the City of Los Angeles River Task Force*, coordinated by the Office of the Mayor, City of Los Angeles, and the Rivers, Trails and Conservation Assistance Program, National Park Service (Los Angeles, 1992).

83. Southern California Institute of Architecture, *Recreating the River: A Prescription for Los Angeles* (Los Angeles, [1990]).

84. Kimball Garrett, e-mail message to the author, 8 December 1997; CSCC, *Park and Recreation Area Study*, 1; Prentiss Williams, "Los Angeles River: Overflowing with Controversy," *California Coast & Ocean*, summer 1993, 19; LACDPW, *Los Angeles River Master Plan*, 314; American Institute of Architects, Los Angeles Chapter, *Taylor Yard Planning and Urban Design Workshop* (Los Angeles, 1992).

85. CSCC, *Park and Recreation Area Study*, 24; LACDPW, *Los Angeles River Master Plan*, 13.

86. Army Corps of Engineers, *Los Angeles County Drainage Area Review*, iii; Duke Helfand, "Controversial L.A. River Project OKd," *Los Angeles Times*, 7 April 1995.

87. E. H. Chin, B. N. Aldridge, and R. J. Longfield, *Floods of February 1980 in Southern California and Central Arizona*, U.S. Geological Survey Professional Paper 1494 (Washington, 1991), 82; Army Corps of Engineers, *Los Angeles County Drainage Area Review*, 5, 21; D. J. Waldie, "The Myth of the L.A. River," *Buzz*, April 1996, 84.

88. Duke Helfand, "High Water: Citing Risk of a Devastating Flood, the Federal Government Wants Southeast Residents to Get Costly and Unpopular Insurance," *Los Angeles Times*, 26 January 1995, Long Beach edition; Army Corps of Engineers, *Los Angeles County Drainage Area Review*, 61–62.

89. Carl Blum, presentation to "Rethinking the River," conference, Long Beach, Calif., 12 November 1994.

90. Barbara Hoag, "Urbanization and Its Effects on the Los Angeles River," unpublished paper, Univ. of California, Los Angeles, 1982 (Los Angeles County Department of Public Works Technical Library, Alhambra, Calif., typescript), 12.

91. Woodward-Clyde Consultants, *Master Environmental Impact Report*, S-1; Army Corps of Engineers, *Los Angeles County Drainage Area Review*, 51–52.

92. Helfand, "High Water"; Helfand, "Controversial L.A. River Project OKd"; Judith Coburn, "Whose River Is It, Anyway? More Concrete versus More Nature: The Battle over Flood Control on the Los Angeles River Is Really a Fight for Its Soul," *Los Angeles Times Magazine*, 20 November 1994, 50.

93. Friends of the Los Angeles River Technical Advisory Board, *The LACDA Public Response Guide: A Guide toward Informed Flood Control Decisions* (Los Angeles, 1994); Tom Bradley to Charles S. Thomas, 13 January 1992, in Woodward-Clyde Consultants, *Final Master Environmental Impact Report: Los Angeles County Drainage Area Project*, prepared for Los Angeles County Department of Public Works (Santa Ana, Calif.: Woodward-Clyde Consultants, 1995); Los Angeles City Planning Department, response to Army Corps of Engineers, *Los Angeles County Drainage Area Review*, January 1992, in Woodward-Clyde Consultants, *Final Master Environmental Impact Report*.

94. FoLAR, *Proposed Flood Control Strategy*.

95. Coburn, "Whose River Is It, Anyway?" 48.

96. Army Corps of Engineers, *Los Angeles County Drainage Area Review*, 92–94, 107.

97. Helfand, "High Water."

98. Helfand, "Controversial L.A. River Project OKd."

99. "Flood Project Battle Moves to State Court," *Current News*, summer 1995; Lewis MacAdams, telephone conversations with the author, 19 July 1995, 11 March 1996; Christopher J. Stone, telephone conversations with the author, 12 March 1996, 5 February 1997; Jeffrey L. Rabin, "Supervisors OK Plan to Raise Walls of L.A. River," *Los Angeles Times*, 4 September 1996; "L.A. River Watershed Task Force Created to Study Wall Alternatives," *Current News*, fall 1996, 1; "Contract Awarded for Wall Alternatives Report," *Current News*, winter 1997, 1; Simons, Li & Associates, *Los Angeles River Alternative Flood Control Study*, vol. 2,

Evaluation of Alternatives (Los Angeles: Los Angeles County Department of Public Works, 1997), i–iv.

100. Coburn, "Whose River Is It, Anyway?" 18.

101. *Los Angeles Times*, 25 April 1994.

102. "A River Doesn't Run through It."

103. Rabin, "Supervisors OK Plan"; "Looking Forward . . . While Revisiting the Past," *Current News*, winter 1997, 1.

104. Christopher J. Stone, telephone conversation with the author, 15 December 1997.

105. MacAdams, interview, 24 October 1997.

106. "Ecological Battle over River Basins in California," *New York Times*, 9 November 1997, national edition. There have been hundreds of articles about the river in the *Los Angeles Times* in recent years. Local columnist Robert A. Jones alone has devoted six of his columns to the river.

107. Patt Morrison, commentary, *Morning Edition*, National Public Radio, 3 May 1995; Warren Olney, moderator, *Which Way L.A.?* radio program, KCRW-FM, Santa Monica, Calif., 15 July 1997; Larry Mantle, moderator, *Air Talk*, radio program, KPCC-FM, Pasadena, Calif., 11 November 1997.

108. Los Angeles County Department of Public Works, *Los Angeles River: "Revitalizing the River,"* poster (Los Angeles, [1997]); Exp Pottery, poster for art sale, 12–13 December 1997, featuring reproduction of Henry Shire's "Confluence," 1981.

109. Suzanne Muchnic, "Gateway to City of Dreams," *Los Angeles Times*, 29 October 1995.

110. Jack Smith, "Driving Down the River," *Westways*, July 1974, 38.

111. "Discovering the River: Perspectives on the L.A. River Watershed," exhibition, Los Angeles Public Library, 21 September 1996–5 January 1997; "Visions of the Los Angeles River/Rivera Promenade," art exhibition, El Pueblo de Los Angeles Historical Monument, Los Angeles, 22 November–31 December 1997; Stephen Callis, "As Water Stories Go," exhibition, El Camino College Art Gallery, Torrance, Calif., 13 March–7 April 1995; Cheri Gaulke, *The Los Angeles: River inside a River* (Los Angeles: Cheri Gaulke, 1991); Robin Rauzi, "A Concept That's (Intentionally) All Wet," *Los Angeles Times*, San Fernando Valley edition, 28 September 1995; Jennifer Fisher, "'Mother Ditch' Delivers Bold Sights, Weak Sound," *Los Angeles Times*, 2 October 1995.

112. Gary Snyder, "Night Song of the Los Angeles Basin," *Whole Earth News*, spring 1995, 62; Luis J. Rodriguez, *The Concrete River* (Willimantic, Conn.: Curbstone Press, 1991); Lewis MacAdams, presentation to "The Los Angeles River: Its Past, Its Present, Its Future, Its Importance," roundtable discussion, Los Angeles Public Library, 12 November 1996. See also L. A. Murillo, *Verses from the Poet to the River of Los Angeles—Porciúncula* (Los Angeles: L. A. Murillo, 1990).

113. E, "L.A. River," on *Broken Toy Shop* (Polydor CD 519 976).

114. "Los Angeles River Virtual Tour," world wide web site created by Kurt Ballash, Jefferson High School, Los Angeles (http://www.lalc.k12.ca.us/target/units/river/riverweb.html).

115. LACDPW, *Los Angeles River Master Plan*, 3–11; Waldie, "Myth of the L.A. River," 84; Jodi Wilgoren, "D-Day for Two Visions of L.A.," *Los Angeles Times*, 8 April 1997.

116. Marc B. Haefele, "Core Problem: Downtown Gets Shabbier as City Thrives," *LA Weekly*, 15–21 August 1997, 18; Dan Rosenfeld, telephone conversation with the author, 17 December 1997; Ira Yellin, presentation to "The Los Angeles River: Its Past, Its Present, Its Future, Its Importance," roundtable discussion at Los Angeles Public Library, 12 November 1996; Stefanos Polyzoides, telephone conversation with the author, 10 December 1997. Rosenfeld, asset manager for the city of Los Angeles, said that "the river is in many ways the home run opportunity to bring back downtown Los Angeles and reunite the city physically."

117. Gayla D. Bechtol, "Infrastructure and Urban Form: The Los Angeles River" (master's thesis, Harvard Univ., 1989); El-Assaad, "Redefining the Role"; Marc Gregory Blake, "A Study of the Los Angeles River" (master's thesis, Univ. of California, Los Angeles, 1990); Ted Young Yoon, "An Emergence of a Riverine Ecology: The Los Angeles River" (master's thesis, Univ. of California, Berkeley, 1992); Dermitzel, "Los Angeles River"; Danza, "Water Quality"; Blake Gumprecht, "Fifty-one Miles of Concrete: The Exploitation and Transformation of the Los Angeles River" (master's thesis, California State Univ., Los Angeles, 1995).

118. American Society of Landscape Architects, *The Los Angeles River: From Infrastructure to Amenity*, CD-ROM (Washington, 1996); James L. Sipes, "Digital Directives: When Design Teams Work Together Common Digital Standards Are Essential," *Landscape Architecture* 87, no. 1 (1997): 32–37; "Universal's River Plan Adds to 'Soul of City,'" *Los Angeles River Master Plan Update*, June 1998, 3.

119. Lewis MacAdams, "The Los Angeles River and Taylor Yard," in *Cruising Industrial Los Angeles* (Los Angeles: Los Angeles Conservancy, 1997), 7; Los Angeles County Department of Public Works and Friends of the Los Angeles River, *Multi-use Study on the Los Angeles River at Taylor Yard* (Los Angeles, [1994]); "FoLAR, Sierra Club to Do Winter Conference on River through Downtown," *Current News*, fall 1997, 1.

120. The conference was held to showcase five new revitalization schemes for the downtown riverfront developed during a design workshop held earlier that month. The other proposals discussed included the creation of parks at the confluence of the Arroyo Seco and the Los Angeles River and on the east side of the river, possible locations for a riverside bikeway through downtown, and the development of a San Antonio-like riverwalk in the abandoned railyards north of Chinatown. See FoLAR, Sierra Club, and Urban Resources Partnership, *The River through Downtown*; Larry Gordon, "River Parks, Shops Proposed," *Los Angeles Times*, 1 March 1998.

121. Melinda Fulmer, "Developer to Turn Railyard into Business Park," *Los An*

geles Times, 31 January 1998; Larry Gordon, "Plans to Build along L.A. River Criticized," *Los Angeles Times*, 28 February 1998.

122. FoLAR, Sierra Club, and Urban Resources Partnership, *The River through Downtown*, 8–11; Christopher Kroll, telephone conversation with the author, 17 June 1998; Lewis MacAdams, telephone conversation with the author, 23 June 1998.

123. Lynnette Kampe, telephone conversation with the author, 2 December 1997; Cynthia D'Agosta, telephone conversation with the author, 17 November 1997; Lynne Dwyer-Hade, "Trees Help Green LA River," *Current News*, summer 1996, 2.

124. Michael J. Kennedy, "Park Hailed as 1st Step to Beautify River," *Los Angeles Times*, 14 July 1995; George Ramos, "The Conservation Movement Comes to Frogtown," *Los Angeles Times*, 17 July 1995; D'Agosta, telephone conversation, 17 November 1997.

125. Michelle Mowery, telephone conversation with the author, 11 December 1997. The agencies and companies that have some authority over the right of way through which the first segment of the bike path was built are the Army Corps of Engineers, Los Angeles County Department of Public Works, California Department of Transportation, Los Angeles Department of Water and Power, Los Angeles Department of Recreation and Parks, and Southern California Edison.

126. Michelle Mowery, telephone conversation with the author, 12 November 1997.

127. Jennifer Fang, telephone conversation with the author, 1 December 1997; Matea Gold, "The Rediscovery of a City River," *Los Angeles Times*, 16 December 1997; "Supervisors OK Funding for Parks along L.A. River," *Los Angeles Times*, 17 December 1997; Bill Stall and Dan Morain, "Prop. 209 Wins, Bars Affirmative Action," *Los Angeles Times*, 6 November 1996; Cynthia D'Agosta, telephone conversations with the author, 17 November 1997, 12 December 1997, 6 July 1998; Deborah Belgum, "$776-Million City Parks Measure Passes—Barely," *Los Angeles Times*, 27 November 1996; Jane Blumenfeld, telephone conversation with the author, 4 November 1997; Sharon Mayer, telephone conversation with the author, 24 June 1998.

128. MacAdams, interview, 24 October 1997.

129. D'Agosta, telephone conversations, 12 December 1997, 6 July 1998.

130. MacAdams, interview, 24 October 1997.

131. D'Agosta, telephone conversation, 12 December 1997. State Assemblyman Scott Wildman introduced a bill into the California legislature in 1998 that would have required any public agency undertaking a public works project along the river to adhere to the principles of the Master Plan. It would also have given the MRCA first right of refusal to purchase excess public lands along the river. The bill was approved by the Assembly in May 1998 and was awaiting action by the Senate. For more information on the Wildman bill (AB 1840, 1998), see the state of California's legislative information web page (http://www.leginfo.ca.gov).

132. Sharon Bernstein, "Thicket of Rules Fuels Flood Fears," *Los Angeles Times*, 12 October 1997.

133. Eric Malnic and Henry Chu, "L.A. Region Faces Major Flood Risk, U.S. Warns," *Los Angeles Times*, 25 October 1997.

134. Sharon Bernstein, "Time to Pay for Clearing Channels," *Los Angeles Times*, 1 December 1997.

135. Lewis MacAdams, "Cleaning Out Flood Channels," *Los Angeles Times*, 12 October 1997; Sharon Bernstein, "Debate over L.A. River Escalates," *Los Angeles Times*, 30 October 1997; Lewis MacAdams, telephone conversation with the author, 4 November 1997. Los Angeles received more than twice its normal annual rainfall during the winter of 1997–98, but no flooding occurred on the river.

136. MacAdams, telephone conversation, 21 November 1997. Cynthia D'Agosta, who was at the meeting, verified the account: "All the while," she said, "Lewis is heating up and Jim is getting annoyed."

137. Kampe, telephone conversation, 2 December 1997.

138. "Ecological Battle over River Basins."

139. Gabby Pelayo, quoted in Gold, "Rediscovery of a City River."

140. D. J. Waldie, response to letter to the editor, *Buzz*, June/July 1996, 114.

Index

Italic page numbers indicate illustrations.

About the Author

BLAKE GUMPRECHT was born in Wilmington, Delaware, in 1959. He was educated at the University of Kansas; Louisiana State University; Temple University; California State University, Los Angeles; and the University of Oklahoma, where he is a member of the faculty of the Department of Geography. Before pursuing a career as a geographer, he was a newspaper reporter (*Los Angeles Times*, *Los Angeles Business Journal*, *Chicago Tribune*, *Long Beach Press-Telegram*), worked in the music business (co-producing the first Soul Asylum album and helping to bring the Replacements to national attention), and was a librarian (Los Angeles Public Library and Temple University). His research interests focus on the cultural and historical geography of the United States and Canada. He has produced studies about early tree planting on the Great Plains; the grain elevators of Enid, Oklahoma; the role of place in the music of West Texas; commercial cultivation of marijuana in California; and liquor-related border settlement in the Oklahoma Territory. He has been published in *Historical Geography*, *Journal of Cultural Geography*, *Southern California Quarterly*, *Chronicles of Oklahoma*, *Great Plains Quarterly*, *Journal of Historical Geography*, and *Weatherwise*. This is his first book.

The Library of Congress has cataloged the hardcover edition
of this book as follows:

Gumprecht, Blake.
  The Los Angeles River : its life, death, and possible rebirth /
Blake Gumprecht.
      p.   cm. — (Creating the North American landscape)
    Includes bibliographical references and index.
    ISBN 0-8018-6047-4 (alk. paper)
    1. Los Angeles River (Calif.)—History. 2. Los Angeles River
(Calif.)—Environmental conditions. I. Title. II. Series.
F868.L8G86 1999
979.4′93—dc21   98-42432

ISBN 0-8018-6642-1 (pbk.)